THE REVELATION OF BAHÁ'U'LLÁH

Mazra'ih and Bahjí 1877–92

By the same author

THE REVELATION OF BAHÁ'U'LLÁH, VOL. 1
Ba<u>gh</u>dád 1853–63

THE REVELATION OF BAHÁ'U'LLÁH, VOL. 2
Adrianople 1863–68

THE REVELATION OF BAHÁ'U'LLÁH, VOL. 3
'Akká, The Early Years 1868–77

THE COVENANT OF BAHÁ'U'LLÁH

THE CHILD OF THE COVENANT
A Study Guide to the Will and Testament of 'Abdu'l-Bahá

TRUSTEES OF THE MERCIFUL
An introduction to Bahá'í Administration

A PRAYER BY BAHÁ'U'LLÁH

In His own handwriting

THE REVELATION OF Bahá'u'lláh

Mazra'ih and Bahjí
1877–92

Adib Taherzadeh

GR
GEORGE RONALD
OXFORD

GEORGE RONALD, Publisher
www.grbooks.com

Reprinted 1988, 1992, 2000, 2009, 2012
Revised 2019
Reprinted 2024

Taherzadeh, Adib
The revelation of Bahá'u'lláh.
Vol. 4 : Mazra'ih and Bahjí, 1877–92
1. Bahá Ullāh 2. Bahai Faith
I. Title
297′.8982 BP392

ISBN 978–0–85398–270–8

To those brilliant souls
the Bahá'í Pioneers and Teachers in every land
who have expended their lives and their substance
in the path of Bahá'u'lláh

Contents

FOREWORD xvii

1. BAHÁ'U'LLÁH AT THE MANSION OF MAZRA'IH 1
    The Life of 'Abdu'l-Bahá in 'Akká 1
    An Air of Freedom 6
2. THE GARDEN OF RIḌVÁN 11
    Trustworthiness: 'ornament of the people of Bahá' 16
    Abu'l-Qásim the Gardener 29
3. *LAWḤ-I-ḤIKMAT* 34
    Teachings for the Spiritualization of Humanity 36
    The Origin of Creation 40
    References to Ancient Philosophy 48
4. VARQÁ, APOSTLE OF BAHÁ'U'LLÁH 52
    Tablets to Varqá 68
5. THE KING AND BELOVED OF THE MARTYRS 77
    Tablets to the Two Brothers 84
    Tablets Revealed after their Martyrdom 92
6. A DIVINE REBUKE: *LAWḤ-I-BURHÁN* 95
7. THE MANSION OF BAHJÍ 108
    The Arrival of Bahá'u'lláh at Bahjí 111
    An Outpouring of Divine Bounty 119
8. THE DAY OF GOD: *TAJALLÍYÁT* 123
    Ustád 'Alí-Akbar-i-Banná 123
    The Station of Bahá'u'lláh 130
        The relationship of God to His Manifestations 134
        The dawn of the new age 143
    Recognition and Steadfastness 145

9. SPLENDOURS OF THE REVELATION: '*ISHRÁQÁT* 152
Jalíl-i-Khú'í 152
Bahá'u'lláh Addresses the People of the Bayán 154
The Meaning of 'Infallibility' 156
Prophecies Fulfilled 161
Religion, a Radiant Light 162

10. GLAD-TIDINGS TO ALL PEOPLES: *BISHÁRÁT* 161

11. TRUTHS OF HIS CAUSE: *ṬARÁZÁT* 168

12. THE LIGHT OF FAITH REACHES INDIA AND BURMA 187

13. THE MEANING OF UNITY 200
Lawḥ-i-Ittiḥád 201
Unity in Society 206
Equality between Men and Women 219

14. *SÚRIY-I-VAFÁ* 216
The Meaning of 'Return' 218
The 'Portals of True Understanding' 223

15. *KALIMÁT-I-FIRDAWSÍYYIH* 226

16. OTHER OUTSTANDING TABLETS 240
Lawḥ-i-Aqdas 240
Lawḥ-i-Maqsúd 249
Lawḥ-i-Siyyid Mihdíy-i-Dahají 250

17. 'THE DOORS OF MAJESTY . . . WERE FLUNG WIDE OPEN' 253
Lawḥ-i-Arḍ-i-Bá 254
The Magnanimity of Bahá'u'lláh 255
The Law of Ḥuqúqu'lláh 263

18. NOTABLE TEACHERS OF THE FAITH 273
Mírzá Abu'l-Faḍl 274
Ḥájí Mírzá Ḥaydar-'Alí 287

19. THE ROLE OF THE HANDS OF THE CAUSE OF GOD 312

20. LIVES OF THE HANDS OF THE CAUSE APPOINTED BY BAHÁ'U'LLÁH 312
Ḥájí Mullá 'Alí-Akbar (Ḥájí Á<u>kh</u>únd) 312
Mírzá 'Alí-Muḥammad (Ibn-i-Aṣdaq) 320
Mírzá Muḥammad-Taqí (Ibn-i-Abhar) 323
Ḥájí Mírzá Ḥasan-i-Adíb 331

21. TABLETS TO THE HANDS OF THE CAUSE 335
The Commandment to Act with Wisdom 341
How Tablets were Delivered to their Recipients 343

22. 'FOR THE ADVANCEMENT OF THE WORLD': *LAWḤ-I-DUNYÁ* 350
Áqá Mírzá Áqáy-i-Afnán (Núru'd-Dín) 350
Circumstances of the Revelation of the *Lawḥ-i-Dunyá* 358
Bahá'u'lláh's Counsels to His Followers 360
Ḥájí Muḥammad-Riḍáy-i-Iṣfahání 364
The Tyrant of Yazd 369
Tablet to *The Times* 371

23. THE CHARTER FOR THE WORLD CENTRE: *LAWḤ-I-KARMIL* 374

24. *EPISTLE TO THE SON OF THE WOLF* 392
<u>Sh</u>ay<u>kh</u> Muḥammad-Taqí, the Son of the Wolf 392
The Re-revelation of Tablets 396
Bahá'u'lláh's Presentation of His Teachings 398
'Shed not the blood of anyone' 402
'The aim . . . is to quench the flame of hate' 408

25. *EPISTLE TO THE SON OF THE WOLF* (continued) 417
The Machinations of the Azalís in Constantinople 417
Ḥájí Mírzá Siyyid Ḥasan (Afnán-i-Kabír) 429
The Supreme Manifestation of God 433
Bahá'u'lláh's Summons to the <u>Sh</u>ay<u>kh</u> 436

26. THE ASCENSION OF BAHÁ'U'LLÁH 441

APPENDIX I: The People of 'Ád and Thamúd; Húd; Ṣáliḥ and the She-Camel 454

APPENDIX II: The House of the Báb in Shíráz 459

APPENDIX III: Notes for the Study of *Epistle to the Son of the Wolf* 462

BIBLIOGRAPHY 470

REFERENCES 475

INDEX 491

Illustrations

A PRAYER BY BAHÁ'U'LLÁH
In His own handwriting *frontispiece*

THE MANSION OF MAZRA'IH
'A lovely place, surrounded by gardens' 19

THE RIḌVÁN GARDEN
The garden, the fountain and the little house 20

ḤÁJÍ MUḤAMMAD-I-YAZDÍ
One of the devoted believers resident in the Holy Land 22

MÍRZÁ 'ALÍ-MUḤAMMAD VARQÁ
An Apostle of Bahá'u'lláh and one of the outstanding Bahá'í poets of the age 65

VARQÁ AND HIS YOUNG SON RÚḤU'LLÁH
In chains in the prison of Ṭihrán where they were martyred 66

MÍRZÁ MUḤAMMAD-ḤASAN OF IṢFAHÁN
Sulṭánu'sh-Shuhadá, King of the Martyrs 81

MÍRZÁ MUḤAMMAD-ḤUSAYN OF IṢFAHÁN
Maḥbúbu'sh-Shuhadá, Beloved of the Martyrs 82

THE MANSION OF BAHÁ'U'LLÁH AT BAHJÍ 115

USTÁD 'ALÍ-AKBAR-I-BANNÁ
The recipient of the Tablet of Tajallíyát who was martyred in Yazd in 1903 126

SULAYMÁN KHÁN-I-TUNUKÁBÁNÍ
Known as Jamálu'd-Dín, he was sent by Bahá'u'lláh to teach in the sub-continent of India 189

SIYYID MUṢṬAFÁY-I-RÚMÍ
An illustrious believer in Burma, posthumously named by Shoghi Effendi as a Hand of the Cause of God 190

MÍRZÁ ABU'L-QÁSIM-I-FARÁHÁNÍ, QÁ'IM-MAQÁM 235

ÁQÁ K_H_ÁN-I-QÁ'IM-MAQÁMÍ
Áqá K_h_án was the grandson of Qá'im-Maqám and an eminent Bahá'í 236

ḤÁJÍ MULLÁ 'ALI-AKBAR-I-S_H_ÁHMÍRZÁDÍ
Hand of the Cause of God appointed by Bahá'u'lláh Known as Ḥájí Ák_h_únd 297

MÍRZÁ MUḤAMMAD-TAQÍ, IBN-I-ABHAR
Hand of the Cause of God appointed by Bahá'u'lláh 298

MÍRZÁ 'ALÍ-MUḤAMMAD, IBN-I-AṢDAQ
Hand of the Cause of God appointed by Bahá'u'lláh 299

MÍRZÁ ḤASAN-I-ADÍB
Hand of the Cause of God appointed by Bahá'u'lláh 300

MEMBERS OF THE FIRST SPIRITUAL ASSEMBLY OF ṬIHRÁN 310

THE HAND OF THE CAUSE IBN-I-ABHAR IN CHAINS
A photograph taken in the prison of Ṭihrán. 'Abdu'l-Bahá's Tablet to him is inscribed at the top of the photograph 329

WILLIAM PATCHIN
An English believer in Ábádih, with Saráju'l-Ḥukamá and his young son 349

ÁQÁ MÍRZÁ ÁQÁ
Entitled Núru'd-Dín, he was the nephew of K_h_adíjih Bagum, the wife of the Báb. He is seen holding the Tablet bearing the seal of Bahá'u'lláh in which his family are nominated custodians of the House of the Báb in S_h_íráz 352

ḤÁJÍ MUḤAMMAD-RIḌÁ
Martyr of the Faith in 'Ishqábád in 1889 367

SITE OF THE FUTURE MASHRIQU'L-ADHKÁR ON MOUNT CARMEL
Marked by an obelisk, the site is near 'the Spot hallowed by the footsteps of Bahá'u'lláh' when He revealed the Tablet of Carmel 387

THE GROVE OF CYPRESS TREES
Here Bahá'u'lláh indicated to 'Abdu'l-Bahá the site of the Shrine of the Báb 387

THE BAHÁ'Í WORLD CENTRE
This aerial view shows the Shrine of the Báb and the Terraces, the International Archives Building, the Centre for the Study of the Texts, the Seat of the Universal House of Justice and the International Teaching Centre Building. The arc and the monument gardens may also be seen 388

THE HAND OF THE CAUSE OF GOD ḤÁJÍ ÁKHÚND IN CHAINS AND STOCKS
This photograph was taken at the request of Náṣiri'd-Dín Sháh 407

SHAYKH MUḤAMMAD-'ALÍ, KNOWN AS NABÍL SON OF NABÍL
A devoted believer from Qazvín, he became a victim of the attacks by the Azalís in Constantinople 431

ḤÁJÍ MÍRZÁ SIYYID ḤASAN, AFNÁN-I-KABÍR
'The Great Afnán', a brother of the wife of the Báb 432

THE SHRINE OF BAHÁ'U'LLÁH AT BAHJÍ 451

Notes and Acknowledgements

The extracts from the Writings of the Báb and Bahá'u'lláh contained in this book are from the matchless translations by Shoghi Effendi, the Guardian of the Bahá'í Faith, and those carried out under the auspices of The Universal House of Justice. Published sources are acknowledged in the references and Bibliography. There are many other quotations from Persian manuscripts and publications, and these I have translated, unless otherwise indicated. Most quotations had to be edited prior to translation. The footnotes to these quotations, however, are mostly mine, and this is indicated explicitly where confusion may arise. Verses taken from the *Qur'án* are numbered in accordance with the Arabic text, although their numbering may differ from that given in English translations. Persian and Arabic names are transliterated in accordance with the system adopted for books on the Bahá'í Faith, but quotations are reproduced in their original form.

The early followers of Bahá'u'lláh seldom sought to be photographed. Occasionally group photographs were taken, from which it has been possible to obtain many of the individual photographs which I have included, in the belief that their historical interest outweighs the fact that some are faded and out of focus. I am deeply indebted to the Audio-Visual Department of the Bahá'í World Centre for supplying most of these photographs. I should like to thank Mr Ruhi Shakibai for his excellent reproduction of one of the photographs printed in this book.

It has taken a long time to finish writing this book, for as before, the only time available has been the late hours of those evenings spent at home in Dublin.

Now that this work is completed, I would like to share

with readers certain facts concerning the force motivating this humble undertaking. The chief factor which has supported and sustained me in writing these volumes has been the deep sense of love I cherish in my heart for those believers throughout the world who are unable to read the Writings of Bahá'u'lláh in their original language, and the hope that this series of volumes, however inadequate and superficial, may convey through the potency of the Words of Bahá'u'lláh Himself a small measure of the greatness of His mighty Revelation.

A contributory factor has been the loving encouragement which the friends everywhere have showered upon me. In particular, I am deeply indebted to Mrs Marion Hofman for her unfailing and genuine support throughout the last fifteen years. I wish to extend to her my heartfelt gratitude and deep appreciation for her wise counsel and loving encouragement which have been of the greatest assistance to me. I am also deeply appreciative of much valuable advice and help given to me by Dr May Hofman Ballerio in the course of her excellent and ably executed editorial work. I wish to express my warmest thanks for her major contributions to the production of this and previous volumes. Another source of encouragement over the years and for which I am truly grateful is my dear wife, Lesley, whose loving support has played an important part in my work.

To Mrs Thelma Batchelor and Mrs Annette Rooney I wish to extend my warmest thanks and appreciation for their excellent typing of the manuscript from my original scribbled notes, great portions of which were difficult to read. My sincere thanks are directed also to Dr Wendi Momen for her skilful production of the Index, and to Mr Harold Boyce for his attention to detail in proofreading and many helpful suggestions.

ADIB TAHERZADEH

Foreword

The Revelation of Bahá'u'lláh has ushered in the Day of God foretold by all the Prophets of the past. So vast has been the outpouring of this Revelation, extending over a period of forty years, that any attempt to describe it must resemble an attempt to place an ocean within a cup. Moreover, His Revelation is possessed of such a potency that to try to fathom its significance or to probe its hidden mysteries is an act beyond the capacity of mortal men.

This puts into perspective the attempt made by the author of these four volumes to capture glimpses of this mighty Revelation and present them to the readers, while knowing only too well how difficult the task is and how inadequately he has treated the subjects. Indeed, all that has been described in these volumes is the outcome of skimming the surface of a tiny part of a boundless ocean.

This fourth volume covers the most momentous period in the Ministry of Bahá'u'lláh, a period during which His Revelation reached its climax, and His own Person, after years of exile and imprisonment, majestically ascended the throne of His sovereignty in a delightful Mansion designated by Him as 'the most sublime vision of mankind'.

The great many Tablets that streamed forth from the Supreme Pen during this period were to a large extent concerned with promulgating those teachings and principles which, in conjunction with the laws of the *Kitáb-i-Aqdas*, constitute the framework of Bahá'u'lláh's World Order. The events associated with this period were highly significant, contributing as they did to the emergence of the Faith in Persia, and demonstrating its universality, its vitality and its invincibility as a young Faith possessed of a dynamism unequalled in the annals of religion. While the Faith was steadily growing in the land of its birth, its healing message had also begun to penetrate the neighbouring countries of the East.

Some of these accounts appear in this volume. The story begins from where it was left off in volume 3 – the arrival of Bahá'u'lláh at the Mansion of Mazra'ih. It continues with the main events during the remainder of His Ministry, and some of the outstanding Tablets revealed by Him until His ascension in the Mansion of Bahjí. It is the hope of the present author to continue the story in future volumes on the subject of the Covenant of Bahá'u'lláh, the most important and significant part of His Revelation.

1

Bahá'u'lláh at the Mansion of Mazra'ih

The departure of Bahá'u'lláh from the prison-city in June 1877 and His transfer to the Mansion of Mazra'ih, a beautiful summer residence of 'Abdu'lláh Páshá in the quiet countryside north of 'Akká, constitute a turning-point in the fortunes of His Ministry. The building at Mazra'ih stood in the middle of a garden, situated on a vast plain. From one side the view was of the Galilee hills and from the other, the sea. One room on the ground floor was used as a reception room by Bahá'u'lláh, and many of the believers attained His presence there. His own room was on the upper floor with a nearby balcony* overlooking beautiful countryside.

'Abdu'l-Bahá, His Mother the saintly Navváb, and His cherished sister the Greatest Holy Leaf all stayed behind in 'Akká. They visited Bahá'u'lláh from time to time, especially the Master, who attained His presence whenever He could.

The Life of 'Abdu'l-Bahá in 'Akká

'Abdu'l-Bahá's main reason for not joining His Beloved Father at Mazra'ih and later at the Mansion of Bahjí was the staggering weight of cares and responsibilities which He had taken upon Himself ever since the days of Adrianople in order to relieve Bahá'u'lláh of the burden of having to attend to daily affairs. In 'Akká these responsibilities weighed so heavily upon Him that He had to remain in the city and take care of a multitude

* see vol. 1, pp. 290–91, for an interesting story of Mírzá Ja'far, who fell down from that balcony.

of problems relating to the Bahá'í community as well as to the inhabitants of 'Akká and its neighbouring towns. He was busy from the early hours of the morning until after midnight meeting government officials, religious dignitaries and men of culture and commerce, as well as attending to the needs of the citizens, the poor, the sick, the old, the dying, the widows and the orphans. Governors and officials often sought His advice on matters of great importance to their work. Religious leaders likewise sat at His feet, and all received a measure of His knowledge and wisdom. He was a counsellor to every man, a true and loving father to the poor and the downtrodden. He would spend many hours every day visiting the sick, providing medical treatment, food and clothing for those who needed them. He was indeed the 'Master of 'Akká'.

His attention to the affairs of the Bahá'í community was no less important and time-consuming. Not only did He guide and direct the individual Bahá'ís living in 'Akká in their personal and community affairs, but He made detailed arrangements for the stream of pilgrims who were coming to attain the presence of Bahá'u'lláh. The Master ensured that each one of the pilgrims was made comfortable in the Pilgrim House, or accommodated elsewhere. He surrounded them with His all-encompassing love, counselled them in their manifold affairs, and prepared them spiritually for that greatest moment in their lives when they would be ushered into the presence of their Lord. In some cases, He even inspected their clothes and if they were found to be worn out or unsuitable, He would arrange for them to wear new outfits worthy of entering the presence of Bahá'u'lláh.

The following are the reminiscences of Ṭúbá Khánum, one of 'Abdu'l-Bahá's daughters, concerning Him in those days:

> The life of the Master in 'Akká was full of work for others' good.
>
> He would rise very early, take tea, then go forth to His self imposed labours of love. Often He would return very late in

the evening, having had no rest and no food.

He would go first to the Bírúní, a large reception room, which had been hired, on the opposite side of the street to our house. We often used to watch from our windows, the people crowding there to ask for help from the Master.

A man who wished to take a shop must ask advice from Him. Another would request a letter of introduction, or recommendation for some government post. Again, it would be a poor woman whose husband had been falsely accused, or had been taken for a soldier, whilst she and the children were left to starve. One would tell Him of children who were ill-treated, or of a woman beaten by husband or brother.

'Abbás Effendi would send a competent person with these poor people to state the case to the judge at the Court House, so that they might have justice.

The Bírúní also received other guests; it came to be looked upon as a centre of interest.

The Muftí, the Governor, Shaykhs, and officials of the Court came singly or in groups to call on the Master at the Bírúní. Here they would be offered a specially delicious make of 'qahviyi-khánigí' (coffee). Sipping this, they would talk over all the news, appealing for explanations, advice, or comment, to the Master, Whom they grew to look upon as learned, wise, full of compassion, practical help, and counsel for all.

When the Court rose the judge invariably came to the Bírúní, where he would speak of any complicated case, sure that 'Abbás Effendi would solve the problem, however difficult . . .

Some days He hardly saw His own family, so hard pressed was He by those who crowded to the Bírúní for some kind of help.

The many sick people, Bahá'í and others, were His constant care; whenever they wished to see Him, He went . . . Never did He neglect anything but His own rest, His own food; the poor were always His first care.

> All sweets, fruits, and cakes which had been sent to Him He would take to the Bírúní for the friends, whom He made very happy . . .
>
> As there was no hospital in 'Akká, the Master paid a doctor, Nikolaki Bey, a regular salary to look after the very poor. This doctor was asked not to say who was responsible for this, 'His right hand was not to know what His left wrought.'
>
> But for those other things the poor needed when they were ill, numberless, various, always to the Master did they turn their eyes . . . [1]

In doing all this 'Abdu'l-Bahá truly shielded His Father from the outside world so that, freed from any involvement in the affairs of the community, He could devote all His time to the Revelation of the Word of God and meeting the believers. 'Abdu'l-Bahá used to visit His beloved Father whenever He could, and this brought much joy to the heart of Bahá'u'lláh.

Ḥájí Mírzá Ḥaydar-'Alí,[*] that spiritual giant immortalized by the title 'The Angel of Carmel', has recorded the following reminiscences of one of his memorable audiences with Bahá'u'lláh. Ḥájí Mírzá Ḥaydar-'Alí recounts the words of Bahá'u'lláh[†] concerning the important role of 'Abdu'l-Bahá in shielding Him from the pressures of the outside world.

> During the days of Baghdád We ourself used to visit the coffee house[‡] and meet with everyone. We associated with people whether they were in the community or outside, whether acquaintances or strangers, whether they came from far or near.
>
> We considered those who were distant from us to be near, and the strangers as acquaintances. We served the Cause of

---

* For his story see vol. 2.

† These are not to be taken as the exact words of Bahá'u'lláh; they are only recollections of His utterances recalled by Ḥájí Mírzá Ḥaydar-'Alí.

‡ see vol. 3, pp. 250–51. (A.T).

> God, supported His Word, and exalted His Name. The Most Great Branch ['Abdu'l-Bahá] carried out all these services, withstood all the difficulties, and endured the sufferings and calamities to a great extent in Adrianople, and now to a far greater extent in 'Akká. Because while in Baghdád, to all appearances We were not a prisoner, and the Cause of God had hardly enjoyed the fame it does today. Those who opposed it and the enemies who fought against it were comparatively few and far between.
>
> In Adrianople We used to meet with some people and gave permission to some to attain Our presence. But while in the Most Great Prison We did not meet with anyone* and have completely closed the door of association with the people. Now the Master has taken upon Himself this arduous task for Our comfort. He is a mighty shield facing the world and its peoples, and so He has relieved Us [from every care]. At first He secured the Mansion of Mazra'ih for Us and We stayed there, then the Mansion of Bahjí. He is so occupied in the service of the Cause that for weeks He does not find the opportunity to come to Bahjí. We are engaged in meeting with the believers and revealing the verses of God, while He labours hard and faces every ordeal and suffering. Because to deal and associate with these people is the most arduous task of all.[2]

'Abdu'l-Bahá's staying in 'Akká served another purpose as well. His brothers, especially Mírzá Muḥammad-'Alí† and his mother, were highly jealous of Him. It was this brother who, after the passing of Bahá'u'lláh, became the Arch-breaker of His Covenant and rose up with all his power to destroy 'Abdu'l-Bahá and the Cause He was promoting. By staying away from Bahá'u'lláh, Who cherished His eldest Son and

* Non-Bahá'ís. (A.T.)

† For more information about the Arch-breaker of the Covenant see *God Passes By*, chapter 15, and *Revelation of Bahá'u'lláh*, vols. 1 and 2.

extolled His station in glowing terms, 'Abdu'l-Bahá succeeded in somewhat dampening the fire of jealousy which was fiercely burning within their breasts. As well as this, Bahá'u'lláh's own practice over the years was, as far as possible, to keep in His company those who were likely to cause trouble or were inwardly unfaithful to Him, so that He could control their mischief and keep them in check. And now that some freedom was given to Him, Bahá'u'lláh chose to live with those members of His household who would prove, in the end, to be disloyal to His Cause.

An explanation has been given in a previous volume* as to why those who were so close to Bahá'u'lláh, such as His brother, His sons and daughters and other members of His family, should have been the first to rebel against His Cause and become a source of dissension among His followers.

An Air of Freedom

In order to appreciate the significance of Bahá'u'lláh's move to Mazra'ih, and why it opened up a new chapter in the annals of the Faith, we may recall the tumultuous years of His Ministry preceding this historic step. As we survey Bahá'u'lláh's eventful life at this juncture, we note that for over a quarter of a century He was the main target of attack by a relentless enemy.

Prior to the birth of His own Revelation, He suffered greatly through persecutions directed at the Bábí community. The appalling bastinado, which was inflicted upon Him in public in His native province of Mázindarán, is one example. The humiliating circumstances in which He was conducted on foot and in chains with bare feet and bared head in the heat of the summer to the Síyáh-Chál of Ṭihrán, His imprisonment in that darksome underground dungeon; the chain of Qara-Guhar which was placed on His neck and which cut through His flesh and left its marks on Him all His life; the hardships He endured during

* see vol. 1, pp. 130–31.

His first exile from His native country to Iraq; the deprivations and sufferings during His solitary retirement in the snow-bound mountains of Kurdistán; His further exile to the capital city of the Ottoman Empire, a city described by Him as the 'seat of tyranny'; His humiliating banishment to Adrianople, the 'remote Prison', travelling in horse-driven carts in sub-zero temperatures; the sufferings He endured in that 'Land of Mystery'; the hardships He was exposed to and the restrictions He underwent on His exile to the desolate city of 'Akká; the unbearable conditions of His solitary cell in the barracks of that city, designated by Him as the 'Most Great Prison'; and His confinement for almost seven years within the walls of a small house devoid of any greenery to please the eye – all these tribulations which He, the Wronged One of the world, had endured with such resignation and forbearance, were at long last coming to an end. His departure from the prison-city signalized the opening of a new era of relative peace and tranquillity in His life.

It was not only the fresh air of the countryside at Mazra'ih and the open fields around it which enhanced the circumstances in which He lived. The major factor which brought about a new phase in His ministry was the unveiling of His greatness, His power and His authority to friends and foe alike. This was made manifest when the highest religious leader in the land knelt before Him in a state of humble adoration and begged Him to leave the prison-city,* a move which the Governor of 'Akká, notwithstanding the strict edict of the Sulṭán, had approved.

The establishment of Bahá'u'lláh's residence in the summer mansion of Mazra'ih also created much excitement and joy in the hearts of His companions. The prophecy uttered by Him on His arrival at 'Akká, that the doors of the prison would be opened, had already been fulfilled when He left the barracks. Now that His confinement within the walls of the city had come to an end the prophecy was fully realized.

* see vol. 3, pp. 416–17, for details.

Bahá'u'lláh loved the beauty of nature and was fond of the outdoor life. Living in the Mansion of Mazra'ih enabled Him to enjoy the scenery after nine years of confinement within the walls of a depressing prison-city. In His Tablets revealed in this period Bahá'u'lláh refers to the beauty of the countryside. In a Tablet to the illustrious Afnán, Áqá Mírzá Áqá, entitled Núru'd-Dín,* He writes about the delightful scenery at Mazra'ih. He describes in cheerful language the view of the sea on the one side and the hills on the other, and speaks of the charm of the trees laden with oranges which He likens to balls of fire!

The believers who came on pilgrimage at this time were also rejoicing in Bahá'u'lláh's freedom. There were many who attained His presence in this Mansion, in an atmosphere far different from that of former times in Adrianople or 'Akká. There was an air of freedom, of victory and ascendancy of the Cause which exhilarated every believing heart. It had been the custom from the days of Baghdád for some of the believers to hold a feast and beg Bahá'u'lláh to honour them with His presence. This practice, however, depended upon His permission and sometimes He obliged the believers by accepting their invitation. Even when He was in the barracks, some of the believers used to save the very meagre rations they received so that they could hold a feast on a special occasion for Bahá'u'lláh to attend.† It is also apparent from some of His Tablets that certain friends in Persia would send funds to Mírzá Áqá Ján, Bahá'u'lláh's amanuensis, and ask him to seek permission to hold a feast in their name for Bahá'u'lláh to attend.

When Bahá'u'lláh moved out of the city, this practice became easier. After seeking His permission, the friends held feasts in the countryside in various outdoor locations. The bounty of God to those disciples who had the unique privilege of being in the presence of their Lord is immeasurable. It is not possible for us who live a hundred years later to fully appreciate, or

* see below, pp. 350–73.
† see vol. 3, p. 53.

even to imagine, the oceans of love, of ecstasy, of devotion and of thanksgiving which must have surged in the hearts of these God-intoxicated people who sat with the Supreme Manifestation of God in places of beauty, or stood as He mingled among them, speaking to them individually or collectively and even joining them in partaking of the food. To what heights of spirituality these souls were uplifted as a result of such gatherings we shall never know. Some who attained His presence have tried to describe the life-giving energies which flowed through their hearts as He spoke to them but have admitted their inability to do so adequately, because to attain the presence of One who embodies within Himself the 'Most Great Spirit'* of God is not an experience one can ever describe.

Ḥájí Muḥammad-Ṭáhir-i-Málmírí† attained the presence of Bahá'u'lláh around 1878–9. When asked by the friends to describe His impressions of the Blessed Beauty, he always recited in answer a Persian poem:

> And wonder at the vision I have dreamed,
> A secret by my muted tongue concealed;
> Beauty that is beyond the poet's word
> By an unhearing world remains unheard.

The same believer has left to posterity an account of one of the feasts at which he had the honour to be present. These are his words recorded in his memoirs:

> In the spring season Bahá'u'lláh used to stay at Mazra'ih for some time.‡ Mazra'ih is situated at a distance of about two farsangs [about 12 kilometres] from the city of 'Akká. To attain His presence I used to go to Mazra'ih in the daytime

* see vol. 3, pp. 144–5.

† The father of the present author. For a story of his life see vol. 1.

‡ Bahá'u'lláh did not live at Mazra'ih or Bahjí all the time. He used to go and stay in 'Akká sometimes; for details see below, p. 110.

and at night I stayed at the Pilgrim House. On the first day of the Ayyám-i-Há [Intercalary days] one of the pilgrims had invited Bahá'u'lláh and all the believers in 'Akká to lunch. I too went to Mazra'ih. Early in the morning a large tent was pitched in front of the entrance to the garden on a delightful open space. That morning all the believers, numbering almost two hundred, consisting of those who were living in the Holy Land and the pilgrims, came to Mazra'ih.

Around the time of noon, the Blessed Beauty came down from the Mansion and majestically entered the tent. All the believers were standing in front of the tent. Then Mírzá Áqá Ján, standing in the presence of Bahá'u'lláh, chanted a dawn prayer for fasting which had been revealed on that day. When the prayer was finished the Blessed Beauty instructed all to be seated. Every person sat down in the place where he was standing. His blessed Person spoke to us and after His utterances were ended He asked, 'What happened to the Feast, is it really going to happen?' Thereupon a few friends hurried away and soon lunch was brought in. They placed a low table in the middle of the tent. His blessed Person and all the Aghṣán* sat around the table and since there was more room, He called some by name to join Him. Among these my name was called; He said, 'Áqá Ṭáhir, come and sit.' So I went in and sat at the table in His presence. At some point Bahá'u'lláh said, 'We have become tired of eating. Those who have had enough may leave.' I immediately arose and His blessed Person left. At first the food which was left over on His plate was divided among the friends, and then group after group entered the tent and had their meal. Everyone at this feast partook of both physical, and spiritual food. I got the prayer of fasting from Mírzá Áqá Ján and copied it for myself. Then in the evening all the friends returned to 'Akká. But the Master was not present that day.

---

* The male descendants of Bahá'u'lláh. (A.T.)

2

The Garden of Riḍván

In addition to Mazra'ih 'Abdu'l-Bahá had earlier on rented the Garden of Na'mayn, an island situated in close proximity to the city of 'Akká. He did this in anticipation of Bahá'u'lláh's release from confinement. After His release Bahá'u'lláh often visited this beautiful spot, usually in the spring, the summer and early autumn seasons. It was designated by Him as the Riḍván Garden (Paradise); in some of His Tablets Bahá'u'lláh refers to the garden as the 'New Jerusalem' and 'Our Verdant Isle'.

This garden was made beautiful through the dedication and hard work of the Persian believers and the constant supervision and guidance of the Master. They brought great quantities of soil from neighbouring places to make flower-beds all around, while from Persia and neighbouring countries the friends brought many shrubs, trees and flowering plants, some of them rare species. Crossing mountains and deserts, which took several months, they took such care that the plants arrived fresh and ready to be planted in the garden. The care with which the believers brought these plants by long hazardous journeys is an indication of a devotion and a love which finds no parallel in the annals of any religion and which is clearly demonstrated in the beauty of the garden itself.

The motive for undertaking this unusual task, which at first seemed impossible, was a deep sense of love for Bahá'u'lláh, a love which knew no bounds. The friends desired to offer Him an earthly gift of beauty which they knew He enjoyed so much. They went so far as to bring to 'Akká the plant of a rare white rose which had been one of His favourite flowers in Ṭihrán. In some of His Tablets Bahá'u'lláh refers to these plants and expresses warm appreciation of the devotion of those who brought them.

The zeal and devotion of the gardeners who tended the plants and laboured day and night to make the Garden of Riḍván a place of beauty for Bahá'u'lláh to enjoy, was no less striking. The Garden of Riḍván was situated on a very small island. The little river, which emptied into the sea, divided itself into two streams surrounding that small area of land. In the time of Bahá'u'lláh the garden was laid out in flower-beds and there were many ornamental shrubs and fruit trees. There was a splashing fountain from which water was fed to all parts of the garden. As it flowed, it came rippling down in a broad stream over a stone platform under two large mulberry trees. The stream which flowed by the island was about fourteen to fifteen feet wide and three feet deep; fish were darting about it in abundance. It was fringed with weeping willows, and the fragrance of jasmine and orange blossoms filled the air. Most of these features are preserved today, except that there is no water circling the garden, for the streams have been diverted in recent times.

Whenever Bahá'u'lláh visited the Garden of Riḍván it was a joyous occasion not only for Himself but for the Master and all the friends. The atmosphere in this oasis of beauty brought some relaxation to Bahá'u'lláh as He sat on a rectangular bench placed in the shade of the two large mulberry trees. Many believers attained His presence there, and they too sat on similar benches.

One believer had an awe-inspiring experience as he gazed upon the face of Bahá'u'lláh in the Garden of Riḍván. He was known by the name of Ḥájí Yahúdá. He grew up in a Jewish family; his father was the chief Rabbi of the city of Ras͟ht and its neighbouring towns in the north of Persia. In his youth, he used to work as a pedlar travelling to various cities. On one of his trips to Hamadán, he encountered a few Bahá'ís who acquainted him with the Mission of Bahá'u'lláh and consequently he was converted to the Faith. Around the year 1888–9 He travelled to 'Akká in order to attain the presence of Bahá'u'lláh. His first meeting with Him took place in the Garden of Riḍván.

As soon as he was ushered into His presence, the scene

of water flowing from the fountain near Bahá'u'lláh's feet as He sat on the bench surrounded by the two streams, vividly brought to his mind the vision of the Prophets of Israel as recorded in the Old Testament:

> There is a river, the streams whereof shall make glad the city of God, the holy place of the tabernacles of the most High. God is in the midst of her; she shall not be moved: God shall help her, and that right early.[1]

> But there the glorious Lord will be unto us a place of broad rivers and streams; wherein shall go no galley with oars, neither shall gallant ship pass thereby.[2]

He was overwhelmed by this vision so suddenly and vividly revealed to him. It came upon him as a thunderbolt and he was carried away into a different world. His whole being was stirred to its depths as he saw himself, standing with awe and wonder in the presence of the Lord of the Old Testament. His instant urge was to prostrate himself at the feet of Bahá'u'lláh, and this he did. The effect of this first meeting, and of hearing the utterances of Bahá'u'lláh on that occasion, was to create a fire of love and adoration which continued to burn within his heart till the end of his life. He was transformed into a new creation and was exultant with joy as he left the Holy Land.

On his return to Persia Ḥájí Yahúdá began to teach the Faith among his people. He emerged as a well-known Bahá'í teacher who succeeded in bringing a number of Jews under the shadow of the Cause, and some of these individuals became prominent Bahá'ís in Persia. Ḥájí Yahúdá also endured hardship and sufferings as a result of severe persecutions which were inflicted upon him by the Jewish community because of his success in teaching the Cause.[3]

Ṭúbá Khánum, 'Abdu'l-Bahá's daughter, has described her childhood memories of Bahá'u'lláh in the Garden of Riḍván:

> Oh the joy of the day when Bahá'u'lláh went to the beautiful Riḍván, which had been prepared for Him with such loving care by the Master, the friends, and the pilgrims!
>
> The Master's heart was gladdened indeed to see the enjoyment of His beloved Father, resting under the big mulberry tree, by the side of the little river rippling by, the fountain which they had contrived splashing and gurgling in sounds refreshing indeed after the long years of confinement in the pestilential air of the penal fortress of 'Akká. Only those who were present there could realize in any degree what it meant to be surrounded by such profusion of flowers, their colours and their scents, after the dull walls and unfragrant odours of the prison city.
>
> I remember well the greatest of our joys was to go with Bahá'u'lláh for the occasional picnics to the Riḍván.
>
> How happy we were with Him. He was indeed the brightness of our lives in that time of difficulty.[4]

There were many occasions when the believers held feasts in that garden and Bahá'u'lláh honoured them with His presence. Such gatherings engendered indescribable joy and spirituality, beyond our imagination. The garden became truly a place of celebration and rejoicing. Siyyid Asadu'lláh-i-Qumí,* an eminent believer, has related that once Bahá'u'lláh Himself entertained all the believers with refreshments in the Garden of Riḍván to celebrate the release of several Bahá'í prisoners in Ṭihrán. These included Mírzá Abu'l-Faḍl, the Hand of the Cause Ḥájí Mullá 'Alí-Akbar,† and Siyyid Asadu'lláh himself. In His all-embracing knowledge Bahá'u'lláh had announced their release and celebrated the occasion, whereas the telegram bearing this news reached 'Akká a day later.

There is a little house at the end of the Garden of Riḍván. Here the small room in which Bahá'u'lláh rested, dined and

* see vol. 1, pp. 35–6, and below, pp. 185–7.

† see vol. 3, also below, pp. 258–70, for Mírzá Abu'l-Faḍl; for Ḥájí Mullá 'Alí-Akbar (Ḥájí Ákhúnd) see below, pp. 312–320.

at times revealed Tablets is kept in its original form. The renowned Ḥájí Mírzá Ḥaydar-'Alí recounts an interesting story of how he was able to see the colour of the head-dress of Bahá'u'lláh for the first time as He was having a meal in that room. This story has been recorded in a previous volume.*

A Tablet of Bahá'u'lláh revealed there and translated into English hangs on the wall of that room today. Its perusal enables the reader to see how much Bahá'u'lláh enjoyed the Garden and how much He loved the beauty of nature. Here is a translation of this Tablet:

He is God, Glorified be He,
Grandeur and Might are His!

On the morning of the blessed Friday we proceeded from the Mansion and entered the Garden. Every tree uttered a word, and every leaf sang a melody. The trees proclaimed: 'Behold the evidences of God's Mercy' and the twin streams recited in the eloquent tongue the sacred verse 'From us all things were made alive'. Glorified be God! Mysteries were voiced by them, which provoked wonderment. Methought: in which school were they educated, and from whose presence had they acquired their learning? Yea! This Wronged One knoweth and He saith: 'From God, the All-Encompassing, the Self-Subsistent.'

Upon Our being seated, Ráḍíyih, upon her be My glory, attained Our presence on thy behalf, laid the table of God's bounty and in thy name extended hospitality to all present. In truth, all that which stimulateth the appetite and pleaseth the eye was offered, and indeed that which delighteth the ear could also be heard as the leaves were stirred by the Will of God, and from this movement a refreshing voice was raised, as if uttering a blissful call inviting the absent to this Feast. God's power and the perfection of His handiwork could enjoyably be seen in the blossoms, the fruits, the trees, the

* see vol. 2, pp. 9–10.

> leaves and the streams. Praised be God who hath thus confirmed thee and her.
>
> In brief, all in the Garden were recipients of the choicest bounties and in the end expressed their thanksgiving unto their Lord. O that all God's beloved would have been present on this day!
>
> We beseech God, exalted be He, to cause to descend upon thee at every moment, a blessing and a mercy and a measure of divine grace from His presence. He is the Forgiving, the All-Glorious.
>
> We send greetings to His loved ones, and supplicate for each one of them that which is worthy of mention and is acceptable in His presence. Peace be upon thee, and upon God's sincere servants. Praise be to Him, the Lord of all mankind.

Rádíyih, who is mentioned in this Tablet, was a sister of Munírih Khánum, the wife of 'Abdu'l-Bahá. The dinner was given on behalf of her husband who was not present at the time. He was her cousin Siyyid 'Alí, the only son of Mírzá Hádí, a distinguished Bábí, and the illustrious Shams-i-Ḍuhá.*

Mírzá Hádí, an uncle of the King of Martyrs and the Beloved of Martyrs,† became an ardent believer in the early days of the Faith. He was present at the Conference of Badasht, suffered persecutions, was attacked in that vicinity and died there. His wife Shams-i-Ḍuhá, a close companion of Ṭáhirih, was described by 'Abdu'l-Bahá as the 'eloquent and ardent handmaid of God'.

Trustworthiness: 'ornament of the people of Bahá'

Other Tablets were revealed in this holy spot. There is a celebrated passage‡ about trustworthiness in which Bahá'u'lláh

* see *Memorials of the Faithful*, pp. 175–90.

† see below, ch. 5.

‡ In a Tablet to His Trustee, Ḥájí Amín, Bahá'u'lláh indicates that a 'Tablet of Trustworthiness' had been revealed in AH 1296 (around AD 1879).

describes a vision He had in the Garden of Riḍván of a Maid of Heaven. This passage appears in the Tablets of Ishráqát, Ṭarázát and also in a Tablet revealed in honour of Ḥájí Mírzá Buzurg-i-Afnán,* one of the illustrious custodians of the House of the Báb in Shíráz. Bahá'u'lláh has often used the symbolic term 'Maid of Heaven' in those of His Tablets which are revealed in the language of imagery. Sometimes, as in this Tablet, Bahá'u'lláh uses this symbolism to describe the revelation of some of the attributes of God.† In others, the term may have different significances which only the deep study of the Holy Writings can reveal.

In such beautiful terms Bahá'u'lláh speaks of the importance of trustworthiness:

> We will now mention unto thee Trustworthiness and the station thereof in the estimation of God, thy Lord, the Lord of the Mighty Throne. One day of days We repaired unto Our Green Island. Upon Our arrival, We beheld its streams flowing, and its trees luxuriant, and the sunlight playing in their midst. Turning Our face to the right, We beheld what the pen is powerless to describe; nor can it set forth that which the eye of the Lord of Mankind witnessed in that most sanctified, that most sublime, that blest, and most exalted Spot. Turning, then, to the left We gazed on one of the Beauties of the Most Sublime Paradise, standing on a pillar of light, and calling aloud saying: 'O inmates of earth and heaven! Behold ye My beauty, and My radiance, and My revelation, and My effulgence. By God, the True One! I am Trustworthiness and the revelation thereof, and the beauty thereof. I will recompense whosoever will cleave unto Me, and recognize My rank and station, and hold fast unto My hem. I am the most great ornament of the people of Bahá, and the vesture of glory unto all who are in the kingdom of creation. I am the

* see below, Appendix II and p. 354.

† For example, see vol. 1, p. 242, and vol. 3, pp. 223–4.

supreme instrument for the prosperity of the world, and the horizon of assurance unto all beings.'[5]

In all His Writings Bahá'u'lláh has exhorted His followers to adorn themselves with the vesture of divine qualities and goodly character. But He has placed a special emphasis on trustworthiness. We cannot imagine a bounty or privilege greater than attaining the presence of the Supreme Manifestation of God. And yet He states in a Tablet to His apostle 'Alí-Muḥammad-i-Varqá* that in the sight of God it is much more meritorious for a believer to become endowed with trustworthiness than to travel all the way on foot and attain His presence. These are His words:

> Were a man in this day to adorn himself with the raiment of trustworthiness it were better for him in the sight of God than that he should journey on foot towards the holy court and be blessed with meeting the Adored One and standing before His Seat of Glory. Trustworthiness is as a stronghold to the city of humanity, and as eyes to the human temple. Whosoever remaineth deprived thereof shall, before His Throne, be reckoned as one bereft of vision.[6]

In the Tablet of Ṭarázát Bahá'u'lláh states:

> The fourth Taráz concerneth trustworthiness. Verily it is the door of security for all that dwell on earth and a token of glory on the part of the All-Merciful. He who partaketh thereof hath indeed partaken of the treasures of wealth and prosperity. Trustworthiness is the greatest portal leading unto the tranquillity and security of the people. In truth the stability of every affair hath depended and doth depend upon it. All the domains of power, of grandeur and of wealth are illumined by its light.[7]

* see below, ch. 4.

THE MANSION OF MAZRA'IH

'A lovely place, surrounded by gardens' (above).
Below, Bahá'u'lláh's reception room on the ground floor.
Here He received his guests and dictated to his amanuenses

THE RIḌVÁN GARDEN

Above, left and right:
the rectangle of benches in the middle of the garden where Bahá'u'lláh used to sit 'under the big mulberry tree, by the side of the little river rippling by, the fountain . . . splashing and gurgling in sounds refreshing indeed after the long years of confinement'.
Below right: the little house where Bahá'u'lláh used to rest

ḤÁJÍ MUḤAMMAD-I-YAZDÍ

One of the devoted believers resident in the Holy Land
(see pp. 23–26)

And in the Tablet of Is͟hráqát He reveals some of his choicest exhortations to His followers:

> Say: O people of God! Adorn your temples with the adornment of trustworthiness and piety. Help, then, your Lord with the hosts of goodly deeds and a praiseworthy character. We have forbidden you dissension and conflict in My Books, and My Scriptures, and My Scrolls, and My Tablets, and have wished thereby naught else save your exaltation and advancement.[8]

and again:

> O Jalíl! Admonish men to fear God. By God! This fear is the chief commander of the army of thy Lord. Its hosts are a praiseworthy character and goodly deeds. Through it have the cities of men's hearts been opened throughout the ages and centuries, and the standards of ascendancy and triumph raised above all other standards.[9]

In one of His Tablets[10] revealed in the year 1882 Bahá'u'lláh, in the words of His amanuensis,* gives details of a case involving two believers in Alexandria who had acted with exemplary honesty and had won His good-pleasure. They were Ḥájí Muḥammad-i-Yazdí and Siyyid 'Alíy-i-Yazdí. These two men were not related but were partners in a successful business establishment. Before going into details of this Tablet about trustworthiness, it is appropriate at this juncture to give a brief account of the life and services of Ḥájí Muḥammad.†

Ḥájí Muḥammad was a son of Ḥájí 'Abdu'r-Raḥím-i-Qannád

* Some Tablets of Bahá'u'lláh are composed in such a way that a part of the Tablet is in the words of His amanuensis, but in fact was dictated by Bahá'u'lláh to appear as if composed by the amanuensis. Every word of the Tablet, therefore, is from Bahá'u'lláh Himself. For more information see vol. 1, pp. 40–42.

† A brief account of the life of Siyyid 'Alíy-i-Yazdí is given in *Chosen Highway*, pp. 131–2.

(candymaker) from Yazd. In his unpublished 'History of the Faith in the Province of Yazd', Ḥájí Muḥammad-Ṭáhir-i-Málmírí has written an account of the life of Ḥájí 'Abdu'r-Raḥím. The following is a summary of a portion of his notes:

> It is very difficult for me to describe his exalted character, his spirituality, and radiance, the depth of his faith and his devotion to the Cause of God. Suffice it to say that when the news of the conversion to the Faith of Ḥájí 'Abdu'r-Raḥím became public knowledge, Mírzá Muḥammad-Taqí, a mujtahid [doctor of Islamic law] of Yazd, was highly disturbed. He was reported to have said, 'If the whole population of Yazd had been converted to this new Faith, I would not have been as much disturbed as I am now over the conversion of Ḥájí 'Abdu'r-Raḥím. Now the back of Islám is broken.'

Because his life was in danger some time after his embracing the Faith, Ḥájí 'Abdu'r-Raḥím was forced to leave Yazd, and eventually went to the Holy Land. He was very dear to Bahá'u'lláh and was permitted by Him to reside there. Among his four sons were Shaykh 'Alí, the eldest, whom Bahá'u'lláh sent on a mission to Khartúm where he established a business and later died. As already mentioned, the other son, Ḥájí Muḥammad, established a business with two other believers in Alexandria. And the youngest son, Aḥmad Effendi, was given the honour by 'Abdu'l-Bahá of marrying His youngest daughter.

In the Tablet mentioned above Mírzá Áqá Ján gives the story of the events following Shaykh 'Alí's death in Khartúm. He says that when he died the Persian Consul sent the full account of his assets to the commercial attaché of the Persian Embassy in Cairo who in turn demanded the payment of the death duties required by law. Shaykh 'Alí's younger brother Ḥájí Muḥammad and one of his partners Siyyid 'Alí, who are both praised in this Tablet by Bahá'u'lláh for their trustworthiness, assured the authorities that they would fulfil their obligation in this regard. A number of leading merchants of the city also assured the Persian attaché that the Bahá'ís were trustworthy people and would honour their obligation. This episode coincided with the bombardment of Alexandria by British forces in 1882 when a great part of the city was ruined and the business house of Ḥájí Muḥammad, together with all its goods, was utterly destroyed.

The two men returned to the Holy Land almost penniless. They succeeded, however, in obtaining a sum of money sufficient to pay their debt to the authorities. Siyyid 'Alí travelled to Cairo and although by then the former commercial attaché had been dismissed from his post, he presented the sum of fifty English guineas* to his successor. Both the merchants and the embassy officials were deeply touched by this action. Knowing that the partners' business had been completely wiped out, the commercial attaché at first refused to accept the money. He is reported to have said that this noble act of honesty demonstrated by the Bahá'ís was sufficient for him. However, in the end he took the money and stated that the best reward in this transaction was that the enemies of the Faith were praising the conduct of its followers.

Bahá'u'lláh in this Tablet describes this action by the two believers as the king of goodly deeds. He prays that His followers in every land may manifest the spirit of trustworthiness among the people.

The story of Ḥájí Muḥammad would not be complete without referring to one of his noble qualities, namely, his utter obedience to the Centre of the Cause. There was a time when Ḥájí Muḥammad had a business concern in 'Akká. One day he was sitting in his office when the Master arrived with an urgent instruction from Bahá'u'lláh that Ḥájí Muḥammad should immediately proceed to Jaddih (Jiddah) in Arabia. He asked 'Abdu'l-Bahá if he could be permitted to attain the presence of

* An obsolete English gold coin. Its value was finally 21 shillings.

Bahá'u'lláh before departing for Jaddih. The Master told him that there was no time, for the boat was leaving at any minute. Ḥájí Muḥammad at once closed the office, and without even paying a visit to his family boarded the ship which sailed away almost immediately. Once on board, he realized that because of the extraordinary rush, he had not even thought to ask the Master the purpose of his trip to Jaddih. But now it was too late, and he knew that Bahá'u'lláh would guide his steps when he arrived in that city. This is the best example of instant, exact and complete obedience to the command of Bahá'u'lláh.

The journey was fraught with danger because the sea was unusually stormy. The danger of the ship sinking was in everyone's mind except for Ḥájí Muḥammad, who was sure that it would sail safely to its destination because God had given him a mission in Jaddih, the nature of which was as yet unknown to him. Soon after disembarking from the ship, he heard two people speaking in Persian among the crowds. When he approached them he soon found out that they were Bahá'ís. They were Ḥájí Mírzá Ḥaydar-'Alí, that illustrious follower of Bahá'u'lláh, and his fellow prisoner Ḥusayn-i-Shírází who had been set free from their ten-year imprisonment in Khartúm and were on their way to 'Akká.* They were in need of help and guidance, for this was their first journey to the Holy Land. Ḥájí Muḥammad knew then that the purpose of his mission in Jaddih was to assist these two souls to go to 'Akká, a task which he then carried out ably.[11]

Concerning trustworthiness, 'Abdu'l-Bahá in a Tablet to Ḥájí Áqá Muḥammad-i-'Aláqih-band, a devoted Bahá'í from Yazd, states that should a believer succeed in carrying out all goodly deeds but fail, even to a small measure, in trustworthiness and faithfulness, all his good deeds will be void.

These are His words:

> If a man were to perform every good work, yet fail in the least scruple to be entirely trustworthy and honest, his good works

* For Ḥájí Mírzá Ḥaydar-'Alí's life and imprisonment see vol. 2.

would become as dry tinder and his failure as a soul-consuming fire. If, on the other hand, he should fall short in all his affairs, yet act with trustworthiness and honesty, all his defects would ultimately be righted, all injuries remedied, and all infirmities healed. Our meaning is that, in the sight of God, trustworthiness is the bedrock of His Faith and the foundation of all virtues and perfections. A man deprived of this quality is destitute of everything. What shall faith and piety avail if trustworthiness be lacking? Of what consequence can they be? What benefit or advantage can they confer? Wherefore 'Abdu'l-Bahá counselleth the friends – nay rather, fervently imploreth them – so vigilantly to guard the sanctity of the Cause of God and preserve their own dignity as individuals that all nations shall come to know and honour them for their trustworthiness and integrity. They can render no greater service than this today. To act otherwise would be to take an axe to the root of the Cause of God – we take refuge with God from this heinous transgression and pray that He will protect His loved ones from committing so flagrant a wrong.[12]

In another Tablet to Jináb-i-Ibn-i-Abhar,* one of the Hands of the Cause of God, 'Abdu'l-Bahá states that in their dealings with each other, the believers must uphold the highest standard of honesty and trustworthiness:

You have written on the question of how the friends should proceed in their business dealings with one another. This is a question of the greatest importance and a matter that deserveth the liveliest concern. In relations of this kind, the friends of God should act with the utmost trustworthiness and integrity. To be remiss in this area would be to turn one's face away from the counsels of the Blessed Beauty and the holy precepts of God. If a man in his own home doth not treat his relations and friends with entire trustworthiness and integrity, his

* see below, pp. 322–31.

> dealings with the outside world – no matter how much trustworthiness and honesty he may bring to them – will prove barren and unproductive. First one should order one's own domestic affairs, then attend to one's business with the public. One should certainly not argue that the friends need not be treated with undue care, or that it is unnecessary for them to attach too great importance to the practice of trustworthiness in their dealings with one another, but that it is in their relations with strangers that correct behaviour is essential. Talk like this is sheer fantasy and will lead to detriment and loss. Blessed be the soul that shineth with the light of trustworthiness among the people and becometh a sign of perfection amidst all men.[13]

Addressing Sulṭán 'Abdu'l-'Azíz, Bahá'u'lláh in the *Súriy-i-Mulúk* (Súrih of the Kings) makes this thought-provoking statement:

> Know thou for a certainty that whoso disbelieveth in God is neither trustworthy nor truthful. This, indeed, is the truth, the undoubted truth. He that acteth treacherously towards God will, also, act treacherously towards his king. Nothing whatever can deter such a man from evil, nothing can hinder him from betraying his neighbor, nothing can induce him to walk uprightly.[14]

For some, especially those who are not Bahá'ís, it may be difficult to accept the statement that a person who does not believe in God is not truthful or trustworthy. Of course there are many who do not believe in God but are honest people. However, the proper time for judging honesty or trustworthiness is the time when a person faces a difficult test. In normal circumstances many people behave truthfully. But when confronted with seemingly insurmountable tests or irresistible temptations, then, if there is no fear of God, one will succumb under pressure. In the final analysis it is belief in God and His Messengers that evokes the urge to obey His teachings even in times of test and provocation. The fear of God, according to Bahá'í teachings, is the only means by which the individual can withstand the onslaught of self and passion in times of temptation. In one of His Tablets Bahá'u'lláh thus reveals:

> The fear of God hath ever been a sure defence and a safe stronghold for all the peoples of the world. It is the chief cause of the protection of mankind, and the supreme instrument for its preservation. Indeed, there existeth in man a faculty which deterreth him from, and guardeth him against, whatever is unworthy and unseemly, and which is known as his sense of shame. This, however, is confined to but a few; all have not possessed and do not possess it.[15]

Some believe that a loving God need not be feared. In a previous volume* we have discussed the significance of the fear of God and explained that without it the believer cannot have the strength to sever his attachment to the material world and fix his gaze upon the heavenly abode of his soul.

Abu'l-Qásim the Gardener

There are many anecdotes about Bahá'u'lláh in the Garden of Riḍván. The following is an account by May Bolles Maxwell† describing in beautiful language her impressions of the garden when she visited it during her pilgrimage. May Maxwell was among the first group of pilgrims from the West to visit the Master in 1898–9. She may be regarded as one of the few spiritual giants of the Faith in the Western world. When she passed away Shoghi Effendi, the Guardian of the Faith, described her as "Abdu'l-Bahá's beloved handmaid and distinguished

* see vol. 2, pp. 94–6.

† For a brief story of her life see *Bahá'í World*, vol. VIII, pp. 631–42.

disciple' and bestowed upon her the rank of martyr.

These are her reminiscences:

After driving for about half an hour we reached the garden where Bahá'u'lláh spent much of His time during His long years of exile in 'Akká. Although this garden is small it is one of the loveliest spots we had ever seen. Bahá'u'lláh frequently said to His gardener, Abu'l-Qásim, '*This is the most beautiful garden in the world.*' With its tall trees, its wealth of flowers, and its fountains, it lies like a peerless gem surrounded by two limpid streams of water just as it is described in the Qur'án; and the atmosphere which pervades it is so fraught with sacred memories, with divine significance, with heavenly peace and calm that one no longer marvels to hear of the traveller who, passing one day before its gates, paused and gazing in saw Bahá'u'lláh seated beneath the shade of the mulberry trees, 'that canopy not made with hands,' and remembering the prophecy in the Qur'án, he recognized his Lord and hastened to prostrate himself at His feet.

We visited the little house at the end of the garden and stood on the threshold of that room where Bahá'u'lláh was wont to sit in hot weather, and one by one we knelt down, and with tears of love and longing kissed the ground where His blessed feet had rested. We returned to the garden, where Abu'l-Qásim made tea for us, and there he told us the story of the locusts. How that during one hot summer there had been a pest of locusts and they had consumed most of the foliage in the surrounding country. One day Abu'l-Qásim saw a thick cloud coming swiftly towards the garden, and in a moment thousands of locusts were covering the tall trees beneath which Bahá'u'lláh so often sat. Abu'l-Qásim hastened to the house at the end of the garden and coming before his Lord besought Him, saying: 'My Lord, the locusts have come, and are eating away the shade from above Thy blessed head. I beg of Thee to cause them to depart.' The Manifestation smiled, and said:

> '*The locusts must be fed, let them be.*' Much chagrined, Abu'l-Qásim returned to the garden and for some time watched the destructive work in silence; but presently, unable to bear it, he ventured to return again to Bahá'u'lláh and humbly entreat Him to send away the locusts. The Blessed Perfection arose and went into the garden and stood beneath the trees covered with the insects. Then He said: '*Abu'l-Qásim does not want you; God protect you.*' And lifting up the hem of His robe He shook it, and immediately all the locusts arose in a body and flew away.
>
> When Abu'l-Qásim concluded this story he exclaimed with strong emotion as he touched his eyes: 'Oh, blessed are these eyes to have seen such things; oh, blessed are these ears to have heard such things.' In parting he gave us flowers, and seemed, like all the oriental believers, unable to do enough to show his love.[16]

Abu'l-Qásim* referred to in this story is the first gardener who dedicated his life to the service of Bahá'u'lláh in that garden. He was a native of the village of Man<u>sh</u>ád in the district of Yazd. It was mainly through his hard work that the garden was built for Bahá'u'lláh. One of Abu'l-Qásim's brothers was Muḥammad-Ibráhím who also served Bahá'u'lláh as a gardener at Bahjí and other places.

Ustád 'Alí-Akbar-i-Banná,† an illustrious martyr of the Faith, has recounted in his detailed history of the Faith in 'I<u>sh</u>qábád the following concerning these two brothers:

> For twenty-seven years‡ these two brothers, Áqá Abu'l-Qásim and Áqá Muḥammad-Ibráhím have been serving in the Holy Land. Áqá Abu'l-Qásim has always been a gardener

* Not to be confused with the renowned Mírzá Abu'l-Qásim-i-<u>Kh</u>urásání, who was the caretaker of the Shrine of Bahá'u'lláh and the gardens.

† see below, pp. 123–30.

‡ He began writing this as yet unpublished history around 1902.

at the Riḍván Gardens while Áqá Muḥammad-Ibráhím was a gardener at Bahjí, the Junayn Gardens, etc. Seventeen years ago when I had the honour of attaining the presence of Bahá'u'lláh, Áqá Muḥammad-Ibráhím in the course of our conversation told me the following story:

'One day the Blessed Beauty was in one of the holy places . . . That place was surrounded by dry reeds and grass. Suddenly these caught fire and the flames rapidly began to spread around. His blessed Person turned to me and said:

"Ibráhím, go and put out the fire." I immediately went towards the fire not knowing how to carry out this task. As I approached, a wind blew and pushed the fire away from me. As if the fire was fleeing from me. I put out the fire by throwing a small amount of earth over it. This incident brought to my mind the verse: "We said, O fire, be Thou cold and a preservation unto Ibráhím . . . "'*

Dr Habíb Mu'ayyad, who travelled to 'Akká in 1907 and was permitted by the Master to study medicine in the University of Beirut, and who later served 'Abdu'l-Bahá in the Holy Land with great dedication, has recorded in his memoirs a brief account of the activities of Abu'l-Qásim in the Garden of Riḍván. The following is a summary of his reminiscences:

Abu'l-Qásim served in the Garden of Riḍván for many years. He worked as a gardener tending the trees, the fruits and flowers. He welcomed the friends to the garden, whether pilgrims or residents, entertained them lovingly, and ensured that they enjoyed their visit. He had devised a master-plan to prevent the Arab inhabitants of 'Akká from entering the Garden.† Whenever he was leaving the Garden to go to 'Akká

* *Qur'án* 21:68. This verse is about Abraham being thrown into the fire by his people, when God turned the fire cold.

† The Garden of Riḍván was a very beautiful oasis in the area, a place full of fruits and flowers which some of the inhabitants were eager to take away. If

> either to attain the presence of the Master or to purchase food or other necessities, he would lock the gate with the instruction that it should remain locked until his return. He had invented two passwords, one which signalled that the gate was to be opened and the other that it should remain shut. When he returned, if there was no one outside the garden wanting to get in, he would call out a fictitious name, 'Shukru'lláh' (Thanks to God). This meant, 'Thanks to God there is no one bothering us', and the gate would open! If, however, there were some people outside, he would call out the name 'Ḥasan' which in Persian sounds phonetically like 'They are', meaning, 'They are waiting outside', and the gate would not open! People thought that Ḥasan was the name of the gardener's servant. And since there was no response from Ḥasan they would eventually leave the garden area and go home. In this way Abu'l-Qásim protected the fruits and flowers of the garden from the inhabitants.[17]

Abu'l-Qásim was tall with broad shoulders, massive in size – a real heavyweight – and 'Abdu'l-Bahá sometimes made humorous remarks about his size and strength, remarks which invoked feelings of joy and gratitude in Abu'l-Qásim.

---

they had been able to gain admission, it would have been impossible to keep the Garden as a holy place. (A.T.)

3

Lawḥ-i-Ḥikmat

As we have stated in previous volumes, many pilgrims, mainly from Persia, travelled to the Holy Land and attained the presence of Bahá'u'lláh. Most of the well-known teachers of the Faith and His apostles had the privilege of meeting Him at least once in their lives, and there were some who had this privilege several times. One such outstanding believer was Áqá Muḥammad-i-Qá'iní, entitled Nabíl-i-Akbar. He came to 'Akká around the year AH 1290 (AD 1873–4) and attained the presence of Bahá'u'lláh in the House of 'Abbúd. His first interview with Him had taken place some years before in Ba<u>gh</u>dád when He recognized the station of Bahá'u'lláh through some interesting incidents.* It was on the occasion of his pilgrimage to 'Akká that Bahá'u'lláh revealed the *Lawḥ-i-Ḥikmat* in his honour.†

All the Tablets revealed by Bahá'u'lláh after the *Kitáb-i-Aqdas* assume a special significance, which will be discussed later. This Tablet in Arabic, revealed before Bahá'u'lláh's move to Mazra'ih, stands out amongst the Writings of Bahá'u'lláh for its philosophical terminology and its references to ancient Greek philosophers, as well as profound explanations of the influence of the Word of God, the cause and origin of creation, the mysterious workings of nature, and many other weighty topics. Nabíl-i-Akbar, its recipient, was a man of great knowledge and learning. He was not only distinguished among his contemporaries in the field of theology, but renowned throughout Persia as an accomplished philosopher whose erudition

---

* For his life see vol. 1, pp. 91–5, and vol. 2, pp. 42–3, 341–6.

† This Tablet has been translated into English in its entirety and is published in *Tablets of Bahá'u'lláh*, pp. 137–52.

had endeared him to men of culture and high intellect before he embraced the Faith.

The following are the words of 'Abdu'l-Bahá paying tribute to this great man of God:

> A sign of guidance he was, an emblem of the fear of God. For this Faith, he laid down his life, and in dying, triumphed. He passed by the world and its rewards; he closed his eyes to rank and wealth; he loosed himself from all such chains and fetters, and put every worldly thought aside. Of wide learning, at once a mujtahid, a philosopher, a mystic, and gifted with intuitive sight, he was also an accomplished man of letters and an orator without a peer. He had a great and universal mind.
>
> Praise be to God, at the end he was made the recipient of heavenly grace. Upon him be the glory of God, the All-Glorious. May God shed the brightness of the Abhá Kingdom upon his resting-place. May God welcome him into the Paradise of reunion, and shelter him forever in the realm of the righteous, submerged in an ocean of lights.[1]

It is therefore not surprising that Bahá'u'lláh chose to reveal this Tablet in the language of an intellectual philosopher. In it He deplores the condition of the world and its peoples. The following words portray His ominous observations.

> We exhort mankind in these days when the countenance of justice is soiled with dust, when the flames of unbelief are burning high and the robe of wisdom rent asunder, when tranquillity and faithfulness have ebbed away and trials and tribulations have waxed severe, when covenants are broken and ties are severed, when no man knoweth how to discern light and darkness or to distinguish guidance from error.[2]

At no time has the perversity of the human race which He describes been more evident than it is today. In many of His

Tablets Bahá'u'lláh warned mankind that unless they recognized and turned to Him, world conditions would deteriorate day by day. And He prophesies that the old order will be rolled up and a new one spread out in its stead. Having described some of the ills afflicting human society, Bahá'u'lláh in the Tablet of Ḥikmat reveals some of the choicest of His counsels which can alone deliver mankind from the abyss of ungodliness into which it has sunk so deeply.

Teachings for the Spiritualization of Humanity

Addressing the peoples of the world, Bahá'u'lláh in this Tablet sets out some of those teachings which are designed to spiritualize the human race and usher in an age in which nobility of character and the acquisition of divine virtues will become the main aim of life for the individual.

> O peoples of the world! Forsake all evil, hold fast that which is good. Strive to be shining examples unto all mankind, and true reminders of the virtues of God amidst men. He that riseth to serve My Cause should manifest My wisdom, and bend every effort to banish ignorance from the earth. Be united in counsel, be one in thought. Let each morn be better than its eve and each morrow richer than its yesterday. Man's merit lieth in service and virtue and not in the pageantry of wealth and riches.[3]

To 'forsake all evil' and become 'shining examples' are not possible to achieve simply by trying. To reach this exalted goal the heart must be touched by the love of God, and this is not possible until the individual recognizes His Manifestation for today and becomes assured of the truth of His Mission. It is then that his strivings to acquire heavenly virtues can be assisted by God. The key is to acquire certitude in one's faith. Bahá'u'lláh in a Tablet[4] to one of his hand-maidens affirms that the heart is the dawning-place of the light of His Countenance, and the treasure-house of the pearls of His love. He urges her to bathe her heart with the waters of certitude, so that it may be cleansed from the remembrance of anyone save Him. Only then can it become the recipient of His boundless favours.

Mírzá Abu'l-Faḍl, the renowned Bahá'í scholar, states in one of his well-known treatises that the way in which an individual can acquire certitude has been given in the *Qur'án* in the following verse:

> Worship Thy Lord until thou attainest certitude.[5]

As we have already stated in a previous volume,* Mírzá Abu'l-Faḍl became the embodiment of divine virtues and perfections to such an extent that 'Abdu'l-Bahá urged the friends to emulate him as their exemplar. Even a cursory study of his life will demonstrate that his noble achievements were mainly due to his deep sense of attachment to God and an irresistible urge to worship Him.

The worship of God is not limited to prayer and acts of devotional service. There are other aspects which are just as important. The essential qualities which man needs in his devotions are sincerity of motive and submissiveness to his Creator. To turn to God at all times with true love, to commune with Him in spirit, to regard Him as always present, to praise and glorify Him by word and by deed, to pray ardently for His confirmations, to promote His Cause, to carry out His teachings and to serve mankind in one's daily work – all these acts constitute the main features of worshipping God. Prayer alone will not be conducive to the good-pleasure of God if it is not followed by service to the Cause. This is confirmed in many of Bahá'u'lláh's Writings.

Returning to the Tablet of Ḥikmat, we note the exhortation, 'Let each morn be better than its eve . . . ' This counsel may

* For his life see vol. 3, and below, pp. 274–87.

be regarded as the application of one of the laws of creation. In this life any living organism is either growing or declining. The same principle applies to the soul of man. The only difference in this case is that the individual has to make the choice of either growing spiritually or not. All the qualities and virtues which the soul acquires in this life, together with one's faith, must be allowed to grow day by day. If not, the person is going to decline, perhaps without realizing it. For in God's creation there is no in-between state of things or remaining stationary. Bahá'u'lláh's counsel to better our spiritual condition every day is thus a fundamental principle of creation. In one of His Tablets[6] he further emphasizes this principle when He states that the believer should arrange his life in such a way that with each breath he may become a new person and with each step arrive at a loftier height, so that in this way he may, at all times, be engaged in the purification of his own self.

In the Tablet of Ḥikmat Bahá'u'lláh further exhorts the peoples of the world in these words:

> Take heed that your words be purged from idle fancies and worldly desires and your deeds be cleansed from craftiness and suspicion. Dissipate not the wealth of your precious lives in the pursuit of evil and corrupt affection, nor let your endeavours be spent in promoting your personal interest. Be generous in your days of plenty, and be patient in the hour of loss. Adversity is followed by success and rejoicings follow woe. Guard against idleness and sloth, and cling unto that which profiteth mankind, whether young or old, whether high or low. Beware lest ye sow tares of dissension among men or plant thorns of doubt in pure and radiant hearts.
>
> O ye beloved of the Lord! Commit not that which defileth the limpid stream of love or destroyeth the sweet fragrance of friendship. By the righteousness of the Lord! Ye were created to show love one to another and not perversity and rancour. Take pride not in love for yourselves but in love for your

> fellow-creatures. Glory not in love for your country, but in love for all mankind. Let your eye be chaste, your hand faithful, your tongue truthful and your heart enlightened. Abase not the station of the learned in Bahá and belittle not the rank of such rulers as administer justice amidst you. Set your reliance on the army of justice, put on the armour of wisdom, let your adorning be forgiveness and mercy and that which cheereth the hearts of the well-favoured of God.[7]

Bahá'u'lláh has often referred to the 'learned in Bahá', as in this Tablet, and extolled their virtues. He has also praised the 'rulers in Bahá'. Shoghi Effendi, the Guardian of the Faith, has explained these two terms in the following passage, which is translated from Persian.

> In this holy cycle the 'learned' are, on the one hand, the Hands of the Cause of God, and, on the other, the teachers and diffusers of His teachings who do not rank as hands, but who have attained an eminent position in the teaching work. As to the 'rulers', they refer to the members of the Local, National and International Houses of Justice.[8]

Bahá'u'lláh has paid glowing tribute to the 'learned in Bahá' in the *Kitáb-i-Aqdas*. We have referred to this in a previous volume.*

The exalted counsels of the Tablet of Ḥikmat are in marked contrast to the way in which the great majority of the peoples of the world are conducting their lives today. However, a careful study of the Mission of Bahá'u'lláh makes it clear that His Faith is destined to embrace the whole of the human race, and that in the fullness of time these exhortations are designed to exert the greatest influence upon the life of man on this planet, to revolutionize human society and shape the conduct of its individual members in accordance with His heavenly teachings.

* vol. 2, p. 265.

But during His Ministry Bahá'u'lláh endured with patience and forbearance the many cruelties which a perverse generation inflicted upon Him. He refers to Himself as the Celestial Bird when he pours out His heart to Nabíl-i-Akbar, saying:

> In such circumstances as thou seest, how can the Celestial Bird soar into the atmosphere of divine mysteries when its wings have been battered with the stones of idle fancy and bitter hatred, and it is cast into a prison built of unyielding stone? By the righteousness of God! The people have perpetrated a grievous injustice.[9]

In this Tablet Bahá'u'lláh alludes to Náṣiri'd-Dín Shah when he says: 'We revealed unto one of the rulers that which overpowereth all the dwellers of the earth.'[10] And, further on, He alludes to the martyrdom of Badí'* when he refers to the lamentations of the 'inmates of the cities of justice and equity'.

The Origin of Creation

The Tablet of Ḥikmat reveals some of the mysteries of God's creation. In one of His Tablets,[11] Bahá'u'lláh states that in each verse of the Tablet of Ḥikmat an ocean is concealed. In answer to a question by Nabíl-i-Akbar concerning the origin of creation, Bahá'u'lláh reveals these words:

> As regards thine assertions about the beginning of creation, this is a matter on which conceptions vary by reason of the divergences in men's thoughts and opinions. Wert thou to assert that it hath ever existed and shall continue to exist, it would be true; or wert thou to affirm the same concept as is mentioned in the sacred Scriptures, no doubt would there be about it, for it hath been revealed by God, the Lord of the worlds. Indeed He was a hidden treasure. This is a station that

* see vol. 3, ch. 9.

> can never be described nor even alluded to. And concerning the question, 'I did wish to make Myself known'; there was God, and His creation had ever existed beneath His shelter from the beginning that hath no beginning, apart from its being preceded by a Firstness which cannot be regarded as firstness and originated by a Cause inscrutable even unto all men of learning.[12]

There are some profound statements in the above passage. Bahá'u'lláh describes two well-known concepts concerning the origin of creation. One is that creation has always existed and that it has no beginning nor will have an end. The other relates to a *ḥadí<u>th</u>* (tradition) of Islám in which the voice of God proclaims, 'I was a hidden treasure, I wished to make Myself known, so I created man that I might be known.'* Bahá'u'lláh explains that these two concepts in the above passage are in reality the same. Bahá'u'lláh and 'Abdu'l-Bahá in many of their Tablets have asserted that creation has existed from the beginning that has no beginning. Since God is eternal and has always existed and will continue to exist till the end that has no end, so His creation has also existed from eternity. It is impossible to imagine that there was a time when 'nothingness' had an existence. For there can be no such thing as absolute non-existence.

The other concept, that God was a hidden treasure and created man in order to make Himself known, seems to imply an interval without a creation. Such a concept is tantamount to saying that there was a time when God was devoid of His attribute 'the Creator'. Bahá'u'lláh in the Tablet of Ḥikmat rejects this theory and confirms that creation had no beginning. He says: '. . . There was God, and His creation had ever

* When in Ba<u>gh</u>dád, Bahá'u'lláh instructed 'Abdu'l-Bahá, who was then in His teens, to write a commentary on the above Islamic tradition. 'Abdu'l-Bahá's detailed commentary was so profound and illuminating that it aroused the admiration of men of knowledge and erudition. For further information see vol. 2, p. 390.

existed beneath His shelter from the beginning that hath no beginning . . . '

Having established this basic truth, He describes the beginning of creation 'being preceded by a Firstness which cannot be regarded as firstness . . . ' In these words Bahá'u'lláh makes a distinction between the eternity of God and the eternity of His creation. The existence of God is not preceded by a cause whereas creation has come into being through a cause. 'Abdu'l-Bahá has explained* that creation emanates from God, and that it does not come about through incarnation. The difference between emanation and incarnation can be explained by the following examples: A book emanates from the author. But no part of the author can be said to be a part of his book, and so he does not incarnate himself in his creation. On the other hand, a seed manifests itself in its creation which is the tree, its branches and its fruits. In this case we note that the seed has become part of the tree. Another example is the sun and its rays. The rays emanate from the sun. It does not break up into pieces to form the rays. It is the same with God and His creation. The creation emanates from God. It has not come into being through incarnation, for if it had, then God would have to be a part of creation, and this would immediately reduce Him to the state of a finite being.

Having established that creation emanates from God, we note a similarity between the sun and its rays. 'Abdu'l-Bahá has spoken about this, as recorded in *Some Answered Questions*:

> Although the rays are always inseparable from the sun, the sun is pre-existent and the rays are originated; for the existence of the rays depends upon that of the sun, but the converse does not hold true: The sun is the bestower of grace and the rays are the grace itself.[13]

Similarly creation cannot be dissociated from God, and the two exist together. But God is pre-existent and self-subsisting.

* see *Some Answered Questions*, ch. 53 and 54.

He is exalted above firstness or lastness or time, whereas creation is preceded by a cause. It is 'preceded by a firstness which cannot be regarded as firstness and originated by a Cause inscrutable even unto all men of learning'.

The relationship between God and His creation is explained by 'Abdu'l-Bahá in these words:

> Therefore, although the contingent world exists, in relation to the existence of God it is non-existence and nothingness. Man and dust both exist, but how great the difference between the existence of the mineral and that of man! The one in relation to the other is non-existence. Likewise, the existence of creation is non-existence in relation to that of God. Thus, even though the universe has existence, in relation to God it is non-existence.[14]

In the *Lawḥ-i-'Abdu'l-Vahháb* revealed in 'Akká Bahá'u'lláh speaks about the immortality of the soul. Of its existence in the spiritual worlds of God He reveals these words:

> Such an existence is a contingent and not an absolute existence, inasmuch as the former is preceded by a cause, whilst the latter is independent thereof. Absolute existence is strictly confined to God, exalted be His glory.[15]

In the Tablet of Ḥikmat Bahá'u'lláh confirms that creation had always existed but not in the same form. These are His words:

> That which hath been in existence had existed before, but not in the form thou seest today.[16]

The universe with all its heavenly bodies is infinite in range and eternal in time. However, change is one of the characteristics of matter. Anything which is composed of matter will eventually decompose. Some heavenly bodies disintegrate while others come into being. But existence as a whole remains eternal and perpetual.

A vital clue to the origin of creation is given in the following statement by Bahá'u'lláh in the Tablet of Ḥikmat:

> The world of existence came into being through the heat generated from the interaction between the active force and that which is its recipient. These two are the same, yet they are different. Thus doth the Great Announcement inform thee about this glorious structure. Such as communicate the generating influence and such as receive its impact are indeed created through the irresistible Word of God which is the Cause of the entire creation, while all else besides His Word are but the creatures and the effects thereof. Verily thy Lord is the Expounder, the All-Wise.[17]

To appreciate the above passage one needs to be well versed in ancient Greek and Islamic philosophy. Bahá'u'lláh has used the terminology of the ancient philosophers to expound the true cause of creation. The theory of the 'active force' and 'its recipient' is related to the four elements, fire, air, water and earth. To those who are familiar with this philosophy, it is clear how the 'active force' and 'its recipient' are the same and yet different. However, this theory, which is very ancient and complicated, is beyond the scope of this book.[18] What is important to the general reader is the disclosure by Bahá'u'lláh that creation has come about through the heat generated by the interaction of this 'active force' and 'its recipient', and that these two were created through the Word of God.

There are many Tablets in which Bahá'u'lláh has elucidated the process of creation. But in all these He has asserted that the Word of God, sent down from the Heaven of Divine Revelation, is the cause of life both physical and spiritual. In a Tablet[19] Bahá'u'lláh states that the life of everything is dependent upon the Word of God.

Not only do the Writings of Bahá'u'lláh bear ample testimony to this truth, but the Holy Books of past Dispensations also confirm it. In the Gospels it is recorded:

> In the beginning was the Word, and the Word was with God and the Word was God.[20]

We read in Isaiah:

> For as the rain cometh down, and the snow from heaven, and returneth not thither, but watereth the earth, and maketh it bring forth and bud . . . So shall my word be that goeth forth out of my mouth: it shall not return unto me void, but it shall accomplish that which I please . . . [21]

It is stated in Islám that when God wanted to create, He uttered one word 'BE',* and then creation came into being. Much has been quoted from Bahá'í scriptures in previous volumes† about the potency of the Word of God and its creative energies.

Bahá'u'lláh in the Tablet of Ḥikmat has disclosed to mankind the mystery of the creative power of God. He has imparted the knowledge of the origin of creation. He thus affirms:

> Every event must needs have an origin and every building a builder. Verily the Word of God is the cause which hath preceded the contingent world . . . [22]

But in the same way that man is unable to know the essence of God, he is also unable to understand the process by which the Word of God has brought creation into being. Of the sacred nature of the Word, Bahá'u'lláh reveals in the Tablet of Ḥikmat:

> Know thou, moreover, that the Word of God – exalted be His

* For further information see vol. 1, p. 30.
† see vol. 1, ch. 3.

> glory – is higher and far superior to that which the senses can perceive, for it is sanctified from any property or substance. It transcendeth the limitations of known elements and is exalted above all the essential and recognized substances. It became manifest without any syllable or sound and is none but the Command of God which pervadeth all created things. It hath never been withheld from the world of being. It is God's all-pervasive grace, from which all grace doth emanate. It is an entity far removed above all that hath been and shall be.[23]

God in His Essence is unknowable to man and His Manifestations. No description or attribute, however exalted, can ever be ascribed to His Essence. The divine attributes such as 'the All-Knowing', 'the All-Wise', 'the Omnipotent' and similar ones, cannot be assigned to God's innermost Being. If they could, then these attributes would impose limitations upon His Essence, which is exalted above any description or praise. These exalted designations are only attributed to God revealed to man and not to His Essence. One of the attributes of God is 'the Creator'. But nor can this attribute be ascribed to the inner reality of God. It seems that somehow the creative force emanates from God and is the source of divine revelation and of creation. It is also referred to as the 'Primal Will' of God or the Universal Reality. 'Abdu'l-Bahá speaks of it in these terms:

> It follows that all things have emanated from God; that is, it is through God that all things have been realized, and through Him that the contingent world has come to exist. The first thing to emanate from God is that universal reality which the ancient philosophers termed the 'First Intellect' and which the people of Bahá call the 'Primal Will'. This emanation, with respect to its action in the world of God, is not limited by either time or place and has neither beginning nor end, for in relation to God the beginning and the end are one and the same. The pre-existence of God is both essential and

temporal, while the origination of the contingent world is essential but not temporal, . . .

Though the First Intellect is without beginning, this does not mean that it shares in the pre-existence of God, for in relation to the existence of God the existence of that universal Reality is mere nothingness – it cannot even be said to exist, let alone to partake of the pre-existence of God. An explanation of this matter was provided on a previous occasion.[24]

Creation in this life takes place through the instrumentality of nature. And nature may be described as the manifestation of the 'Primal Will of God' in this physical universe. Bahá'u'lláh confirms this in the Tablet of Ḥikmat:

Say: Nature in its essence is the embodiment of My Name, the Maker, the Creator. Its manifestations are diversified by varying causes, and in this diversity there are signs for men of discernment. Nature is God's Will and is its expression in and through the contingent world. It is a dispensation of Providence ordained by the Ordainer, the All-Wise. Were anyone to affirm that it is the Will of God as manifested in the world of being, no one should question this assertion. It is endowed with a power whose reality men of learning fail to grasp. Indeed a man of insight can perceive naught therein save the effulgent splendour of Our Name, the Creator. Say: This is an existence which knoweth no decay, and Nature itself is lost in bewilderment before its revelations, its compelling evidences and its effulgent glory which have encompassed the universe.[25]

The subject of creation appears in many Tablets of Bahá'u'lláh and 'Abdu'l-Bahá, who have both shed much light on this theme. Their explanations will be of great assistance in widening the vision of mankind to the realities of God's creation. 'Abdu'l-Bahá has also enriched this knowledge through many of his talks and discourses. Notable among these are the talks given at the dinner table in His home in 'Akká, and compiled under the title *Some Answered Questions*. Another valuable source of information and enlightenment on this subject is *Amr va Khalq* (vol. 1), a compilation of the writings of Bahá'u'lláh and 'Abdu'l-Bahá in Persian.

In the Tablet of Ḥikmat Bahá'u'lláh recalls having explained to Nabíl-i-Akbar the mysteries of creation in the house of Majíd. This person is 'Abdu'l-Majíd-i-Shírází. A brief reference to this interview has been made in a previous volume.*

References to Ancient Philosophy

In the Tablet of Ḥikmat Bahá'u'lláh dwells at length on the work and beliefs of ancient Greek philosophers and sages. He asserts that 'the essence and fundamentals of philosophy have emanated from the Prophets', names some of the Greek philosophers who 'acquired wisdom' from the Prophets of Israel, affirms that the philosophers of old believed in God, praises the work of Socrates and refers to him as 'the most distinguished of all philosophers' who was 'highly versed in wisdom', and gives details of the work and aspirations of several sages of Greece.

It is obvious that some of these details are not to be found in history books, and are indeed revealed for the first time through the knowledge of God and His Revelation. Ethel Rosenberg, one of the early British Bahá'ís, asked 'Abdu'l-Bahá about some of the differences between the historical records and the accounts given by Bahá'u'lláh in the Tablet of Ḥikmat. In reply she received a lengthy Tablet from the Master.[26] In it 'Abdu'l-Bahá explains that records which relate to ancient times before Alexander the Great are not reliable, because they were compiled in later years, mainly from oral traditions. Furthermore, there are many major discrepancies

* see vol. 1, pp. 94–5.

even within reliable historical records. He gives the example of the Holy Book of Torah and states that there are three versions, the Hebrew, the Greek and the Sámerí. But they differ considerably about certain historical events which he enumerates in this Tablet. Having demonstrated the unreliability of ancient historical records, 'Abdu'l-Bahá states that the true version of history is that which is revealed to the Prophets of God. For they are the revealers of the Word of God and have the knowledge of past and future events.

We can find a striking example of this in the *Qur'án*. A great part of that Book consists of the stories found in the Old and the New Testaments. These were all revealed anew to Muḥammad, for He had no access to the Jewish and Christian Scriptures. Indeed, they were not translated into Arabic until centuries after the death of Muḥammad. One of the proofs of the authenticity of the Holy Bible is that its stories were confirmed centuries later through direct revelation in the *Qur'án*. It is interesting to note that the Quranic version of some of these stories contains details which cannot be found in the Old or the New Testaments. In addition, there are in the *Qur'án* some accounts of ancient prophets which are entirely new, and which give a fuller description altogether of the history of religions.

There is a verse in the *Qur'án* which throws light on this subject. In one of the chapters, the voice of God reveals some of the stories relating to Moses, Pharaoh and the children of Israel. Then, as if Muḥammad were in doubt about the veracity of some of the accounts, the voice of God addresses Him in these words:

> And if Thou art in doubt as to what We have revealed unto Thee, then ask those who have been reading the scriptures from before thee. The truth hath indeed come to Thee from Thy Lord so be not of those who doubt.[27]

God is the Knower of all things and if one believes that He manifests Himself to man through His Manifestations, then it follows that their words are the truth and that they have the knowledge of all things. To cite an example: it is well-known that Bahá'u'lláh had not read most of the Writings of the Báb, including the Bayán, the Mother Book of the Bábí Dispensation. He Himself testifies to this fact in these words addressed to the notorious Hádíy-i-Dawlat-Ábádí:*

> God testifieth and beareth Me witness that this Wronged One hath not perused the Bayán, nor been acquainted with its contents . . . I swear by God! This Wronged One, by reason of His constant association with men, hath not looked at these books [The Writings of the Báb], nor gazed with outward eye on these Writings.[28]

Despite this, Bahá'u'lláh, during His forty years' Ministry, quoted profusely from the Writings of the Báb. Innumerable are the passages of the Bayán and other Writings of the Báb that Bahá'u'lláh has quoted in His Tablets. Seen from the human point of view, such a performance is impossible of achievement. But there can be no comparison between God and man. The Manifestation of God is endowed with divine knowledge, whereas man is not. Past, present and future are all before the Chosen Ones of God who represent Him in this world. In the Tablet of Ḥikmat Bahá'u'lláh describes this:

> Thou knowest full well that We perused not the books which men possess and We acquired not the learning current amongst them, and yet whenever We desire to quote the sayings of the learned and of the wise, presently there will appear before the face of thy Lord in the form of a tablet all that which hath appeared in the world and is revealed in the Holy Books and Scriptures. Thus do We set down in writing that which the eye

* see below pp. 183–6.

> perceiveth. Verily His knowledge encompasseth the earth and the heavens.
>
> This is a Tablet wherein the Pen of the Unseen hath inscribed the knowledge of all that hath been and shall be – a knowledge that none other but My wondrous Tongue can interpret. Indeed My heart as it is in itself hath been purged by God from the concepts of the learned and is sanctified from the utterances of the wise. In truth naught doth it mirror forth but the revelations of God. Unto this beareth witness the Tongue of Grandeur in this perspicuous Book.[29]

Nabíl-i-Akbar, for whom the Tablet of Ḥikmat was revealed, was one of the greatest teachers of the Cause and very dear to Bahá'u'lláh. In this Tablet He reveals for him the secret of successfully teaching His Faith. Through His counsels He sets out the most important prerequisites for teaching. Although these exhortations are addressed to Nabíl-i-Akbar, they are equally applicable to other believers in their teaching work. These are the words of Bahá'u'lláh addressed to him:

> Teach thou the Cause of God with an utterance which will cause the bushes to be enkindled, and the call 'Verily, there is no God but Me, the Almighty, the Unconstrained' to be raised therefrom. Say: Human utterance is an essence which aspireth to exert its influence and needeth moderation. As to its influence, this is conditional upon refinement which in turn is dependent upon hearts which are detached and pure. As to its moderation, this hath to be combined with tact and wisdom as prescribed in the Holy Scriptures and Tablets. Meditate upon that which hath streamed forth from the heaven of the Will of thy Lord, He Who is the Source of all grace, that thou mayest grasp the intended meaning which is enshrined in the sacred depths of the Holy Writings.[30]

The Tablet of Ḥikmat is like an ocean. Nabíl-i-Akbar immersed himself in it and obtained a great many of the pearls of wisdom hidden in its depths. He was a distinguished believer who is regarded as one of Bahá'u'lláh's Apostles; he served his Lord with utter dedication until the end of his life. After his passing 'Abdu'l-Bahá conferred on him the rank of Hand of the Cause of God.

4

Varqá, Apostle of Bahá'u'lláh

While Bahá'u'lláh resided in the Mansion of Mazra'ih, many Bahá'ís came on pilgrimage and attained His presence. Notable among them was Ḥájí Mullá Miḥdiy-i-'Aṭrí, a native of Yazd, accompanied by two of his sons – the eldest, Mírzá Ḥusayn, and the youngest, 'Alí-Muḥammad, later surnamed Varqá by Bahá'u'lláh. The latter became one of the luminaries of the Faith, an Apostle of Bahá'u'lláh who in the end laid down his life in His path.

In his unpublished 'History of the Faith in the Province of Yazd', Ḥájí Muḥammad-Ṭáhir-i-Málmírí gives the following account:

> Ḥájí Mullá Mihdí used to produce quantities of rose water and attar of rose each year in Yazd, hence he was known as 'Atrí (distiller of attar) . . . One day he held a large meeting* in his house in Yazd and invited the Bahá'ís, including the members of the Afnán family,† to attend. About two hundred believers attended this meeting. Among them was a certain Dervish Mihdí, who was a Bahá'í and had a melodious voice.‡ He chanted Bahá'í songs in a very loud voice and a few others chanted Tablets. No such meeting had ever been held in Yazd since the Cause began in that city.

* In those days the believers did not assemble in large numbers at a meeting as this was a very unwise action to take. They usually met very discreetly in small numbers to avoid trouble and persecution by the enemies. (A.T.)

† Afnán, literally 'twigs', is a designation used by Bahá'u'lláh to indicate the Báb's kinsmen who are the descendants of the three maternal uncles of the Báb, of the two brothers of the wife of the Báb and of her sister. The Afnán families lived mainly in Shíráz and some in Yazd. (A.T.)

‡ Dervishes were in the habit of chanting the praise of the Lord in public. They were identified as Súfís. Very few of them became Bahá'ís. (A.T.)

The next morning Shaykh Muḥammad-Ḥasan-i-Sabzivárí [a leading mujtahid of Yazd and an inveterate enemy of the Cause] summoned Ḥájí Mullá Mihdí to his office and there ordered his men to flog him brutally in his presence. Then he issued orders for his exile from Yazd. Mírzá Ḥusayn and Mírzá 'Alí-Muḥammad [Varqá], his sons, went into hiding at the time of their father's arrest. The other son, Mírzá Ḥasan, fled to a neighbouring town.

Ḥájí Mullá Mihdí, accompanied by his two sons Mírzá Ḥusayn and Mírzá 'Alí-Muḥammad-i-Varqá, left Yazd on foot and eventually travelled to the Holy Land via Baghdád. Because of old age and fatigue, Ḥájí became ill on the way. They arrived at Mazra'ih by way of Beirut and Sidon. But Ḥájí died on arrival and was buried alongside the road to 'Akká. Whenever the Blessed Beauty passed by his grave on His way to 'Akká or Mazra'ih, He would pause there, put His blessed foot on the grave and stop beside it for a few moments.

Although Ḥájí did not attain the presence of Bahá'u'lláh this time, he had, on a previous occasion, visited Baghdád with his eldest son Mírzá Ḥusayn where he met his Lord face to face. Bahá'u'lláh had revealed Tablets for him for many years, all indicative of his deep love and devotion to the Cause. The outpouring of Bahá'u'lláh's blessings upon him were indeed boundless. In a Tablet addressed to Varqá, Bahá'u'lláh, in the words of His amanuensis* describes the way in which He and some of His companions once on their way to Mazra'ih stopped at the grave of his father and revealed such exalted verses in his honour that no pen could describe the glory with which his soul was invested. Bahá'u'lláh has revealed for him a Tablet of Visitation which clearly indicates how exalted was his rank among the Concourse on High.† 'Abdu'l-Bahá has affirmed that He built his grave with His own hands.

* see above, p. 23n.

† The gathering of the holy souls in the next world.

The following is a tribute paid by 'Abdu'l-Bahá to this noble soul:

> . . . With his two sons, one the great martyr-to-be, Jináb-i-Varqá, and the other Jináb-i-Ḥusayn, he set out for the country of his Well-Beloved. In every town and village along the way, he ably spread the Faith, adducing clear arguments and proofs, quoting from and interpreting the sacred traditions and evident signs.* He did not rest for a moment; everywhere he shed abroad the attar of the love of God, and diffused the sweet breathings of holiness. And he inspired the friends, making them eager to teach others in their turn, and to excel in knowledge.
>
> He was an eminent soul, with his heart fixed on the beauty of God. From the day he was first created and came into this world, he single-mindedly devoted all his efforts to acquiring grace for the day he should be born into the next.† His heart was illumined, his mind spiritual, his soul aspiring, his destination Heaven. He was imprisoned along his way; and as he crossed the deserts and climbed and descended the mountain slopes he endured terrible, uncounted hardships. But the light of faith shone from his brow and in his breast the longing was aflame, and thus he joyously, gladly passed over the frontiers until at last he came to Beirut. In that city, ill, restive, his patience gone, he spent some days. His yearning grew, and his agitation was such that weak and sick as he was, he could wait no more.
>
> He set out on foot for the house of Bahá'u'lláh. Because he lacked proper shoes for the journey, his feet were bruised and torn; his sickness worsened; he could hardly move, but still he went on; somehow he reached the village of Mazra'ih and here, close by the Mansion, he died. His heart found his Well-Beloved One, when he could bear the separation no

* *Qur'án* 3:91.

† *Qur'án* 29:19; 53:48: 56:92.

> more. Let lovers be warned by his story; let them know how he gambled away his life in his yearning after the Light of the World. May God give him to drink of a brimming cup in the everlasting gardens; in the Supreme Assemblage, may God shed upon his face rays of light. Upon him be the glory of the Lord. His sanctified tomb is in Mazra'ih, beside 'Akká.[1]

Mírzá Ḥusayn, the eldest son, was a devoted believer. This pilgrimage was his third, as he had attained the presence of Bahá'u'lláh twice before in Ba<u>gh</u>dád. It was he who took to Yazd for the first time a copy of the *Hidden Words*, which he had obtained on his second visit to Ba<u>gh</u>dád. He also intimated to many Bábís then that Bahá'u'lláh, and no one else, was 'Him Whom God shall make manifest'. This was long before Bahá'u'lláh's declaration. He also informed some of the believers of the defection of Mírzá Yaḥyá, for whom the Bábí community of the time had high regard.

The second son, Mírzá Ḥasan, was also dedicated to the Cause, and Bahá'u'lláh has revealed some Tablets in his honour and showered His confirmations upon his soul.

Mírzá 'Alí-Muḥammad, entitled Varqá, the youngest son, is one of the Apostles of Bahá'u'lláh. He was about twenty-two years old when he left his native city of Yazd. He was a poet of outstanding calibre, knowledgeable in the science of ancient medicine and well-versed in religious subjects. He was an erudite and eloquent teacher of the Cause, one who had truly recognized the station of Bahá'u'lláh; he was filled with His love and radiated the power and the beauty of the Faith to those who came in contact with him.

On his first pilgrimage in AH 1296 (AD 1878–9) when he lost his father, Varqá came in contact with the divine spirit and was utterly magnetized by the onrushing forces of Bahá'u'lláh's Revelation. He truly became a new creation and emerged as one of the spiritual giants of this age. The first time he gazed upon the face of His Lord he was surprised, because he thought that he had previously seen Him somewhere, but he could not remember the occasion or the place. He was puzzled by this until one day after several times coming into His presence, Bahá'u'lláh said to him, 'Varqá! Burn away the idols of vain imaginings!' On hearing these words, Varqá immediately recalled a dream he had had when he was a child. He was in a garden playing with some dolls when 'God' arrived, took the dolls from him and burned them in the fire. When he told this dream to his parents they pointed out to him that no one can see God. However, he had completely forgotten this dream until that day when the words of Bahá'u'lláh exhorting him to burn the idols aroused his memory, and he knew that he had seen Bahá'u'lláh in his dream as a child.

Varqá has told the story[2] that on one occasion a thought entered into his mind as he gazed in adoration upon the countenance of Bahá'u'lláh. He said to himself, 'I know that Bahá'u'lláh is the supreme Manifestation of God, but I wish He would give me a sign to this effect.' At that same instant the following verse from the *Qur'án* flashed into Varqá's mind:

> Thou seest the earth barren and lifeless, but when We pour down rain on it, it is stirred to life, it swells, and it puts forth every kind of luxuriant growth in pairs.[3]

In that very moment, he wished in his heart that Bahá'u'lláh might repeat this verse to fulfil the sign he was looking for.

After some time, in the course of His utterances Bahá'u'lláh recited that same verse from the *Qur'án*. Varqá's wish was fulfilled, but he said to himself, 'Could this have been a mere coincidence?' As soon as this thought occurred to Varqá, Bahá'u'lláh turned and said to him abruptly, 'Was this not a sufficient proof for you?' Varqá was dumbfounded. He was shaken but assured in his heart of the truth of these words of Bahá'u'lláh:

> O heedless ones!
> Think not the secrets of hearts are hidden, nay, know ye of a certainty that in clear characters they are engraved and are openly manifest in the holy Presence.[4]

It is not right for man to test God. Bahá'u'lláh seldom responded positively to those who demanded miracles from Him. But He often revealed a measure of His glory and power to those who had recognized Him in order to strengthen their Faith.*

Varqá never doubted the station of Bahá'u'lláh when such thoughts occurred to him. This is perhaps the human way of reacting when the individual stands face to face with the One whom he knows to be the embodiment of the 'Most Great Spirit' of God. Faith is a relative term. Its intensity varies from person to person. Those who turn to Bahá'u'lláh with absolute sincerity in their hearts and submit themselves to Him can reach the pinnacle of faith. Certainly Varqá, as a result of this and other experiences in the presence of Bahá'u'lláh, reached the highest level of certitude and assurance. He was so carried away into the realms of the spirit that this mortal life was of no value to him any longer. He begged Bahá'u'lláh to enable him to lay down his life in the path of God, and this he did.

Varqá returned to Persia as a flame of fire, a tower of strength, a mine of knowledge and virtues. He served the Faith with heroism and wisdom. It is beyond the scope of this book to go into the details of his distinguished services, or to recount the stories of his turbulent life. He chose the city of Tabríz as his main place of residence, but in the year AH 1300 (AD 1882–3) he went to his native city of Yazd to meet his only sister, Bíbí Ṭúbá, who was very lonely after the exile of her father and brothers from Yazd. However, Varqá was arrested and imprisoned there. He was kept in custody for about one year and later transferred to the prison of Iṣfahán where he succeeded in converting certain tribal leaders to the Faith of

* For a fuller discussion of this theme see vol. 3, pp. 300–305 and 389–91.

Bahá'u'lláh. When released he returned to Tabríz.

Varqá was granted the privilege of a second pilgrimage to the presence of His Lord. This was about a year before the ascension of Bahá'u'lláh. This time, however, he was accompanied by two of his sons, 'Azízu'lláh and Rúḥu'lláh, and his father-in-law Mírzá 'Abdu'lláh-i-Núrí, a devoted believer of note who was prominent among the government officials in Tabríz.

This time, as on the first occasion, Bahá'u'lláh showered upon Varqá much praise and admiration for his services to the Faith. The blessings and bounties that he received from His Lord were indeed boundless. He and his sons, though young in age, basked in the sunshine of Bahá'u'lláh's presence. They all became filled with the spirit of joy and certitude, and intoxicated with the wine of His presence.

In order to please Varqá, Bahá'u'lláh once told him that since he was knowledgeable in medicine he ought to prescribe a remedy for Him, as He did not feel well; later He told him that He had taken the medicine.

Once Varqá asked Bahá'u'lláh, 'How will the Cause of God be universally adopted by mankind?' Bahá'u'lláh said that first, the nations of the world would arm themselves with infernal engines of war, and when fully armed would attack each other like bloodthirsty beasts. As a result, there would be enormous bloodshed throughout the world. Then the wise from all nations would gather together to investigate the cause of such bloodshed. They would come to the conclusion that prejudices were the cause, a major form being religious prejudice. They would therefore try to eliminate religion so as to eliminate prejudice. Later they would realize that man cannot live without religion. Then they would study the teachings of all religions to see which of the religions conformed to the prevailing conditions of the time. It is then that the Cause of God would become universal.*

Once Bahá'u'lláh spoke to Varqá about the station of

* These and the following accounts are not the exact words of Bahá'u'lláh, but convey the gist of what He said to Varqá.

'Abdu'l-Bahá and extolled His virtues and heavenly qualities. He said that in this world of being there was a phenomenon which He had referred to in some Tablets as the 'Most Great Elixir'. Any person who possessed this power would be able to exert enormous influence in the world through his work and could do anything he desired. Consider Christ after His crucifixion: the Jews had completely ignored Him. They had not even mentioned His name in their books. But since He possessed this power, He could not remain unrecognized. He revolutionized the world. Yet Christ used to avoid fools. And now, look at the Master. Observe with what patience and compassion He dealt with all types of people. He possessed this power, therefore immeasurable was the extent of the influence He would exert upon the world of humanity.

When Varqá heard this, he was so filled with joy and excitement that he fell prostrate at Bahá'u'lláh's feet and begged Him to make it possible for him and one of his sons to lay down their lives in the path of the Master. Bahá'u'lláh favoured him with His acceptance. When he returned to Persia, Varqá wrote to Bahá'u'lláh and renewed his plea for martyrdom, a plea to which He again favourably responded. And, as we shall see later, this happened; he was martyred during the Ministry of 'Abdu'l-Bahá.

It is not possible for those of us who have not reached that level of utter devotion to Bahá'u'lláh, and have not become intoxicated with the wine of His Revelation, to understand the motive of a high-minded person, talented and well-balanced, in seeking to give his life for the Cause. These people who sought martyrdom must have attained the pinnacle of faith and assurance. They must have seen with their spiritual eyes a glimpse of the inner reality of their Lord, and have become magnetized by His glory. These souls, the moth-like lovers of His beauty, were so dazzled by the splendours of the light of His countenance that they wished to sacrifice themselves in His path.

But in most cases Bahá'u'lláh has discouraged the believers

from seeking martyrdom. He has, in His Tablets, urged the friends to protect their lives by all means possible, so as to be able to teach the Cause of God to others. Indeed, Bahá'u'lláh has given the station of martyr to those who teach the Cause with wisdom.*

Some who had the privilege of attaining the presence of Bahá'u'lláh begged Him to accept them as martyrs in His path, knowing that only if He gave His assent would it come about. We shall see a noble example of this in the lives of the two illustrious brothers of Iṣfahán entitled by Bahá'u'lláh the 'King of Martyrs' and the 'Beloved of Martyrs'.

Varqá's two children 'Azízu'lláh and Rúḥu'lláh who accompanied him to 'Akká also had the honour of attaining the presence of Bahá'u'lláh several times. Contact with the Supreme Manifestation of God left an abiding impression on their souls. Though young in age they both became charged with the spirit of faith. Rúḥu'lláh in particular flourished spiritually in those holy surroundings. He may be regarded as one of the spiritual prodigies which the hand of God has raised up in this Dispensation. Although He was only about eight years old when He came into the presence of Bahá'u'lláh, his understanding of the Faith was very profound.

To cite one example: One day Bahá'u'lláh asked Rúḥu'lláh, 'What did you do today?'

He replied, 'I was having lessons from - [a certain teacher].'

Bahá'u'lláh asked, 'What subject were you learning?'

'Concerning the return [of the prophets]', said Rúḥu'lláh.

'Will you explain what this means?' Bahá'u'lláh demanded.

He replied: 'By return is meant the return of realities and qualities.'

Bahá'u'lláh, questioning him further, said: 'These are exactly the words of your teacher and you are repeating them like a parrot. Tell me in your own words your own understanding of the subject.'

---

* For further discussion see vol. 2, p. 94.

'It is like cutting a flower from a plant this year,' answered Rúḥu'lláh. 'Next year's flower will look exactly like this one, but it is not the same.'

The Blessed Beauty praised the child for his intelligent answer and often called him Jináb-i-Muballigh (His honour, the Bahá'í teacher).

On another occasion Bahá'u'lláh asked Rúḥu'lláh how he spent his time at home. He answered, 'We teach the Faith and tell the people that the "Promised One" has come.' Bahá'u'lláh, obviously enjoying this conversation, then asked him what he would do if it were found that the Message of the Báb was not authentic and the true Promised One appeared. 'I would try to teach him the Faith,' was his prompt reply.

Varqá had four sons. We have already mentioned the first two. The third son was Valíyy'u'lláh, who lived longest and distinguished himself as an outstanding servant of the Faith. He was Trustee of the Ḥuqúqu'lláh,* appointed by Shoghi Effendi, the Guardian of the Faith. Later in 1951 Shoghi Effendi appointed him as one of the Hands of the Cause of God. He passed away in 1955.

The fourth son, Badí'u'lláh, died at a young age. All four were the recipients as children of Tablets revealed by Bahá'u'lláh in their honour and in each case He has abundantly favoured them with His bounties and blessings.

After the ascension of Bahá'u'lláh, Varqá, together with the same two children, went on pilgrimage to the presence of 'Abdu'l-Bahá. As in the past, 'Abdu'l-Bahá and His sister the Greatest Holy Leaf showed admiration and love for Rúḥu'lláh, and both enjoyed talking to him.

One day the Greatest Holy Leaf noticed that Rúḥu'lláh and his older brother 'Azízu'lláh were playing in the garden. She called them in and they sat in her presence. Also present were Mírzá Badí'u'lláh and Mírzá Díyá'u'lláh, the two sons of

---

* see below, pp. 263–72.

Bahá'u'lláh who later joined hands with Mírzá Muḥammad-'Alí,* the Arch-breaker of the Covenant of Bahá'u'lláh. The Greatest Holy Leaf, often referred to as 'Khánum', asked them what they said to people when teaching the Faith.

'We tell them', Rúḥu'lláh answered, 'that God has manifested Himself.'

Surprised at this remark, Khánum told them that surely they could not say such a thing straight away to people!

'We don't tell this to everybody,' responded Rúḥu'lláh, 'we only say it to those who have the capacity to hear such a statement.'

'How would you know such people?' asked Khánum.

'We look into their eyes and then know whether we can give them the Message,' replied Rúḥu'lláh.

Khánum laughed heartily and then beckoned Rúḥu'lláh to come close and look into her eyes to find out whether she had the capacity for hearing such words. In obedience to her request Rúḥu'lláh sat down opposite the Greatest Holy Leaf, looked intently into her eyes and then said, 'You already believe in these words.'

Then it was the turn of the two sons of Bahá'u'lláh. Rúḥu'lláh went close to them, looked searchingly into their eyes and sadly said to Khánum, 'They are not worth looking into!'

Truly, Rúḥu'lláh was no ordinary child. He was an inspired being and acted as a spiritual giant. At a young age he wrote beautiful poetry which clearly demonstrates how deep was his love for Bahá'u'lláh and 'Abdu'l-Bahá, how vast his knowledge of the Faith and how profound his understanding of the real purpose of life. He used to speak about the Faith in gatherings of divines and men of learning with such eloquence and knowledge, and produce such irrefutable proofs of the truth of the Faith that many were confounded after hearing him. His answers were profound yet simple and very compelling.

* For a further discussion of the Covenant and Covenant-breaking see *God Passes By* and *Revelation of Bahá'u'lláh*, vols. 1, 2 and 3.

There are some delightful stories related to this indefatigable child-teacher of the Cause of God. To cite an example: Although only twelve years of age, Rúḥu'lláh attended with his father several meetings in Zanján at which the divines of the city were present. The Governor of Zanján, 'Alá'u'd-Dawlih, had especially arranged these meetings in order that Varqá might confront the divines in defence of his Faith. Ḥájí Mírzá Ḥaydar-'Alí has written about this in his celebrated book of reminiscences, the *Bihjatu'ṣ-Ṣudúr*:

> Varqá . . . was prepared to prove, by the power of divine assistance, the authenticity of this most great Revelation which is promised in all the heavenly Books, and to establish the validity of the basic principles, laws both spiritual and physical, and even secondary matters in the Faith using the *Qur'án* as the basis of his argument . . .
>
> This prompted 'Alá'u'd-Dawlih, the Governor of Zanján, to convene several meetings. He ordered the divines of Zanján to attend, and arranged for Bahá'í books and Tablets to be taken to these meetings. After reading some of these, the objections of the divines were adequately answered sometimes by Varqá and sometimes by Rúḥu'lláh. The answers, which were all supported by the verses of the *Qur'án*, were convincing and irrefutable.
>
> Since the defeat of the divines in their argument became evident to the Governor, who was a powerful and courageous personality, the divines did not dare to label Varqá as an infidel and issue his death warrant. In these meetings 'Alá'u'd-Dawlih often permitted the twelve-year-old Rúḥu'lláh to speak with the divines. He used to prove the subject with amazing courage, eloquence and profundity. His talks were so sweet that the Governor admitted that the proofs which that child had adduced were a great miracle in his sight . . . [5]

MÍRZÁ ʻALÍ-MUḤAMMAD VARQÁ

An Apostle of Bahá'u'lláh and one of the outstanding Bahá'í poets of the age

VARQÁ AND HIS YOUNG SON RÚḤU'LLÁH

In chains in the prison of Ṭihrán where they were martyred

Another story goes like this: Once Rúḥu'lláh and his older brother were walking in town. A Muslim clergyman riding on his donkey spotted the two boys and from their appearance he knew they were strangers in Zanján. So he went to them and said, 'Who are you?'

Rúḥu'lláh answered, 'We are sons of Varqá, a native of Yazd.'

'What is your name?' the clergyman demanded.

'My name is Rúḥu'lláh,' came the answer.

'That is a great name,' said the clergyman. 'Christ was Rúḥu'lláh* and He used to raise the dead and give them life.'

'Sir, if you slow down the pace of your donkey,' Rúḥu'lláh declared with great enthusiasm, 'I too shall raise you from the dead and give you a new life!'

The clergyman hurriedly left saying, 'You two must be Bábí† children!'

The full story of the circumstances which led to the martyrdom of Varqá and his twelve-year-old son Rúḥu'lláh is beyond the scope of this book. Both of them were engulfed in a series of arrests and imprisonments. They were transferred from prison to prison weighed down with chains, their feet placed in stocks. As a result they suffered much hardship and torture until at the end Varqá was martyred when in a rage Ḥájibu'd-Dawlih, the chief steward in charge of the Prison of Ṭihrán, pierced his stomach with a dagger. Rúḥu'lláh saw his father fall to the ground, and then his body was cut into pieces. A short while later, refusing to recant his faith and earnestly wishing to join his father, that noble and heroic child was strangled to death. This was in May 1896.

Thus ended the life of two immortal heroes of the Bahá'í Dispensation. Both father and son have immeasurably enriched the annals of the Faith and shed such a lustre upon it

* 'Rúḥu'lláh' literally means the 'Spirit of God', a title of Christ mentioned in the *Qur'án*.

† For many years in Persia Bahá'ís were known as 'Bábís'.

that generations yet unborn will be inspired by the example of their lives and moved to scale the lofty heights of service in the promotion of the Cause of God.

Tablets to Varqá

There are numerous Tablets revealed by Bahá'u'lláh for Varqá which, if compiled, would make up a large volume. A common feature of them all is the outpouring of grace and manifold favours upon him. Bahá'u'lláh refers to Varqá as one who has truly recognized the exalted station of His Lord, and has had the honour of attaining His presence. He testifies that Varqá has immersed himself in the ocean of His words, soared in the heaven of His love, drunk deep of the living waters of His remembrance, turned himself wholly towards Him, and served His Cause with utter dedication. He showers praises upon him for his devotion and love, his steadfastness, his sincerity, his faithfulness and his meritorious teaching activities.

In one of His Tablets revealed about 1888–9[6] Bahá'u'lláh highly commends Varqá for having adorned his being with the mantle of servitude and assures him that it is God who has desired that same mantle for him.

We have stated in previous volumes* that the only station that God has destined for man in this life is that of servitude. Great powers will descend from on high upon a believer only when he renders service to the Cause in a spirit of utter humility and servitude. To seek to exalt oneself above others will inevitably lead to pride, spiritual decline and even downfall. A service motivated by selfish desires is not acceptable in the sight of God. 'Humble Thyself before Me that I may graciously visit thee', are the Words of Bahá'u'lláh.[7] But it is not possible for man to become humble and attain the station of servitude until he discovers a motivating force to direct him in his path.

There is a beautiful story in verse by the renowned Persian

* For further discussion see vol. 1, pp. 133–4, and vol. 3, p. 405.

poet Sa'dí. It is the story of a drop of rain falling from the clouds. The drop knew itself to be the water of life, the most precious element that God had created, and so it was very proud of itself. Boasting all the way down it suddenly saw an ocean beneath. It was then that it recognized its own insignificance and exclaimed, 'If this exists, then what am I?' And when the ocean heard this expression of humility, it attracted the drop to itself and caused it to become the companion of the pearl.

The Revelation of Bahá'u'lláh is like the ocean and the believer like a drop. Whenever, through his own endeavours and with the help of prayer, the individual succeeds in seeing a glimpse of the majesty and grandeur of Bahá'u'lláh, he will, like the drop when it saw the ocean, become the embodiment of self-effacement and utter nothingness which are the highest attainments for man and the essential makings of a spiritual giant. For not until a soul recognizes the greatness of the Cause of God can it truly become humble.

The Revelation of Bahá'u'lláh has ushered in the 'Day of God', a day that all the Prophets and Founders of the world religions have foretold. It is essential for a believer who wishes to attain the station of servitude to acquire steadily, through reciting the Holy Writings and the study of the history of the Faith, a clearer understanding of the station of Bahá'u'lláh and a keener insight into His stupendous Revelation, a revelation which 'stands unparalleled in the annals of the past, nor will future ages witness its like'.[8] No Bahá'í can ever claim that he has fully understood the greatness of this Revelation.* This is a never-ending goal. Since faith and understanding are relative terms, people are all positioned at different levels on this path. The more an individual recognizes the glories of the Faith, the more humble he becomes.

The Tablets of Bahá'u'lláh to Varqá are replete with

* For a fuller discussion of the greatness of the Revelation of Bahá'u'lláh see vols. 1, 2, 3, and below, pp. 130–45.

passages in which He extols with great eloquence the loftiness and grandeur of the Cause He has revealed, glorifies the Person of its Author, unravels some of the mysterious and superhuman forces which have been released by Him in this age and lays bare some of the truths which are enshrined in His Writings.

In a lengthy Tablet revealed for Varqá in about 1887–8,[9] several years before His ascension, Bahá'u'lláh lauds in glowing terms the greatness of His Revelation, affirms that the verses of God have been sent down in great profusion, that proofs and testimonies of His Cause have encompassed the world, that the pearls of wisdom and utterance have been brought forth for all to see, and that the Tongue of Grandeur has uttered His call to the nations, and yet in spite of this outpouring of God's grace and bounty the people of the world have remained for the most part uninformed. Some have heard the Call of God but remained heedless. Only a few have witnessed the glory of His Revelation and embraced His Cause.

Deploring the blindness and perversity of humanity in this age, Bahá'u'lláh states that people are brought up to believe in their old and antiquated traditions which are, for the most part, the product of vain imaginings. These traditions, though but a drop, are considered by them to be an ocean; while the ocean of God's Revelation, surging with the billows of knowledge and truth, seems to be but a drop in their sight. The cause of this blindness He attributes to waywardness and ignorance, to pride and unseemly deeds. He prays that God may vouchsafe to the people of the world the capacity to realize that He has released enormous spiritual forces for the regeneration of mankind. He further affirms that the Cause of God stands transcendent and supreme and that the influence it will exert upon the human race is irresistible.

In this Tablet Bahá'u'lláh calls upon the believers to render Him victorious by the hosts of goodly deeds and praiseworthy character. He states that day and night His tongue is engaged in exhorting His loved ones to a virtuous life and saintly conduct, through which His Cause will be glorified and His Word exalted. He urges the believers to teach His Cause, but counsels them to carry out this injunction with great wisdom, reminds them that speech in moderation acts as the water of life for the soul, whereas if it is carried beyond the bounds of moderation it will give birth to fanaticism and malice.

In an earlier Tablet to Varqá revealed about 1880–81[10] Bahá'u'lláh describes the condition of humanity as grievous. Man can clearly see the instability of this mortal life and the continued disturbances and changes which overtake the world. He can witness at all times in every created thing the signs and tokens of ultimate extinction. And yet he is utterly heedless of his own extinction. Wayward and negligent he roams over the earth, occupies himself with that which perishes, and commits such deeds as will bring upon him everlasting loss and deprivation.

Bahá'u'lláh explains that all created things speak out at all times, but their call is muted. Only those who are endowed with hearing ears can hear them speak eloquently of their evanescent life. For example, the sun tells its own story; it rises in the morning and sets in the evening. The call of change and eventual perishing may be heard from all sides, but human beings with deaf ears cannot hear it. In a Tablet,[11] Bahá'u'lláh metaphorically describes the sad plight of man, saying that this material world laughs at those who have attached themselves to it and become its bond-slaves. It addresses them scornfully, saying, 'Pity on you, people who have failed to find someone greater than me to follow.'

The main cause of man's blindness and perversity is his attachment to the things of this world. The subject of detachment repeatedly appears in the Holy Writings and we have discussed it in previous volumes. Man is usually attracted to material things. The heart is a focal point of warmth and love. The characteristic of the heart is to fall in love with another party, and it is the individual who finds and chooses that party. For example, if man turns his affections to the material world, his heart will become attached to material things very easily. But if he turns to God and spiritual things, then his heart can fall in love with Him provided he fulfils the condition stated by Bahá'u'lláh in the *Hidden Words*:

> O Son of Being! Thy heart is My home; sanctify it for My descent . . . [12]

Elsewhere in the same book Bahá'u'lláh explains:

> O Son of Dust! All that is in heaven and earth I have ordained for thee, except the human heart, which I have made the habitation of My beauty and glory; yet thou didst give My home and dwelling to another than Me; and whenever the manifestation of My holiness sought His own abode, a stranger found He there, and, homeless, hastened unto the sanctuary of the Beloved . . . [13]

and again:

> O My Friend in Word! Ponder a while. Hast thou ever heard that friend and foe should abide in one heart? Cast out then the stranger, that the Friend may enter His home.[14]

It is a fascinating thought that God has given man an infinite number of things – all that is in heaven and earth. This means that everything in this creation belongs to man except one thing, and that is his own heart. 'The stranger' mentioned above is none other than man's attachment to this world and the most formidable type of attachment is the love of one's own self. This type of attachment manifests itself mainly in the form of pride in one's own knowledge and other accomplishments such as rank and position. It is the love of one's own self that renders the individual opinionated, self-centred, proud and egotistical. In fact, it denudes him of spiritual qualities. Such a person has indeed harboured within his heart a great enemy, namely, 'the stranger'.

That the heart is entrusted to man by God for the descent of His love and bestowals and not for harbouring passion and worldly desires is the very basis of the spiritual life of the individual. How vast is the gap between this concept and that of the great majority of the human race today who live their lives forgetful of the purpose for which they are created!

The heart pulsates within the body and through its life-giving energies every organ becomes active. The eyes, the ears, the tongue, the mind, the hands, all function in harmony with the heart. Since the heart is meant to be the dawning-place of the love of God, it is only logical that these organs should follow suit. Indeed, Bahá'u'lláh has confirmed this in many of His Tablets. 'Know thou', He states, 'that the ear of man hath been created that it may hearken unto The Divine Voice on this day . . . '[15] And in His Book of the Covenant he states: Verily I say, the tongue is for mentioning what is good, defile it not with unseemly talk.[16] In one instance He states that the ears are created to hear His Melodies, the eyes to behold the effulgent light of His Countenance, the tongue to utter His praise and glorification and the hands to hold His Epistles and Tablets.[17]

These are very exalted teachings, all pointing to a new way of life in which the believer must be vigilant not to abuse his God-given powers. To the extent that the individual can abide by these standards in his daily life, and is able to harmonize his thoughts, his words and his deeds with the Will of his Creator, he can succeed in reaching the goal of nearness to God. Returning to the theme of a perverse humanity, Bahá'u'lláh in a Tablet to Varqá[18] declares that in this day the whole world has been immersed in the ocean of God's Revelation; verses have been sent down from the heaven of the Will of God; the Sun of Truth has shone forth, all testimonies and proofs have been fulfilled; the Speaker on Sinai* has ascended the Throne of His Sovereignty, and the Shrill Voice† of His exalted Pen has been heard far and wide. But the people are found to be in palpable error, and deprived of any sense to discover the truth.

Such sentiments, with their sad features depicting the perversity of the human race in this age, are to be found in abundance among the Writings of Bahá'u'lláh. He grieves over humanity's blindness and in His prayers He invokes the power of God to bestow upon mankind the gift of a new vision so that it can see the Glory of God manifested in this day.

In another Tablet to Varqá,[19] and expounding the same theme, Bahá'u'lláh states that even the German Templers,‡ who had discovered through the Gospels that the coming of the Lord was nigh, and had gone to the Holy Land with the express purpose of coming face to face with Him, had utterly failed to recognize their Lord when He manifested Himself to them.

Now, almost a century later, the Cause of God has spread throughout the world, multitudes of people from all walks of life and of every colour and class have embraced it, and the rising institutions of its embryonic world order have been reared throughout the globe; yet still the generality of mankind and its leaders, both secular and ecclesiastic, have so far remained unmoved or uninformed.

Humanity is desperately seeking solutions to the horrific perils with which it is faced today. It experiments with every ideology or creed that it may come across in order to halt the destructive process which in ever-increasing acceleration is threatening to destroy the fabric of its present-day society. But so far it has not found a solution. Religious leaders, who are witnessing the bankruptcy of their time-honoured institutions and the inapplicability of old standards to the modern age,

* One of the titles of Bahá'u'lláh, see *God Passes By*, p. 94.

† For an explanation of this term see vol. 1, p. 35n.

‡ A group of German Protestants who left their homes and took up residence mainly on the slopes of Mt. Carmel, Haifa, in anticipation of the return of Christ. For further details see vol. 3, pp. 28–31.

try to adapt new standards through making compromises, but these in their turn seriously undermine those religious teachings which had remained unchanged for centuries. The strict standards of truth which in older days were to be found in religious teachings are now in many parts of the world replaced by public opinion. The incompatibility of the two has forced religious leaders to walk a tight-rope, while people become increasingly disenchanted with religion. Many have swelled the ranks of agnostics and atheists in this century, while others are creating cults and religious sects mainly based on trivial or sensational ideologies.

While the religious leaders are constantly engaged in finding a way out, a great many people embrace these cults which become fashionable for a time. But when the novelty wears off or dissatisfaction sets in, or the movements become impotent and disintegrate, then they look for another saviour, another movement or another sect, and there are many to turn to throughout the world. And so the experiment to find peace and tranquillity in one's life continues. But so far few have found happiness or peace of mind.

On the other hand, the political leaders and the world's statesmen are struggling both individually and collectively to solve the problems facing mankind. Like religious leaders, they too are trying very hard to discover a formula. But since their actions are based on expediency and short-term interests, the world's horizons become darker every day. Neither religious leaders nor those in the political and social spheres have as yet found an answer to the ills of mankind.

And so the struggle goes on. Humanity will try everything until it reaches the stage of utter hopelessness and despair. Bahá'u'lláh forecasts the outcome in these words:

> The world is in travail, and its agitation waxeth day by day. Its face is turned towards waywardness and unbelief. Such shall be its plight, that to disclose it now would not be meet

> and seemly. Its perversity will long continue. And when the appointed hour is come, there shall suddenly appear that which shall cause the limbs of mankind to quake. Then, and only then, will the Divine Standard be unfurled, and the Nightingale of Paradise warble its melody.[20]

We can see from the history of past religions too that each one has been ignored by the people in its own day. For instance, for some centuries the Message of Christ was ignored. But as it was the Message of God, it eventually penetrated into the hearts of people. Bahá'u'lláh in His Writings has made a very interesting statement concerning the future of His Cause. He unequivocally proclaimed that God has manifested Himself in this day and that there is no way out for the human race except to embrace His Cause. But it is apparent, from the world conditions now prevailing, that humanity will have to go through great suffering and tribulation and become chastised before reaching the final stage of turning its attention to the Cause of Bahá'u'lláh and entering into that tabernacle of unity of which He speaks in these words:

> How vast is the tabernacle of the Cause of God! It hath overshadowed all the peoples and kindreds of the earth, and will, ere long, gather together the whole of mankind beneath its shelter.[21]

5

The King and Beloved of the Martyrs

A grievous event of great consequence occurred in Iṣfahán during the last few months of Bahá'u'lláh's residence in the Mansion of Mazra'ih. This was the martyrdom of two distinguished followers of Bahá'u'lláh, the 'twin shining lights' Mírzá Muḥammad-Ḥasan and his elder brother Mírzá Muḥammad-Ḥusayn, surnamed respectively by Bahá'u'lláh 'Sulṭánu'sh-Shuhadá' (King of the Martyrs) and 'Maḥbúbu'sh-Shuhadá' (Beloved of the Martyrs). Reminiscent of the martyrdom of Badí',* this tragic event caused the Pen of the Most High to lament their loss for several years. In no less than one hundred Tablets He recounts their story, discloses their exalted station and praises their virtues.

In a Tablet[1] to one of the Afnáns, Bahá'u'lláh, in the words of Mírzá Áqá Ján His amanuensis, makes a statement that can be described only as astounding. He states that the martyrdom of these brothers made a greater impression, exerted more influence and was more heart-breaking than the Martyrdom of their Lord, the Báb, whom they served and worshipped.

The King of the Martyrs and Beloved of the Martyrs were born to a noble family in Iṣfahán. They were nine and ten years of age respectively when the Declaration of the Báb took place in 1844.

Their two illustrious uncles, Mírzá Hádí and Mírzá Muḥammad-'Alí (the father of Munírih Khánum, the wife of 'Abdu'l-Bahá) had embraced the Faith of the Báb in the early days of its Revelation. They both took part in the Conference

* see vol. 3, ch. 9.

of Badasht. But their father, Mírzá Ibráhím, was not a believer at the time; he recognized the truth of the Faith later. He was engaged in the service of Mír Siyyid Muḥammad, the Imám-Jum'ih* of Iṣfahán, as manager of his financial affairs. When the Báb went to that city He stayed part of the time as a guest in the home of the Imám-Jum'ih.

Because of his close association at that time with the Báb, Mírzá Ibráhím, though not a believer, entertained Him one day in his home. On that occasion the two young brothers and their uncles† attained the presence of the Báb. This meeting left an abiding impression on the two youths, who became ardent believers through the efforts of their uncles, especially Mírzá Muḥammad-'Alí who later accompanied them to Baghdád where they attained the presence of Bahá'u'lláh. As a result of their meeting with Him, they became aware of His exalted Station and were filled with the spirit of faith and certitude. The splendours of the Face of their Lord brightly illumined their beings and they returned home radiant as shining lights.

In those days merchants occupied an important position in the community. The King and the Beloved of the Martyrs were held in high esteem as merchants of note by the inhabitants of Iṣfahán. These two brothers had established a very prosperous business there, but they were not attached to earthly possessions. Through their generous support they were able to alleviate some of the hardships which Bahá'u'lláh and His companions had to endure in the course of His successive exiles and confinements. They also spent much of their enormous wealth on the poor, and lovingly harboured the distressed and the needy at all times. For example, they provided food and other necessities for a great many starving people during a famine in Iṣfahán. In their dealings with people they were renowned for their trustworthiness, honesty, compassion, loving-kindness

* A high religious dignitary of the city.
† For the story of Mírzá Muḥammad-'Alí, who begged the Báb that his childless wife might bear him a child, see vol. 2, pp. 203–4.

and generosity. They were shining embodiments of all Bahá'í ideals. Their love and devotion for Bahá'u'lláh knew no bounds. The praise that Bahá'u'lláh has lavishly showered upon them is ample testimony to the loftiness of their station, the nobility of their character and the purity of their souls.

After the death of Mír Siyyid Muḥammad, the host to the Báb, the position of Imám-Jum'ih went to his brother, Mír Muḥammad-Ḥusayn. This man, the new Imám, left the management of his financial affairs in the hands of the two brothers who were the most trustworthy persons he could find.

Time passed, during which the Imám-Jum'ih became rich and prosperous through the many financial transactions negotiated for him. He was quite satisfied with the handling of his financial affairs until he was informed that he owed the two brothers a considerable sum of money. It was at this point that the ferocious and beastly nature of the Imám-Jum'ih came to the surface and he turned his evil thoughts to one course of action only – to take the lives of the two who had served him with absolute faithfulness and honesty. How appropriate is Bahá'u'lláh's denunciation of this wicked Imám as 'Raqshá' (the She-Serpent), poised to strike mercilessly at the two embodiments of loving-kindness and compassion.

To carry out his evil intentions, he combined forces with another equally wicked member of the clergy, an inveterate enemy of the Cause, Shaykh Báqir, the leading mujtahid* of the city whom Bahá'u'lláh later denounced as *Dhi'b* (Wolf). They both knew that taking the lives of the two brothers would not be difficult. All that the mujtahid had to do was to write their death warrant on the grounds that they were Bahá'ís. Having realized that carrying out this evil plan would fulfil not only their long-cherished ambition of inflicting a serious blow upon the community of the Most Great Name by extinguishing the light of two of its shining luminaries, but would also place at their disposal enormous wealth, these two embodiments

* Doctor of Islamic Law.

of wickedness approached Mas'úd Mírzá, the Ẓillu's-Sulṭán* (Shadow of the King), the Governor of Iṣfahán, and asked him to implement their sinister designs. They demanded the execution of the brothers and promised him a giant share of their estate after its confiscation.

The detailed story of their arrest and execution is beyond the scope of this book – a brief account will suffice here. On the anniversary of the birth of the Prophet Muḥammad, a day on which the whole nation celebrates this event, Mírzá Ḥasan, the King of the Martyrs, and his older brother Mírzá Ḥusayn, the Beloved of the Martyrs, together with their youngest brother Mírzá Ismá'íl, were arrested by the servants of the Imám and brought to government headquarters. The youngest brother was later freed, but the other two were several times interviewed by the Prince. It is reported that in his first interview he appealed to the two brothers to recant their faith and be freed. He begged them several times to do so but was met with silence each time. He then became angry and violently demanded recantation of the Faith and the cursing of its Founder. Refusing to comply, Mírzá Ḥasan is reported to have remarked, 'If only you knew what I know, you would never demand this of me.'

This remark provoked such anger in the Prince that several times he reached for his sword but hesitated to pull it out fully. Instead he grabbed his walking stick, struck Mírzá Ḥasan violently several times in the face and sent the brothers to prison.

In the meantime, Náṣiri'd-Dín Sháh was informed of this. He sent a telegram ordering the Prince to despatch the two brothers to Ṭihrán. This resulted in a bitter struggle by the two clergymen, who disliked this new development and wanted the execution to take place in Iṣfahán. The Prince was now torn between the two – the king and the clergy. In the end the clergy won. They roused the fanatic populace against the new Faith;

* He was a son of Náṣiri'd-Dín Sháh, extremely cruel and lacking in humanity. At one stage in his life he ruled over Iṣfahán and many other provinces in the south.

MÍRZÁ MUḤAMMAD-ḤASAN OF IṢFAHÁN

Bahá'u'lláh gave him the title Sulṭánu'sh-Shuhadá, King of the Martyrs

MÍRZÁ MUḤAMMAD-ḤUSAYN OF IṢFAHÁN

Bahá'u'lláh gave him the title Maḥbúbu'sh-Shuhadá, Beloved of the Martyrs

a great commotion seized the city, and crowds shouting anti-Bahá'í slogans poured into the streets. Headed by the clergy they surrounded the government house and with wild and ferocious cries demanded the execution. The death warrant had already been written and signed by a number of leading divines of the city.

The Prince succumbed under the pressure, but fearing the wrath of the king for disobeying his orders, he is reported to have withdrawn the services of his official executioner. It was at this juncture that Shaykh Muḥammad-Taqí,* the son of Shaykh Báqir (the Wolf), rolled up his sleeves and volunteered to be the executioner himself, several others followed suit. But eventually the Prince issued orders for the execution to take place. This he did after his final appeal to the captives asking them to recant their faith and be saved, an appeal met by their refusal to do so.

It must be noted that many among the crowds demanding the death of the two brothers were deeply indebted to them for their charitable and philanthropic assistance in the past. Many of them owed their lives to them for all the help they had received in difficult times over the years. Yet, blinded by the deep prejudice provoked by the Imám and his partner, they were clamouring for the death of their benefactors. Even the executioner himself, a man by the name of Ramaḍán, had been the recipient of a great many favours over the years. He was loath to carry out the execution and was ashamed to look into the faces of his noble victims. And when he expressed his revulsion for the task allotted to him, the King and the Beloved of the Martyrs assured him of their forgiveness and told him to perform his duty. Indeed Mírzá Ḥasan, the King of the Martyrs, took a precious ring from his finger and gave it to Ramaḍán, the executioner, as a gift.

On the sixth day of their imprisonment, 17 March 1879, watched by the Raqshá (the She-Serpent) and the Dhi'b (the

* Years later the *Epistle to the Son of the Wolf* was addressed to him.

Wolf), these noble brothers, the twin 'shining lights', stood with their arms around each other ready to give their lives in the path of God. Their faces portrayed the beauty and the strength of their faith as they communed in spirit with their Lord, invoking Him to accept from them the sacrifice of their earthly lives and admit them into the spiritual realms of nearness to Him. At the time of execution, each one pleaded with the other to be the first. The younger brother, Mírzá Ḥasan, the King of the Martyrs, was beheaded first, followed immediately by Mírzá Ḥusayn, the Beloved of the Martyrs.

On the orders of the evil perpetrators of this infamous act, ropes were tied to their feet and their bodies dragged through the city for everyone to see and then left in the ruins of a dilapidated building. Afterwards their remains were buried secretly by the youngest brother. Thus ended the lives of the two most illustrious of Bahá'u'lláh's followers. The story of their martyrdom shook the Bahá'í community to its depths and brought great sorrow to the heart of Bahá'u'lláh.

While the King and Beloved of the Martyrs were in prison, the Imám-Jum'ih (the Raqshá) ordered his men to confiscate their whole estate. Not only did he seize all their financial assets, including their vast merchandise, but he plundered their homes and took away every item of furniture, most of which were of exquisite quality and some consisting of priceless articles rarely to be found in anyone's possession. They ransacked the house in such a way that even some of the trees in the garden were taken out. At the same time the bereaved family lived in an empty house which was surrounded by a hostile crowd. They were terrified, grief-stricken and without any succour or help.

Tablets to the Two Brothers

Bahá'u'lláh revealed many Tablets in honour of each of these two brothers. Since the days that the two came face to face with Him in Baghdád and became ignited by the fire of His love, the

Pen of the Most High had addressed Tablets to them from time to time bestowing upon them His blessings, infusing into their souls the forces of His Revelation and indeed preparing them for that day of days when they would lay down their lives in His path. It is not practicable to refer to all these Tablets in this volume. We can only skim the surface and mention a few.

In a Tablet[2] to the Beloved of the Martyrs Bahá'u'lláh exhorts him to hearken to the melodies of the spirit from His Lord and to turn away from those who have repudiated the Cause of God and denied the verses sent down by Him. This is an implied reference to the Bábís who remained heedless of His Revelation. He calls on him to arise for the triumph of His Faith, to hold the reins of the Faith in his hands and never to allow the Cause to fall into the hands of the unfaithful. This is what God had destined for him.

It must be remembered that in the early days of His Declaration Bahá'u'lláh focused His main attention upon the followers of the Báb. This is because these people had been prepared by the Báb to recognize and embrace the Cause of 'Him Whom God shall make manifest'. The teachers of His Cause in those early days were primarily concerned with teaching the Bábís. Those among the Bábís who turned away from Bahá'u'lláh were addressed by Him as, among other things, the 'evil ones' who had 'repudiated the Cause of God', been 'unfaithful to Him', 'joined partners with God', or 'shown enmity and malice toward His loved ones'. Phrases such as these revealed soon after His Declaration often refer to those followers of the Báb who sided with Mírzá Yaḥyá* and rose up in opposition against Bahá'u'lláh.

In the fore-mentioned Tablet which seems to have been revealed in Adrianople, Bahá'u'lláh alludes to the story of Joseph and refers to the actions of Mírzá Yaḥyá. He refers to Himself allegorically as the One who has been thrown into a

* A half-brother of Bahá'u'lláh, the Arch-breaker of the Covenant of the Báb. For his life see vols. 1 and 2.

deep well by reason of the envy of those who had been among His servants, who were created through one word from Him and who have now arisen against their Lord. Thus He alludes to the sufferings which He had endured from some of the Bábís who had not recognized the truth of His Cause. He confers authority on the Beloved of the Martyrs to employ the power of the word of God and, sword-like, separate the faithful believers from the company of the unfaithful who had repudiated Him.

From the early days of the Faith, Bahá'u'lláh made provision for the breakers of the Covenant of God (in this case the followers of Mírzá Yaḥyá) to be kept out of the community of the believers. In this Tablet, as in many others, Bahá'u'lláh exhorts the believers not to associate with these people. 'Abdu'l-Bahá describes this action as similar to that of isolating an ill person who might otherwise spread a contagious disease* to others.

In a moving prayer[3] revealed for the King of the Martyrs, Bahá'u'lláh bestows such bounties upon his soul and upon that of his brother as no pen can adequately describe. He testifies that he has wholly detached himself from all earthly things, and that he has succeeded in attaching himself with the cord of servitude to the exalted dominion of his Lord. This description by Bahá'u'lláh of the relationship of a servant to his Lord, the ties of the truly poor with the riches of an Almighty God, amply demonstrates, as does the study of His other Tablets, that the greatest achievement for man in this life is to empty himself of every desire, recognize his own utter nothingness, follow the commandments of God revealed by His Manifestation and become filled with the power of the Almighty. Bahá'u'lláh testifies that the King of the Martyrs had indeed achieved this exalted station. His wealth and that of his brother did not become a barrier between them and God.

These words of Bahá'u'lláh in *The Hidden Words* are truly applicable to these twin shining lights of the Cause of God:

* For a fuller discussion on this subject see vols. 1 and 2.

> O ye that pride yourselves on mortal riches! Know ye in truth that wealth is a mighty barrier between the seeker and his desire, the lover and his beloved. The rich, but for a few, shall in no wise attain the court of His presence nor enter the city of content and resignation. Well is it then with him, who, being rich, is not hindered by his riches from the eternal kingdom, nor deprived by them of imperishable dominion. By the Most Great Name! The splendour of such a wealthy man shall illuminate the dwellers of heaven, even as the sun enlightens the people of the earth![4]

In a brief Tablet[5] to the King of the Martyrs Bahá'u'lláh reveals the sadness of His heart when He speaks of the heedlessness of some of His followers. He states that in most of His Tablets He had exhorted all to rectitude of conduct and praiseworthy character. They had all read these Tablets and become aware of the teachings of God, yet some followed their own passions and desire. He had directed them to be loving and united with each other, but instead they created disunity. He had urged them to act with wisdom, but they acted contrary to this. He had clearly asked the believers in many of His Tablets not to go to the Holy Land to attain His presence, yet groups of pilgrims arrived every day without His permission. In this Tablet Bahá'u'lláh expresses His displeasure at the waywardness and misbehaviour of some of His followers. He directs the King of the Martyrs to strive with all his strength to teach the weaker souls, to deepen their understanding of the teachings of God, and to exhort them to unity and love.

That some of the believers in the time of Bahá'u'lláh did not live up to the high standards of behaviour demanded of them in the Holy Writings, is one of the most unfortunate situations in the history of the Bahá'í community. We have already stated in a previous volume* that in some of His Tablets Bahá'u'lláh has clearly indicated that if the believers

* see vol. 3, p. 360.

had carried out His teachings faithfully, lived their lives in accordance with the divine standards and achieved absolute detachment from earthly things, they would have moved the peoples of the world and the majority of the human race would have embraced the Cause of God.

In this Tablet to the King of the Martyrs mentioned above there is a reference to the presence of many pilgrims in the Holy Land. Normally, the established practice among the believers was to seek permission from Bahá'u'lláh before setting out on pilgrimage. But there were some who, either through ignorance or impelled by an extreme enthusiasm and eagerness to attain the presence of their Lord, did not follow this practice. Indeed, Bahá'u'lláh in a Tablet to 'Andalíb[6*] has stipulated certain conditions for pilgrimage. These are: the person should be healthy, should be able to provide his means of travel including finance and, above all, should seek permission before setting off on the journey.

In that same Tablet to 'Andalíb, Bahá'u'lláh states that a great part of His affliction is due to the assemblage in the Holy Land of a large group of believers numbering about three hundred including men, women and children. Some were steadfast in the Cause and staunch in their faith, but there were a number of vacillating souls among them. He states that, nevertheless, He had treated them all with the utmost love and had manifested to them His most excellent favours and blessings. God is very gracious indeed.

An interesting example of seeking permission to attain the presence of Bahá'u'lláh is that of 'Abdu'l-Majíd-i-Marághi'í. He was an outstanding believer in the district of Ádhirbáyján. His great enthusiasm to meet Bahá'u'lláh prompted him to leave his home for the abode of the Beloved. Without seeking permission he set off on the journey, travelling on foot until he reached Díyár-Bakr in Turkey where he became ill and

* A devoted follower of Bahá'u'lláh, a gifted poet and a Bahá'í teacher of wide repute.

had to remain during the months of winter. There he attracted many people. His fame spread through the town and soon the divines and men of learning came and sat at his feet to receive a portion of his knowledge and wisdom. To show their respect for him, they would, before entering his room, call out to him in Turkish and say, "Abdu'l-Majíd! Do we have permission to come in?' He heard these words every day and the phrase became familiar to him.

At last the cold of the winter passed and 'Abdu'l-Majíd continued his journey towards the Holy Land. When he came close to 'Akká, he wrote a letter to Bahá'u'lláh seeking permission, and asked Nabíl-i-A'ẓam to present it to Him. The reply came in the form of a Tablet to Nabíl, saying that 'Abdu'l-Majíd should have sought permission before leaving his home in Persia, rather than coming all the way and then seeking permission from a nearby city such as Haifa or Beirut. However, He forgives him for this and extends to him His loving invitation. But He asks him to be satisfied with staying for only a few days and then to depart, even as a life-giving breeze wafting over all regions to vivify the souls of the believers. This was shortly after Bahá'u'lláh had moved to the Mansion of Bahjí.

An amusing part of the story is that the first time 'Abdu'l-Majíd attained the presence of Bahá'u'lláh, He who is the All-Knowing, seeing and hearing everything we do, turned to him and in a humorous tone and in the Turkish language quoted the phrase he had been used to hearing every day in Díyár-Bakr. He said, "Abdu'l-Majíd! Do we have permission to come in?'

Through this remark, not only did 'Abdu'l-Majíd reach the state of absolute certitude in his faith, witnessing that the Supreme Manifestation of God has the knowledge of all things, but he was also reminded indirectly and in a loving way of his negligence to seek permission.

'Abdu'l-Majíd was to stay for only a few days, but he begged 'Abdu'l-Bahá to intercede for him so that he might stay for a longer period. Graciously, Bahá'u'lláh gave His consent and he stayed for over three months. During this time he became magnetized by the power of God and intoxicated with the wine of His presence. He acquired such radiance and attraction that through the remainder of his life he became a successful teacher of the Faith to seekers and a tower of strength for the believers. When he was to leave 'Akká, Bahá'u'lláh directed him to go to the Caucasus, and here he stayed for some years and succeeded in guiding many souls to the Cause of God.

Those who arrived in 'Akká without Bahá'u'lláh's permission were nevertheless received by Him with great love and compassion. Bahá'u'lláh always looked upon the believers with a sin-covering eye, concealing their shortcomings and transgressions, while showering upon them so much blessing and bounty that none was made to feel unhappy or dejected. This is because God's forgiveness, His manifold favours and bestowals, by far outweigh His justice. In many of His Tablets Bahá'u'lláh expounds this theme. The following is one such reference:

> Every time My name 'the All-Merciful' was told that one of My lovers hath breathed a word that runneth counter to My wish, it repaired, grief-stricken and disconsolate to its abode; and whenever My name 'the Concealer' discovered that one of My followers had inflicted any shame or humiliation on his neighbour, it, likewise, turned back chagrined and sorrowful to its retreats of glory, and there wept and mourned with a sore lamentation. And whenever My name 'the Ever-Forgiving' perceived that any one of My friends had committed any transgression, it cried out in its great distress, and, overcome with anguish, fell upon the dust, and was borne away by a company of the invisible angels to its habitation in the realms above.[7]

Only if a believer committed an act which brought disgrace upon the Faith, or rose up actively in opposition to the Centre of the Cause, as Mírzá Yaḥyá did, was God's justice invoked; then Bahá'u'lláh condemned his actions and even expelled him from His community. In spite of this, however, He always prayed God that the individual might mend his ways, repent and return to his Lord.

In the following Tablet too, revealed in the Holy Land, Bahá'u'lláh confirms that through His mercy and loving-kindness God conceals the sins of His creatures.

> He Who is the Eternal Truth knoweth well what the breasts of men conceal. His long forbearance hath emboldened His creatures, for not until the appointed time is come will He rend any veil asunder. His surpassing mercy hath restrained the fury of His wrath, and caused most people to imagine that the one true God is unaware of the things they have privily committed. By Him Who is the All-Knowing, the All-Informed! The mirror of His knowledge reflecteth, with complete distinctness, precision and fidelity, the doings of all men. Say: Praise be to Thee, O Concealer of the sins of the weak and helpless! Magnified be Thy name, O Thou that forgivest the heedless ones that trespass against Thee![8]

Bahá'u'lláh at times allowed some of the believers to travel for the purpose of attaining His presence. But in many cases, especially during His days in the Holy Land, He advised the would-be pilgrims not to make the journey, as for most of the time circumstances in 'Akká did not warrant the arrival of great numbers for pilgrimage. In most cases He assured the believers concerned that God would instead bestow upon them the same reward as He bestowed on those who had attained His presence. He often stated that there were some who had been in His presence for long periods of time but who were not able to receive their portion of the bounties which were bestowed freely upon all in His company. Yet there were others who never came face to face with their Lord but who became the recipients of His glory and were rewarded by God as though they had in fact attained His presence.

The practice of seeking permission from the Centre of the Cause to visit the Bahá'í Holy Places continued after the ascension of Bahá'u'lláh. The believers requested 'Abdu'l-Bahá or Shoghi Effendi to grant them permission to make their pilgrimage, and today the Universal House of Justice is the body which performs this function.

There is a Tablet[9] addressed to the King of the Martyrs which is significant in its allusions to martyrdom. Revealed some time before his martyrdom, Bahá'u'lláh states that the believers should act with wisdom and prudence to protect themselves. But if the occasion demands it they should be willing to lay down their lives in the path of God. He affirms that since death is inevitable for everyone, it is much more praiseworthy, if the situation requires it, to die as a martyr than by a natural cause. He further explains that a believer who has truly recognized Him will not even become saddened by the terror and persecution of the enemies, much less be frightened by them.

In this Tablet, as in others revealed in honour of the King of the Martyrs or his noble brother the Beloved of the Martyrs, Bahá'u'lláh assures them both of His unfailing grace and bounties. In view of their later martyrdom this Tablet is significant in its contents and prophetic in its outcome.

Tablets Revealed after their Martyrdom

After the martyrdom of the two illustrious brothers, the Pen of the Most High continued for some years to make mention of them in most tender and moving language in almost one hundred Tablets. He extolled their noble virtues and disclosed their exalted station. The story of their early pilgrimage to the presence of Bahá'u'lláh is given in a Tablet to Varqá.[10] In it, Bahá'u'lláh in the words of His amanuensis describes how they went to 'Iráq and attained His presence in Baghdád. They came face to face with their Lord and it was on that occasion that they hearkened to the Voice of God and were transformed into a new creation. He states that although they were not known among the people, the Tongue of Grandeur showered upon them so much praise and bounty that some believers became very surprised. Afterwards they returned to their native land on His instructions. He affirms that the Hand of Power exalted them among the people and conferred upon them honour and glory. From the clouds of the heaven of generosity He rained down upon them wealth, good fortune and fame. Well-known as Bahá'ís, they became beloved of all. He mentions that even the enemies of the Cause were so touched by their integrity that they showed respect to them.

In a Tablet to Shaykh Káẓim-i-Samandar[11]* Bahá'u'lláh states that the soul of the Prophet Muḥammad in the highest paradise laments the martyrdom of the two brothers and denounces the people of Islám for the wicked crime they had perpetrated. In this Tablet Bahá'u'lláh affirms that until his martyrdom, He had not disclosed the station of the King of the Martyrs. This had been due to the weakness and immaturity of people around. But since his ascension to the realms on high, He had revealed in His Tablets a measure of the bounties that God had bestowed upon him.

In His various Tablets Bahá'u'lláh has referred to these two shining lights, among many other designations, as 'the great trust of God', 'the spirit which appeared in the form of a human temple to serve God', 'the tree of love', 'the breeze of God that wafted over the city', 'the luminous stars', 'the ocean of the love of God', 'a fruit upon the tree of fidelity' whose martyrdom had constituted the most great sacrifice in this Cause, and through whom the standards of victory 'were hoisted', and 'the horizon of steadfastness illumined'.

Bahá'u'lláh has conferred great spiritual rewards upon

* One of the Apostles of Bahá'u'lláh, see vol. 3.

the believers who entertain true love for them in their hearts and who visit their graves and chant the Tablets of Visitation revealed in their honour.

In a Tablet to Varqá[12] Bahá'u'lláh pays glowing tribute to the King and Beloved of the Martyrs for their exalted qualities. He affirms that God vouchsafed unto them special favours, and they appeared among people as embodiments of honour and glory. To their goodly virtues both friends and foes had testified. Earlier on they had expressed to Bahá'u'lláh their longing to lay down their lives in His path. In order to describe their exalted station, Bahá'u'lláh states that people would be dumbfounded if the station of even those who worked for them as servants were to be disclosed.

In another Tablet[13] Bahá'u'lláh testifies that many believers had not realized that these two holy souls were already accounted as martyrs while they lived. While they walked on this earth they had utterly sacrificed themselves for the Cause of God and they had achieved the station of martyrdom twice: once when they lived and again when they died. Bahá'u'lláh further states that many would be astonished if they knew how glorious was their first martyrdom. He testifies in one of His Tablets[14] that the Messengers of God and His Chosen Ones are desirous of attaining to their exalted station.

Sentiments and truths such as these flowed from the Pen of Bahá'u'lláh in great profusion for some years after the martyrdom of the 'twin shining lights'. Only when these Tablets are translated and studied in full will one be enabled to see a glimpse of the mysteries which God has, in abundance, enshrined in His Revelation. Among them is the mystery that when a man reaches the stage of utter nothingness in relation to His Lord, his soul will be endowed with such transcendent glory as to stagger one's imagination.

6

A Divine Rebuke

Lawḥ-i-Burhán

Soon after the martyrdom of the King and Beloved of the Martyrs, Bahá'u'lláh wrote the *Lawḥ-i-Burhán* (Tablet of the Proof) addressed to Shaykh Báqir (the Wolf). In it He strongly condemned his evil action. He also addressed Mír Muḥammad Ḥusayn (the She-Serpent) and sternly rebuked him for his part. The strong language that Bahá'u'lláh uses in this Tablet* is indicative of the wrath of God descending upon these two embodiments of wickedness.

Between the two, they have been stigmatized by Bahá'u'lláh as 'the heedless one', 'the perverse hater', 'the ignorant' who had 'gone far astray', who was 'engulfed in evident folly', 'wrapped in thick veil', and had 'joined partners with God'. Both are denounced for a heinous crime as a result of which the 'Apostle' (the Prophet Muḥammad) lamented, 'the hearts of the Concourse on high' were consumed, 'the soul of the Chaste One'† melted, the inmates of Paradise' wept, 'Gabriel'‡ was made to groan, 'all created things' lamented, 'the limbs of the holy ones' quaked, and 'darkness fell upon all regions'.

To Shaykh Báqir, the Wolf, who had penned the death warrant, Bahá'u'lláh declares:

> When thou didst pen Thy judgement, Thou wast accused by Thy very pen.[1]

---

* Translated into English and published in *Tablets of Bahá'u'lláh*, pp. 205–16.

† Fáṭimih, daughter of the Prophet Muḥammad, the holiest woman in Islám.

‡ The Angel which appeared to Muḥammad as the embodiment of the Holy Spirit.

In another instance He affirms:

> Hadst thou realized that which thou hast done, thou wouldst have cast thyself into the fire, or abandoned thine home and fled into the mountains, or wouldst have groaned until thou hadst returned unto the place destined for thee by Him Who is the Lord of strength and of might.[2]

In this Tablet Bahá'u'lláh rebukes the Shaykh in these words:

> O thou who hast gone astray! Thou hast neither seen Me, nor associated with Me, nor been My companion for the fraction of a moment. How is it, then, that thou hast bidden men to curse Me? Didst thou, in this, follow the promptings of thine own desires, or didst thou obey thy Lord? Produce thou a sign, if thou art one of the truthful. We testify that thou hast cast behind thy back the Law of God, and laid hold on the dictates of thy passions.[3]

In the above passage Bahá'u'lláh speaks of cursing by the people. It was a common practice by the enemies of the Faith to curse its Founders. When a Bahá'í was condemned to die for his faith, he would invariably be given a chance to recant. If he did, his life would be saved. But often the mere act of recanting was not considered sufficient. The basic reason for this was that dissimulation of one's faith was considered by the followers of Shí'ah Islám to be a legitimate action to take at times of danger. The practice of dissimulation was widespread among the population of Persia for centuries. Although it amounted to telling a lie concerning one's beliefs, no blame was attached to it. It was considered to be an acceptable way of life, and even some believers in the early days of the Faith followed this practice in order to save their lives. This is why at times some of the enemies of the Faith insisted that it was not sufficient for a Bahá'í to recant his faith. In addition to recanting he had to curse Bahá'u'lláh, the Founder of the Faith, in order that his life might be saved. Cursing was considered to be a test of sincerity for the one who was asked to recant. It must be noted that it is forbidden for a Bahá'í to dissimulate his faith.

The practice of cursing was not limited to these occasions only; it was much more widespread. Cursing Bahá'u'lláh and other Central Figures of the Faith was considered by the Muslim clergy in Persia to be an act of devotion to God and a great service to Islám. They often cursed the Faith from the pulpit during their sermons. Many a devout Muslim of the Shí'ah sect would take pride in hurling imprecations at the Founders of the Faith in public when a Bahá'í passed him by. This was one form of severe mental persecution which many Bahá'ís had to endure day after day. Sometimes it could provoke serious incidents in which the individual Bahá'í might be hurt, or the troubles might even spill over to a wider area involving part or the whole of the Bahá'í community.

Bahá'í children too suffered from this. In some areas Bahá'í children would be surrounded by groups of stone-throwing children who chanted anti-Bahá'í slogans. The abusive language aimed at the Founders of the Faith had a deep psychological effect on Bahá'í children. Parents played a very important role in dispelling the gloom and sadness of their sensitive hearts. What was most helpful for the children was the Bahá'í teaching that it is enjoined on the followers of Bahá'u'lláh to have pity on the enemies of the Faith and not entertain hatred for them in their hearts. Bahá'u'lláh and 'Abdu'l-Bahá have often taught that those who attack the Faith are ignorant people. They are foolish and ignoble, their hearts are full of enmity and rancour; they are already punished by their own actions, for the greatest punishment for an ignorant person is his own ignorance. The Bahá'ís are not to look for vengeance, but look upon these people with the eyes of compassion and pity. They are enjoined by Bahá'u'lláh to pray that God may show mercy to their enemies and open their eyes so that they may see the truth. Otherwise they are condemned by their own actions to spiritual deprivation and everlasting loss.

Addressing the Shaykh, Bahá'u'lláh in the Tablet of Burhán reveals these challenging words:

> Thinkest thou that We fear thy cruelty? Know thou and be well assured that from the first day whereon the voice of the Most Sublime Pen was raised betwixt earth and heaven We offered up Our souls, and Our bodies, and Our sons, and Our possessions in the path of God, the Exalted, the Great, and We glory therein amongst all created things and the Concourse on high. Unto this testify the things which have befallen Us in this straight Path.[4]

The power and ascendancy of Bahá'u'lláh, deriving from the all-pervasive influence of the Most Great Spirit of God, are clearly manifested in this Tablet when He proclaims His station in unequivocal language and with forcefulness and supreme authority to a man who at that time wielded the sceptre of power in his hands. A human being, however capable, however aided by his own knowledge and strength, will never be able to utter commanding words such as these:

> By God! Troubles have failed to unnerve Me, and the repudiation of the divines hath been powerless to weaken Me. I have spoken, and still speak forth before the face of men: 'The door of grace hath been unlocked and He Who is the Dayspring of justice is come with perspicuous signs and evident testimonies from God, the Lord of strength and of might!' Present thyself before Me that thou mayest hear the mysteries which were heard by the Son of 'Imrán* upon the Sinai of Wisdom. Thus commandeth thee He Who is the Dawning-Place of the Revelation of thy Lord, the God of Mercy, from His great Prison.[5]

---

* Moses, who heard the voice of God, the Speaker on Sinai. (A.T.)

Thus the summons of the Lord of Hosts was issued with the hands of power and might, and called the Shaykh to come into His presence and see what the Prophets of God had longed to witness.

In this Tablet Bahá'u'lláh through His loving-kindness counsels this inveterate enemy of His Cause to meditate on the tragic fate of Sulṭán 'Abdu'l-'Azíz of Turkey after Bahá'u'lláh had warned him of his downfall and extinction, reminds him also of Napoleon III whose downfall He had clearly prophesied, urges him to peruse the *Kitáb-i-Íqán* so that his eyes may behold the truth, and warns him in these words:

> O Báqir! Rely not on thy glory, and thy power. Thou art even as the last trace of sunlight upon the mountain-top. Soon will it fade away, as decreed by God, the All-Possessing, the Most High. Thy glory and the glory of such as are like thee have been taken away, and this verily is what hath been ordained by the One with Whom is the Mother Tablet.[6]

One of the attributes of God is mercy. He manifests this attribute to all his creatures. This is the reason why Bahá'u'lláh in His Tablets has exhorted even those who were the embodiments of tyranny to change their ways and turn to God. This feature is noticeable in His Tablets addressed to enemies of the Cause whose actions He has severely condemned. Such condemnation, however, is not due to hatred, nor is it vengeful. Indeed, in the *Lawḥ-i-Burhán* Bahá'u'lláh, addressing the Shaykh, confirms this when He states: 'There is no hatred in Mine heart for Thee nor for anyone.' [7]

That God is merciful and kind to His enemies may be seen in this Tablet. Having denounced the Shaykh most vehemently, rebuked him for his evil doings, and even through His foresight announced his extinction by describing his earthly glories as 'the last traces of sunlight upon the mountain-top', Bahá'u'lláh yet urges him to open his eyes, to discover the truth, to mend his ways and repent so that God may forgive him.

In these words the Pen of the Most High unveils His glorious station to the Shaykh and then invites him to return to his God:

> O foolish one! Know thou that he is truly learned who hath acknowledged My Revelation, and drunk from the Ocean of My knowledge, and soared in the atmosphere of My love, and cast away all else besides Me, and taken firm hold on that which hath been sent down from the Kingdom of My wondrous utterance. He, verily, is even as an eye unto mankind, and as the spirit of life unto the body of all creation. Glorified be the All-Merciful Who hath enlightened him, and caused him to arise and serve His great and mighty Cause. Verily, such a man is blessed by the Concourse on high, and by them who dwell within the Tabernacle of Grandeur, who have quaffed My sealed Wine in My Name, the Omnipotent, the All-Powerful. O Báqir! If thou be of them that occupy such a sublime station, produce then a sign from God, the Creator of the heavens. And shouldst thou recognize thy powerlessness, do thou rein in thy passions, and return unto thy Lord, that perchance He may forgive thee thy sins which have caused the leaves of the Divine Lote-Tree to be burnt up, and the Rock to cry out, and the eyes of men of understanding to weep.[8]

And again:

> . . . Open thine eyes that thou mayest behold this Wronged One shining forth above the horizon of the will of God, the Sovereign, the Truth, the Resplendent. Unstop, then, the ear of thine heart that thou mayest hearken unto the speech of the Divine Lote-Tree that hath been raised up in truth by God, the Almighty, the Beneficent . . . Reflect, that haply thou mayest

recognize thine iniquity and be numbered with such as have repented.[9]

In this Tablet, Bahá'u'lláh denounces the Imám-Jum'ih, the Raq<u>sh</u>á (She-Serpent) in wrathful language. In some ways He addresses him in a more condemnatory tone than his evil accomplice, the Wolf. He rebukes him in these words:

> O She-Serpent! For what crime didst thou sting the children* of the Apostle of God, and pillage their possessions? Hast thou denied Him Who created thee by His command 'be, and it was'? Thou hast dealt with the children of the Apostle of God as neither 'Ád hath dealt with Húd, nor <u>Th</u>amúd with Ṣáliḥ,† nor the Jews with the Spirit of God, the Lord of all being.[10]

Reminding him that he cannot destroy the Cause of God, Bahá'u'lláh addresses the She-Serpent in these words:

> . . . O perverse hater! Didst thou imagine that martyrdom could abase this Cause? Nay, by Him Whom God hath made to be the Repository of His Revelation, if thou be of them that comprehend. Woe betide thee, O thou who hast joined partners with God, and woe betide them that have taken thee as their leader, without a clear token or a perspicuous Book.[11]

And finally He foreshadows his extinction:

> . . . O heedless outcast! Ere long will the breaths of chastisement seize thee, as they seized others before thee. Wait, O thou who hast joined partners with God, the Lord of the visible and the invisible.[12]

---

* The King of the Martyrs and the Beloved of the Martyrs were descendants of the Prophet of Islám. (A.T.)

† See Appendix I.

And again:

> Thou hast clung to tyranny and cast away justice; whereupon all created things have lamented, and still thou art among the wayward. Thou hast put to death the aged, and plundered the young. Thinkest thou that thou wilt consume that which thine iniquity hath amassed? Nay, by Myself! Thus informeth thee He Who is cognizant of all. By God! The things thou possessest shall profit thee not, nor what thou hast laid up through thy cruelty. Unto this beareth witness Thy Lord, the All-Knowing. Thou hast arisen to put out the light of this Cause; ere long will thine own fire be quenched, at His behest. He, verily, is the Lord of strength and of might.[13]

As we shall see, divine chastisement descended upon him almost at the same time as these words were being revealed by Bahá'u'lláh. It began with a series of grave setbacks culminating in his exile from his native city and later his death in miserable circumstances.

In the *Lawḥ-i-Burhán* Bahá'u'lláh also addresses the divines of Islám collectively and proclaims His Mission to them in such challenging words as these:

> . . . O concourse of divines! This is the day whereon nothing amongst all things, nor any name amongst all names, can profit you save through this Name which God hath made the Manifestation of His Cause and the Dayspring of His Most Excellent Titles unto all who are in the kingdom of creation. Blessed is that man that hath recognized the fragrance of the All-Merciful and been numbered with the steadfast. Your sciences shall not profit you in this day, nor your arts, nor your treasures, nor your glory. Cast them all behind your backs, and set your faces towards the Most Sublime Word through which the Scriptures and the Books and this lucid Tablet have been distinctly set forth. Cast away, O concourse

> of divines, the things ye have composed with the pens of your idle fancies and vain imaginings. By God! The Day-Star of Knowledge hath shone forth above the horizon of certitude.[14]

In this Tablet Bahá'u'lláh further addresses the divines of Persia, points to their corrupt practices, their incompetence, their foolishness and their war-mongering. And finally He blames them for the downfall of Islám altogether. These are His ominous warnings:

> O concourse of divines! Because of you the people were abased, and the banner of Islám was hauled down, and its mighty throne subverted.[15]

The Revelation of Bahá'u'lláh has abolished priesthood. Ever since this took place, religious leaders have lost their power and authority. 'From two ranks amongst men', Bahá'u'lláh declares, 'power hath been seized: Kings and ecclesiastics.'[16] In a Tablet,[17] Bahá'u'lláh warns the divines that as of then they could not expect to hold on to their honour and glory any more, for He had taken these from them and given them to those who had believed in God in this day.

There are many reproachful passages in the Writings of Bahá'u'lláh addressed to the divines. The following are merely examples:

> Say: O concourse of divines! Pronounce ye censure against this Pen unto which, as soon as it raised its shrill voice, the kingdom of utterance prepared itself to hearken, and before whose mighty and glorious theme every other theme hath paled into insignificance? Fear ye God and follow not your idle fancies and corrupt imaginings, but rather follow Him Who is come unto you invested with undeniable knowledge and unshakeable certitude.[18]

And again:

> O concourse of divines! When My verses were sent down, and My clear tokens were revealed, We found you behind the veils. This, verily, is a strange thing . . . We have rent the veils asunder. Beware lest ye shut out the people by yet another veil. Pluck asunder the chains of vain imaginings, in the name of the Lord of all men, and be not of the deceitful. Should ye turn unto God, and embrace His Cause, spread not disorder within it, and measure not the Book of God with your selfish desires. This, verily, is the counsel of God aforetime and hereafter . . . Had ye believed in God, when He revealed Himself, the people would not have turned aside from Him, nor would the things ye witness today have befallen Us. Fear God, and be not of the heedless . . . This is the Cause that hath caused all your superstitions and idols to tremble . . .
>
> O concourse of divines! Beware lest ye be the cause of strife in the land, even as ye were the cause of the repudiation of the Faith in its early days. Gather the people around this Word that hath made the pebbles to cry out: 'The Kingdom is God's, the Dawning-Place of all signs!' . . . [19]

The Tablet of Burhán must have been revealed by Bahá'u'lláh very soon after the martyrdom of the King and Beloved of the Martyrs. Mírzá Abu'l-Faḍl, the great Bahá'í scholar, has stated that thirty-eight days after the martyrdom of the two brothers, the believers in Ṭihrán received a copy of the Tablet. He made two copies in his own handwriting and, as bidden by Bahá'u'lláh, sent a copy each to Shaykh Báqir (the Wolf), and the Imám, Mír Muḥammad-Ḥusayn (the She-Serpent).

It took only a few days after the martyrdom of the 'twin shining lights' before a serious quarrel broke out between the Prince and the Imám-Jum'ih (the She-Serpent) over the sharing out of the plundered wealth. About twenty-five days after the martyrdom, the Imám gathered a great number of his followers who accompanied him to the government house to pressurize the Prince for a much larger share than previously envisaged for him. The crowd gathered and soon there was a commotion outside the government headquarters. Day by day the situation grew worse and soon the central government in Ṭihrán became involved. Soldiers were secretly despatched. They arrested the Imám, ransacked his home, plundered all his possessions and took him to Khurásán as an exile. Eventually he was permitted to return to his native town and retire to his home where he died in great misery. This was two years after the martyrdom of the King and Beloved of the Martyrs.

As to Shaykh Muḥammad Báqir, the Wolf, he was sent in disgrace by the Prince to the city of Najaf in 'Iráq. Prevented from returning home and unable to enjoy all the wealth he had accumulated, he died grief-stricken in remote lands in 1883. Shoghi Effendi describes the end of these two in these words:

> Shaykh Muḥammad Báqir, surnamed the 'Wolf', who, in the strongly condemnatory Lawḥ-i-Burhán addressed to him by Bahá'u'lláh, had been compared to 'the last trace of sunlight upon the mountain-top', witnessed the steady decline of his prestige, and died in a miserable state of acute remorse. His accomplice, Mír Muḥammad-Ḥusayn, surnamed the 'She-Serpent', whom Bahá'u'lláh described as one 'infinitely more wicked than the oppressor of Karbilá', was, about that same time, expelled from Iṣfahán, wandered from village to village, contracted a disease that engendered so foul an odor that even his wife and daughter could not bear to approach him, and died in such ill-favor with the local authorities that no one dared to attend his funeral, his corpse being ignominiously interred by a few porters.[20]

The disease mentioned above is said to have been a cancer of the throat which caused a huge abscess on his neck; the pain and the foul odour were intolerable. It is reported that when the martyrdom of the King and Beloved of the Martyrs was being discussed, some were hesitant to put them to death. The Imám became very angry at this: placing his hands upon his neck he said, 'If there be any sin in this let it be upon my neck!'

The Prince, Ẓillu's-Sulṭán, whom Bahá'u'lláh has stigmatized as 'the infernal tree' also fell from grace. He who once ruled over two-thirds of Persia, who made the greatest effort and even secured the support of the British government in fulfilling his long-cherished ambition to become the heir to the throne, and who had assembled such pomp and majesty around himself as to rival those of the King – such a man went steadily into decline, his position and authority lowered, and his hopes and aspirations frustrated. In the end he was sent to Europe as an exile, and was only allowed to return home when suffering from melancholia. Later he died in ignominy.

It is interesting to note that this ignoble Prince had the temerity to send a letter in his own handwriting to Bahá'u'lláh asking Him to allow His followers to support him to overthrow the King, his own father. In return, he undertook to assist the Bahá'ís if he became king. He sent this letter through Ḥájí Muḥammad-'Alíy-i-Sayyáh,* a two-faced political figure whom Bahá'u'lláh has stigmatized as Jáhil (the Ignorant One). Bahá'u'lláh responded firmly, telling Sayyáh that it was incumbent upon the Prince to pray for the King and be his well-wisher and not to wish to overthrow him. He stated that it was not His mission to interfere in political affairs but to improve the character of men. He also forbade him to make such a request of Him ever again.

Ḥájí Mírzá Ḥabíb-i-Afnán† has recorded in his memoirs that he was present when Bahá'u'lláh referred to the Prince's letter and said, 'Were We to send his letter to Náṣiri'd-Dín Sháh, he would skin him [the Prince] alive, but God is the

* Not to be confused with 'Alíy-i-Sayyáh, a faithful disciple of the Báb and Bahá'u'lláh.

† see below, pp. 353–7.

Concealer, He draws a veil over the deeds of His servants.'

When in Europe, the Prince met 'Abdu'l-Bahá a few times. Wishing to absolve himself of the heinous crimes he had committed, he transferred the blame onto his father, Náṣiri'd-Dín Sháh, saying that it was he who had ordered the execution of the two brothers. In this way he thought he could hide the truth from the Master, but the Master, with his sin-covering eye, showed his usual kindness to him.

7

The Mansion of Bahjí

A few miles outside 'Akká stands a beautiful mansion surrounded by magnificent landscaped gardens. Next to it at the centre of converging avenues bordered by beautiful flowers, shrubs and trees in that same garden, stands a small building, the Shrine of Bahá'u'lláh. There His earthly remains are laid to rest, and for the Bahá'ís it is the holiest spot on earth. Today Bahá'í pilgrims from all over the world come to pray at the Shrine of Bahá'u'lláh and visit the Mansion.

Bahá'u'lláh moved to this Mansion in September 1879 and lived there almost thirteen years till 1892, the end of His life. But there were no formal gardens in His time; these were created after His ascension. Nevertheless, the Mansion was built in the countryside close to some beautiful pine trees away from the forbidding city of 'Akká with its narrow gloomy streets and its depressing atmosphere. 'Údí Khammár, in whose house Bahá'u'lláh resided for several years in 'Akká, built the Mansion for himself and his family. The appellation Bahjí (Delight) is truly appropriate for this Mansion when one considers the beauty of the open fields around it, the charm of the building itself and the pleasing sight of the pine trees close by, some of which still stand in the grounds.

Towards the end of Bahá'u'lláh's residence in the Mansion of Mazra'ih, an epidemic broke out in the area. People panicked. Many left their homes and many died. 'Údí Khammár died and was buried by the wall of the Mansion of Bahjí. Soon after this 'Abdu'l-Bahá rented the Mansion for Bahá'u'lláh. The inscription in Arabic placed by Khammár over the entrance in 1870 can be seen in no other light than an inspirational sentiment foreshadowing all the wonderful events which were to take place within its walls. It says:

> Greetings and salutations rest upon this mansion which increaseth in splendour through the passage of time. Manifold wonders and marvels are found therein, and pens are baffled in attempting to describe them.

Shoghi Effendi, the Guardian of the Bahá'í Faith, writes:

> . . . the palace of 'Údí Khammár, on the construction of which so much wealth had been lavished, while Bahá'u'lláh lay imprisoned in the barracks, and which its owner had precipitately abandoned with his family owing to the outbreak of an epidemic disease, was rented and later purchased for Him – a dwelling-place which He characterized as the 'lofty mansion,' the spot which 'God hath ordained as the most sublime vision of mankind.' [1]

In one of His Tablets[2] Bahá'u'lláh describes the Mansion as the scene of His transcendent glory and asserts that it was specially built to serve as the Seat of God in His Day. He refers to its builder, 'Údí Khammár, stating that during his life he had no idea for whom he was building it. He bestows the bounties of God upon his soul through His loving-kindness. He rebukes His enemies, who through their waywardness and ignorance had condemned Him to life imprisonment in the Most Great Prison. However, as a sign of His sovereignty and power He has transformed the prison into a lofty Mansion. He further states that he who was the ruler (i.e. Sulṭán 'Abdu'l-'Azíz) had returned to the fire of hell, while the builder of the Mansion was taken under the canopy of God's mercy and favours.

Before moving to the Mansion of Bahjí, Bahá'u'lláh's residence was at Mazra'ih. But at the actual time of the move to Bahjí He was staying in 'Akká, and it was from the city that He set off for the Mansion. It must be remembered that during the period when Bahá'u'lláh lived in the Mansions of Mazra'ih and Bahjí, He used to go to 'Akká from time to time and stay there for various lengths of time.

Núru'd-Dín-i-Zayn, the son of one of the Apostles of Bahá'u'lláh, Zaynu'l-Muqarrabín, has left to posterity the following account of Bahá'u'lláh's movements in 'Akká and its surrounding areas.

> Normally, during the spring, summer and part of the autumn season, the Blessed Perfection resided in the Mansion of Bahjí and the remainder of the year in the city of 'Akká. He used to ride a white donkey. It was called Barq [lightning] because of its ability to move fast. Any time He went from the Mansion to the Garden of Riḍván, to Mazra'ih, to the Garden of Junaynih, or to 'Akká, He rode on that donkey, and returned in the same way to the Mansion. On these trips a servant always accompanied Him. Later when Barq died they brought another donkey from Persia . . . it was called Ra'd [thunder].[3]

In a Tablet[4] Bahá'u'lláh declares that through the power of His sovereignty, He left the prison-city in spite of the Sulṭán's decree. His footsteps ennobled the Mansion and the Garden of Riḍván. But because He had been accustomed to life in the prison-city, He chose to return there from time to time. In several of His Tablets Bahá'u'lláh indicates that through the years He had become attached to calamities and sufferings. In one instance[5] He declares that He was as fond of sufferings as a lover is of his beloved. In another[6] He states that He is attached to adversities and afflictions as a suckling child is to his mother's milk or a thirsty one longs for a fount of water.

In a Tablet[7] written in the words of Mírzá Áqá Ján, His amanuensis, it is stated that it is beyond man to comprehend the ways of God. For instance, Bahá'u'lláh had been to the Garden of Riḍván and the Mansion, but on one occasion He said that He preferred to be in the Most Great Prison.

The Arrival of Bahá'u'lláh at Bahjí

Returning to the story of Bahá'u'lláh transferring His residence to the Mansion of Bahjí, it was 'Abdu'l-Bahá who had rented the Mansion, and prepared it for Bahá'u'lláh's arrival. First, members of His household moved in. This did not include 'Abdu'l-Bahá, His mother or His sister, the Greatest Holy Leaf; these all remained in 'Akká. When all arrangements were completed Bahá'u'lláh moved to the Mansion. He left the House of 'Abbúd, passed through the Land Gate of 'Akká and arrived at Bahjí in the evening. Ḥájí Muḥammad-Ṭáhir-i-Málmírí, who was in 'Akká at the time, used to live in a room next to Nabíl-A'ẓam's in the vicinity of the Súq-i-Abyaḍ. Their rooms were next to each other; in practice they shared both rooms. Their rooms overlooked the street through which Bahá'u'lláh passed on His way to the Mansion of Bahjí. In his memoirs Ḥájí Muḥammad Ṭáhir describes an amazing episode connected with Bahá'u'lláh's arrival in the Mansion. The event may be regarded as one of the highlights of his nine months' pilgrimage in the presence of the Blessed Beauty.

He writes:

> On the evening that the Blessed Beauty, exalted be His glory, was to move to the Mansion of Bahjí, this servant and Nabíl-i-A'ẓam were staying at our residence, which was a room we both shared. It was situated on the upper floor of the Khán-i-Súq-i-Abyaḍ. The room had five glass windows overlooking the road. We were both sitting at the windows looking out, waiting to behold His blessed Person as He passed by. It was nearly two hours after sunset, when we saw Him pass in front of our room riding on a special white donkey. A few steps behind Him, riding on, his donkey, was Khádimu'lláh (the Servant of God) Mírzá Áqá Ján. When He passed out of our sight, Nabíl suggested that we follow Him on foot to the Mansion to circumambulate it and then return home.

With much enthusiasm I welcomed the suggestion. We both ran down the stairs immediately and walked quickly behind Him, keeping a distance of about fifty steps. That evening an oil lamp was burning inside the Mansion and we could see its light from outside. It was a very large oil lamp which had three wicks. I was familiar with this lamp because we [Ḥájí Muḥammad Ṭáhir and Muḥammad Khán-i-Balúch] had brought it with us to the Holy Land. It was presented to the Blessed Beauty by Ḥájí Siyyid Mírzáy-i-Afnán from Bombay.

When the Blessed Perfection dismounted and went inside the Mansion, we walked toward the building in order to circumambulate. But when we came a little closer we saw to our amazement that the footpaths around the walls of the Mansion were packed with people, who were standing. Crowds had assembled around the four sides of the Mansion and we could hear their murmuring as well as their breathing. Of course we knew that no one had come from 'Akká to circumambulate the Mansion, and we two had gone there without permission. Anyhow, since there was no room to walk on the footpath we stepped back, and at a distance of about thirty steps from the Mansion we circumambulated. To do this we had to walk in some wheatfields and, as it happened, the ground had been recently watered, so we had to walk through muddy fields. As we circled the Mansion we could sense the presence of the multitude on the four sides of the building at some distance from us. In the end we prostrated ourselves on the ground opposite the Gate of the Mansion, and returned to 'Akká. On the way back heavy rain poured down on us, and just as we arrived at the gate of 'Akká, the guards were about to close it. Normally they used to close the gate every night four hours after sunset.

When we arrived home, Nabíl suggested that we ought not to sleep that night and instead keep vigil.* He said to me, 'I will

* The practice of keeping vigil at night is carried out to commemorate a sacred event which has taken place at night. For example, one such event is the ascension of Bahá'u'lláh, which took place in the early hours of the morning. (A.T.)

compose poems and you make tea.' I made tea several times during the night and Nabíl was engaged in writing poetry. He was a gifted poet, he used to compose extemporaneously. By the morning, he had produced poems written on both sides of a large sheet of paper. We sent a copy of his poems, together with two sugar cones,* to the Blessed Beauty. His poems were mainly about history, the history of Bahá'u'lláh's imprisonment, His banishment to Baghdád, Istanbul, Adrianople and 'Akká, the sufferings He had endured in the barracks, the story of the building of the Mansion by 'Údí Khammár, and 'Abdu'l-Bahá renting it to serve as a residence for the Blessed Perfection.

He then described the events of the evening Bahá'u'lláh went to the Mansion, and how we both followed Him, the account of our circumambulation when we saw the souls of all the Prophets and Messengers and the Concourse on high assembled outside the Mansion, circumambulating the throne of their Lord. In these poems Nabíl described in detail our keeping vigil, his own writing poems, and my making tea.

When His Blessed Person received the poems of Nabíl, He revealed a Tablet in honour of Nabíl and myself. In it He graciously accepted our pilgrimage to the Mansion, conferred upon Nabíl the title of Bulbul (Nightingale) and upon myself Bahháj (the Blissful).

Circumambulation of the holy places is an act of devotion and love. It is an expression of the individual's humility, submissiveness and adoration toward the Holy Ones. It is also a sign of one's utter dependence on them. We note that the same act takes place in nature. A satellite circles around a planet and is held in orbit by the force of attraction. It originates from, and its very existence depends upon, the planet. There is a special

* In the old days solid sugar was made in the form of a large cone. It was a very popular gift to present to friends. (A.T.)

relationship between the two: one acts as the master, the other as a servant.

We have in previous volumes described the greatness of the Revelation of Bahá'u'lláh and the exalted station of its author. It was He at whose advent 'the hearts of the entire company' of God's Messengers and Prophets were proved, 'whose presence' Moses 'hath longed to attain', for 'whose love' the spirit of Jesus 'ascended to heaven', and the Day of whose Revelation 'all the Prophets and the Chosen Ones, and the holy ones have wished to witness'.*

The Author of such a transcendent Revelation has, in many of His Tablets, described how the souls of God's Messengers and the company of the Concourse on high circumambulated His throne of sovereignty. Of course this is not a physical circling around such as could be seen in this life. It may be regarded as one of the many mysteries which surround the Supreme Manifestation of God. The early believers who had the inestimable bounty of attaining His presence sometimes witnessed supernatural events at one time or another through His special favours, events which completely overwhelmed their souls and which they recorded in their memoirs. But these may be considered as personal experiences only; they are not valid for others.

The story of Ḥájí Muḥammad-Ṭáhir and Nabíl falls into this category. They had the vision in which they saw the souls of the Prophets and the company of the Concourse on high circling around the Mansion at the time that Bahá'u'lláh ascended the throne of His sovereignty in that hallowed spot. But such a soul-stirring experience is valid for those two privileged souls only: it can never be adduced as a conclusive proof of the station of Bahá'u'lláh. We have already discussed this subject in a previous volume:† miracles are not a proof of the authenticity of the Manifestation of God. If miracles take place, they

* For further discussion see vols. 1, 2, 3 and below, pp. 130–45.

† see vol. 3, pp. 37–46, and vol. 1, p. 291n.

THE MANSION OF BAHÁ'U'LLÁH AT BAHJÍ

Above: local Bahá'ís and pilgrims approaching.
Below: looking over the fields from the pine trees towards the Shrine of Bahá'u'lláh and the Mansion

THE MANSION OF BAHJÍ

The doorway of the Mansion (left) with detail (top right) of the inscription placed over the door by ‘Udí Khammár (see p. 104).
Below, Bahá’u’lláh’s room inside the Mansion where he received pilgrims and revealed Tablets

BAHJÍ

Aerial view of Bahjí, taken in the early 1950s, during the early development by the Guardian of the north-western quadrant, the Ḥaram-i-Aqdas (Most Holy Precincts). The hill has not yet been raised, nor the homes of the Covenant-breakers demolished.

are proof only for those who witness them. Bahá'u'lláh has explained that the proof of the sun is the sun itself; similarly, He states that the proof of the Manifestation of God is in the first place His own Self; in the second place, His Revelation; and for those who are in need of further proof, His words.

Those who attained the Presence of Bahá'u'lláh with pure hearts and spiritual vision had the bounty of being able to recognize Him through 'His own Self'. As a result of coming in contact with His Person these believers became a new creation completely detached from the things of this world, intoxicated by the wine of His presence and carried away into new realms of the spirit. They enjoyed such nearness to the Blessed Beauty that they became the intimates of His mysteries. Some of them saw glimpses of His hidden glory and power and were awe-struck at the revelation of His supreme station.

An Outpouring of Divine Bounty

The transfer of Bahá'u'lláh's residence to the Mansion of Bahjí begins a new and final chapter in His Ministry which constitutes one of the most glorious periods in His life. The King of Glory, the Supreme Manifestation of God, ascended the throne of His sovereignty, the spot which 'God hath ordained as the most sublime vision of mankind'. It was here that the majesty of Bahá'u'lláh and His grandeur were outwardly manifested to both friend and foe. And it was here that the climax of forty years of Revelation was consummated. The verses that streamed from His Pen and the Tablets which were revealed in the latter part of His life released a special potency through which the teachings and principles of His Faith were further enunciated in conjunction with the laws of the *Kitáb-i-Aqdas*, and through which their application to the building of His new world order became apparent.

The prodigious outpouring of the Word of God during Bahá'u'lláh's residence in the Mansion of Bahjí staggers the imagination. The rapidity with which His Tablets were revealed, the manner in which His amanuensis, Mírzá Áqá Ján, though devoid of a proper education, was empowered by Him to cope with recording His words at an amazing speed,* the zeal and enthusiasm with which several of His servants spent long hours every day in transcribing His Writings, all these resulted in the dissemination of innumerable Tablets unprecedented in their range and content during any period of His Ministry. Parallel with the revelation of divine verses, which released their creative energies within human society in general and the Bahá'í community in particular, was the inestimable bounty experienced by a considerable number of His devoted followers of attaining His presence in an atmosphere of freedom and delight. Those who were privileged to come into contact with the divine spirit were magnetized by the energizing forces radiating from His Person. Each one became a new creation and returned home with a new vision and capacity enabling him to scale loftier heights of service in His path.

These two sources of divine bounty – the Person of Bahá'u'lláh on the one hand and His Revelation on the other – endowed the Bahá'í community with a vigour and vitality which it had never experienced before. The many soul-stirring Tablets revealed in this period inspired and enraptured their recipients and transformed them into spiritual giants who, in turn, were able to set on fire the hearts of their fellow believers and thus create a dynamic and flourishing community in Persia. The Cause of God was then securely established in the land of its birth. The teaching exploits of some of its outstanding teachers were highly successful. The expansion of the community, in spite of much persecution, was taking place at a remarkable pace, and the pernicious influence of Mírzá Yaḥyá in creating dissension and doubt had been reduced to a considerable extent. Above all, the prestige of the Faith and its Author in the Holy Land had been mounting steadily towards

* For further information see vol. 1, chapter 3.

a climax, ushering in the last and the most momentous chapter in the history of the Revelation of Bahá'u'lláh.

The Revelation of Bahá'u'lláh may be likened to a tree which in the early years of His Ministry in Baghdád and Sulaymáníyyih had produced its blossoms in a magnificent display of beauty and splendour, dazzling the eyes of those enchanted lovers who were endowed with spiritual vision. They were awestruck as they gazed at its glory and became conscious of its hidden potentialities. Later, towards the end of His sojourn in Adrianople and within the citadel of 'Akká, this tree of divine Revelation yielded its choicest fruits. And now during the latter part of His Ministry when He was residing in the Mansion of Bahjí, the fruits of this exalted tree were ripening and were ultimately garnered. His Mission was coming to a climax and His Revelation reaching its consummation as His earthly life neared its close.

Since its beginnings in the Síyáh-Chál of Ṭihrán the outpouring of the Revelation of Bahá'u'lláh had continued at different periods. This latter part of His Ministry served to crown the inestimable bounties which God had chosen to bestow upon humanity in this Dispensation. Indeed, everything which needed to be revealed by God for humanity in this age has been revealed.

In a Tablet in honour of His Trustee, Ḥájí Abu'l-Ḥasan-i-Amín,[8*] Bahá'u'lláh states that the bounty of God has so encompassed the peoples of the world that the meanings and the inner meanings of every word, every statement and every mystery revealed by Him, have been divulged in this day.

It is interesting to note that for reasons that Bahá'u'lláh Himself has given,[†] He did not choose to reveal the laws of His Dispensation in the early days of His Ministry. Indeed, it was half-way through it that He revealed the Laws of the *Kitáb-i-Aqdas*. And even then He withheld their release to

---

* For a brief account of His life and services see vol. 3, pp. 75–86.

† For further discussion see vol. 2, pp. 353–4, and vol. 3, pp. 277–80.

His followers for some time. The formulation of the laws of the *Kitáb-i-Aqdas*, however, enabled Him, in the latter part of His Ministry, to complete the structure of His all-encompassing Revelation through the revelation of the many important Tablets which streamed from His Pen. Shoghi Effendi describes this process in these words:

> The formulation by Bahá'u'lláh, in His Kitáb-i-Aqdas, of the fundamental laws of His Dispensation was followed, as His Mission drew to a close, by the enunciation of certain precepts and principles which lie at the very core of His Faith, by the reaffirmation of truths He had previously proclaimed, by the elaboration and elucidation of some of the laws He had already laid down, by the revelation of further prophecies and warnings, and by the establishment of subsidiary ordinances designed to supplement the provisions of His Most Holy Book. These were recorded in unnumbered Tablets, which He continued to reveal until the last days of His earthly life, among which the 'Ishráqát' (Splendors), the 'Bishárát' (Glad Tidings), the 'Ṭarázát' (Ornaments), the 'Tajallíyát' (Effulgences), the 'Kalimát-i-Firdawsíyyih' (Words of Paradise), the 'Lawḥ-i-Aqdas' (Most Holy Tablet), the 'Lawḥ-i-Dunyá' (Tablet of the World), the 'Lawḥ-i-Maqsúd' (Tablet of Maqsúd), are the most noteworthy. These Tablets – mighty and final effusions of His indefatigable pen – must rank among the choicest fruits which His mind has yielded, and mark the consummation of His forty-year-long ministry.[9]

8

The Day of God
Tajallíyát

Ustád 'Alí-Akbar-i-Banná

The Tablet of Tajallíyát* was revealed after the *Kitáb-i-Aqdas* around the year AH 1303 (AD 1885–6) in honour of Ustád 'Alí-Akbar-i-Banná (builder-architect),† a native of Yazd, a believer of staunch faith and devotion and one who at the end laid down his life in the path of His Lord. He was a building contractor of wide repute, well respected in government circles, and he was often engaged in construction work for the Governor of Yazd and other high-ranking officials.

When Ustád 'Alí-Akbar embraced the Cause he became filled with the spirit of faith. His soul was illumined by his intense love for Bahá'u'lláh, and he became a shining light among the members of the Bahá'í community of Yazd. His dedication to the Cause and enthusiasm for teaching it aroused the passions of the fanatical clergy who wrote his death warrant. This was in the year AH 1295 (AD 1878) when Nabíl-i-Akbar‡ had gone on a visit to Yazd. The Governor, who was on friendly terms with Ustád 'Alí-Akbar, advised both men to leave the city immediately for their safety. They went to Iṣfahán, stayed a few days in the home of the King of the

---

* This Tablet has been translated in full into English and published in *Tablets of Bahá'u'lláh*, pp. 47–54.

† In the old days in Persia there were no colleges or universities in which students might graduate in the fields of science, art or technology. Those who were described as 'builder-architects' had learned their trade through practical experience working as apprentices to the great master-builders of the time.

‡ see above, ch. 3.

Martyrs and Beloved of the Martyrs and then Ustád went to Ṭihrán while Nabíl-i-Akbar remained in Iṣfahán.

Ustád 'Alí-Akbar was so dedicated to the Cause that he could never withhold himself from teaching the Faith. Although he was a stranger in Ṭihrán, he succeeded in teaching some individuals who were enabled to embrace the Cause. He stayed nine months in the capital before returning to his native city of Yazd. On his return, the enemies of the Faith began agitating the authorities in the hope of taking his life. The clergy again issued his death warrant and handed it to the Governor for execution. But his qualities of service and loving-kindness had endeared him to the authorities and high-ranking officials, who extended their protection to him. However, his life was still in danger, for having failed to put him to death officially, his enemies plotted assiduously to assassinate him. For several years he was the target of many an intrigue, but the Almighty protected him for greater tasks ahead. During this time he succeeded in guiding many souls to the Cause of God.

It must be remembered that during the Heroic Age of the Faith all the believers lived and laboured under very dangerous conditions. The male members of the Bahá'í community were in greater danger than the female, because in those days women lived a secluded life and did not as a general rule appear in public. Any man who was a Bahá'í could not be sure when he left his home in the morning that he would be alive to return home in the evening. This was especially true if the individual was an educated person and an active teacher of the Cause. Ustád 'Alí-Akbar certainly was one of these. During the few years that he remained in Yazd many incidents took place which were fraught with danger. Eventually, after consultation with the Afnáns,* it was decided that Ustád 'Alí-Akbar should go to 'Ishqábád. He arrived there in the year AH 1301 (AD 1883–4).

---

* see above, p. 53n. In the absence of spiritual assemblies, Bahá'í teachers, or the Afnáns, or Bahá'ís with deeper knowledge of the Faith took counsel together on the affairs of the community.

For some time a few members of the Afnán family had taken great interest in 'I<u>sh</u>qábád. Ḥájí Mírzá Muḥammad-'Alí, a maternal cousin of the Báb, had purchased some properties in that city on the advice of his younger brother Ḥájí Mírzá Muḥammad-Taqí* who was then living in Yazd. When the news of this purchase was communicated to Bahá'u'lláh, He ordered that a certain plot of land purchased from a person called A'ẓam should be set aside for the building of a Ma<u>sh</u>riqu'l-A<u>dh</u>kár in 'I<u>sh</u>qábád. This was done and later the first Bahá'í House of Worship in the world was erected on that site.†

For about two years Ustád 'Alí-Akbar was engaged in building shops, a caravanserai and houses for the Afnáns. He then received permission from Bahá'u'lláh to go on pilgrimage to 'Akká. He attained the presence of Bahá'u'lláh in AH 1303 (AD 1885–6). His coming in contact with the Supreme Manifestation of God left an abiding impression on this devoted believer. The fire of the love of Bahá'u'lláh, already burning within his heart, was fanned into a mighty flame as a result of this pilgrimage, He returned to 'I<u>sh</u>qábád radiating the light of the Faith to all souls whom he met. These are the words of Bahá'u'lláh as He addresses Ustád 'Alí-Akbar in the Tablet of Tajallíyát:

> We testify that thou hast set thy face towards God and travelled far until thou didst attain His presence and gavest ear unto the Voice of this Wronged One, Who hath been cast into prison through the misdeeds of those who have disbelieved in the signs and testimonies of God and have denied this heavenly grace through which the whole world hath been made to shine. Blessed thy face, for it hath turned unto Him, and thine ear, for it hath heard His Voice, and thy tongue, for it hath celebrated the praise of God, the Lord of lords. We pray God to graciously aid thee to become a standard for the promotion

* For a brief account of his life see vol. 1, pp. 198–201.

† Ma<u>sh</u>riqu'l-A<u>dh</u>kár: literally, 'the Dawning-place of the Mention of God'. Unfortunately the building was damaged as a result of an earthquake in 1963 and had to be demolished.

USTÁD ʻALÍ-AKBAR-I-BANNÁ

The recipient of the Tablet of Tajallíyát
martyred in Yazd in 1903

> of His Cause and to enable thee to draw nigh unto Him at all times and under all conditions.[1]

In 'Ishqábád, Ḥájí Mírzá Muḥammad-'Alí, the cousin of the Báb, financed the construction of a two-storey building on the corner of the land which he had purchased from A'ẓam and which had been set aside by Bahá'u'lláh's direction as a site for the future Mashriqu'l-Adhkár. Ustád 'Alí-Akbar constructed the building, which was dedicated as a Bahá'í centre in the year AH 1305 (AD 1887–8). All Bahá'í activities, such as meetings and receptions, were held in this building until some years later when the House of Worship was built through the dedicated and sacrificial efforts of Ḥájí Mírzá Muḥammad-Taqí, a younger cousin of the Báb.

Ustád 'Alí-Akbar went on pilgrimage to the Holy Land once again in AH 1311 (AD 1893–4) during the Ministry of 'Abdu'l-Bahá. It was on this occasion that under the direction of 'Abdu'l-Bahá, who conceived the plan for a nine-sided building, he designed the main features of the House of Worship which were approved by the Master. In his last Tablet to Ustád 'Alí-Akbar, 'Abdu'l-Bahá confirms that this design was drawn when Ustád was in the Holy Land, and asks him to send a few copies to one of the Hands of the Cause in Persia. It was, however, a Russian architect who planned and executed the details of the construction; this began in 1902 when the foundation stone was laid in a moving ceremony in the presence of the Czar's representative General Krupatkin, the Governor-General of Turkistán. Of the significance of this House of Worship and its historic importance, Shoghi Effendi, the Guardian of the Faith, writes:

> More conspicuous than any of these undertakings,* however,

* Referring mainly to the restoration of the House of the Báb and the establishment of schools by the Bahá'í community of Persia during the Ministry of 'Abdu'l-Bahá. (A.T.)

> was the erection of the first Mas͟hriqu'l-Ad͟hkár of the Bahá'í world in the city of 'Is͟hqábád, a center founded in the days of Bahá'u'lláh, where the initial steps preparatory to its construction, had been already undertaken during His lifetime. Initiated at about the close of the first decade of 'Abdu'l-Bahá's ministry (1902); fostered by Him at every stage in its development; personally supervised by the venerable Ḥájí Mírzá Muḥammad-Taqí, the Vakílu'd-Dawlih, a cousin of the Báb, who dedicated his entire resources to its establishment, and whose dust now reposes at the foot of Mt. Carmel under the shadow of the Tomb of his beloved Kinsman; carried out according to the directions laid down by the Center of the Covenant Himself; a lasting witness to the fervor and the self-sacrifice of the Oriental believers who were resolved to execute the bidding of Bahá'u'lláh as revealed in the Kitáb-i-Aqdas, this enterprise must rank not only as the first major undertaking launched through the concerted efforts of His followers in the Heroic Age of His Faith, but as one of the most brilliant and enduring achievements in the history of the first Bahá'í century.[2]

Ustád 'Alí-Akbar took a leading role in the building of the House of Worship. But God had other plans for him. Barely six months had passed from the laying of the foundation stone when he received a Tablet from 'Abdu'l-Bahá urging him to go on a visit to Yazd in the spring. He advised him not to hesitate or delay his departure. Ustád 'Alí-Akbar immediately arranged his affairs and in the spring of 1903, after twenty years of absence, he arrived in his native city. His arrival coincided with a period of unusual activity by the Bahá'ís of Yazd. Some well-known teachers of the Cause were coming and going, and the Bahá'ís were very active in teaching the Faith. The arrival of Ustád 'Alí-Akbar in particular created a stir among the non-Bahá'ís, who circulated rumours that he was about to build a Bahá'í House of Worship in Yazd. The people who lived in his neighbourhood were particularly angry, because over the years he had succeeded in converting many souls to the Faith in that area.

In the meantime, 'Abdu'l-Bahá despatched Jináb-i-Ibn-i-Abhar, one of the Hands of the Cause, to Yazd with a special mission. Some large gatherings were held and Ibn-i-Abhar aroused the believers to great heights of spirituality and particularly prepared them for martyrdom should the occasion arise. Consequently a great many souls stood ready to sacrifice their lives in the path of God. This was the summer of 1903, a few months after the arrival of Ustád 'Alí-Akbar. Ibn-i-Abhar left Yazd; he had hardly reached a neighbouring town when suddenly a great uprising against the Bahá'ís erupted in the city, which soon spread to several villages around Yazd. This was the greatest upheaval that had occurred in Persia during the Ministries of Bahá'u'lláh and 'Abdu'l-Bahá since the blood-bath of Ṭihrán after the attempt on the life of Náṣiri'd-Din Sháh in 1852.

The upheaval within the city of Yazd lasted a few days. Every Bahá'í who could be found was put to death. A great many believers laid down their lives for the Cause of God in most moving circumstances. *The History of the Martyrs of Yazd* published in Cairo describes in detail the martyrdom of these souls. However, it is a well-known fact that few people have succeeded in reading this book all the way through; its heartrending stories are so piercing that most people stop reading after a few pages.

Ustád 'Alí-Akbar was among those martyred. The first fatal shot was fired by one of his close relatives. He fell to the ground and shouted, 'Yá Bahá'u'l Abhá'! Then crowds of people attacked, smashed his head with a pickaxe, tied a rope to his feet and dragged his corpse through the city where hundreds of people hurled stones at it and inflicted blows upon it. His disfigured body was then lowered into a deep unused well on the outskirts of the city in which the bodies of other martyrs had been deposited.

Thus ended the life of a believer who served the Cause of

God with exemplary devotion and self-sacrifice. Although he had only an elementary education, he is the author of some beautiful poems and a book on proofs of the Faith (unpublished). He also wrote a detailed account of the early days of the Faith in 'Ishqábád which has not as yet been published. His achievements in the teaching field were truly outstanding. According to his own testimony written about two years before his martyrdom, three hundred souls embraced the Cause of God as a direct result of his teaching work. Ustád 'Alí-Akbar was certainly one of the favoured ones of God; Bahá'u'lláh has revealed twenty-seven Tablets in his honour. 'Abdu'l-Bahá also honoured him with many Tablets.

When Ustád 'Alí-Akbar received the Tablet of Tajallíyát he was particularly fascinated by it, as Bahá'u'lláh had sent him pages of 'revelation-writing' along with the text of the Tablet. When Tablets were revealed, Mírzá Áqá Ján, Bahá'u'lláh's amanuensis, usually took them down. But the speed of revelation was so fast that his handwriting, known as revelation-writing, was practically illegible. We have discussed this subject more fully in a previous volume.*

The Station of Bahá'u'lláh

In the Tablet of Tajallíyát Bahá'u'lláh reveals a glimpse of the transcendent splendour of His Revelation. In a few passages He extols the Mission of its Author in such wise that some may find it difficult to appreciate. It is interesting to note that Bahá'u'lláh often repeats a certain subject in His Writings, but each time it is freshly revealed and expressed in a different way. One subject, however, appears more than any other in the Writings of Bahá'u'lláh: one can hardly come across a Tablet which does not expound the greatness of His Revelation and the exalted station of its Author.

---

* see vol. 1, ch. 3. For a facsimile of a page of the Tablet of Tajallíyát in revelation-writing see vol. 1, facing p. 110.

This recurring theme is the cornerstone of Bahá'u'lláh's Message to mankind. He constantly reiterates that He has ushered in the Day of God. For instance, the following utterances selected at random reveal this outstanding feature of His transcendent Revelation. These highly significant passages are the cause of supreme felicity and exhilaration for His loved ones who have truly recognized His station. On the other hand, the same passages may be misconstrued by those who are not endowed with true understanding, or by those motivated by malice. Indeed, many of Bahá'u'lláh's adversaries falsely accused him of identifying Himself with that Invisible Reality, the Essence of Deity itself.

> Verily I say! No one hath apprehended the root of this Cause. It is incumbent upon every one, in this day, to perceive with the eye of God, and to hearken with His ear. Whoso beholdeth Me with an eye besides Mine own will never be able to know Me. None among the Manifestations of old, except to a prescribed degree, hath ever completely apprehended the nature of this Revelation.[3]

> Great indeed is this Day! The allusions made to it in all the sacred Scriptures as the Day of God attest its greatness. The soul of every Prophet of God, of every Divine Messenger, hath thirsted for this wondrous Day. All the divers kindreds of the earth have, likewise, yearned to attain it.[4]

> By the righteousness of God! These are the days in which God hath proved the hearts of the entire company of His Messengers and Prophets, and beyond them those that stand guard over His sacred and inviolable Sanctuary, the inmates of the celestial Pavilion and dwellers of the Tabernacle of Glory.[5]

> This is the Day whereon human ears have been privileged to hear what He Who conversed with God (Moses) heard

upon Sinai, what He Who is the Friend of God (Muḥammad) heard when lifted up towards Him, what He Who is the Spirit of God (Jesus) heard as He ascended unto Him, the Help in Peril, the Self-Subsisting.[6]

This is the Day whereon the unseen world crieth out, 'Great is thy blessedness, O earth, for thou hast been made the footstool of thy God, and been chosen as the seat of His mighty throne.'[7]

Be fair, ye peoples of the world . . . is it meet and seemly for you to question the authority of one Whose presence 'He Who conversed with God' (Moses) hath longed to attain, the beauty of Whose countenance 'God's Well-beloved' (Muḥammad) had yearned to behold, through the potency of Whose love the 'Spirit of God' (Jesus) ascended to heaven, for Whose sake the 'Primal Point' (the Báb) offered up His life? [8]

He it is* . . . Who in the Old Testament hath been named Jehovah, Who in the Gospel hath been designated as the Spirit of Truth, and in the Qur'án acclaimed as the Great Announcement . . . But for Him no Divine Messenger would have been invested with the robe of prophethood, nor would any of the sacred scriptures have been revealed. To this bear witness all created things.[9]

In the Tablet of Tajallíyát Bahá'u'lláh acknowledges that the mere mention of His Station may cause people to become perturbed and filled with consternation. He intimates to the recipient of that Tablet that He would not have disclosed the exalted nature of His Station had it not been for the Báb who had repeatedly announced it in His Writings. These are the words of Bahá'u'lláh in the Tablet of Tajallíyát:

* Bahá'u'lláh. (A.T.)

> By the righteousness of God! But for the anthem of praise voiced by Him Who heralded the divine Revelation, this Wronged One would never have breathed a word which might have struck terror into the hearts of the ignorant and caused them to perish. Dwelling on the glorification of Him Whom God shall make manifest – exalted be His Manifestation – the Báb in the beginning of the Bayán saith: 'He is the One Who shall proclaim under all conditions, "Verily, verily, I am God, no God is there but Me, the Lord of all created things. In truth all others except Me are My creatures. O, My creatures! Me alone do ye worship."' Likewise in another instance He, magnifying the Name of Him Who shall be made manifest, saith: 'I would be the first to adore Him.' Now it behoveth one to reflect upon the significance of the 'Adorer' and the 'Adored One', that perchance the people of the earth may partake of a dewdrop from the ocean of divine knowledge and may be enabled to perceive the greatness of this Revelation. Verily, He hath appeared and hath unloosed His tongue to proclaim the Truth. Well is it with him who doth acknowledge and recognize the truth, and woe betide the froward and the wayward.[10]

It is obvious that the great majority of the people at this time in history will not be able to accept Bahá'u'lláh's claims to such an exalted position. In the above passage He confirms that such a claim would strike 'terror into the hearts of the ignorant'. Even some of His followers whose hearts have been touched by His love but who have not had the opportunity to deepen themselves in the verities of His Faith and discover the inner significances of His Revelation may find themselves severely tested when they come across Bahá'u'lláh's utterances revealing some of the awe-inspiring features of His transcendent Revelation. They may be equally tested by the statement of the Báb, Himself a Manifestation of God, saying that He would be 'the first to adore' Bahá'u'lláh. The mind is bewildered when it attempts to contemplate the station of the 'Adorer' – the Báb, a Manifestation of God, the 'Primal Point', the 'King of Messengers', one 'round Whom the realities of the Prophets and Messengers revolve'. The 'Adored One' is Bahá'u'lláh, and it was noted in the above passage that the Báb describes Him as 'the One Who shall proclaim under all conditions, "Verily, verily, I am God, no God is there but Me, the Lord of all created things. In truth all others except Me are My creatures. O, My creatures! Me alone do ye worship."' The Writings of the Báb are replete with passages* such as this one. Bahá'u'lláh Himself in one of His Tablets[11] makes a striking statement when He testifies that the Cause is so mighty that whenever His Pen moves to inscribe its greatness, it trembles and swoons away.

This subject – the greatness of the Revelation of Bahá'u'lláh – has been discussed repeatedly in previous volumes, each time from a slightly different point of view. In this instance let us examine the main obstacles which may prevent the seeker of truth from appreciating the exalted nature of the Revelation of Bahá'u'lláh and the lofty station of its Author. These obstacles appear to be based on two misunderstandings. One is Bahá'u'lláh's identification with the Godhead. The other, the apparent contradiction between the belief that all the Manifestations of God are one and the statement that Bahá'u'lláh is the supreme Manifestation of God.

The relationship of God to His Manifestations

As to the first question, we can do no better than to turn to Shoghi Effendi's explanation. He writes:

> Let no one meditating . . . on the nature of the Revelation of Bahá'u'lláh, mistake its character or misconstrue the intent of its Author. The divinity attributed to so great a Being and the complete incarnation of the names and attributes of

* For further information see vol. 1, ch. 18.

> God in so exalted a Person should, under no circumstances, be misconceived or misinterpreted. The human temple that has been made the vehicle of so overpowering a Revelation must, if we be faithful to the tenets of our Faith, ever remain entirely distinguished from that 'innermost Spirit of Spirits' and 'eternal Essence of Essences' – that invisible yet rational God Who, however much we extol the divinity of His Manifestations on earth, can in no wise incarnate His infinite, His unknowable, His incorruptible and all-embracing Reality in the concrete and limited frame of a mortal being. Indeed, the God Who could so incarnate His own reality would, in the light of the teachings of Bahá'u'lláh, cease immediately to be God. So crude and fantastic a theory of Divine incarnation is as removed from, and incompatible with, the essentials of Bahá'í belief as are the no less inadmissible pantheistic and anthropomorphic conceptions of God – both of which the utterances of Bahá'u'lláh emphatically repudiate and the fallacy of which they expose . . . [12]

It is essential to differentiate between the 'Essence of God' which Shoghi Effendi describes as the 'innermost Spirit of Spirits' or 'Eternal Essence of Essences', and 'God revealed' to humanity. The former is unknowable, while the latter is comprehensible to man. We note in the Writings of Bahá'u'lláh that the Manifestations of God do not have any knowledge of God's Essence. One can understand his own equal or an inferior being, but knowledge of a superior being is impossible. Therefore, if the Manifestations of God were able to understand the Essence of Divinity they should be equal to Him, and this is blasphemy.

In one of His Tablets Bahá'u'lláh has made a categorical statement that the Manifestations of God do not have any access to the Essence of God, that invisible Reality. These are His Words:

> From time immemorial . . . He, the Divine Being, hath been veiled in the ineffable sanctity of His exalted Self, and will everlastingly continue to be wrapt in the impenetrable mystery of His unknowable Essence . . . Ten thousand Prophets, each a Moses, are thunderstruck upon the Sinai of their search at God's forbidding voice, 'Thou shalt never behold Me!'; whilst a myriad Messengers, each as great as Jesus, stand dismayed upon their heavenly thrones by the interdiction 'Mine Essence thou shalt never apprehend!' [13]

Bahá'u'lláh Himself has testified in many of His Tablets that He too has no knowledge or understanding of the innermost reality of God. In one instance He thus testifies:

> How bewildering to me, insignificant as I am, is the attempt to fathom the sacred depths of Thy knowledge! How futile my efforts to visualize the magnitude of the power inherent in Thine handiwork – the revelation of Thy creative power! [14]

In one of His celebrated prayers Bahá'u'lláh refers to Himself as the Day-Spring of God's signs and the Revealer of His clear tokens. He also testifies to the immensity of His own wisdom and the loftiness of His knowledge. Nevertheless, the possessor of such an exalted station affirms that He is unable to know the innermost Essence of God. These words are part of His prayer as He communes with God:

> I swear by Thy Beauty, O King of eternity Who sittest on Thy most glorious Throne! He Who is the Day-Spring of Thy signs and the Revealer of Thy clear tokens hath, notwithstanding the immensity of His wisdom and the loftiness of His knowledge, confessed His powerlessness to comprehend the least of Thine utterances, in their relation to Thy most exalted Pen – how much more is He incapable of apprehending the nature of Thine all-glorious Self and of Thy most august Essence! [15]

From these and many other Writings of Bahá'u'lláh we arrive at the conclusion that there can be no direct path or relationship between Him Who is the Essence of Divinity and all others, including His Manifestations. There is no door which could lead His creatures to His innermost Reality. We read in the Long Obligatory Prayer that He is far exalted above the reach of man's prayers.

> Too high art Thou for the praise of those who are nigh unto Thee to ascend unto the heaven of Thy nearness, or for the birds of the hearts of them who are devoted to Thee to attain to the door of Thy gate. I testify that Thou hast been sanctified above all attributes and holy above all names. No God is there but Thee, the Most Exalted, the All-Glorious.[16]

We note that God is 'sanctified above all attributes'. In many of His Tablets and prayers Bahá'u'lláh has testified that one cannot attach any attributes to the Essence of God. This can be easily appreciated, for any attribute which may be related to Him will have a limiting effect on Him, and consequently He will cease to be God. Those familiar with mathematics and the term 'infinity' know that it is impossible to evaluate it in terms of a number, however large. It would cease immediately to be 'infinity' if it were identified with any item other than itself.

God is the infinite Being. The attributes 'the All-Knowing', the All-wise', 'the Incomparable' and others cannot be related to the Innermost Reality of God, His Essence.

In a Tablet[17] 'Abdu'l-Bahá states that a great many people are bondslaves of vain imaginings. They confess that they worship God, but if they were asked which God they were worshipping, the response would be 'the God which comes to mind'. 'Abdu'l-Bahá then explains in this Tablet that whatever the individual can think about God in his mind is the fabric of his own imagination, and is not God. He emphasizes that the only way for one's mind to visualize God is to turn to His Manifestations. The explanations of 'Abdu'l-Bahá may be summarized by saying that the Infinite cannot be comprehended by man's finite mind.

In another Tablet[18] 'Abdu'l-Bahá states that we may attach some attributes to God. We do this not because we wish to prove that God is the possessor of exalted attributes – attributes which are beyond our understanding – but rather to dissociate from Him the lack of such attributes. In his celebrated Tablet to Dr Forel, 'Abdu'l-Bahá states:

> As to the attributes and perfections such as will, knowledge, power and other ancient attributes that we ascribe to that Divine Reality, these are the signs that reflect the existence of beings in the visible plane and not the absolute perfections of the Divine Essence that cannot be comprehended. For instance, as we consider created things we observe infinite perfections, and the created things being in the utmost regularity and perfection we infer that the Ancient Power on whom dependeth the existence of these beings, cannot be ignorant; thus we say He is All-Knowing. It is certain that it is not impotent, it must be the All-Powerful; it is not poor, it must be All-Possessing; it is not non-existent, it must be Ever-Living. The purpose is to show that these attributes and perfections that we recount for that Universal Reality are only in order to deny imperfections, rather than to assert the perfections that the human mind can conceive. Thus we say His attributes are unknowable.[19]

God, Who in the Kingdom of His Own Self is exalted above any attribute, reveals Himself in His Kingdom of Revelation. It is in this Kingdom that all the attributes of God are manifested, and it is from this Kingdom that all the Manifestations are sent down. These embodiments of Holiness, the Manifestations of God, are the bearers of God's attributes. All the superlative attributes such as 'the Omnipotent', 'the All-Knowing', 'the

All-glorious' and other similar attributes refer to God revealed to man. It may be noted in all the heavenly Books and in the Bahá'í Writings that the Manifestations of God, the Founders of world religions, are all the recipients of the Holy Spirit of God. And it is through the aid of the Holy Spirit that at each age they have revealed the attributes of God to Man.

Bahá'u'lláh, as far back as His days in the Síyáh-Chál* of Ṭihrán, has categorically claimed that it was the 'Most Great Spirit' of God which was revealed to Him. And it is clear from the study of His Writings that it never left Him, and that He was animated and sustained throughout His Ministry by this 'Most Great Spirit'. In the *Súriy-i-Haykal*† Bahá'u'lláh affirms that the Holy Spirit revealed to the Manifestations of God has come into being through the agency of this 'Most Great Spirit', whatever that is. These are His words:

> Naught is seen in My temple but the Temple of God, and in My beauty but His Beauty, and in My being but His Being, and in My self but His Self, and in My movement but His Movement, and in My acquiescence but His Acquiescence, and in My pen but His Pen, the Mighty, the All-Praised. There hath not been in My soul but the Truth, and in Myself naught could be seen but God. The Holy Spirit Itself hath been generated through the agency of a single letter revealed by this Most Great Spirit, if ye be of them that comprehend.[20]

The Most Great Spirit is therefore the begetter of the Holy Spirit and the Revealer of God's attributes to man. Through it all Revelations have been sent down and all created things called into being. This 'Most Great Spirit' which has existed from eternity and which will exist for eternity had never before revealed Itself directly to mankind. God had waited for millions of years for man to develop spiritually and intellectually

* Dungeon in Ṭihrán where Bahá'u'lláh was imprisoned.
† see vol. 3, chapter 7.

to a point where he could receive this Most Great Revelation. Bahá'u'lláh has declared that this was indeed God's purpose in creating man. In a Tablet He thus reveals:

> The purpose underlying all creation is the revelation of this most sublime, this most holy Day, the Day known as the Day of God, in His Books and Scriptures – the day which all the Prophets and the Chosen Ones, and the holy ones, have wished to witness.[21]

In past Dispensations God's Revelation had been indirect through the intermediary of the Holy Spirit. In this Dispensation, however, for the first time the Most Great Spirit of God has revealed Itself directly to Bahá'u'lláh and ushered in the Day of God. The most important point which can help clarify any misunderstanding about the station of Bahá'u'lláh is the dissociation of His human temple from the 'Most Great Spirit' which animated it. When we refer to Bahá'u'lláh, we are referring to the 'Glory of God', the 'Most Great Spirit' and not to a human being. When He speaks, the words are not His. They issue from the 'Most Great Spirit' which speaks in the language of man through a mouthpiece – the Person of Bahá'u'lláh. We often come across the words of Bahá'u'lláh saying 'I am God'. In many instances He declares that all creation has come into being through one of His words, or announces that He has sent all the Messengers in the past. The following passage is a typical example.

> But for Him [Bahá'u'lláh] no Divine Messenger would have been invested with the role of prophethood.[22]

None of these utterances come from the Person of Bahá'u'lláh. They represent the Voice of God which speaks to us through the instrumentality of a human being. Bahá'u'lláh Himself has expressed this phenomenon in these words:

> When I contemplate, O my God, the relationship that bindeth me to Thee I am moved to proclaim to all created things 'verily I am God!'; and when I consider my own self, lo, I find it coarser than clay![23]

From all these explanations one may conclude that the greatness of the Revelation of Bahá'u'lláh and His transcendent glory is due to the Manifestation of the 'Most Great Spirit' which revealed itself directly to Him. Never before had God sent a Manifestation of His 'Most Great Spirit' to mankind, His Supreme Manifestation, or the Universal Manifestation Who appeared in His Greatest Name, Bahá (Glory).*

Shoghi Effendi, the Guardian of the Faith, has given the following explanation through his secretary:

> By Greatest Name is meant that Bahá'u'lláh has appeared in God's Greatest Name, in other words, that He is the Supreme Manifestation of God . . . There are no Prophets, so far, in the same category as Bahá'u'lláh, as He culminates a great cycle begun with Adam.[24]

Although one must distinguish between the Spirit which animated Bahá'u'lláh and His own Person, and be on one's guard not to attribute the glory of His Revelation to His human frame, it is nevertheless clear that the Person of the Manifestation cannot be dismissed altogether. On the contrary, the human temple which becomes the carrier of such a mighty Spirit moves and acts with the majesty and authority of God. The overwhelming and all-pervasive power of God is so infused into every atom of His Being that in every action He portrays the signs and tokens of divine power. Those endowed with spiritual insight can see in every move of the Manifestation of God, the attributes of God unmistakably apparent. His

* For further discussion of the term 'Universal Manifestation' see vol. 1, pp. 309–11.

thoughts, His words, His actions are all motivated not by a human soul but by the Divine Spirit.

Ḥájí Mírzá Ḥaydar-'Alí, to whom much reference has been made in this and previous volumes, has described his own observations of Bahá'u'lláh in these words:

> His blessed person appeared in the form of a human being, but His very movements, His manners, His way of sitting or standing, eating or drinking, even His sleep or wakefulness, were each a miracle to me. Because His perfections, His exalted character, His beauty, His glory, His most excellent titles and most august attributes revealed to me that He was peerless and without parallel. He was matchless with no one to join partners with Him, unique with no peer or equal, the One and Single without a deputy . . . I saw a Person Who, from the human point of view, was like the rest of humanity. However, if one were to add the love, mercy and compassion of all the peoples of the world together, they would appear as a drop when compared with the ocean of His tender mercy and loving-kindness. I even seek God's forgiveness for making such a comparison. Similarly, if one brought together all the knowledge of science, crafts, philosophy, politics, natural history and divinity possessed by mankind, it would seem, in comparison with His knowledge and understanding, as an atom compared to the sun. If one weighed the might and power of kings, rulers, Prophets and Messengers against His omnipotence and sovereignty, His grandeur and glory, His majesty and dominion, they would be as insignificant as a touch of moisture compared with the waters of the sea . . . As I observed every one of His attributes, I discovered my inability to emulate Him, and realized that all the peoples of the world will never be able to attain to His perfections.[25]

The dawn of the new age

The other cause of misunderstanding about the station of Bahá'u'lláh is the apparent contradiction between His being the 'Supreme Manifestation', and the principle of the equality and oneness of all the Manifestations. To appreciate this point the reader would be well advised to study the *Kitáb-i-Íqán*, in which Bahá'u'lláh explains that the difference between the Manifestations lies in the intensity of their Revelations. We have also discussed this matter in detail in a previous volume.*

In the Tablet of Tajallíyát Bahá'u'lláh reveals the following:

> God testifieth that there is none other God but Him and that He Who hath appeared is the Hidden Mystery, the Treasured Symbol, the Most Great Book for all peoples, and the Heaven of bounty for the whole world. He is the Most Mighty Sign amongst men and the Dayspring of the most august attributes in the realm of creation. Through Him hath appeared that which had been hidden from time immemorial and been veiled from the eyes of men. He is the One Whose Manifestation was announced by the heavenly Scriptures, in former times and more recently. Whoso acknowledgeth belief in Him and in His signs and testimonies hath in truth acknowledged that which the Tongue of Grandeur uttered ere the creation of earth and heaven and the revelation of the Kingdom of Names. Through Him the ocean of knowledge hath surged amidst mankind and the river of divine wisdom hath gushed out at the behest of God, the Lord of Days.[26]

The Revelation of Bahá'u'lláh has endowed the human race with new capacity and bestowed upon it immense potentialities. In the above passage Bahá'u'lláh asserts that through Him has 'appeared that which had been hidden from time immemorial and been veiled from the eyes of men'. As we look back

* see vol. 1, pp. 64–6 and 118–19.

upon the progress of humanity throughout the ages we can clearly see that the advent of every Manifestation of God has coincided with a time when the older Dispensation had come to its end* and was enveloped in darkness. But the Dispensation of Bahá'u'lláh is different in that it has brought to light all that was hidden from man because of his lack of capacity in the past.

The dawn of this new age coincided with the advent of the Báb and Bahá'u'lláh. This phenomenon is similar to the appearance of the dawn banishing the darkness of the night. During the night no one can see and all is dormant, but at the break of day eyes begin to see and everything comes to light. The dawn of this new era, which occurred in the middle of the nineteenth century at the appearance of the Báb, caused the minds and hearts of people to be illumined. The masses of the people, who in olden days followed their leaders almost blindly, were now able to see for themselves and think independently. The night season had passed and the morning light had dawned. As this process of enlightenment continued, people viewed life and all that pertains to it with a critical eye. A multiplicity of ideas resulted in the clash of differing opinions. Hundreds of sects were created in religions and many left religion altogether and swelled the ranks of agnostics and atheists. Many contrasting political and social systems were created and many controversial philosophies were introduced and established throughout the world.

These divisive developments in the fields of religion, politics and social affairs are threatening to plunge the human race into a deep and dangerous abyss. On the other hand, there has occurred such an explosion of arts and sciences in this new era as bids fair to usher in an age in which spiritual and material forces will combine together to bring about a new civilization which will be well-balanced and world-embracing. These manifestations of human activity, with all their constructive as well as destructive consequences, are unprecedented in the

* see below, pp. 163–4.

annals of the past and owe their origins to the dawning of the Sun of Truth in this new age.

Although the human world has been illumined in this day, the generality of mankind has not been able to find the source of this illumination. Returning to our analogy of the dark night and the appearance of the dawn, we can see a striking similarity between the plight of humanity today and the fate of those who are confined in their rooms when the dawn appears. They can witness the area brightening, but may fail to see the sun because of closed doors and drawn curtains. The veils that shut people out from the Sun of Truth are many and varied. The veil of knowledge, of pride and vainglory, of time-honoured traditions to which people usually become bondslaves, of various forms of prejudice, of religious indoctrination and many more – all these veils act as barriers for man and prevent him from recognizing the Revelation of Bahá'u'lláh as the Source of a revolutionizing process which is at work in the world of humanity in this age. Only by the lifting of these 'veils' and through an earnest search for truth can the individual become assured in his heart that Bahá'u'lláh, and no one else, has ushered in this revolutionizing process to which He Himself testifies in these words from the *Kitáb-i-Aqdas*:

> The world's equilibrium hath been upset through the vibrating influence of this most great, this new World order. Mankind's ordered life hath been revolutionized through the agency of this unique, this wondrous System – the like of which mortal eyes have never witnessed.[27]

Recognition and Steadfastness

In the Tablet of Tajallíyát Bahá'u'lláh states that no one can recognize God save through Him. Statements such as these are to be found in many of His Writings. These are His words in this Tablet:

> The first Tajallí which hath dawned from the Day-Star of Truth is the knowledge of God – exalted be His glory. And the knowledge of the King of everlasting days can in no wise be attained save by recognizing Him Who is the Bearer of the Most Great Name. He is, in truth, the Speaker on Sinai Who is now seated upon the throne of Revelation. He is the Hidden Mystery and the Treasured Symbol. All the former and latter Books of God are adorned with His praise and extol His glory. Through Him the standard of knowledge hath been planted in the world and the ensign of the oneness of God hath been unfurled amidst all peoples. Attainment unto the Divine Presence can be realized solely by attaining His presence. Through His potency everything that hath, from time immemorial, been veiled and hidden, is now revealed. He is made manifest through the power of Truth and hath uttered a Word whereby all that are in the heavens and on the earth have been dumbfounded, except those whom the Almighty was pleased to exempt. True belief in God and recognition of Him cannot be complete save by acceptance of that which He hath revealed and by observance of whatsoever hath been decreed by Him and set down in the Book by the Pen of Glory.[28]

The 'Bearer of the Most Great Name', the 'Speaker on Sinai', the 'Hidden Mystery' and the 'Treasured Symbol' mentioned in the above passage all refer to Bahá'u'lláh. One of the basic teachings of Bahá'u'lláh is that man can never know God directly. The only way open to him to know God is through knowing His Manifestations. Bahá'u'lláh has fully expounded this subject in the *Kitáb-i-Íqán*, and we have referred to it in a previous volume.* Similarly, 'attainment unto the Divine presence', which Bahá'u'lláh testifies to be none other than attaining His Own presence, is also discussed previously.†

---

* see vol. 1, pp. 175–80.

† see vol. 1, pp. 185, 299n.

It is interesting to note Bahá'u'lláh's statement that He 'uttered a Word whereby all that are in the heavens and on the earth have been dumbfounded'. In another Tablet He makes a similar statement and reveals that the word in question is the changing of 'He' into 'I'. Again this statement has been referred to and explained in a previous volume.*

Another subject to which Bahá'u'lláh has attached great importance in His Writings is that of steadfastness in the Cause of God. These are His words in the Tablet of Tajallíyát:

> The second Tajallí is to remain steadfast in the Cause of God – exalted be His glory – and to be unswerving in His love. And this can in no wise be attained except through full recognition of Him; and full recognition cannot be obtained save by faith in the blessed words: 'He doeth whatsoever He willeth.' Whoso tenaciously cleaveth unto this sublime word and drinketh deep from the living waters of utterance which are inherent therein, will be imbued with such a constancy that all the books of the world will be powerless to deter him from the Mother Book. O how glorious is this sublime station, this exalted rank, this ultimate purpose! [29]

The Cause of God has been steadily growing since its inception. It has been, and still is, subjected to continuous opposition and harrowing persecutions. That it has survived, and indeed flourished, in spite of encountering many grievous upheavals in the course of its history, is partly due to the protection vouchsafed to it by the Almighty God, and partly to the steadfastness of its adherents. The heroic spirit of self-sacrifice demonstrated by thousands of its martyrs, its saints and scholars, its teachers and administrators, is indicative of an unshakeable faith and certitude unprecedented in the annals of religion. If it were not for the steadfastness of the followers of the Báb and Bahá'u'lláh in the face of brutal attacks and persecutions, the

* see vol. 1, p. 46.

Bahá'í community could not have won such remarkable victories within so short a period of time.

The steadfastness of a believer depends upon the extent to which he has recognized the station of Bahá'u'lláh. Those who have truly reached the pinnacle of faith and certitude have become so steadfast in the Cause of God as to fulfil the conditions for steadfastness that Bahá'u'lláh has laid down in the Tablet of Aḥmad:*

> And be thou so steadfast in My love that thy heart shall not waver, even if the swords of the enemies rain blows upon thee and all the heavens and the earth arise against thee.

It is interesting to note that in the same Tablet Bahá'u'lláh has made the following promise:

> By God! Should one who is in affliction or grief read this Tablet with absolute sincerity, God will dispel his sadness, solve his difficulties and remove his afflictions.

People often wonder how to recite this Tablet with absolute sincerity. It may be said that reading with absolute sincerity takes place when the reader can truly reach to such heights of faith and assurance that 'his heart shall not waver, even if the swords of the enemies rain blows upon him'. In one of His Tablets[30] Bahá'u'lláh states that a person will become steadfast in the Cause when he is absolutely assured in his heart that he does not need to turn to any religion other than this Most Great Revelation.

One of the teachings of Bahá'u'lláh is the unfettered search after truth. Some misunderstand this important teaching to mean that even after discovering the Truth in the Revelation of Bahá'u'lláh and recognizing Him as the Manifestation of God, one ought to continue the search, perchance one may find

* For further information see vol. 2, ch. 5.

it elsewhere. To hold such a view is a clear indication that the person has not discovered the truth in the first place and has not reached the stage of assurance in his faith. On the other hand, having found the truth, one never reaches the end of his journey; for as long as one lives there is scope for a better and deeper understanding of the truth he has found.

In *The Seven Valleys* Bahá'u'lláh describes how the wayfarer passes from one stage to another. It begins with the Valley of Search when the individual seeks to find the Truth. When he discovers the object of his search he moves forward to other valleys, the Valleys of Love, of Knowledge and the rest. To remain in the Valley of Search for ever is an evident sign of failure to find the Truth. The recognition of the Manifestation of God must be followed by steadfastness in His Covenant, which means simply obedience* to the Centre of the Cause and carrying out His laws and teachings.

When we study human nature we notice there are two forces within man which are always at work in opposition to each other. One is the force of the animal nature which tends to drag him down into the animal kingdom. The other is the force of the spiritual nature which elevates man to great heights of nearness to God. A human being may be likened to an aircraft which is also under the influence of two opposing forces. The first is the force of gravity which tends to pull the machine down toward the earth; the second, the lifting force of the engine which propels the machine upwards. By its nature the former is always present and effortlessly pulls down the craft, while the latter force is applied only when the engine is switched on and kept running. As long as the engine is running, the aircraft can fly. As soon as it stops, the force of gravity will instantly pull the machine down.

There is a striking similarity between the aircraft and the functioning of a human being. The animal nature is similar to the force of gravity. It is always present and can easily

* For a further discussion of the subject of obedience see vol. 3.

and swiftly degrade the station of the individual to that of the animal and far beyond. The spiritual nature, if allowed to exert its influence, can subdue the animalistic inclinations and lift man to great heights of spirituality just as the aircraft engine provides the force to lift the aircraft. This upliftment and spiritual growth occurs when the individual recognizes the Manifestation of God and acquires faith and assurance.

Although having faith in Bahá'u'lláh will cause the human soul to be uplifted spiritually, it will not be sufficient for the individual to overcome the many tests and trials he encounters in life. There is yet another important step which must be taken after having recognized the station of Bahá'u'lláh and embraced His Faith. To elucidate this point we may use the analogy of the flying machine again, as it can throw further light on this subject. A powerful engine will not necessarily guarantee the safe landing of an aircraft at its destination. It is the navigational instruments continuously receiving signals from a central point, that guide the pilot to navigate the aeroplane throughout its flight. The safety of the plane and its landing at a destination depends upon the pilot who must unquestionably obey the signals he gets from the control centre.

A similar situation faces a believer in Bahá'u'lláh. To have recognized Him as a Manifestation of God is not sufficient. What is needed in addition is steadfastness in the Covenant, a term which may be summed up as turning to the Centre of the Cause and obeying His guidance. In the days of Bahá'u'lláh He, Himself, was the Centre of the Cause to whom the believers turned. After Him they turned to 'Abdu'l-Bahá as the Centre of His Covenant, and then to Shoghi Effendi, the Guardian of the Faith, and today to the Universal House of Justice. It is by turning to the Centre of the Cause as an infallible source of guidance that the believer can be protected from many pitfalls in his life and, like the pilot in the analogy who follows the navigational instructions, arrive at his spiritual abode in the worlds beyond.

In the Tablet of Tajallíyát Bahá'u'lláh enjoins upon everyone the study of arts and sciences, but disapproves of those which begin with words and end with words. This subject has been stressed repeatedly by Bahá'u'lláh in His Tablets and will be discussed later.*

* see below, pp. 170, 249–50.

9

Splendours of the Revelation

I<u>sh</u>ráqát

Jalíl-i-<u>Kh</u>ú'í

The Tablet of I<u>sh</u>ráqát* was addressed to Jalíl-i-<u>Kh</u>ú'í, a coppersmith who lived in the province of Á<u>dh</u>irbáyján and was a well-known believer. It was revealed in answer to his questions, particularly those on the subject of supreme infallibility. He had the inestimable privilege of attaining the presence of Bahá'u'lláh, and became the recipient of many bounties from Him.

But Jalíl deprived himself of all the blessings which were showered on him, and perished spiritually. After the ascension of Bahá'u'lláh, he violated the Covenant and joined hands with Muḥammad-'Alí,† the Arch-breaker of the Covenant of Bahá'u'lláh. He was influenced by Jamál-i-Burújirdí, who was foremost among the Covenant-breakers in Persia and had the ambition of becoming the undisputed leader of the community in that country. We have already given a brief account of his infamous career, his swift downfall and eventual extinction.‡ About four years after the ascension of Bahá'u'lláh, Jamál went to Á<u>dh</u>irbáyján, appointed Jalíl as his agent in the area and urged him to meet the believers secretly and sow the seeds of Covenant-breaking among them. Jalíl was further encouraged when Muḥammad-'Alí despatched to Á<u>dh</u>irbáyján a

* The full text of this Tablet has been translated into English and published in *Tablets of Bahá'u'lláh*, pp. 101–34.

† For more information about him see *God Passes By* and *Revelation of Bahá'u'lláh*, vols. 1, 2 and 3.

‡ For further information see vol. 2.

series of letters against the Centre of the Covenant.

In the meantime the Master sent Ibn-i-Abhar, one of the Hands of the Cause, to the area to assist the believers to remain steadfast in the Covenant. Jalíl failed to make appreciable headway in his subversive activities; the believers in Ád͟hirbáyján stood firm, rallied around 'Abdu'l-Bahá and defended the Cause of God heroically from the onslaught of the unfaithful.

In AH 1315 (AD 1897–8) 'Abdu'l-Bahá addressed a lengthy Tablet known as the *Lawḥ-i-Hizár Bayti* (Tablet of One Thousand Verses) to Jalíl. In this celebrated Tablet He showers upon him much loving-kindness, exhorts him to faithfulness in the Cause, explains in detail the authenticity of the Covenant of Bahá'u'lláh, sets forth convincing proofs in support of His argument and provides one of the most illuminating insights into the subject of the Covenant as a whole. We have referred to this Tablet and discussed an important subject contained in it in a previous volume.* Writing at a time of great agitation and danger in the Holy Land and wishing not to add fuel to the fire already lit by the Covenant-breakers, which threatened to engulf the community of the believers, the Master sent a trusted servant of the Cause, Mírzá Maḥmúd-i-Zarg͟hání, to Tabríz, the capital of Ád͟hirbáyján, with instructions to read aloud the full contents of the Tablet to Jalíl, but not to hand him a copy. Jalíl heard this highly enlightening Tablet in full but, alas, the lust of leadership had blinded his eyes and stopped his ears. He later witnessed the futility of his efforts and died in ignominy.

The Tablet of Is͟hráqát revealed by Bahá'u'lláh in his honour contains some of the choicest fruits of His Revelation. Towards the end of the Tablet Bahá'u'lláh outlines some of His basic teachings and principles under nine headings, each one designated as an 'Is͟hráq' (Splendour). The first few paragraphs of this Tablet are revealed in a language of mystery, the

* see vol. 1, p. 127n.

unravelling of which depends partly upon a deep understanding of Islamic theology and its terminology and of the Arabic language, and partly upon the individual's insight into the inner significances of the words of Bahá'u'lláh. For these reasons, and in order not to enter into unauthorized interpretation of the Holy Writings, we refrain from discussing these. However, there is a certain Tablet by 'Abdu'l-Bahá (in Persian)[1] which may help the reader to appreciate the significance of some of Bahá'u'lláh's statements.

Bahá'u'lláh Addresses the People of the Bayán

In the Tablet of Ishráqát Bahá'u'lláh refers to the Báb as the 'Point', the 'Herald of His Name and the Harbinger of His Great Revelation'. He affirms that God ordained the Báb 'to be an ocean of light for the sincere' and 'a flame of fire to the froward' among the people.

The advent of every Manifestation of God brings about the same situation. His coming causes humanity to be divided into believers and unbelievers. This is similar to the holding of a school examination. When the students enter into the examination hall, they all have equal status, but as they walk out the division has already taken place as some have passed the examination while others have failed. Similarly the appearance of the Manifestation of God is the harbinger of universal testing. Before His appearance all humanity is placed on the same plane, but as soon as the Manifestation of God reveals Himself, some are elevated to a higher plane by embracing His Cause while others are left behind.

When the Báb appeared He announced the glad-tidings of the coming of 'Him Whom God shall make manifest': Bahá'u'lláh. He prepared His followers for His coming and made of them a new creation worthy to recognize the Supreme Manifestation of God. But when Bahá'u'lláh revealed Himself to humanity in general and to the followers of the Báb in particular, the scene was set for yet another universal test of faith. With the unveiling of Bahá'u'lláh's station, the Bábí community became divided; most of the followers of the Báb embraced His Cause while a small number deprived themselves of His Faith. The Revelation of Bahá'u'lláh became thereby the cause of felicity and bounty for some but brought about remoteness and misery for others. Bahá'u'lláh confirms this process in the Tablet of Is͟hráqát when He states:

> This is the Day that God hath ordained to be a blessing unto the righteous, a retribution for the wicked, a bounty for the faithful and a fury of His wrath for the faithless and the froward. Verily He hath been made manifest, invested by God with invincible sovereignty. He hath revealed that wherewith naught on the earth or in the heavens can compare.[2]

In this Tablet Bahá'u'lláh rebukes the people of the Bayán, meaning the followers of the Báb, for their waywardness and blindness which had prevented them from recognizing His own mighty Revelation. He admonishes them to cast away their idle fancies and turn with pure hearts to Him. These are some of His words addressed to them:

> Fear ye God and abandon vain imaginings to the begetters thereof and leave superstitions to the devisers thereof and misgivings to the breeders thereof. Advance ye then with radiant faces and stainless hearts towards the horizon above which the Day-Star of certitude shineth resplendent at the bidding of God, the Lord of Revelations.[3]

In the course of these admonitions Bahá'u'lláh mentions the sufferings which had been inflicted on Him, twice in the 'Land of Tá' (Ṭihrán) and once in the 'Land of Mím' (Mázindarán).* The first time that Bahá'u'lláh was made captive at the hands

* For details see *The Dawn-Breakers*, pp. 278–9, 368–74.

of his enemies was in Ṭihrán. This was almost four years after the Declaration of the Báb. His second imprisonment, when the bastinado was inflicted on Him, took place a few months later in Ámul in the Province of Mázindarán. The third imprisonment, the most afflictive of all, was in August 1852 in the Síyáh-Chál of Ṭihrán.*

The Meaning of 'Infallibility'

Jalíl, for whom the Tablet of Ishráqát was revealed, had asked Bahá'u'lláh to explain for him the meaning of the 'Most Great Infallibility'. In response Bahá'u'lláh reveals these thought-provoking words:

> Thou hast asked this Wronged One to remove for thee its veils and coverings, to elucidate its mystery and character, its state and position, its excellence, sublimity and exaltation. By the life of God! Were We to unveil the pearls of testimony which lie hid within the shells of the ocean of knowledge and assurance or to let the beauties of divine mystery which are hidden within the chambers of utterance in the Paradise of true understanding, step out of their habitation, then from every direction violent commotion would arise among the leaders of religion and thou wouldst witness the people of God held fast in the teeth of such wolves as have denied God both in the beginning and in the end . . . Verily the birds abiding within the domains of My Kingdom and the doves dwelling in the rose-garden of My wisdom utter such melodies and warblings as are inscrutable to all but God, the Lord of the kingdoms of earth and heaven; and were these melodies to be revealed even to an extent smaller than a needle's eye, the people of tyranny would utter such calumnies as none among former generations hath ever uttered, and would commit such deeds as no one in past ages and centuries hath ever committed.[4]

* see vol. 1, pp. 8–11.

In this Tablet Bahá'u'lláh describes some aspects of infallibility and makes a distinction between 'conferred' and 'the Most Great' infallibility. The former derives its authority from the latter. We have already discussed this subject in a previous volume* and stated that Bahá'u'lláh possesses the Most Great Infallibility, while He conferred infallibility upon 'Abdu'l-Bahá, Shoghi Effendi and the Universal House of Justice. These are the words of Bahá'u'lláh in the Tablet of Is͟hráqát:

> Know thou that the term 'Infallibility' hath numerous meanings and divers stations. In one sense it is applicable to the One Whom God hath made immune from error. Similarly it is applied to every soul whom God hath guarded against sin, transgression, rebellion, impiety, disbelief and the like. However, the Most Great Infallibility is confined to the One Whose station is immeasurably exalted beyond ordinances or prohibitions and is sanctified from errors and omissions. Indeed He is a Light which is not followed by darkness and a Truth not overtaken by error. Were He to pronounce water to be wine or heaven to be earth or light to be fire, He speaketh the truth and no doubt would there be about it; and unto no one is given the right to question His authority or to say why or wherefore.[5]

In many of His Tablets Bahá'u'lláh has made similar statements to those in this Tablet. He states that if He were to explain the inner meaning of His Words, or reveal the exalted station of His own Person or the greatness of His Revelation, then those devoid of true understanding would be so shocked and filled with such anger as to arise in vehement opposition to His Cause and His loved ones. The religious leaders of Islám, and some of the followers of the Báb who were not endowed with true knowledge, used some of Bahá'u'lláh's utterances about the greatness of the Cause in order to misrepresent Him.

* vol. 3, pp. 300–305.

Later, others both in the East and the West joined in and misrepresented His Writings in order to oppose His Cause. There are innumerable passages revealed by Bahá'u'lláh in which He glorifies the exalted nature of His Revelation.* The immensity of His claims overwhelms the believers and antagonizes His enemies. It is increasingly evident that the generality of mankind is getting further away from the concept of spirituality and religious truth. Added to this is the fact that man's intellectual capacity to understand God and His Manifestations is limited. There are also other barriers in his way such as bias, prejudice of all kinds, vain imaginings, superstition and many more. It is not surprising, therefore, that Bahá'u'lláh, appearing in a society poor in spiritual perception, should find it necessary to withhold His Pen from revealing the exalted nature of God's power and glory with which He was invested. Indeed, it was man's unworthiness that prompted Bahá'u'lláh to order His amanuensis to obliterate a considerable portion of His Tablets in His own handwriting and cast them into the river during His banishment in 'Iráq.

Mírzá Abu'l-Faḍl,† the great Bahá'í scholar, has described an interesting incident which took place when he was residing in Cairo, an incident which sheds further light upon the above subject. Mírzá Abu'l-Faḍl emerged in circles of learning and erudition in Cairo as the foremost authority on religious history and teachings. A great many professors and students of the famous Al-Azhar University, as well as many divines and men of culture, crowded into his presence and sat at his feet to partake of his vast knowledge and insight into spiritual matters. This is the story as he himself recounts:

> When the Protestant Evangelical Society published the book *Maqálih-Fí-Al-Islám* (Treatise on Islám), certain of the religious leaders (Muslims) of these parts, such as the erudite

* For a fuller discusson of this subject see above, pp. 130–45.

† For a brief account of his life see vol. 3.

Shaykh Badru'd-Dín Al Ghazzí . . . and others from the fields of Islamic jurisprudence and divinity, suggested to this servant that it would be appropriate, in view of the extent of knowledge of the holy books of ancient faiths which God, exalted be His Glory, has vouchsafed unto him . . . that he should write an adequate and satisfactory reply to the aforementioned 'treatise' and expose its errors of fact and its historical calumnies so that the weak ones amongst the people might not be misled by its inaccuracies, and doubt might not be implanted in their minds.

To this request I replied: 'Please let me be excused; for there are difficulties in this path which are very hard to overcome. For many years, indeed centuries, the ears of the people of Islám have become accustomed to hearing 'tawdry speech',* and their minds have been nourished on the superficialities of literalism. Now if the veil be lifted off the true meaning of all the Qur'ánic allusions, and thus all the objections of those who promote doubts among people are cleared away (such as the objections of the 'treatise'), then these very same people who are Muslims in name will rise up in enmity and engage in vehement opposition. They would be content to see the objections and doubts raised by these people not removed from the *Qur'án*, but retained for ever. They would rather see the standard of the people of Islám be trampled upon by the misguided, than allow that through the emanations of the Supreme Pen (of Bahá'u'lláh) the 'maids' of true meaning step forth out of their 'cloistered mansions'† of the divine verses . . . so that all the objections be answered and indeed all the thick clouds of criticism and cavilling be dispelled and made to disappear.[6]

This argument put forward by Mírzá Abu'l-Faḍl concerning Islám is valid for other religions too. For example, Christianity

* Refers to *Qur'án* 6:112. (A.T.)

† Refers to *Qur'án* 55:72. (A.T.)

as practised today is so far removed from the pure teaching of Christ that if its Founder could return in person He would never be able to reconcile His Faith with all the man-made dogmas and rituals and so many divided churches. Bahá'u'lláh and 'Abdu'l-Bahá have explained in their Writings the reality of Christ, the truth of His Message and the true meaning of the words recorded in the Gospels. But to present the picture of Christianity as given by Bahá'u'lláh in the *Kitáb-i-Íqán*, or to approach some Christian subjects with the explanations given by 'Abdu'l-Bahá in *Some Answered Questions* will undoubtedly be met with strong disapproval by many Christians today. It is in fact much more difficult to explain the reality and truth of the Christian Faith to a practising Christian than to an unbiased person of a different background. It is indeed a grievous situation in which the followers of the religions have placed themselves. They have gone astray from the true path which the Manifestations of God laid down for them, and consequently have been unable to recognize the truth of the Revelation of Bahá'u'lláh. It is concerning such people that the Pen of the Most High reveals these despairing words in the *Lawḥ-i-Ishráqát*:

> They have rejected the bounty of God and His proofs and have repudiated the testimony of God and His signs. They have gone astray and have caused the people to go astray, yet perceive it not. They worship vain imaginings but know it not. They have taken idle fancies for their lords and have neglected God, yet understand not. They have abandoned the most great Ocean and are hastening towards the pool, but comprehend not. They follow their own idle fancies while turning aside from God, the Help in Peril, the Self-Subsisting.[7]

Prophecies Fulfilled

Quoting from a Tablet He had revealed previously,* Bahá'u'lláh in the Tablet of Is͟hráqát enumerates some of the Islamic prophecies concerning the advent of the Day of God. He employs a dialogue between the voice of Truth and the voice of those who are bereft of true understanding and have denied His Cause. There are many passages such as these in this Tablet:

> 'Have the verses been sent down?' Say 'Yea, by Him Who is the Revealer of clear tokens! . . . And they say: 'Hath the Catastrophe come to pass?' Say: 'Yea, by the Lord of Lords!' 'Is the Resurrection come?' 'Nay, more; He Who is the Self-Subsisting hath appeared with the Kingdom of His signs.' 'Seest thou men laid low?' 'Yea, by my Lord, the Most High, the Most Glorious!' 'Have the tree-stumps been uprooted?' 'Yea, more; the mountains have been scattered in dust; by Him the Lord of attributes!' They say: 'Where is Paradise, and where is Hell?' Say: 'The one is reunion with Me; the other thine own self, O thou who dost associate a partner with God and doubtest.' They say: 'We see not the Balance.' Say: 'Surely, by my Lord, the God of Mercy! None can see it except such as are endued with insight.' They say: 'Have the stars fallen?' Say: 'Yea, when He Who is the Self-Subsisting dwelt in the Land of Mystery. Take heed, ye who are endued with discernment!'[8]

The falling of stars is a reference to the well-known prophecy of the Gospels concerning the return of Christ, and the 'Land of Mystery' is a designation given by Bahá'u'lláh to the city of Adrianople. We have already described the significance of the

* see below, pp. 396–8, for the manner in which Bahá'u'lláh quotes from His own Writings. The passage that follows is part of a Tablet originally revealed in honour of Ḥájí Muḥammad-Ibráhím, entitled by Bahá'u'lláh '*Muballi͟gh*' (teacher, proclaimer). He quotes it again at length in *Epistle to the Son of the Wolf.*

falling stars in a previous volume.*

To appreciate the inner meanings of the prophecies quoted in this Tablet referring to the coming of the Lord, one needs to study the *Kitáb-i-Íqán*. This is the Book in which the mysteries hidden in the heavenly books of past religions are explained and the significance of the prophecies contained in them revealed. Before the revelation of the *Kitáb-i-Íqán* the purpose and meaning of the words were concealed. With the coming of Bahá'u'lláh the 'time of the end' as prophesied by Daniel was fulfilled:

> And I heard, but I understood not: then said I, O my Lord, what shall be the end of these things? And he said, Go thy way, Daniel: for the words are closed up and sealed till the time of the end.[9]

The *Kitáb-i-Íqán* unsealed the heavenly Books of the past. Like the morning sun which brightens the eye, it illumined the hearts and imparted knowledge and understanding to the minds. Since then many Bahá'í scholars and teachers have written volumes on the interpretation of prophecies given by prophets of the past.

Religion, a Radiant Light

Under the nine headings in the Tablet of Ishráqát known as 'Ishráq' (Splendour), Bahá'u'lláh elucidates some of His teachings 'revealed specially for the rulers and ministers of the world'; teachings which are 'conducive to safety and protection, tranquillity and peace'. In the first Ishráq He attaches the greatest importance to religion and describes it as 'a radiant light and an impregnable stronghold for the protection and welfare of the peoples of the world'. He further prophesies that

* see vol. 2, pp. 270–72, and Appendix I.

'should the lamp of religion be obscured, chaos and confusion will ensue, and the lights of fairness and justice, of tranquillity and peace cease to shine'. This is already happening.

A basic principle which applies to all religions is that there is a special relationship between a religion and the one which appears immediately after it. When a new Manifestation of God appears, the spirit of faith is extinguished in the older religion and at the same time is breathed into the new one. For instance, with the coming of Christ, the Jewish Faith lost its vigour and vitality; these were instilled into the Christian Faith. In the *Qur'án* it is stated:

> Unto every nation there is a preordained term; therefore when their term is expired, they shall not have respite for an hour, neither shall they be anticipated.[10]

This means that every Dispensation has a beginning and an end. The Bahá'í Dispensation began with the advent of the Báb and all the major religions of the world lost a great deal of their spiritual power. The influence which they used to exert upon the hearts of men has been diminishing with every passing day. A contributing factor to this process has been the inability of religious leaders to adhere to the fundamental truths enshrined in each religion. Instead of understanding the reality of their religions and explaining the verities of their Faiths to their followers, they have, in their ignorance, introduced so many dogmas and man-made interpretations that the light of true religion has become obscured. Consequently many intelligent and honest people have discarded religion altogether and have swelled the ranks of agnostics and atheists. No one can blame a person, endowed with commonsense, who rejects the claim of certain religious leaders that the body of Christ rose into space, or that one day the stars shall fall upon the earth!

It is only since the coming of Bahá'u'lláh and through His Writings that the true meaning of all the abstruse passages in the Holy Books of past religions are so clearly explained that not a single statement remains which would appear contrary to reason and commonsense. Indeed, it is one of the teachings of Bahá'u'lláh that religious truth and scientific theories must be in harmony. But unfortunately religious leaders, through their lack of understanding of true religious teachings, have widened the gap between religion and science. Today, the word 'religion' is generally associated with ignorance, narrow-mindedness and vain imaginings by a vast number of enlightened people. On the other hand, some have made a mockery of religion by creating sects which have proved to be nothing short of nests of corruption and profiteering. The sacredness of many religious acts, which were the mainstay of communities in olden times, have now been either completely eroded or corrupted, expediently transformed into political or commercial activities. It is for this reason that in introducing the Bahá'í Faith to the public, the followers of Bahá'u'lláh will have to explain that the word 'religion' as commonly understood by people is not applicable to the Faith. It is a religion in its pure form and freed from corruption or adulteration. This is one of the distinguishing features of the Faith of Bahá'u'lláh.

Today, when the light of religion is fading away, the prophecy of Bahá'u'lláh in the 'First Ishráq' has been fulfilled. 'Chaos and confusion' have indeed ensued, and 'the lights of fairness and justice, of tranquillity and peace' have ceased to shine. This process will continue and the world's horizons become darker until the warnings by Bahá'u'lláh issued over a hundred years ago come to pass. We have already quoted this passage:

> The world is in travail, and its agitation waxeth day by day. Its face is turned towards waywardness and unbelief. Such shall be its plight, that to disclose it now would not be meet and seemly. Its perversity will long continue. And when the appointed hour is come, there shall suddenly appear that

> which shall cause the limbs of mankind to quake. Then, and only then, will the Divine Standard be unfurled, and the Nightingale of Paradise warble its melody.[11]

These words of Bahá'u'lláh foreshadow great sufferings in store for mankind. It is important to appreciate that these sufferings are not visited upon humanity as vengeance on the part of God. On the contrary, they are entirely man-made and the consequences of man's own actions. For God has created man in His own image, which means that He has bestowed upon man His attributes. He has also given him free-will. He has created laws which govern the relationship of all things – cause and effect, action and reaction, reward and punishment. These laws are part of God's creation. Where people live and act in unity, the result is peace and harmony. Where they disregard this basic principle and groups of people rise up in enmity against each other the result is destruction and suffering. It is not God's pleasure that millions die in war or perish through starvation. All these calamitous happenings are the product of man disobeying the laws and teachings of God which have been revealed in this age.

In many of His Tablets Bahá'u'lláh has confirmed that a great part of human suffering is man-made. In a Tablet[12] He states that the peoples of the world are encompassed by punishment for their deeds, and at each period this punishment manifests itself in a different form. In another Tablet[13] He states that God has created all human beings to recognize His great Revelation in this day, but their failure to embrace His Cause is in itself a chastisement for their deeds. Reward and punishment are the mainstay of human society; this is the law of creation and cannot be altered.

Elsewhere in a Tablet[14] Bahá'u'lláh declares that people are the bondslaves of vain imaginings and corrupt desires. God enables them to busy themselves with their idle fancies and worldly affections as a punishment* in their lives.

* For further discussion see vol. 3, pp. 294–7.

In another Tablet He states:

> Had the world been of any worth in His sight, He surely would never have allowed His enemies to possess it, even to the extent of a grain of mustard seed. He hath, however, caused you to be entangled with its affairs, in return for what your hands have wrought in His Cause. This, indeed, is a chastisement which ye, of your own will, have inflicted upon yourselves, could ye but perceive it. Are ye rejoicing in the things which, according to the estimate of God, are contemptible and worthless, things wherewith He proveth the hearts of the doubtful?[15]

But the main purpose of the Revelation of Bahá'u'lláh is to instil into the hearts of men a measure of God's love and endow their souls with the spirit of faith. Only when this happens on a universal scale will man-made sufferings and calamities be replaced by the Most Great Peace. When humanity attains to this exalted state and the causes of disunity are thus eliminated, then trials and tribulations will be limited to those which God ordains for each individual. The sufferings which come from God are essential for the spiritual development of the soul. Whereas manmade sufferings today are intolerable, God-sent ordeals and difficulties are never imposed upon a soul beyond its capacity.

Numerous are the exhortations of Bahá'u'lláh to His followers in the Tablet of Ishráqát urging them to follow the teachings of God. The following passage, which also appears in the Bishárát, demonstrates the exalted nature of these exhortations:

> O people of Bahá! Ye are the dawning-places of the love of God and the daysprings of His loving-kindness. Defile not your tongues with the cursing and reviling of any soul, and guard your eyes against that which is not seemly. Set forth

> that which ye possess. If it be favourably received, your end is attained; if not, to protest is vain. Leave that soul to himself and turn unto the Lord, the Protector, the Self-Subsisting. Be not the cause of grief, much less of discord and strife. The hope is cherished that ye may obtain true education in the shelter of the tree of His tender mercies and act in accordance with that which God desireth. Ye are all the leaves of one tree and the drops of one ocean.[16]

In each I<u>sh</u>ráq of the Tablet of I<u>sh</u>ráqát Bahá'u'lláh reveals some of His weighty counsels to mankind in general and to His followers in particular. He enjoins upon all mankind to establish the Lesser Peace,* urges His followers to 'observe God's holy commandments', reminds them that the Cause of God will become victorious through 'praiseworthy deeds and upright character', addresses special counsels to the Universal House of Justice (the supreme body ordained by Bahá'u'lláh which came into being in 1963), affirms that its members 'have been charged with the affairs of the people', refers to it 'all matters of state', and asserts that this instruction is to be considered as 'part of the Most Holy Book'. He moreover affirms that justice is 'upheld by two pillars, reward and punishment', counsels 'everyone regarding the instruction and education of children', announces the purpose of religion to be the establishment of 'unity and concord amongst the peoples of the world', forbids His followers to make religion the cause of dissension and strife, advocates the adoption of a universal auxiliary language, and enjoins upon the Trustees of the House of Justice 'either to choose one language from among those now existing or to adopt a new one'.

It is interesting to note that in the Tablet of Bi<u>sh</u>árát Bahá'u'lláh enjoins upon the governments of the world to adopt the international language. These two statements, which seem to be contradictory, may be regarded as two different

* For further discussion of this subject see vol. 3, pp. 314–15.

stages in bringing about a world auxiliary language. The first stage will be the adoption of a universal language by the governments, while the second will have to wait until such time that the Universal House of Justice has emerged as the supreme institution of the World Order of Bahá'u'lláh and its authority is recognized. It is only then that it can possibly reconsider the choice of the language so as to either retain the one chosen by the governments or alter it altogether.

In one of His Tablets[17] revealed in 'Akká, Bahá'u'lláh emphasizes the importance of adopting the auxiliary international language ordained in the *Kitáb-i-Aqdas*. He states that its implementation will provide a means for safeguarding the unity of the human race and will facilitate intercourse and understanding among the peoples of the world. In this Tablet Bahá'u'lláh praises the Arabic language for its expressiveness and eloquence, and remarks that no other language can match its vast possibilities. He further states that God would be pleased if all the peoples of the world were to speak the Arabic language. But He does not require humanity necessarily to adopt it as the international language; rather He leaves the choice to the appropriate institutions.

10

Glad-Tidings to All Peoples

Bis͟hárát

It has not been possible so far to identify the person for whom the Tablet of Bis͟hárát (Glad-Tidings) was revealed.* On the other hand, Bahá'u'lláh after the preamble addresses the peoples of the world. The tone of His utterances throughout the Tablet indicate that possibly it was addressed to mankind as a whole and not to a particular individual.

In this Tablet there are fifteen headings, each one designated as a Bis͟hárát. Many of the subjects addressed relate to existing beliefs, to practices carried out by the followers of past religions. The first of these Glad-tidings is the abolition of the law of holy war practised by the Muslims. The teachings of Bahá'u'lláh, all revolving around the principle of love and unity among the peoples of the world, are utterly incompatible with war of any kind. In most of His Tablets Bahá'u'lláh has clearly stated that any action which could bring about coolness between people or cause unhappiness among them is unacceptable in the sight of God today.

In a Tablet[1] He describes the qualification of a true believer by saying: he is to be counted among the 'People of Bahá', who when retiring at night can say that his heart is completely devoid of any trace of hate or enmity towards his fellowman, and who in his prayers he is a well-wisher of all that dwell on earth. Among the followers of former religions there are many who shun members of other Faiths; Bahá'u'lláh has ordained the opposite. He declares in the Tablet of Bis͟hárát:

---

* This Tablet has been translated in full into English and published in *Tablets of Bahá'u'lláh*, pp. 21–9.

> O people! Consort with the followers of all religions in a spirit of friendliness and fellowship.[2]

In this Tablet Bahá'u'lláh advocates the adoption of a universal language, advises the sovereigns of the world or their ministers* to choose a new or an existing language for the purpose, confirms the establishment of the Lesser Peace,† exhorts His followers to honesty and truthfulness towards the governments of the world, recommends constitutional monarchy in preference to a presidential system‡ and permits the study of arts and sciences which 'would redound to the progress and advancement of the people'. That Bahá'u'lláh uses the word 'permission' for the study of sciences is due to the fact that the Muslim clergy in their fanaticism had forbidden the study of modern science. They claimed that such sciences were satanic as they had originated from those who did not believe in Islám.

One of the Glad-tidings concerning some of the duties of the Universal House of Justice is cited also in the *Lawḥ-i-Is͟hráqát*. Occasionally in some of His writings, Bahá'u'lláh includes passages from Tablets previously revealed, often with slight changes.§

One of the great bounties of this Dispensation is that Bahá'u'lláh has abolished the practice of idleness in the name of religion. There are many who think that a godly and spiritual person is one who renounces the world, leads an ascetic life and goes into seclusion. These practices are against the teachings of Bahá'u'lláh. In many of His Tablets He has stated that leading a cloistered life is not conducive to spirituality; it has the opposite effect. There are also a group of people, among them religious leaders, who spend many hours a day reciting the Holy Books or indulging in various acts of worship.

---

* see above, p. 167.

† see above, p. 167.

‡ for further discussion of this subject see vol. 3, pp. 156–61.

§ see below, pp. 396–8.

Bahá'u'lláh states in one of His Tablets:[3] should a person spend all his life worshipping God, but be deprived of those virtues and qualities which help to exalt His Cause, all his acts of worship are void in the sight of God. Bahá'u'lláh teaches that every person must take an interest in this life, work for the betterment of human affairs and continuously strive to serve his fellow men. He has indeed exalted work carried out in the spirit of service to the rank of worship. These are His exalted words in the Tablet of Bis͟hárát:

> The pious deeds of the monks and priests among the followers of the Spirit* – upon Him be the peace of God – are remembered in His presence. In this Day, however, let them give up the life of seclusion and direct their steps towards the open world and busy themselves with that which will profit themselves and others. We have granted them leave to enter into wedlock that they may bring forth one who will make mention of God, the Lord of the seen and the unseen, the Lord of the Exalted Throne.[4]

And again:

> It is enjoined upon every one of you to engage in some form of occupation, such as crafts, trades and the like. We have graciously exalted your engagement in such work to the rank of worship unto God, the True One. Ponder ye in your hearts the grace and the blessings of God and render thanks unto Him at eventide and at dawn. Waste not your time in idleness and sloth. Occupy yourselves with that which profiteth yourselves and others. Thus hath it been decreed in this Tablet from whose horizon the day-star of wisdom and utterance shineth resplendent.
>
> The most despised of men in the sight of God are those who sit idly and beg. Hold ye fast unto the cord of material

* Jesus Christ.

> means, placing your whole trust in God, the Provider of all means. When anyone occupieth himself in a craft or trade, such occupation itself is regarded in the estimation of God as an act of worship; and this is naught but a token of His infinite and all-pervasive bounty.[5]

Another practice abrogated by Bahá'u'lláh is that of the confession of sins which is practised in some Christian churches. These are His own words revealed in the Tablet of Bis͟hárát:

> When the sinner findeth himself wholly detached and freed from all save God, he should beg forgiveness and pardon from Him. Confession of sins and transgressions before human beings is not permissible, as it hath never been nor will ever be conducive to divine forgiveness. Moreover such confession before people results in one's humiliation and abasement, and God – exalted be His glory – wisheth not the humiliation of His servants. Verily He is the Compassionate, the Merciful. The sinner should, between himself and God, implore mercy from the Ocean of mercy, beg forgiveness from the Heaven of generosity . . . [6]

Another custom of which Bahá'u'lláh disapproves is that of undertaking long journeys to the resting-places of the dead. The majority of Muslims consider this practice to be conducive to the forgiveness of sins and regard it as a means of winning the good-pleasure of God. They call upon the dead to act as an intermediary for them and fulfil their wishes in this life. In olden days there was considerable traffic to the various cities in which the tombs of saints were located. A number of travellers were poor and often had to walk long distances covering hundreds of miles. Bahá'u'lláh states that 'if the people of substance and affluence offer the cost of such journeys to the House of Justice, it will be pleasing and acceptable in the presence of God'.

Bahá'u'lláh's disapproval of special journeys to visit the graves of the dead does not mean that there is no spiritual value in praying at the resting-place of the departed. On the contrary, the teachings of Bahá'u'lláh emphasize the great blessings which may descend upon the individual through the influence of the departed holy souls. In one of His Tablets[7] 'Abdu'l-Bahá states that a person may become the recipient of the confirmations of Bahá'u'lláh when he prays at the graveside of a holy soul because that soul is endowed with divine bounties. In another Tablet[8] He states that the resting-places of the holy souls deserve to be honoured and respected. But the honour is not given to the earth, rather it is intended for the soul which is sanctified from all material things. However, since the soul was once associated with the body, it is only natural that we respect the earthly remains of holy ones. But it is not proper to seek assistance and confirmations from any source except from the Blessed Beauty.

In a Tablet[9] 'Abdu'l-Bahá explains the difference between travelling from country to country with the specific intention of visiting graves of the departed (which is the act disapproved by Bahá'u'lláh) and that of visiting those which are accessible to the individual either in his own country or if he comes across them elsewhere, a practice which is encouraged by the teachings of the Faith. Visits, for instance, to the graves of the martyrs or great teachers of the Faith are conducive to attracting divine bounties. Indeed, Bahá'u'lláh and 'Abdu'l-Bahá have both revealed several Tablets of visitation for specific individuals after their death, which are intended to be recited at their graveside. And in some cases 'Abdu'l-Bahá has asked certain individual Bahá'ís to visit the grave of a devoted believer and chant a special Tablet of visitation on His behalf.

The prohibition by Bahá'u'lláh of making special long journeys to the resting-places of the dead does not in any way refer to pilgrimage to the Holy Shrines of the Faith which normally requires the pilgrim to travel long distances. On the contrary,

Bahá'u'lláh has enjoined formal pilgrimages* to the House of the Báb in Shíráz and that of Bahá'u'lláh in Baghdád, and has ordained the performance of certain rituals in connection with these pilgrimages. The pilgrimage to the Shrines of Bahá'u'lláh and the Báb is free from these rites and is considered as one of the greatest bounties which the soul may receive on this earth.

Another law which Bahá'u'lláh has abolished in the Tablet of Bishárát is the destruction of Books. This is a reference to the Báb's advice in the *Bayán* to destroy the Books of the past, on the basis that a new Revelation includes everything from the past and that Books of past Dispensations become abrogated by the advent of the new. Some of the laws ordained by the Báb are harsh and severe. This is because of the nature of His Mission, which was to release enormous spiritual energies within an unusually short Dispensation. It was similar to applying a mighty force to an object in one short stroke. The effect of the Báb's Revelation in Persia proved to be so dynamic, and His influence so revolutionary, that within a very short period of time the whole country was stirred to its depths. The laws of the *Qur'án* were abrogated at a stroke. The prophetic cycle within which several Manifestations of God had appeared was now closed and new laws, some of them severe, were enjoined, but at the same time the promise of the imminent advent of the Day of God was given unequivocally, and consequently great excitement and a deep sense of awe and wonder filled the hearts of His faithful followers. Actually many of the laws were not carried out, partly because circumstances did not permit it, and partly because the Dispensation came to an end within a very short period of time. The abrogation of the old laws and the severity of the new ones made a deep impression on the Bábís, galvanized them into action and prepared the way for the advent of 'Him Whom God shall make manifest'.

Shoghi Effendi has made the following comment on the severity of some of the laws of the Báb.

* see vol. 2, p. 240.

> . . . The severe laws and injunctions revealed by the Báb can be properly appreciated and understood only when interpreted in the light of His own statements regarding the nature, purpose and character of His own Dispensation. As these statements clearly reveal, the Bábí Dispensation was essentially in the nature of a religious and indeed social revolution, and its duration had therefore to be short, but full of tragic events, of sweeping and drastic reforms. These drastic measures enforced by the Báb and His followers were taken with the view of undermining the very foundations of Shí'ah orthodoxy, and thus paving the way for the coming of Bahá'u'lláh. To assert the independence of the new Dispensation, and to prepare also the ground for the approaching Revelation of Bahá'u'lláh the Báb had therefore to reveal very severe laws, even though most of them were never enforced. But the mere fact that He revealed them was in itself a proof of the independent character of His Dispensation and was sufficient to create such widespread agitation, and excite such opposition on the part of the clergy that led them to cause His eventual martyrdom.[10]

Bahá'u'lláh's closing remarks in the *Lawḥ-i-Bishárát* are indicative of the importance of this and similar Tablets revealed after the *Kitáb-i-Aqdas*, Tablets which set out basic teachings and principles of His Faith.

> In former religions such ordinances as holy war, destruction of books, the ban on association and companionship with other peoples or on reading certain books had been laid down and affirmed according to the exigencies of the time; however, in this mighty Revelation, in this momentous Announcement, the manifold bestowals and favours of God have overshadowed all men, and from the horizon of the Will of the Ever-Abiding Lord, His infallible decree hath prescribed that which We have set forth above.

We yield praise unto God – hallowed and glorified be He – for whatsoever He hath graciously revealed in this blessed, this glorious and incomparable Day. Indeed if everyone on earth were endowed with a myriad tongues and were to continually praise God and magnify His Name to the end that knoweth no end, their thanksgiving would not prove adequate for even one of the gracious favours We have mentioned in this Tablet. Unto this beareth witness every man of wisdom and discernment, of understanding and knowledge.[11]

11

Truths of His Cause

Ṭarázát

The Tablet of Ṭarázát[*] was revealed in honour of an individual believer whose identity has not as yet been discovered. In the same fashion as in the preceding Tablets of Is͟hráqát, Bis͟hárát and Tajallíyát, Bahá'u'lláh here reveals some of His choicest teachings and exhortations. The Tablets of Bahá'u'lláh are always full of significances. Every line, every word of His Writings is pregnant with meaning.[†] Some are easily comprehended and some become apparent to a believer through prayer and meditation, and detachment from all earthly things.[‡] The opening paragraphs of this Tablet contain many levels of meaning.

In My Name, which standeth supreme above all names

> Praise and glory beseem the Lord of Names and the Creator of the heavens, He, the waves of Whose ocean of Revelation surge before the eyes of the peoples of the world. The Day-Star of His Cause shineth through every veil and His Word of affirmation standeth beyond the reach of negation. Neither the ascendancy of the oppressor nor the tyranny of the wicked hath been able to thwart His Purpose. How glorified is His sovereignty, how exalted His dominion!
>
> Great God! Although His signs have encompassed the

* The text of this Tablet is translated in full into English, see *Tablets of Bahá'u'lláh*, pp. 33–44.

† Bahá'u'lláh states that the meaning of the Word of God cannot be exhausted. For further information see vol. 1, p. 32.

‡ For further discussion see vol. 3, pp. 94–6.

> world and His proofs and testimonies are shining forth and manifest as the light, yet the ignorant appear heedless, nay rather, rebellious. Would that they had been content with opposition. But at all times they are plotting to cut down the sacred Lote-Tree. Since the dawn of this Revelation the embodiments of selfishness have, by resorting to cruelty and oppression, striven to extinguish the Light of divine manifestation. But God, having stayed their hands, revealed this Light through His sovereign authority and protected it through the power of His might until earth and heaven were illumined by its radiance and brightness. Praise be unto Him under all conditions.[1]

A perusal of these utterances brings into focus a vast difference between the vision of Bahá'u'lláh and that of mankind. While outwardly He was living an austere life as an exile, confined in one of the most desolate cities of the world, bitterly opposed by two powerful despots of the Islamic world, His followers severely persecuted, Himself a target of attacks by enemies from within and without, His Cause in utter obscurity and His own person unknown to the nations and peoples of the world, Bahá'u'lláh's vision of His Cause was so glorious that in the above passage He states that the waves of the ocean of His Revelation 'surge before the eyes of the peoples of the world'.

Knowing the reality of His own Mission and being at the centre of the Orb of God's Revelation, Bahá'u'lláh could see the end in the beginning. While others cannot observe anything but darkness surrounding the world, He beholds the rays of the Sun of Truth enveloping the earth. Proclaiming these glad-tidings, He declares in these words the triumph of His Cause: 'God . . . revealed this light through His sovereign authority and protected it through the power of His might until the earth and heaven were illumined by its radiance and brightness.'

This contrast may be attributed to the fact that in the sight of God there is no past, present or future. All three are the same. We may appreciate this if we examine the relationship between the sun and our planet. For those who live on earth there is a concept of time in relation to the sun. But if one could live in the sun there would be no passage of time as experienced on earth. The Manifestation of God and His knowledge of the future may be likened to an experienced farmer who can see, in his mind's eye, inside a tiny seed a large tree laden with fruit. He knows that once it is sown in the soil, the seed will germinate and a tree will begin to grow in its place.

There are many stories attributed to Bahá'u'lláh, 'Abdu'l-Bahá and Shoghi Effendi which further illustrate this point. For example, Dr Ḥabíb Mu'ayyad has left to posterity the following account in his memoirs. It describes in vivid terms the vision of 'Abdu'l-Bahá about the future of Mount Carmel and the Shrine of the Báb. When 'Abdu'l-Bahá spoke these ords Mount Carmel was a heap of rocks and uninhabited; today much of His vision has been fulfilled.

> On one occasion when 'Abdu'l-Bahá was strolling in the gardens [near the Shrine of the Báb] His eyes were focused upon the sea and the city of 'Akká for some time. After a few moments of silence, He said, 'I have seen many places abroad, but nowhere has the fresh air and the beautiful scenery of the Shrine of the Báb.* Ere long this mountain will become habitable. Many fine buildings will be built on it. The Shrine of the Báb will be constructed in the most exquisite fashion and will appear with the utmost beauty and magnificence. Terraces will be built from the bottom of the mountain to the top. Nine terraces from the bottom to the Shrine and nine terraces from the Shrine to the summit. Gardens with colourful flowers will be laid down on all these terraces. A single street lined with flower beds will link the seafront to the Shrine. Pilgrims who arrive by ship will be able to see the dome of the Shrine from a long distance out at sea. The kings of the earth, bare-headed,

* At the time the Shrine of the Báb consisted of six rooms built in stone.

> and the queens, will walk up the street of the Shrine carrying bouquets of flowers. With bowed heads they will arrive as pilgrims, and prostrate themselves at the sacred threshold . . . [2*]

The same chronicler has recounted that on another occasion 'Abdu'l-Bahá spoke on the same subject to a number of believers in the Holy Land:

> . . . The future of Mount Carmel is very bright. I can see it now covered all over with a blanket of light. I can see many ships anchored at the Port of Haifa. I can see the kings of the earth with vases of flowers in their hands walking solemnly toward the Shrine of Bahá'u'lláh and the Báb with absolute devotion and in a state of prayer and supplication. At the time that they put a crown of thorns on His head, Christ could see the kings of the earth bowing before Him, but others could not see this.
>
> And now I can see not only powerful lamps which will floodlight this mountain brightly, but I can also see Houses of Worship, hospitals, schools, homes for the handicapped, orphanages and all the other humanitarian institutions erected on Mount Carmel.[3†]

These prophecies, of which many have been fulfilled, amply demonstrate that the chosen ones of God behold the past and the future in the present. All the persecutions that a heedless generation can heap upon Him will not deter Him from executing His purpose. He speaks and acts with authority and confidence because He sees victory in defeat and glory in abasement. With one believer in a country He envisages a whole nation embracing His Faith. And in the end all His visions come true, He becomes victorious and His Cause spreads throughout many nations.

* These are not the exact words of 'Abdu'l-Bahá, but they are very close to what he had said.

† Again, these words are not the exact words of 'Abdu'l-Bahá.

This is the story of all the Manifestations of God. In this day the Faith of Bahá'u'lláh, in spite of the opposition from its enemies, has spread throughout the world. Shoghi Effendi, the Guardian of the Faith, encouraged the believers to pioneer to virgin territories of the globe. As each one arrived at his post he hailed that historic event as the spiritual conquest of that country and announced the Bahá'í pioneer as its conquerer. He saw in one individual believer the whole country entering the Faith. He was the spiritual gardener, guided by Bahá'u'lláh. He planted the seed of the Cause in many lands, and from the very start he had the vision to see that it would grow into a mighty tree.

There is a passage in the opening paragraph of the Tablet of Ṭarázát which is significant in its implications:

> The Day-Star of His Cause shineth through every veil and His Word of affirmation standeth beyond the reach of negation.[4]

Everything which is derived from the Revelation of Bahá'u'lláh, be it His words, His teachings, His laws or His Covenant, are all revealed in the affirmative. And everything which comes from the ungodly, the enemies and the Covenant-breakers, are all in the negative. In the Tablet of Salmán Bahá'u'lláh explains that in the Islamic Dispensation the letter of negation stood above that of affirmation. Those among the followers of Muḥammad who disregarded His wishes about the appointment of His successor and violated His wishes after His passing, dominated over the faithful ones and ruled over them for centuries. In that same Tablet Bahá'u'lláh gives the reasons for this and emphatically states that in this Dispensation He has taken out the letter of negation and substituted for it the letter of affirmation, meaning that the enemies of the Cause, and particularly the Covenant-breakers, will never be able to dominate or rule over the community of the Most Great Name. 'This is a day that shall not be followed by night', is a promise of Bahá'u'lláh.

The subject of 'affirmation' and 'negation' is a deep and fascinating one, but to discuss it any further would result in the repetition of some of the contents of previous volumes, as we have referred to this subject in detail previously.*

In the same opening paragraph, Bahá'u'lláh refers to the 'ascendancy of the oppressor' and the 'tyranny of the wicked'. These terms often appear in the Writings of Bahá'u'lláh. In one of His Tablets revealed in 1882–3[5] He categorically states that the terms revealed in the Writings such as 'veils', 'oppressors', 'wicked ones', 'embodiments of tyranny' and any other word from which the odour of wrath is inhaled, means the divines and religious leaders† the world over, those who appear to be walking in the pathway of error.

Several themes of the Tablet of Ṭarázát are taken up in Tablets already described in preceding chapters. These include the celebrated passage about trustworthiness,‡ Bahá'u'lláh's exhortations to associate with all kindreds and peoples of the earth, and the commandment to study arts and sciences. In this Tablet Bahá'u'lláh asserts that 'in this Day whatsoever serveth to reduce blindness and to increase vision is worthy of consideration'.[6] He also states that 'keenness of understanding is due to keenness of vision'. He exhorts His followers to adorn themselves with the 'saintly attributes and character of the Concourse on High', urges them to fix their gaze 'under all conditions upon justice and fairness', admonishes them not to 'deny any soul the reward due to him', advises them to appreciate the craftsmanship of the people of the West, asks them to treat such craftsmen with deference, and enjoins on them not to 'defile their tongues with abuse'.

In this Tablet, too, Bahá'u'lláh grieves that 'truthfulness and sincerity are sorely afflicted in the clutches of falsehood,

---

* see vol. 2, pp. 286–90.

† Concerning Bahá'u'lláh's condemnation of religious leaders see the *Kitáb-i-Íqán* and vol. 1, pp. 163–4.

‡ see above, p. 18.

and justice is tormented by the scourge of injustice', observes that corruption has spread throughout the world, deplores the arming of the nations and the clashing of the swords, describes the pages of newspapers as the 'mirror of the world', and delineates guidelines for their editorial staff, urging the 'writers thereof to be purged from the promptings of evil passions and desires and to be attired with the raiment of justice and equity. They should enquire into situations as much as possible and ascertain the facts, then set them down in writing.' How vast is the difference between these guidelines and the system which prevails at present!

Towards the end of the Tablet of Ṭarázát, Bahá'u'lláh turns His attention, as He has done in many other Tablets, to the people of the Bayán who had followed the promptings of their own selves and passions, and denied the Cause of Bahá'u'lláh whom the Báb designated 'Him Whom God shall make manifest'. Bahá'u'lláh particularly addresses Hádíy-i-Dawlat-Ábádí in this Tablet. He was at the time Mírzá Yaḥyá's representative in Persia and later became his successor. He was a Muslim clergyman in Iṣfahán who became a Bábí in the early days of the Faith and followed Mírzá Yaḥyá when the latter announced himself as the Báb's successor. Very corrupt and ambitious, Hádí succeeded in misleading some of the Bábís to follow Mírzá Yaḥyá. He instilled into the minds of his supporters much falsehood about the Cause of Bahá'u'lláh. Although the followers of Mírzá Yaḥyá were very few in number, Bahá'u'lláh admonishes them lovingly in innumerable Tablets to leave the path of error and turn to the Cause of God. He likewise addresses Hádí in many of His Tablets, as in this one, and invites him to open his eyes to find the truth. But Bahá'u'lláh's exhortations fell on deaf ears.

In the Tablet of Ṭarázát Bahá'u'lláh addresses the followers of Mírzá Yaḥyá in these words:

> O people of the Bayán! It is men like unto Hádí Dawlat-Ábádí who, with turban and staff, have been the source of opposition

> and hindrance and have so grievously burdened the people with superstitions that even at the present time they still expect the appearance of a fictitious person from a fictitious place. Be ye warned, O men of understanding.[7]

In this passage Bahá'u'lláh warns the followers of the Bayán that Hádí is misleading them just as the Muslim clergy misled the Islamic people. They had led the Shí'ah community to believe that the Qá'im, the Promised One, had been living for more than a thousand years in an underground city to which no one had access. The clergy promise their followers that one day this fictitious person will come out of this fictitious place and rule over the faithful.

In this Tablet Bahá'u'lláh reminds Hádí of his despicable act in recanting his faith. He alludes to this by rebuking him for being two-faced. These are His words:

> O Hádí! Be thou of one face in the path of God. When in company with the infidels, thou art an infidel and with the pious, thou art pious. Reflect thou upon such souls as offered up their lives and their substance in that land, that haply thou mayest be admonished and roused from slumber. Consider: who is to be preferred, he who preserveth his body, his life and his possessions or the one who surrendereth his all in the path of God? Judge thou fairly and be not of the unjust. Take fast hold of justice and adhere unto equity that perchance thou mayest not, for selfish motives, use religion as a snare, nor disregard the truth for the sake of gold.[8]

In the year AH 1306 (AD 1888) a believer of wide repute by the name of Mírzá Ashraf* was martyred in Iṣfahán. Soon afterwards the Mujtahid of the city, Shaykh Muḥammad-Taqí,

* For a brief account of his martyrdom see below, pp. 411–2. He should not be confused with Mírzá Ashraf of Zanján to whose martyrdom reference is made in vol. 2, pp. 223–30.

known as the 'Son of the Wolf', demanded the death of Hádí, whereupon the latter ascended the pulpit in a mosque in Iṣfahán and recanted his faith in public. This recantation of faith was followed by a series of imprecations which he hurled, in the most vile language, at the Báb and Bahá'u'lláh. Shaykh Muḥammad-Taqí was satisfied by Hádí's performance and absolved him of the charges made against him of being a Bábí. The news of his recantation was publicized throughout the city and reached the ears of many people far and near.

In the Tablet known as *Kalimát-i-Firdawsíyyih** Bahá'u'lláh refers to Hádí in these words:

> The disbelievers among the people of the Bayán are like the followers of the Shí'ih sect and walk in their footsteps. Leave them to their idle fancies and vain imaginings. They are in truth accounted with the lost in the Book of God, the All-Knowing, the All-Wise. The Shí'ih divines, one and all, are now engaged in reviling and denouncing the True One from their pulpits. Gracious God! Dawlat-Ábádí too hath followed suit. He ascended the pulpit and gave voice to that which hath caused the Tablet to cry out in anguish and the Pen to wail. Meditate upon his conduct and the conduct of Ashraf – upon him be My glory and My tender mercy – and likewise consider those loved ones who hastened to the place of martyrdom in My Name, and offered up their lives in the path of Him Who is the Desire of the world.[9]

In spite of such shameful conduct, which was widely discussed in various circles in the country, Hádí continued his leadership of the Azalís, the followers of Mírzá Yaḥyá in Persia. For some years the Pen of Bahá'u'lláh continued to admonish Hádí and urge him to change his ways. These are a few lines gleaned from some lengthy passages in the Tablet of Ṭarázát exhorting him to follow the path of Truth.

---

* see below, ch. 15.

> O Hádí! Give ear unto the Voice of this trustworthy Counsellor: direct thy steps from the left unto the right, that is turn away from idle fancy unto certitude. Lead not the people into error. The divine Luminary shineth, His Cause is manifest and His signs are all-embracing. Set thy face towards God, the Help in Peril, the Self-Subsisting. Renounce thy leadership for the sake of God and leave the people unto themselves. Thou art ignorant of the essential truth, thou art not acquainted therewith.[10]

Hádíy-i-Dawlat-Ábádí soon passed on to the realm of ignominy and extinction. His influence utterly failed to undermine the foundation of the Cause of God; but it stained the annals of the Faith and armed a few misguided souls, enabling them to arise in opposition to the Supreme Manifestation of God. Their action resembled that of darkness challenging the sun.

12

The Light of Faith Reaches India and Burma

A number of outstanding believers had been travel teaching in Persia from the early days of the Faith. By the time Bahá'u'lláh entered the city of 'Akká, the Faith had also reached a few of the neighbouring countries and its light had illumined the hearts of some of their inhabitants. Towards the end of Bahá'u'lláh's Ministry, the Cause of God was introduced to fifteen countries, mainly the Islamic lands stretching from Turkmenistan in the east to Egypt and the Sudan in the west. Several teachers of the Cause travelled through these territories, among them some eminent Bahá'ís such as Nabíl-i-Akbar and Mírzá Abu'l-Faḍl.

To the vast sub-continent of India, whose inhabitants were mainly non-Muslim, Bahá'u'lláh despatched the zealous, untiring and renowned travel-teacher Sulaymán Khán-i-Tunukábání, surnamed by Him Jamálu'd-Dín and usually referred to as Jamál Effendi. He came from the province of Mázindarán in northern Persia. His Bahá'í career began in Ṭihrán, where he had moved in order to obtain an important position in government circles. There he found the Faith and became an ardent believer. The fire of the love of Bahá'u'lláh began to burn brightly within his heart, so he changed his plans completely. The first thing he did was to dress as a dervish,* which was the most convenient appearance for a person who wished to roam around the country with freedom. Sulaymán

* A Persian mendicant who usually lives on alms and roams the country freely. Sometimes men of culture and means also dressed as dervishes in order to enjoy freedom of movement. Often these men, by virtue of their knowledge and erudition, became the centre of attraction for those who inclined towards Sufism.

Khán had a strong urge to travel to 'Akká and attain the presence of His Lord. So he set off on the journey and travelled to the Holy Land via Tabríz. He achieved his heart's desire and basked for some time in the sunshine of Bahá'u'lláh's presence.

When the time of his pilgrimage came to an end, he did not return to Persia, but instead travelled extensively and for a long time in the Ottoman territory. Being a man of culture and dressed as he was in the garb of a dervish, he hoped to become a centre of attraction for many souls in that vast country, so that he could teach the Faith to them.

Shaykh Káẓim-i-Samandar* states that he met Sulaymán Khán in Istanbul in the year AH 1291 (AD 1874) when the latter was travelling around the country after his pilgrimage to the presence of Bahá'u'lláh. Samandar writes:

> His [Sulaymán Khán's] intention in putting on the garb of a dervish was to be able to diffuse the divine fragrances and teach the Cause of the Lord of Revelation in those regions. Gradually, after his association with the public, he realized that these people for the time being did not have the capacity to embrace the Faith, and also his activities were not conducive to wisdom. Therefore he returned to 'Akká and attained the presence of the Blessed Perfection. From there he went to India . . . [1]

Some years before this episode, a few members of the Afnán family had established a trading company and later a printing press bearing the trade mark 'Náṣirí' in Bombay, India. This was the first printing press in the Bahá'í world to produce several volumes of Bahá'í writings. As a result of this enterprise Bombay became a place where Bahá'ís would congregate and to which Persian Bahá'í pilgrims travelled on their way to and from 'Akká. When the Afnáns realized that there was receptivity towards the Faith among the Indians, they sent a petition to Bahá'u'lláh for a Bahá'í teacher with knowledge

* For an account of his life see vol. 3. pp. 88–91.

SULAYMÁN KHÁN-I-TUNUKÁBÁNÍ

Known as Jamálu'd-Dín, he was sent by Bahá'u'lláh to teach in the sub-continent of India

SIYYID MUṢṬAFÁY-I-RÚMÍ

An illustrious believer in Burma, posthumously named by Shoghi Effendi as a Hand of the Cause of God

and experience to go to India, and offered financial assistance towards this meritorious enterprise.

Their request coincided with the time that Sulaymán Khán was in 'Akká. Bahá'u'lláh chose him for this purpose and instructed him to go to India and teach the Cause of God in that vast sub-continent. With a happy heart and radiant countenance, this old man of God set off for India in his dervish dress, his dignified bearing enhanced by a long cloak and a special headdress which immediately put him in the category of men of culture and leaders of thought. He took with him a relative of his, Mírzá Ḥusayn, as his companion. He arrived in Bombay in 1878, around the time Bahá'u'lláh was in Mazra'ih, and from there began his teaching activities. He travelled extensively throughout India, then went to Ceylon where he encountered great opposition from Buddhist leaders. His companion died in Ceylon. He travelled to Burma for a short visit and continued travel teaching for over ten years. During this period he met many leaders of thought and men of culture from every background and religion. He associated with people with genuine friendship and love; his pleasant manners and good character, his attractive talks and dignified way of listening, all contributed to his success in the teaching field.

People from all walks of life turned to Sulaymán Khán, whom they knew as Jamál Effendi, for enlightenment and spiritual blessing. He published *The Seven Valleys* in Persian and disseminated it among certain people. He attracted many souls to the Cause; some became ardent believers, others remained admirers of the Faith till the end of their lives. Bahá'u'lláh addressed several encouraging Tablets to him, showering His confirmations upon his work and assuring him of His good-pleasure. To others who had embraced the Faith in India, Bahá'u'lláh also addressed some Tablets.

In the city of Madras Sulaymán Khán came across Siyyid Muṣṭafáy-i-Rúmí, a youth of about twenty years whose parents were originally from 'Iráq. He was deeply attached to Islám and diligently observed every religious rite. This youth became greatly attracted to Sulaymán Khán whose charming personality and radiance of spirit had left an abiding impression on him. Siyyid Muṣṭafá listened with great interest to Sulaymán Khán's explanations about religion in general and the Bahá'í Faith in particular. He became highly attracted to the Person of Bahá'u'lláh as he sat spellbound, listening to the discourses of his new-found teacher. Soon Siyyid Muṣṭafá recognized the truth of the Cause and became filled with excitement at the knowledge that the Supreme Manifestation of God had at last revealed Himself to mankind. He was the most illustrious of Jamál Effendi's converts in the sub-continent of India. He served the Cause with distinction, mainly in Burma, and was posthumously named by Shoghi Effendi, the Guardian of the Faith, as one of the Hands of the Cause of God. After his death, Shoghi Effendi, in a cable to the Bahá'í world, referred to him as a 'DISTINGUISHED PIONEER' of the Faith of Bahá'u'lláh, a 'STAUNCH AND HIGH-MINDED SOUL', the record of whose 'SUPERB SERVICES IN BOTH TEACHING AND ADMINISTRATIVE FIELDS SHED LUSTRE ON BOTH THE HEROIC AND FORMATIVE AGES OF BAHÁ'Í DISPENSATION', and whose resting-place 'SHOULD BE REGARDED FOREMOST SHRINE IN THE COMMUNITY OF BURMESE BELIEVERS'.

For over ten years Sulaymán Khán travelled throughout the sub-continent; then he departed for the Holy Land to attain the presence of Bahá'u'lláh. He was accompanied by two believers whom he had brought under the shadow of the Cause of God. He also took with him a young lad to work as a domestic helper in the household of Bahá'u'lláh. He attained the presence of His Lord in 'Akká for the third time, but his sojourn in the Holy Land was cut very short, for Bahá'u'lláh instructed him to return to India and continue his teaching exploits in that vast country. This time he again took one of the believers to accompany him in his travels, arriving back in India on the eve of Naw-Rúz* 1888.

* 21 March, the Bahá'í New Year.

In some of his letters Siyyid Muṣṭafáy-i-Rúmí has named a number of countries and provinces that were visited by Sulaymán Khán. In each place he had sown the seeds of the Message of Bahá'u'lláh in many hearts. Among the places he visited were Ceylon, Punjab, Burma, Malaya, Siam, Java, and the islands of Celebes and Bali. On one of his trips, which lasted one and a half years, he visited Lahore, Punch, Yarkand, Kashmir, Laddakh (Ladakh), Tibet, Balkh and Badakhshán. Siyyid Muṣṭafá has written a brief account about this journey, a summary of which is translated below:

> On this journey, according to Jamál Effendi's own account, his feet became frost-bitten so severely owing to the extreme cold that for about six months he was confined to bed in Yarkand. When recovered, he went to Balkh and Badakhshán (both in Afghanistan) but his feet were still wounded – and he walked with difficulty. The road between Kashmir and Tibet, where one has to climb high mountains, was extremely difficult for him to negotiate. All his luggage containing many Bahá'í books and Tablets, which was carried on the backs of bullocks, fell into a river and could not be recovered.
>
> Between Kashmir and Tibet, Jamál Effendi had to encounter great numbers of the Ismá'ílí sect, followers of Áqá Khán-i-Maḥallátí. The majority of these people were bloodthirsty and savage. Because of much ill-treatment, he was disappointed and with a heavy heart . . . went to Balkh and Badakhshán in Afghanistan. The people in that area also treated him very badly, . . . so he returned to Kashmir in 1889. From there he resumed his customary trips to various parts of India and later went to Burma . . . [2]

After the ascension of Bahá'u'lláh, Sulaymán Khán was instructed by 'Abdu'l-Bahá to remain on the sub-continent and continue his meritorious activities. As the years went by his achievements became clearly visible, and the foundations he laid in those vast countries and islands remained unassailable with the passage of time. Through his travel teaching many people were attracted to the Cause, especially in the islands of Java where some rulers and dignitaries were influenced by his teaching work. In Burma he achieved greater success. In the city of Mandalay, it is reported that no less than six thousand Muslims were converted to the Faith. But he did not disclose to them that Bahá'u'lláh had ushered in a new Dispensation with new laws and teachings, because they were not ready for them at the time. These people, according to the testimony of some local believers, acknowledged the truth of the Message of Bahá'u'lláh, but at the same time were practising Muslims and carried out the religious laws and rituals of Islám.

In the early days of His Ministry, some time after Sulaymán Khán had ended his services on the sub-continent and had returned to the Holy Land, 'Abdu'l-Bahá sent Mírzá Maḥram, a teacher of the Faith, to Mandalay with clear instructions to announce the independence of the Faith to these people and acquaint them with the laws of the new Dispensation and the abrogation of the laws of Islám. Mírzá Maḥram carried out this mission faithfully. But on hearing such far-reaching deviations from Islamic laws, almost two-thirds of this community angrily rejected the Cause of Bahá'u'lláh and later some of them came together to kill Mírzá Maḥram. One day a great crowd assembled outside his residence and had it not been for the prompt action of a British police officer, they would have succeeded in putting him to death. It is reported that the British officer, who was a Christian, asked Mírzá Maḥram, 'What did you say to these people who have now assembled to take your life?' 'I said', Mírzá Maḥram replied, 'the same thing that Christ said in His day.' Mírzá Maḥram nonetheless succeeded in remaining in Mandalay for some time. He deepened the knowledge of the remainder of the community and enabled them to embrace the Cause of God fully and to carry out its laws and teachings in their daily lives.

As to Sulaymán Khán, he spent altogether about twenty years continually teaching the Cause of God in India and adjoining countries. He succeeded in converting peoples of various religions to the Faith. Among them were Muslims of the Sunní and Shí'ah sects, Ismá'ílís, Hindus and Buddhists. However, the hardships he underwent during these years, his travelling in climates of extreme heat and cold, riding on bullocks and elephants, passing through so many inhospitable regions and encountering some inhuman opposition, all took their toll on his strength and he returned to 'Akká. This was about five years after the ascension of Bahá'u'lláh.

After some time in the Holy Land, 'Abdu'l-Bahá sent him on an important mission to Persia. The background to this story goes back to the days of Bahá'u'lláh when two outstanding believers, the Hand of the Cause of God Mullá 'Alí-Akbar, known as Ḥájí Ákhúnd, and Ḥájí Abu'l-Ḥasan, known as Ḥájí Amín, the Trustee of Bahá'u'lláh, were both cast into the prison of Qazvín in 1891 for about two years.[*] The prime minister at the time was 'Alí-Aṣghar Khán, the Amínu's-Sulṭán. He was sympathetic to their case, knew that they were unjustly imprisoned, and made kind remarks about them. Bahá'u'lláh was pleased about this and wished 'Abdu'l-Bahá to send a message to him. 'Abdu'l-Bahá describes this in these words:

> Not long before His passing, Bahá'u'lláh had said: 'Should someone go to Persia, and manage to convey it, this message must be delivered to Amínu's-Sulṭán: "You took steps to help the prisoners; you freely rendered them a befitting service; this service will not be forgotten. Rest assured that it will bring you honor and call down a blessing upon all your affairs. O Amínu's-Sulṭán! Every house that is raised up will one day fall to ruin, except the house of God; that will grow more massive and be better guarded day by day. Then serve the Court of God with all your might, that you may discover

* see below, pp. 358–60.

the way to a home in Heaven, and found an edifice that will endure forever.'"[3]

Soon after this the ascension of Bahá'u'lláh took place. 'Abdu'l-Bahá was able to carry out Bahá'u'lláh's wishes shortly after the following incident took place in Persia. Early on during the Ministry of 'Abdu'l-Bahá, Siyyid Asadu'lláh-i-Qumí,* who was then in 'Akká, had a dream: in his dream Bahá'u'lláh placed a few Tablets inside some envelopes, wrote on them in red ink, handed the envelopes to Siyyid Asadu'lláh and directed him to proceed to Persia. In the morning the Siyyid recounted his dream to 'Abdu'l-Bahá and asked permission to leave for Persia. 'Abdu'l-Bahá warned him that on this journey he would be severely persecuted in a special manner. This prophecy was fulfilled when Siyyid Asadu'lláh reached the city of Ardabíl in the province of Ádhirbáyján. A few of the clergy became aware of his teaching activities in the city and plotted to take his life. One day he was conducted to a place where several men surrounded him and beat him so severely that they thought he was dead. They dragged his body into a disused stable. After some time he regained consciousness but was taken into prison by the orders of the governor. Later he was sent to the prison of Tabríz in which he languished for a few days. Eventually orders arrived that he should be sent to Ṭihrán under escort. However, instead of taking him to a prison there, the Prime Minister gave instructions that the Siyyid should be brought to his own home, where he was received with kindness and consideration.

On his way to Ṭihrán, while escorted by the soldiers, Siyyid Asadu'lláh recalled the words of Bahá'u'lláh a few years earlier when on a certain occasion he had attained His presence in the Mansion of Mazra'ih in AH 1306 (AD 1888–9). He said to him, 'Asadu'lláh, I want to send you to visit Náṣiri'd-Dín Sháh, but remember that he does not kill Bahá'ís any more.

* For a brief reference to him see vol. 1, p. 35.

Do you wish to go?"* And Siyyid Asadu'lláh bowed as a sign of his submission to his Lord. Now he was a prisoner on his way to the capital and he knew that somehow he was going to meet the Sovereign:

> Amínu's-Sulṭán came to the prisoner's assistance and, in his own office, provided Asadu'lláh with a sanctuary. One day when the Prime Minister was ill, Náṣiri'd-Dín Sháh arrived to visit him. The Minister then explained the situation, and lavished praise upon his captive; so much so that the Sháh, as he left, showed great kindness to Asadu'lláh, and spoke words of consolation. This, when at an earlier time, the captive would have been strung up at once to adorn some gallows-tree, and shot down with a gun.[4]

The Prime Minister's act of kindness in harbouring Siyyid Asadu'lláh prompted 'Abdu'l-Bahá to carry out the wishes of Bahá'u'lláh and send him a message. The person to whom 'Abdu'l-Bahá entrusted this task was Sulaymán Khán.

> After a time Amínu's-Sulṭán lost the Sovereign's favor. Hated, in disgrace, he was banished to the city of Qum. Thereupon this servant dispatched Sulaymán Khán to Persia, carrying a prayer and a missive written by me. The prayer besought God's aid and bounty and succor for the fallen Minister, so that he might, from that corner of oblivion, be recalled to favor. In the letter we clearly stated: 'Prepare to return to Ṭihrán. Soon will God's help arrive; the light of grace will shine on you again; with full authority again, you will find yourself free, and Prime Minister. This is your reward for the efforts you exerted on behalf of a man who was oppressed.' That letter and that prayer are today in the possession of the family of Amínu's-Sulṭán.
>
> From Ṭihrán, Sulaymán Khán journeyed to Qum, and

* These are not to be taken as the exact words of Bahá'u'lláh.

according to his instructions went to live in a cell in the shrine of the Immaculate.* The relatives of Amínu's-Sulṭán came to visit there; Sulaymán Khán inquired after the fallen Minister and expressed the wish to meet him. When the Minister learned of this, he sent for Sulaymán Khán. Placing all his trust in God, Sulaymán Khán hastened to the Minister's house and, meeting him in private, presented the letter from 'Abdu'l-Bahá. The Minister rose, and received the letter with extreme respect. Then addressing the Khán he said: 'I had given up hope. If this longing is fulfilled, I will arise to serve; I will preserve and uphold the friends of God.' Then he expressed his gratitude, indebtedness and joy, and added, 'Praise be to God, I hope again; I feel that by His aid, my dream will come true.'

In brief, the Minister pledged himself to serve the friends, and Sulaymán Khán took his leave. The Minister then desired to give him a sum of money to defray the expenses of his journey, but Sulaymán Khán refused and, despite the Minister's insistence, would accept nothing. The Khán had not yet reached the Holy Land on his return journey when Amínu's-Sulṭán was recalled from exile and immediately summoned to the Premiership again. He assumed the position and functioned with full authority; and at first he did indeed support the believers, but toward the end, in the case of the Yazd† martyrdoms, he was neglectful. He neither helped nor protected the sufferers in any way, nor would he listen to their repeated pleas, until all of them were put to death. Accordingly he too was dismissed, a ruined man; that flag which had flown so proudly was reversed, and that hoping heart despaired.[5]

Before embarking on this journey Sulaymán Khán was advised by 'Abdu'l-Bahá not to divulge to anyone the nature of the

* Qum is the shrine city of Fáṭimih 'the Immaculate'. Sister of the eighth Imám, Imám Riḍá, she was buried here in AD 816.

† This refers to the upheaval of 1903 in Yazd in which a great number of Bahá'ís were martyred. (A.T.)

mission with which he was entrusted. It took only a month after receiving 'Abdu'l-Bahá's Tablet before Amínu's-Sulṭán was again installed as Prime Minister and the promise of 'Abdu'l-Bahá was fulfilled. Soon after this happened, Sulaymán Khán in his enthusiasm made a mistake and intimated the whole story to the proud and egotistical Jamál-i-Burújirdí,* the notoriously unfaithful Bahá'í teacher who soon after became a Covenant-breaker. When Jamál heard of the success of the mission and the reverence shown by Amínu's-Sulṭán for the Tablet from 'Abdu'l-Bahá, the fire of jealousy raged in his heart and prompted him to establish contact with the Prime Minister in order to claim credit for himself. He made preparations and soon a meeting took place between the two. The satanic influence which Jamál-i-Burújirdí exerted upon the Prime Minister in this interview was fatal.

There is nothing more damaging to a soul than meeting a person who is infected with the disease of Covenant-breaking. 'Abdu'l-Bahá has stated[6] that the reason for Amínu's-Sulṭán's failure to keep his promise of support for the Faith was twofold. One was the chilling effect of meeting Jamál-i-Burújirdí, the other was pride in his position of supreme authority.

As for Sulaymán Khán, he returned to the Holy Land, but it did not take long before he passed away to the realms above. This was in the year AH 1316. He was buried in 'Akká, having achieved everlasting renown as the spiritual conqueror of the sub-continent of India and of Burma.

---

* see vol. 2.

13

The Meaning of Unity

Bahá'u'lláh has deposited the priceless treasure of His love within the heart of every believer, and therefore the distinguishing feature by which a true Bahá'í may be identified is his love for Bahá'u'lláh. He has also decreed the chief characteristic of the Bahá'í community to be unity.

Love of Bahá'u'lláh in the heart of the individual, and the spiritual unity of the community, which is born of His love, are very closely linked together. Unity among the believers is not merely an acknowledgement of their common beliefs and practices. It transcends human limitations and finds its highest form when the believers appear as one soul in many bodies. It is then that the individual will reach such heights of spiritual unity that he exalts other believers above himself.

In one of his letters to the Persian Bahá'ís,[1] Shoghi Effendi, the Guardian of the Faith, has said that love and compassion were the counsels of older dispensations. In this day the people of Bahá are exhorted to sacrifice their all for each other. These words of Shoghi Effendi are not to be taken as mere utopian visions of an unattainable goal. On the contrary, the history of the Cause amply demonstrates that some of its followers have attained to this exalted station. The unity of the Bahá'í community is the glory and the promise of the future. It guarantees the unity of the human race on a spiritual as well as a social level. It is a model which, as it grows in strength and develops further towards maturity, can and will inspire generations yet unborn to come under its world-embracing tabernacle of unity which the hand of God has raised in this day.

Lawḥ-i-Ittiḥád

There is a Tablet known as the *Lawḥ-i-Ittiḥád* (Tablet of Unity) revealed by Bahá'u'lláh in 'Akká. In it He describes different features of unity. This Tablet was addressed to Siyyid Asadu'lláh, a believer from the city of Rasht, in answer to his question about the meaning of unity. He was one of the five brothers entitled by Bahá'u'lláh as Sádát-i-Khamsih (The Five Siyyids*). All five were believers. At one time Siyyid Asadu'lláh lived in Qazvín, a city where Mírzá Yaḥyá's followers were actively engaged in misrepresenting the Cause of Bahá'u'lláh. These people succeeded in poisoning the mind of Siyyid Asadu'lláh to a point where he became confused in his faith. However, this situation did not last very long. The purity of his heart coupled with the devoted efforts of the renowned Shaykh Káẓim-i-Samandar who clarified all the misrepresentations of the Azalís, enabled Siyyid Asadu'lláh to regain his faith and become a steadfast believer. He then went on pilgrimage to 'Akká and attained the presence of Bahá'u'lláh. He saw with his own eyes the Glory of God and was made the recipient of His grace and bounties. His youngest brother, Siyyid Naṣru'lláh, also had the great privilege of attaining the presence of Bahá'u'lláh in 'Akká. Both brothers, survivors of the five, were great servants of the Cause till the end of their lives.

In the Tablet of Ittiḥád, Bahá'u'lláh describes in some detail several features of unity. He states that unity in the first place is the unity of religion, meaning that people must follow the same religion which is His Faith in this day. He declares that when the majority of the people in a country embrace His Cause, then the government will be able to put into practice His teachings and commandments. He asserts that in past dispensations such a unity has always brought victory to the Cause of God.

Bahá'u'lláh explains that unity on another level is in the

* Siyyid is a title for one who is a descendant of the Prophet Muḥammad.

realm of speech. He gives the example of two believers who might contradict each other on a subject. In such a case they would become the cause of depriving themselves, and others who hear them, of the bounty of unity. He also reveals that a speech about the Cause, if given in moderation, will attract divine bounty, but if carried to excess may become the cause of the perishing of the souls. In this Tablet He further counsels the believers to teach the people with tenderness and moderation, so that their words may have the same effect as milk has for the infant. In several of His Tablets Bahá'u'lláh has given the same advice for teaching His Cause. An example is this quotation from the *Lawḥ-i-Ḥikmat*:

> Say: Human utterance is an essence which aspireth to exert its influence and needeth moderation. As to its influence, this is conditional upon refinement which in turn is dependent upon hearts which are detached and pure. As to its moderation, this hath to be combined with tact and wisdom as prescribed in the Holy Scriptures and Tablets. Meditate upon that which hath streamed forth from the heaven of the Will of thy Lord, He Who is the Source of all grace, that thou mayest grasp the intended meaning which is enshrined in the sacred depths of the Holy Writings.[2]

He has warned His followers not to overwhelm the listener with too much information in the early stages, and has likened such an act to giving a big meal to an infant which, instead of giving life, could kill it.

Bahá'u'lláh further reveals that unity of deeds follows that of words. When the believers carry out His teachings and adorn themselves with divine virtues they will become united in their deeds. He deplores the divisions which have occurred in past religions, attributes this to disunity among the followers and states that the foundation of the Cause of God in past Dispensations was shattered as a result of such differences.

Another aspect of unity described by Bahá'u'lláh concerns the station of the believers. The unity of their station will exalt the Cause of God amidst the people. The world is in a grievous state because some have considered themselves superior to others. He states that the believers, who have quaffed from the ocean of His Revelation and have truly turned their faces towards His most exalted Horizon, should regard themselves as being on one plane, occupying the same position and having equal rank. He prophesies that if this happens, the world of humanity will become a paradise. Throwing further light on this subject, Bahá'u'lláh declares that although man is a glorious being endowed with divine attributes, it is a grave transgression to consider oneself superior to others.

This teaching of Bahá'u'lláh, if implemented, will create in the heart the feeling of humility and self-effacement. If not, pride and vainglory will tend to dominate and man will become a prisoner of his own self and passion. His Saviour in this case is none other than the Manifestation of God.

By recognizing Bahá'u'lláh as the Revealer of the Word of God for today and wholeheartedly following His exhortations and counsels, the soul becomes freed from the fetters of self and material attachments. It is then that the individual can understand the purpose of life. And it is then that he can become truly united with his fellow believers.

One of the great bounties of the Revelation of Bahá'u'lláh is that He has abolished the institution of priesthood. Although greatly abused, and now almost ineffective, this institution was perhaps necessary and useful in past ages when the great majority of people were illiterate and had to be shepherded by leaders. But today it is totally unnecessary. In the Tablet of Ittiḥád Bahá'u'lláh states that if the religious leaders and divines of Persia had not regarded themselves as superior beings, their followers would not have engaged in bitter opposition to His Cause. He describes their pride and vainglory as a fire which has engulfed and consumed the whole nation.

Not only has the Cause of Bahá'u'lláh rid itself of the institution of priesthood, which breeds disunity and corruption, but intrinsically it does not harbour egotistical personalities within its divinely ordained institutions. Its hallmark is servitude to God which, in practice, is servitude to man. Those who serve on Bahá'í institutions can experience unity in action because there is no scope for anyone to promote personal ambitions or demonstrate superior talents within these institutions. Indeed, should one member try to exalt himself above others his effectiveness is greatly impaired. Great tests and trials ensue once the framework of unity within a Bahá'í institution is upset through the egotistical attitude of one of its members. Should this happen, the members will go through great pressures and sufferings and that Assembly, in the words of 'Abdu'l-Bahá, will be brought to naught.

In the Tablet of Ittiḥád Bahá'u'lláh states that if He were to expound fully upon the various levels of unity in all things, His Pen would have to move upon the Tablets for several years, and since this is not feasible He concludes His explanations by describing one more aspect of unity, namely, the unity of peoples. He states that the unity of peoples can be realized through the love of God and the influence of the Word of God. When human beings turn to the Word and adhere to it, they will become united.

The followers of Bahá'u'lláh have already brought about a real unity of hearts in their communities. Although coming from so many diverse backgrounds and speaking different languages, they are motivated by a strong bond of love which binds them together spiritually. This love is not produced artificially, nor is it due to any special talents which the believers may possess. Without any effort on the part of the individual other than turning to Bahá'u'lláh, it descends from on high into the hearts of the believers. This love is generated through the influence of the Revelation of Bahá'u'lláh. It is like the flow of electric current in a vast network, energizing every circuit which is connected to it. The mere belief in Bahá'u'lláh as the Bearer of the Message of God for this age opens up the channels of grace, and the believer finds himself able to empty his heart of inborn prejudices and become the bearer of the love of God. This love, in turn, manifests itself among the body of the believers as the most potent force within the Bahá'í community. It unites the hearts together in such wise that a true believer will see a trace of the love of Bahá'u'lláh in the face of another believer, and thus never dwell on the shortcomings of his friend. There are innumerable passages in the Writings of Bahá'u'lláh concerning the power of unity and the destructive effects of disunity. In one of His Tablets[3] Bahá'u'lláh states that if the loved ones of God were able to achieve unity in every region, the whole world would be illumined with its light. He grieves over the existence of disunity among the believers in some areas, and declares that this has brought abasement and disgrace upon the Faith. In this Tablet He further explains that if all the peoples of the world were to rise up against the Cause no harm would come to it, rather their opposition would become the cause of its exaltation, but disunity among His loved ones will damage the good name of the Cause, hinder its progress, and inflict untold sufferings and pain upon its Author.

In another Tablet[4] Bahá'u'lláh exhorts His followers to shun any word which might become the cause of disunity, even if such a word is uttered by those who are closest to Him and continually circle the throne of His sovereignty. He describes disunity, in yet another Tablet,[5] as a burning fire which ought to be quenched with the waters of wisdom and utterance. In one of His Tablets[6] 'Abdu'l-Bahá states that anyone who becomes the cause of disunity in the Cause will not see happiness in his life.

Concerning the unity of earthly possessions, Bahá'u'lláh in the *Lawḥ-i-Ittiḥád* states that there are two stages of unity. One is that of generosity, when the individual does not deprive his fellow human beings of the things God has given him, and bestows some of his earthly riches upon them. This praiseworthy deed Bahá'u'lláh describes as the state of *musávát* (equality). It is a state in which a person generously gives to others as to himself. The other stage is that of *muvását*, which means that the individual sacrifices his own needs for the sake of others and gives preference to them. Bahá'u'lláh regards this attitude as the highest and noblest quality in man. But he emphasizes that this preference is meant to be exercised only in the realm of earthly possessions and does not apply to anything else.

In the Tablet known as *Kalimát-i-Firdawsíyyih*,* Bahá'u-'lláh declares what amounts to the highest statement of the Golden Rule:

> O son of man! If thine eyes be turned towards mercy, forsake the things that profit thee and cleave unto that which will profit mankind. And if thine eyes be turned towards justice, choose thou for thy neighbour that which thou choosest for thyself.[7]

Unity in Society

The main purpose of the Revelation of Bahá'u'lláh is to establish unity among the peoples of the world. 'So powerful is the light of unity', Bahá'u'lláh states, 'that it can illuminate the whole earth.'[8] So destructive today is the influence of disunity in society that Bahá'u'lláh and 'Abdu'l-Bahá have made it clear in their Writings that if religion becomes the cause of disunity it is better to be without it. The call to unity has been raised by Bahá'u'lláh in this day, and the creative power of the Word of God leaves mankind with no alternative but to establish a sound and impregnable foundation for the unity of all the peoples and kindreds of the earth. These exalted words of Bahá'u'lláh have revolutionized the equilibrium of human society on a world scale:

* see below, ch. 15.

> O well-beloved ones! The tabernacle of unity hath been raised; regard ye not one another as strangers. Ye are the fruits of one tree, and the leaves of one branch.[9]

Today a great many among the peoples of the world are clamouring for peace. The fear of large-scale destruction and annihilation has driven people towards the idea of peace and the abolition of war. There is great activity in many quarters with the aim of bringing this dream to reality, ranging from lecturing to societies, debating on the issues, arranging peaceful demonstrations, propaganda campaigns, protest marches and even large-scale violence. But peace cannot be established by these activities. It is not an isolated goal; it is closely related to human behaviour and depends on the attitude of one man towards another. Not until there is unity among people can there be peace. And unity cannot be produced artificially by superficial measures. So long as mankind tries to settle its affairs through compromise on principles, instead of seeking out and then following the truth, there can be no way of bringing about goodwill among all the nations of the world. Today wherever there is disunity, the people involved will be encompassed by sufferings and tribulations. Bahá'u'lláh has clearly stated in his Writings that mankind will not experience peace and tranquillity unless it creates unity among the peoples and nations of the world:

> The well-being of mankind, its peace and security, are unattainable unless and until its unity is firmly established. This unity can never be achieved so long as the counsels which the Pen of the Most High hath revealed are suffered to pass unheeded.[10]

In a Tablet Bahá'u'lláh reveals these exalted words concerning unity:

> O contending peoples and kindreds of the earth! Set your faces towards unity, and let the radiance of its light shine upon you. Gather ye together, and for the sake of God resolve to root out whatever is the source of contention amongst you. Then will the effulgence of the world's great Luminary envelop the whole earth, and its inhabitants become the citizens of one city, and the occupants of one and the same throne. This wronged One hath, ever since the early days of His life, cherished none other desire but this, and will continue to entertain no wish except this wish. There can be no doubt whatever that the peoples of the world, of whatever race or religion, derive their inspiration from one heavenly Source, and are the subjects of one God. The difference between the ordinances under which they abide should be attributed to the varying requirements and exigencies of the age in which they were revealed. All of them, except a few which are the outcome of human perversity, were ordained of God, and are a reflection of His Will and Purpose. Arise and, armed with the power of faith, shatter to pieces the gods of your vain imaginings, the sowers of dissension amongst you. Cleave unto that which draweth you together and uniteth you. This, verily, is the most exalted Word which the Mother Book hath sent down and revealed unto you. To this beareth witness the Tongue of Grandeur from His habitation of glory.[11]

Recognition of the oneness of mankind is the most essential prerequisite for world peace. However, the establishment of unity on any level will in its turn create a form of peace on that same level. For example, the establishment of political unity among all the nations of the world will bring about a political peace on a world scale, which is referred to in the Writings of Bahá'u'lláh as the 'Lesser Peace'.* In the distant future, when the generality of mankind will have recognized the station of Bahá'u'lláh as the Mouthpiece of God on this

* For further study of the Lesser Peace see vol. 3, pp. 314–15.

earth and the redeemer of all humanity, when the outpouring of His Revelation will have penetrated into the hearts of men, creating thereby a bond of spiritual unity among the peoples and kindreds of the earth, then the human race will witness the establishment of the 'Most Great Peace' promised by Bahá'u'lláh as one of the noblest fruits of His Revelation.

Unity of the human race should not be confused with uniformity, which is against the fundamental laws of creation. The teachings of Bahá'u'lláh emphasize the principle of unity in diversity. In God's creation there is only one of everything. No two things are the same. The best way to appreciate the reason for this uniqueness is to study the Bahá'í Writings and also observe nature. We understand from the Writings of Bahá'u'lláh and 'Abdu'l-Bahá that every created thing, be it from the mineral, vegetable or animal kingdom, manifests some of the attributes of God. The differences between these kingdoms are due to the varying degrees of the manifestation of these attributes. For instance, there are fewer attributes of God manifested in the mineral kingdom than there are in the vegetable. The same is true of the vegetable in relation to the animal. Many attributes possessed by the latter are not to be found in the former. And within man are deposited all the attributes of God.

However, there are some attributes which are commonly manifested in all created things, but in each kingdom appear with different intensity. Among these is the attribute of love, which is the prime cause of creation. It manifests itself in the mineral as cohesion. Within the vegetable there is also cohesion but the attribute of love attains a further dimension when the tree stretches its boughs and branches towards the sun to receive its rays as a lover reaches for its beloved. In the animal the attribute of love appears with greater intensity. The love of a mother for her young is an example. And in the world of man, the attributes of love manifest themselves in their highest intensity.

Another attribute of God which manifests itself within the whole of creation is the attribute of God the Incomparable. This attribute appears in every created thing and therefore everything is unique. These are the words of Bahá'u'lláh in one of His Tablets:

> Consider, in like manner, the revelation of the light of the Name of God, the Incomparable. Behold, how this light hath enveloped the entire creation, how each and every thing manifesteth the sign of His Unity, testifieth to the reality of Him Who is the Eternal Truth, proclaimeth His sovereignty, His oneness, and His power. This revelation is a token of His mercy that hath encompassed all created things.[12]

Just as no two things are the same, so in the world of humanity there is no absolute equality between people. Each person is a unique creation of God. The equality which is often referred to in the Writings is that of rights and privileges. Otherwise, every person is distinct from every other human being in his talents, capacities, character and all other virtues.

Equality between Men and Women

One of the basic teachings of Bahá'u'lláh is the equality of men and women. From the beginning of recorded history up until recently, men have dominated in almost every activity. During this period mankind has been going through the stages of infancy and childhood, and the social circumstances have been such that the principle of the equality of men and women has not been taught in the Holy Books of past religions. On the contrary, men have been considered to be endowed with superior powers and women have had to remain under their domination. In the *Qur'án* it is unequivocally stated: 'Men have superiority over women.'[13]

Bahá'u'lláh, for the first time in the history of religion,

has firmly proclaimed the equality of men and women. Like every other teaching revealed from the Pen of the Most High, this particular teaching has released enormous spiritual forces, which are irresistible and have revolutionized human society in this respect. Consequently, there is a movement for bringing about this equality nowadays everywhere in the world. In many of His Tablets Bahá'u'lláh refers to this subject and unequivocally emphasizes the equality of the sexes.

> Exalted, immensely exalted is He Who hath removed differences and established harmony. Glorified, infinitely glorified is He Who hath caused discord to cease, and decreed solidarity and unity. Praised be God, the Pen of the Most High hath lifted distinctions from between His servants and handmaidens and, through His consummate favours and all-encompassing mercy, hath conferred upon all a station and rank on the same plane. He hath broken the back of vain imaginings with the sword of utterance and hath obliterated the perils of idle fancies through the pervasive power of His might.[14]

The words 'servants' and 'handmaidens' signify 'men' and 'women' respectively. In another Tablet He states:

> In this Day the Hand of divine grace hath removed all distinction. The servants of God and His handmaidens are regarded on the same plane. Blessed is the servant who hath attained unto that which God hath decreed, and likewise the leaf moving in accordance with the breezes of His will. This favour is great and this station lofty. His bounties and bestowals are ever present and manifest. Who is able to offer befitting gratitude for His successive bestowals and continuous favours?[15]

The word 'leaf' is a designation used by Bahá'u'lláh to refer to a female believer.

Bahá'u'lláh revealed these words at a time when the Islamic world in which He appeared took it for granted that women were inferior beings. There were some schools of thought among the Muslim clergy which used to conduct debates as to whether a woman had a soul or not! The laws within the Islamic society were based on polygamy. Legally men could have as many as four wives and countless concubines. A woman had no say in the choice of her husband, was commonly illiterate, and generally would not be allowed to take part in public affairs. She would be mostly confined to the house of her father before marriage and to the house of her husband afterwards. It was like being a piece of furniture.

The custom of the time was that when a young man was about to marry, his female relatives, such as his mother or sister, would choose his future wife for him. He would not even be allowed to gaze upon the face of his bride, who would be heavily veiled, until after the marriage ceremony was concluded. Within such a system it was not possible for women to know what was happening in the world around them. Very few parents provided education for their daughters. Even then, they had no opportunity to utilize their talents in public.

One of the few public activities that women were allowed to undertake in the community of Shí'ah Islám was to attend special meetings known as *rawdih-khání* (a form of lamentation meeting) held in commemoration of the martyrdom of Imám Ḥusayn. They would be seated in a separate corner and when the speaker, who was usually a priest, recounted the episode of the martyrdom with great passion and fervour, thus exciting the people into a frantic display of emotion, the women would be allowed to wail and shriek so loudly as to drown the voice of the speaker completely and arouse the whole neighbourhood with their hysterical screams!

Within such a society, over a hundred years ago, Bahá'u'lláh granted equal rights to men and women. He revealed Tablets to many of the female members of the community, showered His favours and bounties upon them, praised their actions, assured them of God's purpose in this day to bring about their equality with men, encouraged them to teach the Cause with wisdom among women, and exhorted them to live their lives in accordance with His teachings. The following words of Bahá'u'lláh are gleaned from a Tablet addressed to a Bahá'í woman:

> By My Life, the names of handmaidens who are devoted to God are written and set down by the Pen of the Most High in the Crimson Book. They excel over men in the sight of God. How numerous are the heroes and knights in the field who are bereft of the True One and have no share in His recognition, but thou hast attained and received thy fill.[16]

There are innumerable Tablets revealed by Bahá'u'lláh in honour of Bahá'í women. The following is cited as another example:

> He is the All-Seeing from the Horizon of the Heaven of Knowledge! O My handmaiden, O My leaf! Verily the Pen of the Most High hath borne witness unto thy recognition of Him, thy love for Him and thy turning towards the Ancient Countenance at a time when the world hath rejected Him, save those whom God, the Most High, hath willed . . .
>
> Well is it with thee for having adorned thyself with the ornament of the love of God and for having been enabled to make mention of Him and utter His praise. Divine grace, in its entirety, is in the mighty grasp of God, exalted be He. He conferreth it upon whomsoever He willeth. How many a man considered himself a celebrated divine and a repository of heavenly mysteries, and yet when the slightest test visited him, he arose with such opposition and denial as to cause the Concourse on high to moan and lament. Through the bestowals of the Lord, however, and His infinite favour, thou hast attained unto the hidden secret and the well-guarded

> treasure. Preserve then, in the name of God, this lofty station and conceal it from the eyes of betrayers. The glory shining from the horizon of My Kingdom be upon thee and upon every handmaiden who hath attained the splendours of My sublime Throne.[17]

'Abdu'l-Bahá too, both in His numerous Tablets and in His talks, has elaborated on the theme of the equality of men and women. He regarded it as one of the fundamental prerequisites for the establishment of a well-balanced and healthy society. There are innumerable references in His Writings to this subject. To cite an example, the following is part of one of His Tablets:

> And among the teachings of Bahá'u'lláh is the equality of women and men. The world of humanity has two wings – one is women and the other men. Not until both wings are equally developed can the bird fly. Should one wing remain weak, flight is impossible. Not until the world of women becomes equal to the world of men in the acquisition of virtues and perfections, can success and prosperity be attained as they ought to be.[18]

One aspect of the equality of the sexes is that of rights and privileges. But identical functions – as sought by so many people today – are not always possible. While in certain functions men and women can perform equally well, there are some areas of work in which women excel men and others for which men are better suited than women, and there are some areas in which it is impossible for one sex to carry out the functions of the other.

The most important aspect of equality, and one which has completely escaped the attention of many present-day sociologists promoting the principle of the equality of men and women, is equality in the realm of the spirit. The equality of the sexes, so emphatically proclaimed by Bahá'u'lláh, has its origin in the act of creation itself. Although God has created men and women to be physically different in some respects, spiritually they are one.

There is no difference between the soul of a man and the soul of a woman. Both possess the same attributes of God, the same powers and the same qualities. In one of His Tablets 'Abdu'l-Bahá states:

> Know thou, O handmaid, that in the sight of Bahá, women are accounted the same as men, and God hath created all humankind in His own image, and after His own likeness. That is, men and women alike are the revealers of His names and attributes, and from the spiritual viewpoint there is no difference between them. Whosoever draweth nearer to God, that one is the most favoured, whether man or woman. How many a handmaid, ardent and devoted, hath, within the sheltering shade of Bahá, proved superior to the men, and surpassed the famous of the earth.[19]

As the soul is the supreme reality in a human being, far greater than the mortal frame, and is the most sacred trust of God within an individual, therefore the fundamental and the most valid reason for the equality of men and women lies in the equal status of their souls. This most important aspect of equality is often overlooked, in the same way and for the same reason that the soul itself is a subject commonly neglected by humanity in general.

14

Súriy-i-Vafá

In a Tablet known as the *Súriy-i-Vafá** Bahá'u'lláh refers to the immensity and boundlessness of the spiritual worlds. This Tablet was revealed in honour of a devoted believer from Shíráz who lived in Nayríz. He was Shaykh Muḥammad-Ḥusayn, surnamed Vafá (fidelity) by Bahá'u'lláh, and was one of the survivors of the upheaval in Nayríz. His father Mullá Báqir was the Imám-Jum'ih† of that city. When Vahíd arrived in Nayríz, Mullá Báqir and a great many people embraced the Bábí Faith, but most of them were massacred in that upheaval.‡ Mullá Báqir and his sons, including Vafá, were among the believers. However, because of his high office and his close links with the Imám-Jum'ih of Shíráz, who was a man of great influence, he and his sons were not persecuted and were among the survivors of that heroic struggle.

Vafá was a gifted poet and was respected by the inhabitants of Nayríz for his noble qualities as well as his learning and knowledge. He became a devoted follower of Bahá'u'lláh, one whose heart was overflowing with His love. The *Súriy-i-Vafá* was revealed in 'Akká in answer to some of his questions.

Concerning the spiritual worlds of God Bahá'u'lláh reveals these words:

> As to thy question concerning the worlds of God. Know thou of a truth that the worlds of God are countless in their number, and infinite in their range. None can reckon or comprehend

* This Tablet has been translated into English and is published in *Tablets of Bahá'u'lláh*, pp. 181–91.

† High-ranking religious leader of a city.

‡ For details see *The Dawn-Breakers*.

them except God, the All-Knowing, the All-Wise. Consider thy state when asleep. Verily, I say, this phenomenon is the most mysterious of the signs of God amongst men, were they to ponder it in their hearts. Behold how the thing which thou hast seen in thy dream is, after a considerable lapse of time, fully realized. Had the world in which thou didst find thyself in thy dream been identical with the world in which thou livest, it would have been necessary for the event occurring in that dream to have transpired in this world at the very moment of its occurrence. Were it so, you yourself would have borne witness unto it. This being not the case, however, it must necessarily follow that the world in which thou livest is different and apart from that which thou hast experienced in thy dream. This latter world hath neither beginning nor end. It would be true if thou wert to contend that this same world is, as decreed by the All-Glorious and Almighty God, within thy proper self and is wrapped up within thee. It would equally be true to maintain that thy spirit, having transcended the limitations of sleep and having stripped itself of all earthly attachment, hath, by the act of God, been made to traverse a realm which lieth hidden in the innermost reality of this world. Verily I say, the creation of God embraceth worlds besides this world, and creatures apart from these creatures. In each of these worlds He hath ordained things which none can search except Himself, the All-Searching, the All-Wise.[1]

Bahá'u'lláh highly praises Vafá, the recipient of the Tablet, for his faithfulness to the Covenant of God. Equally, He condemns the unfaithful – the followers of the Bayán, the Bábís – who had failed to recognize Him. About them He says:

For indeed they erred grievously, misguided the people, ignored the Covenant of God and His Testament and joined partners with Him, the One, the Incomparable, the All-Knowing. Verily they failed to recognize the Point of the Bayán,

> for had they recognized Him they would not have rejected His manifestation in this luminous and resplendent Being. And since they fixed their eyes on names, therefore when He replaced His Name 'the Most Exalted' by 'the Most Glorious' their eyes were dimmed. They have failed to recognize Him in these days and are reckoned with those that perish.[2]

The 'Point of the Bayán' in the above passage is a reference to the Báb. His name 'Alí' means 'Exalted', and therefore one of His titles is 'the Lord, the Most Exalted'. This term is used to identify the author of the Bábí Revelation. The word 'Bahá' means 'Glory'; it is the Greatest Name of God.* The term 'the Most Glorious' is thus distinctive of Bahá'u'lláh's Revelation and is associated with His person. In the above passage He states that a mere change of names and attributes has caused some of the Bábís to become deprived of His Revelation. In another instance in this Tablet, Bahá'u'lláh, referring to His Own Person, states:

> Verily this is the Primal Point, arrayed in His new attire and manifested in His glorious Name . . .
>
> Say, God is my witness! The Promised One Himself hath come down from heaven, seated upon the crimson cloud with the hosts of revelation on His right, and the angels of inspiration on His left, and the Decree hath been fulfilled at the behest of God, the Omnipotent, the Almighty.[3]

The Meaning of 'Return'

In this Tablet Bahá'u'lláh describes the meaning of return in the Day of Resurrection, which is the day of the appearance of the Manifestation of God. It is the day that the 'dead' will arise from their sepulchres. In the *Kitáb-i-Íqán* Bahá'u'lláh has explained that when a Manifestation of God appears, by

* see vol. 1, pp. 116–17.

recognizing Him the spiritually 'dead' becomes alive through the spirit of faith.*

In the *Súriy-i-Vafá* Bahá'u'lláh further explains:

> Know thou moreover that in the Day of His Manifestation all things besides God shall be brought forth and placed equally, irrespective of their rank being high or low. The Day of Return is inscrutable unto all men until after the divine Revelation hath been fulfilled. He is in truth the One Who ordaineth whatsoever He willeth. When the Word of God is revealed unto all created things whoso then giveth ear and heedeth the Call is, indeed, reckoned among the most distinguished souls, though he be a carrier of ashes. And he who turneth away is accounted as the lowliest of His servants, though he be a ruler amongst men and the possessor of all the books that are in the heavens and on earth.[4]

Another aspect of return described by Bahá'u'lláh is that God can, through His All-pervasive power and in the station of absolute authority, manifest in any soul the return of the qualities of another. He gives the example of the Báb, who pronounced Mullá Ḥusayn, the first to believe in Him, to be the return of the Prophet Muḥammad. These are the words of Bahá'u'lláh as revealed in the *Súriy-i-Vafá*:

> Consider thou the Revelation of the Point of the Bayán – exalted is His glory. He pronounced the First One† to believe in Him to be Muḥammad, the Messenger of God. Doth it beseem a man to dispute with Him by saying that this man is from Persia, the Other from Arabia, or this one was called Ḥusayn while the Other bore the name of Muḥammad? Nay, I swear by God's holy Being, the Exalted, the Most Great. Surely no man of intelligence and insight would ever pay

* see the *Kitáb-i-Íqán* and *The Revelation of Bahá'u'lláh*, vol. 1, pp. 184–5.

† Mullá Ḥusayn. (A.T.)

> attention unto limitations or names, but rather unto that with which Muḥammad was invested, which was none other than the Cause of God. Such a man of insight would likewise consider Ḥusayn and the position he occupied in the Cause of God, the Omnipotent, the Exalted, the Knowing, the Wise. And since the First One to believe in God in the Dispensation of the Bayán was invested with command similar to that with which Muḥammad, the Messenger of God, was invested, therefore the Báb pronounced him to be the latter, namely His return and resurrection. This station is sanctified from every limitation or name, and naught can be seen therein but God, the One, the Peerless, the All-Knowing.[5]

The Revelation of the Báb, being the harbinger of the advent of the Day of God, was invested with a special distinction and endowed with enormous potentialities. Similar to a seed which holds within itself the potentialities of a tree, His Cause gave birth to a mightier Revelation than His own. The Báb has been extolled by Bahá'u'lláh as the 'Point round Whom the realities of the Prophets and Messengers revolve', 'Whose rank excelleth that of all the Prophets', 'the King of Messengers' and 'the Essence of Essences'.

The bearer of such a Revelation, who on the day of His declaration to Mullá Ḥusayn inaugurated the Bahá'í Cycle destined to last for no less than five thousand centuries, had among the first contingent of His followers some souls who were the return* of the realities of Prophets and Chosen Ones. For instance, the Báb bestowed upon Mullá 'Alíy-i-Baṣṭámí, the fourth Letter of the Living, the station of Imám 'Alí, who in the view of Shí'ah Islám is the true successor of Muḥammad. This He did when He sent Mullá 'Alí to deliver His newly-revealed words into the hands of Shaykh Muḥammad-Ḥasan-i-Najafí, one of the leading religious leaders in 'Iráq. In His Message to this divine, the Báb clearly stated that the bearer of the message

* see also vol. 2, p. 182.

was the return of the reality of Imám 'Alí.

Mullá Ḥusayn, the first Letter of the Living, was acclaimed by Bahá'u'lláh as one 'But for him, God would not have been established upon the seat of His mercy, nor ascended the throne of eternal glory'.[6] It was he who in the last year of his life attired his head with one of the Báb's green turbans which had been sent to him by his Lord, mounted his steed at Mashhad in Khurásán, unfurled the Black Standard and marched at the head of two hundred and two of his fellow Bábís towards Mázindarán where most of them laid down their lives in the path of their Beloved.* On such a person the Báb conferred the station of the Prophet of Islám.

Upon Quddús, the last Letter of the Living but the most eminent among His disciples, the Báb conferred a far greater station than that of Mullá Ḥusayn's. When the Báb was held in captivity in the mountains of Ádhirbáyján it was to Quddús that all the believers turned with the same degree of devotion, love and obedience, as they had done in relation to their Lord. Notable among those who did this was Mullá Ḥusayn. He showed the same humility and subordination to Quddús as he did to the Báb Himself. The recognition of the station of Quddús came to Mullá Ḥusayn in a mysterious way reminiscent of his memorable experience of his first meeting with the Báb some years earlier.

Nabíl has recorded this fascinating story, the perusal of which unfolds before the eyes a magnificent spectacle in which the hands of the Almighty can be seen directing every act of a moving drama performed by a band of men whose ranks equal those of Prophets and Messengers of God.[7]

One of the Báb's titles is the 'Primal Point'. Bahá'u'lláh

* For further information about this heroic episode, see *The Dawn-Breakers*, chapters XIV and XIX. In those days the type of one's head-dress was indicative of one's status in the community. The significance of the Black Standard comes from the ḥadíth (tradition) of Islám which states that whenever it was unfurled at Khurásán, it would signalize the advent of God's new Revelation on earth.

conferred the sublime title of 'the last Point' upon Quddús, stated that he was one of the 'Messengers charged with imposture' mentioned in the *Qur'án*, and elevated him to a rank next to that of the Báb. To contemplate these issues may be perplexing to some. The mind staggers at the thought that owing to the greatness of this Revelation some of its early disciples have been given the station of the Messengers of God. In the *Súriy-i-Vafá* Bahá'u'lláh has clarified this point by stating that God is the 'One Who doeth and ordaineth all things', and to no one is given the right to object. These are some of His words in that Tablet:

> Verily God is fully capable of causing all names to appear in one name, and all souls in one soul. Surely powerful and mighty is He . . .
>
> For instance, were He to take a handful of earth and declare it to be the One Whom ye have been following in the past, it would undoubtedly be just and true, even as His real Person, and to none is given the right to question His authority. He doeth what He willeth and ordaineth whatsoever He pleaseth. Moreover, in this station take thou heed not to turn thy gaze unto limitations and allusions, but rather unto that whereby the Revelation itself hath been fulfilled and be of them that are discerning . . .
>
> Know thou moreover that in the Day of Revelation were He to pronounce one of the leaves* to be the manifestation of all His excellent titles, unto no one is given the right to utter why or wherefore, and should one do so he would be regarded as a disbeliever in God and be numbered with such as have repudiated His Truth.[8]

In the *Súriy-i-Vafá* Bahá'u'lláh explains the meaning of heaven and hell. Heaven is not a place, but nearness to God, and hell is remoteness from Him. In this Tablet He states that in this world

* A designation for women. (A.T.)

heaven 'is realized through love of Me and My good-pleasure'. He further asserts that 'for every act performed there shall be a recompense according to the estimate of God'.[9] Indeed, within every action is embodied its reward or punishment. For instance, punishment for an ignorant man is his ignorance, and the reward for a learned person is his knowledge.

There is another subject in this Tablet, which concerns Mírzá Yaḥyá. Bahá'u'lláh alludes to him and those who supported him when he mentions Sámirí and the calf.[10] This is a reference to the verses of the *Qur'án*[*] in which the story of Sámirí is told. According to the *Qur'án*, he was the one who made the golden calf for the children of Israel to worship during the absence of Moses.

The 'Portals of True Understanding'

There is a passage in the *Súriy-i-Vafá* which may be regarded as one of the most edifying counsels which the Pen of the Most High has revealed. It is an exhortation to the believers which, if carried out, can lead to greater understanding of the verities enshrined in the Cause of God.

> O servant! Warn thou the servants of God not to reject that which they do not comprehend. Say, implore God to open to your hearts the portals of true understanding that ye may be apprised of that of which no one is apprised. Verily, He is the Giver, the Forgiving, the Compassionate.[11]

When a person recognizes Bahá'u'lláh as the Manifestation of God for this age and embraces his Faith, he knows that the words revealed by Him are the Words of God. All the teachings, laws and ordinances are therefore based on the truth of God's Revelation. The knowledge which is derived from His words is the standard against which all human understanding

* see *Qur'án* 20:87–98.

and knowledge must be weighed. In the *Kitáb-i-Aqdas* Bahá'u'lláh thus admonishes the leaders of religion:

> Say: O leaders of religion! Weigh not the Book of God with such standards and sciences as are current amongst you, for the Book itself is the unerring balance established amongst men. In this most perfect balance whatsoever the peoples and kindreds of the earth possess must be weighed, while the measure of its weight should be tested according to its own standard, did ye but know it.[12]

It is, of course, natural that a believer may not understand the wisdom of a certain teaching, or may have difficulty in adjusting his own views on an issue to the teachings of the Faith. The way to resolve such a conflict is to study the Holy Writings further and to discuss the problem with knowledgeable believers. But if every approach fails, and the person does not succeed in reconciling his views with the teachings of the Faith, the only sure way to bring confirmation to his soul is to carry out Bahá'u'lláh's exhortation in the above passage in the *Súriy-i-Vafá*. According to this, two steps must be taken. First, not to reject those teachings which the individual cannot comprehend. This can be done through having faith in the truth of the Word of God and becoming humble before Him. Indeed, the believer becomes filled with heavenly strength when he can acknowledge in his heart that man is a fallible being, whereas the teachings of God are based on truth. To insist that one is right in his views and opinions is to erect a barrier between himself and God. The mere acknowledgement of one's imperfections and inadequacies is a major steppingstone to resolving the conflict and finding the truth.

The second step is to pray ardently that God may open to one's heart 'the portals of true understanding'. This is a stage in which the light of knowledge will shine within the heart of the believer and he will be 'apprised' of the things he could not comprehend earlier. The knowledge of God and a true understanding of His teachings can come about when the believer approaches Him in a spirit of utter humility and submissiveness, and opens his heart fully to the outpourings of His Revelation. Then and only then will the vernal showers of His unfailing grace cause the tree of knowledge and wisdom to grow within the heart, and enable him to bring forth, in the fullness of time, the fruit of understanding. When this stage is reached, the individual will be aided to comprehend the truth of the Word and discover the manifold mysteries that are enshrined within God's Revelation. Knowledge of spiritual truth comes through the heart of man. The intellect will then grasp the subject and reason will emerge. There is a tradition in Islám which Bahá'u'lláh confirms in the *Kitáb-i-Íqán*, stating that 'knowledge is a light which God sheddeth into the heart of whomsoever He willeth'. This is a knowledge which wells out of the heart of the believer and is independent of academic learning.

15

Kalimát-i-Firdawsíyyih

Another Tablet in which Bahá'u'lláh proclaims some of His basic teachings is the *Kalimát-i-Firdawsíyyih* (Words of Paradise).* This Tablet was revealed about two years before His ascension in honour of His trusted disciple Ḥájí Mírzá Ḥaydar-'Alí. Bahá'u'lláh's exhortations and counsels in this Tablet are no less soul-stirring and significant than those in His other Tablets mentioned previously in this book.

In this Tablet Bahá'u'lláh calls upon 'the People of Bahá to render the Lord victorious through the power of their utterance and to admonish the people by their goodly deeds and character'. He declares that man will be exalted through 'honesty, virtue, wisdom and saintly character'; considers the 'fear of God' to be 'a sure defence and a safe stronghold for all the peoples of the world';† enjoins upon the world's rulers, its divines and the wise 'to uphold the cause of religion' and regard it as 'the chief instrument for the establishment of order in the world and of tranquillity amongst its peoples'; acclaims the greatness of His Day;‡ counsels His followers 'to adhere tenaciously to unity and concord'; urges them 'to labour diligently in promoting the Cause of God'; admonishes the 'men of wisdom among nations' to shut their 'eyes to estrangement', to fix their 'gaze upon unity', to 'cleave tenaciously unto that which will lead to the well-being and tranquillity of all mankind'; declares that 'this span of earth is but one homeland and one habitation'; asserts that the 'basis of world order

* A full translation of this Tablet is published in *Tablets of Bahá'u'lláh*, pp. 57–80.

† For a further discussion on this subject see above, pp. 27–9.

‡ see above, pp. 130–45.

hath been firmly established upon reward and punishment';* warns that the world's corruptions, so deeply rooted, cannot be purged 'unless the peoples of the world unite in pursuit of one common aim and embrace one universal faith'; advocates that 'schools must first train the children in the principles of religion';† urges the establishment of a universal language; and states that 'in all matters moderation is desirable', explaining that 'if a thing is carried to excess, it will prove a source of evil'.

Furthermore, in the *Kalimát-i-Firdawsíyyih* Bahá'u'lláh disapproves of 'living in seclusion or practising asceticism',‡ saying that these practices are 'sprung from the loins of idle fancy', or 'begotten of the womb of superstition', and that they 'ill beseem men of knowledge'. He also refers to the mystics,§ 'some of whom indulge in that which leadeth to idleness and seclusion'. He condemns their way of life which 'lowereth man's station and maketh him swell with pride', and teaches that 'man must bring forth fruit. One who yieldeth no fruit is, in the words of the Spirit [Jesus], like unto a fruitless tree, and a fruitless tree is fit but for fire.'

Most of these teachings extracted from the *Kalimát-i-Firdawsíyyih* have already been mentioned in other Tablets and quoted in more detail in this book.

In this Tablet Bahá'u'lláh authorizes the members of the Universal House of Justice 'to take counsel together regarding those things which have not been outwardly revealed in the Book', and commands them 'to ensure the protection and safeguarding of men, women and children'.

Bahá'u'lláh has revealed the laws of this Dispensation, which must last for at least one thousand years. These laws are described as the warp and woof of His World Order, and

---

* For an explanation of the need for punishment see vol. 3, pp. 294–7.

† see vol. 3, pp. 326–331.

‡ see vol. 2, pp. 34–7, and above, pp. 170–2.

§ see vol. 2, pp. 24–8.

no one can abrogate them except the next Manifestation of God. But there are some laws which Bahá'u'lláh, through His wisdom, has not ordained. Some of these are temporary and may be changed with the passage of time. The Universal House of Justice has the authority to enact such laws. It can also resolve any matters which are not specified in the Writings, as well as deciding on the application of the laws revealed by Bahá'u'lláh.*

Expounding the greatness of His Revelation, Bahá'u'lláh reveals these thought-provoking words in the *Kalimát-i-Firdawsíyyih*:

> O people of God! Great is the Day and mighty the Call! In one of Our Tablets We have revealed these exalted words: 'Were the world of the spirit to be wholly converted into the sense of hearing, it could then claim to be worthy to hearken unto the Voice that calleth from the Supreme Horizon; for otherwise, these ears that are defiled with lying tales have never been, nor are they now fit to hear it.' Well is it with them that hearken; and woe betide the wayward.[1]

These words clearly indicate that no one in this world is worthy to embrace the Cause of God. How immeasurable is the gap between the immensity of the 'world of the spirit . . . wholly converted into the sense of hearing', and the feebleness of a human being. How vast is the difference between the glory of God's heavenly Revelation and the human's attachments to earthly things. That some have recognized the station of Bahá'u'lláh in this Day and embraced His faith is due to the bounty of God and not man's worthiness. Creation has come into being through the bounty of God, and not through His justice; so has His Revelation. Man, a finite being, does not merit such a glorious gift from his Creator. To this a Bahá'í testifies every day when he performs one of the Obligatory Prayers:

* see vol. 3, pp. 275–94.

. . . O God, my God! Thy forgiveness hath emboldened me, and Thy mercy hath strengthened me, and Thy call hath awakened me, and Thy grace hath raised me up and led me unto Thee. Who, otherwise, am I that I should dare to stand at the gate of the city of Thy nearness, or set my face toward the lights that are shining from the heaven of Thy will? Thou seest, O my Lord, this wretched creature knocking at the door of Thy grace, and this evanescent soul seeking the river of everlasting life from the hands of Thy bounty. Thine is the command at all times, O Thou Who art the Lord of all names; and mine is resignation and willing submission to Thy will, O Creator of the heavens![2]

Although man is unworthy, he can nevertheless become an embodiment of heavenly attributes once he attires himself with the vesture of faith. For it is through having faith and believing in the Manifestation of God for this age that the individual becomes the recipient of divine assistance from on high.

'Abdu'l-Bahá is reported to have said these words in the course of His parting address to the first group of western pilgrims who visited Him in 'Akká in 1899:

And now I give you a commandment which shall be for a covenant between you and Me – that ye have faith; that your faith be steadfast as a rock that no storms can move, that nothing can disturb, and that it endure through all things even to the end; even should ye hear that your Lord has been crucified, be not shaken in your faith; for I am with you always, whether living or dead, I am with you to the end. As ye have faith so shall your powers and blessings be. This is the balance – this is the balance – this is the balance.[3]

In the *Kalimát-i-Firdawsíyyih* Bahá'u'lláh issues these challenging words to the divines:

> Say: O concourse of divines! Pronounce ye censure against this Pen unto which, as soon as it raised its shrill voice, the kingdom of utterance prepared itself to hearken, and before whose mighty and glorious theme every other theme hath paled into insignificance? Fear ye God and follow not your idle fancies and corrupt imaginings, but rather follow Him Who is come unto you invested with undeniable knowledge and unshakeable certitude.[4]

The 'shrill voice' of the Pen of Bahá'u'lláh has been raised amidst the peoples of the world, but few have yet been awakened by its clarion call proclaiming to all mankind the advent of the Day of God. The significance of the term 'shrill voice of the Pen' which repeatedly appears in the Writings has been briefly explained in a previous volume.* The term 'kingdom of utterance' also appears in many of Bahá'u'lláh's Writings. The word 'Kingdom' has been used by Bahá'u'lláh to express the spiritual realms of God which are beyond the understanding of man. For instance, we come across such terms as 'the Kingdom of Revelation', 'the Kingdom of Creation', 'the Kingdom of divine power', 'the Kingdoms of earth and heaven', 'the Kingdom of glory', 'the Kingdom of names', and more. That the 'Kingdom of utterance' – the realm from which the word of God is revealed – has 'prepared itself to hearken' to the outpourings of the 'Supreme Pen' is an amazing statement, and an indication of the greatness of Bahá'u'lláh's Revelation. He further reveals these words:

> The Ocean of utterance exclaimeth and saith: 'O ye dwellers on the earth! Behold My billowing waters and the pearls of wisdom and utterance which I have poured forth. Fear ye God and be not of the heedless.'
>
> In this Day a great festival is taking place in the Realm above; for whatsoever was promised in the sacred Scriptures

* see vol. 1, p. 35.

> hath been fulfilled. This is the Day of great rejoicing. It behoveth everyone to hasten towards the court of His nearness with exceeding joy, gladness, exultation and delight and to deliver himself from the fire of remoteness.[5]

In a Tablet[6] revealed in 1887–8 to Ḥájí Áqá Muḥammad-i-'Aláqih-band, one of His devoted followers in Yazd, Bahá'u'lláh states that when He is revealing the verses of God all the inmates of the highest Paradise, and the Concourse on High, present themselves before Him to hear His Voice raised between earth and heaven. In another Tablet He testifies that if the divines and men of learning were able to be in His presence* when revelation of the Word of God takes place, they would be so influenced as to be left with no other choice but to acknowledge the truth of His Cause. To another believer, Bahá'u'lláh intimates in a Tablet[7] that if he were present at the time of revelation he would be so exhilarated that his soul would take its flight into the realms of the spirit which are hidden from the eyes of men.

In one of His Tablets[8] Bahá'u'lláh discloses the intensity with which the verses of God have been sent down in this Dispensation. From the tone of this Tablet it appears that it was revealed towards the end of His earthly life. In it He states that His amanuensis, Mírzá Áqá Ján, used to take down the verses of God which were revealed continuously from morning till evening. He describes how in earlier days He had been engaged in revealing the Words during both day and night, and would only interrupt His utterances in order to attend to other matters. In those days, He affirms, the Tongue of Grandeur was continually revealing the verses of God. But now, at the time of revealing this Tablet, He intimates that owing to physical weakness He has had to bring His utterances to a close after one hour of revelation. But whenever He resumes, all the members of His body will be activated and the verses of

* For further information see vol. 2, p. 254.

God will transform His whole Being. This condition of physical weakness Bahá'u'lláh attributes to the sufferings inflicted on Him by the people of tyranny. They have been the cause of the withholding of the further diffusion of divine fragrances among mankind. But he assures the recipient of this Tablet that until His spirit takes its flight to His other Dominions, the Tongue of Grandeur shall continue to speak and the Pen of the Most High move upon His Tablets.

In the *Kalimát-i-Firdawsíyyih* as in His other Tablets Bahá'u'lláh rebukes the people of the Bayán, the followers of Mírzá Yaḥyá, for their waywardness and ignorance. He thus addresses them:

> Glorified be God! One wondereth by what proof or reason the disbelievers among the people of the Bayán have turned away from the Lord of being. In truth the station of this Revelation transcendeth the station of whatever hath been manifested in the past or will be made manifest in the future.[9]

And then He makes this statement which may only be described as astounding:

> Were the Point of the Bayán* present in this day and should He, God forbid, hesitate to acknowledge this Cause, then the very blessed words which have streamed forth from the wellspring of His Own Bayán would apply to Him. He saith, and His word is the truth, 'Lawful is it for Him Whom God will make manifest to reject him who is the greatest on earth.' Say, O ye that are bereft of understanding! Today that Most Exalted Being is proclaiming: 'Verily, verily, I am the first to adore Him.' How shallow is the fund of men's knowledge and how feeble their power of perception. Our Pen of Glory beareth witness to their abject poverty and to the wealth of God, the Lord of all worlds.[10]

* The Báb. (A. T.)

He also addresses Mírzá Yaḥyá, His unfaithful brother, in these challenging words reminding him of earlier days when he used to take down the words of Bahá'u'lláh and with His permission disseminate them among the Bábís in his own name as the leader of the Bábí community:

> Say: O Yaḥyá (Azal), produce a single verse, if thou dost possess divinely-inspired knowledge. These words were formerly spoken by My Herald Who at this hour proclaimeth: 'Verily, verily, I am the first to adore Him.' Be fair, O My brother. Art thou able to express thyself when brought face to face with the billowing ocean of Mine utterance? Canst thou unloose thy tongue when confronted with the shrill voice of My Pen? Hast thou any power before the revelations of Mine omnipotence? Judge thou fairly, I adjure thee by God, and call to mind when thou didst stand in the presence of this Wronged One and We dictated to thee the verses of God, the Help in Peril, the Self-Subsisting. Beware lest the source of falsehood withhold thee from the manifest Truth.[11]

Another person, a Muslim, who is rebuked by Bahá'u'lláh in this Tablet is Ḥájí Mullá Hádíy-i-Sabzavárí, a noted philosopher of the time and a renowned poet, who died in 1873. He was the author of several books on divine philosophy, and his works are available both in verse and prose. In one of his poems Mullá Hádí boasts about his own spiritual perception. It is believed that Moses heard the voice of God from the Burning Bush; Mullá Hádí states in his poem that nowadays there is no Moses around and the voice 'I am God' can be heard from every tree. It is because of this claim that Bahá'u'lláh in several of His Tablets condemned this man as worthless, as he had failed to hearken to His voice in this great Day of God. He thus refers to him in the *Kalimát-i-Firdawsíyyih*:

> The sage of Sabzivár hath said: 'Alas! Attentive ears are

lacking, otherwise the whisperings of the Sinaic Bush could be heard from every tree.' In a Tablet to a man of wisdom who had made enquiry as to the meaning of Elementary Reality, We addressed this famous sage in these words: 'If this saying is truly thine, how is it that thou hast failed to hearken unto the Call which the Tree of Man hath raised from the loftiest heights of the world? If thou didst hear the Call yet fear and the desire to preserve thy life prompted thee to remain heedless to it, thou art such a person as hath never been nor is worthy of mention; if thou hast not heard it, then thou are bereft of the sense of hearing.' In brief, such men are they whose words are the pride of the world, and whose deeds are the shame of the nations.

Verily We have sounded the Trumpet which is none other than My Pen of Glory, and lo, mankind hath swooned away before it, save them whom God pleaseth to deliver as a token of His grace. He is the Lord of bounty, the Ancient of Days.[12]

A person who is remembered with affection in the *Kalimát-i-Firdawsíyyi*h is Mírzá Abu'l-Qásim-i-Faráhání, entitled Qá'im-Maqám. He is not named, but is referred to in this Tablet as 'Prince of the City of Statesmanship and Literary Accomplishment'. He was a contemporary of Bahá'u'lláh's father and a faithful friend of his, highly acclaimed at the court of Fatḥ-'Alí Sháh* for his wisdom, uprightness, benevolence, courage and dignity as well as his learning and knowledge. He was a highly gifted writer whose compositions are considered to be among the best in the literary field. As a statesman he was very capable; 'Abdu'l-Bahá has described him as foremost in the whole of Persia. He became Prime Minister in 1821 and continued to hold this position until the reign of Muḥammad Sháh (1834–48). In a country where injustice and corruption were rife he upheld standards of justice and honesty. As a result his enemies conspired against him, poisoned the mind of

* Reigned 1797–1834.

the monarch and made him believe that his Prime Minister was about to overthrow him. These falsehoods gained credibility and Muḥammad Sháh became filled with fear. In 1835 Qá'im-Maqám was executed in Ṭihrán by his orders.

In the Writings of Bahá'u'lláh one can hardly find a word of praise directed at any of the authorities in Persia. The tribute He has paid to Qá'im-Maqám is unique, and indicative of the greatness of this man. Bahá'u'lláh finds that no actions on the part of Muḥammad Sháh were more heinous than the banishment of the Báb to the fortress of Máh-Kú and the murder of Qá'im-Maqám.

But God rewards His faithful servants in mysterious ways. One of Qá'im-Maqám's grandsons, Mírzá Áqá Khán (entitled Qá'im-Maqámí) had inherited all the outstanding qualities of his paternal grandfather. He was the embodiment of dignity, benevolence and courage, a man of culture and erudition. He grew up in the luxurious home of his ancestors in Arák. On one of his teaching trips, Siyyid Asadu'lláh-i-Qumí, a renowned teacher of the Faith,* arrived in Arák. The father of Mírzá Áqá Khán, being an open-minded and liberal person, invited Siyyid Asadu'lláh to his home knowing that he was a Bahá'í teacher. At that time Mírzá Áqá Khán was a youth and an enthusiastic Muslim. He became highly indignant that his father was entertaining a Bahá'í in the house, and decided to put an end to it. Believing that he would win the good-pleasure of God if he killed a Bahá'í, he proceeded to attack Siyyid Asadu'lláh, but the latter through his charm and loving personality succeeded in calming him down. Soon in that same house Mírzá Áqá Khán found himself sitting spellbound at the feet of Siyyid Asadu'lláh, listening to his words as he produced proofs of the authenticity of the station of Bahá'u'lláh. So profound and convincing were his arguments and so radiant his spirit that Mírzá Áqá Khán and his cousin both became ardent believers.

As time went by Mírzá Áqá Khán became a truly

* see above, pp. 195–6.

MÍRZÁ ABU'L-QÁSIM-I-FARÁHÁNÍ, QÁ'IM-MAQÁM (left) and ÁQÁ KHÁN-I-QÁ'IM-MAQÁMÍ (right)

Áqá Khán was the grandson of Qá'im-Maqám and an eminent Bahá'í

outstanding Bahá'í. To the nobility and courage of his character was now added the power of faith. He arose to serve the Cause with a zeal and devotion which few among his contemporaries could match. At first he began to earn a modest living and became independent of his father's wealth, but soon he was faced with serious financial difficulties. Then he had a dream: Bahá'u'lláh appeared to him, pointed to a hill nearby, and directed him to dig out some valuable relics which were buried on the side of the hill. Believing his dream to be true, Mírzá Áqá Khán carried out the excavation and recovered a great quantity of priceless relics and jewels. He thus became one of the richest men in Arák and the most influential of its residents. Throughout his long years of life he used his enormous wealth and influence to further the interests of the Cause he loved and served so well. Although he was wealthy, he lived a very simple life. He was a tower of strength for the believers and a guide and refuge for the downtrodden and the needy. His generosity, magnanimity and care for the welfare of people earned him the love and respect of the public in general and the Bahá'ís in particular.

In a Tablet addressed to him[13] 'Abdu'l-Bahá states that his grandfather, Qá'im-Maqám, is rejoicing in the Abhá Kingdom, for God has enabled his grandson to become a sign of guidance to the people, a bearer of the standard of the Kingdom and a manifestation of the bounties of heaven.

Kalimát-i-Firdawsíyyih was revealed about two years before the passing of Bahá'u'lláh, as we have said. Yet in it He reveals these prophetic words which were realized decades later through the discovery of nuclear energy:

> Strange and astonishing things exist in the earth but they are hidden from the minds and the understanding of men. These things are capable of changing the whole atmosphere of the earth and their contamination would prove lethal.[14]

It is noteworthy that in 1911 in Paris in the course of a conversation with Viscount Arawaka, the Japanese Ambassador to Spain, 'Abdu'l-Bahá spoke these words:

> Scientific discoveries have increased material civilization. There is in existence a stupendous force, as yet, happily, undiscovered by man. Let us supplicate God, the Beloved, that this force be not discovered by science until spiritual civilization shall dominate the human mind. In the hands of men of lower material nature, this power would be able to destroy the whole earth.[15]

In a previous volume* there is a reference to the words of Bahá'u'lláh concerning the discovery of alchemy, the transmutation of elements, which He links with the coming of a great calamity for the whole world. It is known that the transmutation of elements is now possible through certain nuclear processes.

The following passage in the *Kalimát-i-Firdawsíyyih* needs some explanation. In many Tablets revealed during the latter part of His Ministry Bahá'u'lláh describes to some of His faithful disciples the anguish of His heart because of the misdeeds of a few of His so-called followers who had joined hands with the supporters of Mírzá Yaḥyá in Constantinople in attempting to dishonour the good name of the Faith and its Author. This distressing episode brought great sorrow to Bahá'u'lláh towards the end of His earthly life.

> O thou who hast turned thy gaze towards My face! In these days there occurred that which hath plunged Me into dire sadness. Certain wrong-doers who profess allegiance to the Cause of God committed such deeds as have caused the limbs of sincerity, of honesty, of justice, of equity to quake. One known individual to whom the utmost kindness and favour

* see vol. 2, p. 268.

> had been extended perpetrated such acts as have brought tears to the eye of God. Formerly We uttered words of warning and premonition, then for a number of years We kept the matter secret that haply he might take heed and repent. But all to no purpose. In the end he bent his energies upon vilifying the Cause of God before the eyes of all men. He tore the veil of fairness asunder and felt sympathy neither for himself nor for the Cause of God. Now, however, the deeds of certain individuals have brought sorrows far more grievous than those which the deeds of the former had caused. Beseech thou God, the True One, that He may graciously enable the heedless to retract and repent. Verily He is the Forgiving, the Bountiful, the Most Generous. [16]

The 'one known individual' mentioned above is a certain Muḥammad-'Alíy-i-Iṣfahání, not to be confused with Siyyid Muḥammad-i-Iṣfahání, the Anti-Christ of Bahá'u'lláh's Revelation. A brief account of this episode is given in Chapter 25.

16

Other Outstanding Tablets

Innumerable are the Tablets which streamed forth from the Most Exalted Pen after the *Kitáb-i-Aqdas* was revealed. Most of these are not as yet available in English. The few which are may be studied in *Tablets of Bahá'u'lláh revealed After the Kitáb-i-Aqdas*.

Lawḥ-i-Aqdas

This Tablet,* otherwise known as the 'Tablet to the Christians', is in Arabic and addresses a believer of Christian background. It is believed by some that it was revealed in honour of the Syrian convert to the Faith, Fáris Effendi, the fascinating circumstances of whose conversion have been described in a previous volume,† but there is so far no conclusive evidence to prove this. All we can say is that possibly he was the recipient of this Tablet. Prior to its revelation Bahá'u'lláh had addressed some Tablets‡ to people of the Christian Faith, but the *Lawḥ-i-Aqdas* seems to be the first major Tablet to a believer of Christian background.

In this Tablet Bahá'u'lláh proclaims His message to the Christian people. In clear and unequivocal terms He declares His station to be that of the Father whose advent Jesus Christ had promised, and through whom the Spirit of Truth has been manifested to man. He describes His Supreme Revelation in these words to the Christians, whom He addresses as 'followers of the Son':

---

* Not to be confused with the *Kitáb-i-Aqdas*, the full text of this Tablet has been translated into English and published in *Tablets of Bahá'u'lláh*, pp. 9–17.

† see vol. 3, pp. 5–11.

‡ see vol. 3, p. 244.

> The river Jordan is joined to the Most Great Ocean, and the Son, in the holy vale, crieth out: 'Here am I, here am I, O Lord, my God!', whilst Sinai circleth round the House, and the Burning Bush calleth aloud: 'He Who is the Desired One is come in His transcendent majesty.' Say, Lo! The Father is come, and that which ye were promised in the Kingdom is fulfilled! This is the Word which the Son concealed, when to those around Him He said: 'Ye cannot bear it now.' And when the appointed time was fulfilled and the Hour had struck, the Word shone forth above the horizon of the Will of God. Beware, O followers of the Son, that ye cast it not behind your backs. Take ye fast hold of it. Better is this for you than all that ye possess.[1]

In another passage He admonishes the Christians for not having recognized Him, and likens them to the Jews at the time of Christ:

> Say, O followers of the Son! Have ye shut out yourselves from Me by reason of My Name? Wherefore ponder ye not in your hearts? Day and night ye have been calling upon your Lord, the Omnipotent, but when He came from the heaven of eternity in His great glory, ye turned aside from Him and remained sunk in heedlessness.
>
> Consider those who rejected the Spirit* when He came unto them with manifest dominion. How numerous the Pharisees who had secluded themselves in synagogues in His name, lamenting over their separation from Him, and yet when the portals of reunion were flung open and the divine Luminary shone resplendent from the Dayspring of Beauty, they disbelieved in God, the Exalted, the Mighty. They failed to attain His presence, notwithstanding that His advent had been promised them in the Book of Isaiah as well as in the Books of the Prophets and the Messengers. No one from among them

* Jesus Christ. (A.T.)

> turned his face towards the Dayspring of divine bounty except such as were destitute of any power amongst men. And yet, today, every man endowed with power and invested with sovereignty prideth himself on His Name. Moreover, call thou to mind the one who sentenced Jesus to death. He was the most learned of His age in His own country, whilst he who was only a fisherman believed in Him. Take good heed and be of them that observe the warning.
>
> Consider likewise, how numerous at this time are the monks who have secluded themselves in their churches, calling upon the Spirit, but when He appeared through the power of Truth, they failed to draw nigh unto Him and are numbered with those that have gone far astray.[2]

In this Tablet Bahá'u'lláh addresses the priests, the bishops and the monks, and announces to them the joyful tidings of His Revelation.

> O concourse of bishops! Ye are the stars of the heaven of My knowledge. My mercy desireth not that ye should fall upon the earth. My justice, however, declareth: 'This is that which the Son hath decreed.' And whatsoever hath proceeded out of His blameless, His truth-speaking, trustworthy mouth, can never be altered.[3]

This is a reference to the passage in the Gospels about the falling of the stars which must signalize the advent of the Lord. In His Tablets Bahá'u'lláh has explained that by 'stars' are meant the clergy, who were shining in the firmament of Christendom but who have now fallen for not recognizing Him in this day when He has returned in the glory of the Father. This subject, along with the falling stars of 1866, has been discussed in greater detail in a previous volume.*

In other Tablets Bahá'u'lláh addresses similar statements

* see vol. 2, p. 270, and Appendix I, pp. 422–6.

to the aristocracy of the Church, exhorting and admonishing them in these challenging words:

> Say: O concourse of archbishops! He Who is the Lord of all men hath appeared. In the plain of guidance He calleth mankind, whilst ye are numbered with the dead! Great is the blessedness of him who is stirred by the Breeze of God, and hath arisen from amongst the dead in this perspicuous Name.
>
> Say: O concourse of bishops! Trembling hath seized all the kindreds of the earth, and He Who is the Everlasting Father calleth aloud between earth and heaven. Blessed the ear that hath heard, and the eye that hath seen, and the heart that hath turned unto Him Who is the Point of Adoration of all who are in the heavens and all who are on earth.[4]

> O concourse of priests! The Day of Reckoning hath appeared, the Day whereon He Who was in heaven hath come. He, verily, is the One Whom ye were promised in the Books of God, the Holy, the Almighty, the All-Praised. How long will ye wander in the wilderness of heedlessness and superstition? Turn with your hearts in the direction of your Lord, the Forgiving, the Generous.[5]

In the Tablet of Aqdas too Bahá'u'lláh addresses the priests of Christendom. This is part of His call:

> O concourse of priests! Leave the bells, and come forth, then, from your churches. It behoveth you, in this day, to proclaim aloud the Most Great Name among the nations. Prefer ye to be silent, whilst every stone and every tree shouteth aloud: 'The Lord is come in His great glory!'[6]

With these commanding words Bahá'u'lláh has summoned the Christian clergy to come out of their churches and proclaim His Cause to all mankind. His summons has for the most part fallen on deaf ears. Very few among leading Christian ecclesiastics have so far paid any attention to Bahá'u'lláh's clarion call of the Advent of the Day of God.

Notable among those few churchmen who have recognized His station and arisen to serve His Cause was an Irishman, George Townshend, sometime Canon of St. Patrick's Cathedral in Dublin and Archdeacon of Clonfert. A remarkable man, a spiritual giant, a writer and scholar of note, he dedicated almost forty years of his life to the promotion of the Faith of Bahá'u'lláh and was appointed towards the end of his life as a Hand of the Cause of God by the Guardian of the Bahá'í Faith. George Townshend was born in Ireland around the time that the 'Tablet to the Christians' was revealed. The news of the coming of Bahá'u'lláh reached him towards the end of 1916 during the Ministry of 'Abdu'l-Bahá. As he moved from the valley of search into the city of certitude, he made his declaration of faith in the form of a moving poem addressed to 'Abdu'l-Bahá, a poem which indicates the depth of his faith and understanding:

> Hail to Thee, Scion of Glory, Whose utterance poureth abroad
> The joy of the heavenly knowledge and the light of the greatest of days!
> Poet of mysteries chanting in rapture the beauty of God,
> Unto Thee be thanksgiving and praise!
>
> Child of the darkness that wandered in gloom but dreamed of the light,
> Lo! I have seen Thy splendour ablaze in the heavens afar
> Showering gladness and glory and shattering the shadows of night,
> And seen no other star.
>
> Thy words are to me as fragrances borne from the garden of heaven,
> Beams of a lamp that is hid in the height of a holier world,

> Arrows of fire that pierce and destroy with the might of the
> levin
> Into our midnight hurled.
>
> Sword of the Father! None other can rend the dark veil from
> my eyes,
> None other can beat from my limbs with the shearing blade
> of God's might
> The sins I am fettered withal and give me the power to rise
> And come forth to the fullness of light.
>
> Lo! Thou hast breathed on my sorrow the sweetness of faith
> and of hope,
> Thou hast chanted high paeans of joy that my heart's echoes
> ever repeat
> And the path to the knowledge of God begins to glimmer and
> ope
> Before my faltering feet.
>
> Weak and unworthy my praise. Yet, as from its throbbing
> throat
> Some lone bird pours its song to the flaming infinite sky,
> So unto Thee in the zenith I lift from a depth remote
> This broken human cry.[7]

In the *Lawḥ-i-Aqdas* Bahá'u'lláh states:

> In the East the Light of His Revelation hath broken; in the West the signs of His dominion have appeared.[8]

From the early days of His Revelation, Bahá'u'lláh has prophesied that His Cause will be taken to the West and from there its light will be diffused to all regions. When He was in Constantinople before the proclamation of His Faith, Bahá'u'lláh in His *Mathnaví** calls on Himself to unveil His glory to mankind, so that the Sun of His Revelation may arise from the West.

'Abdu'l-Bahá has likewise declared:

> From the beginning of time until the present day, the light of Divine Revelation hath risen in the East and shed its radiance upon the West. The illumination thus shed hath, however, acquired in the West an extraordinary brilliancy. Consider the Faith proclaimed by Jesus. Though it first appeared in the East, yet not until its light had been shed upon the West did the full measure of its potentialities be manifest.
>
> The day is approaching when ye shall witness how, through the splendour of the Faith of Bahá'u'lláh, the West will have replaced the East, radiating the light of Divine Guidance.
>
> In the books of the Prophets certain glad-tidings are recorded which are absolutely true and free from doubt. The East hath ever been the dawning-place of the Sun of Truth. In the East all the Prophets of God have appeared . . . The West hath acquired illumination from the East but in some respects the reflection of the light hath been greater in the Occident. This is specially true of Christianity.[9]

During the lifetime of Bahá'u'lláh His Message was at first confined to countries in Asia. Later it spread to other continents. It was first taken to Europe when He was exiled to Adrianople. Next it was taken to Africa and later during 'Abdu'l-Bahá's Ministry to America and then to Australasia. When 'Abdu'l-Bahá passed away, the Cause of God had been introduced into thirty-five countries.

The Heroic Age of the Faith was closed by the ascension of 'Abdu'l-Bahá, and the Formative Age began with the Ministry

* see vol. 2, p. 30.

of Shoghi Effendi, the Guardian of the Faith. It was during his Ministry that the rising institutions of the Administrative Order of the Cause, the channels through which the vivifying forces of Bahá'u'lláh's Revelation are canalized, were gradually reared and progressively consolidated. By virtue of the primacy conferred on the North American Bahá'í community, he built the pattern of the Administrative Order within that community which he described as 'the champion-builders of an Order which posterity will hail as the harbinger of a civilization to be regarded as the fairest fruit of the Revelation proclaimed by Bahá'u'lláh'.[10] While Persia is the cradle of the Faith, North America became the cradle of the Administrative Order. The Words of Bahá'u'lláh that 'the signs of His Dominion have appeared in the West' have been fulfilled, and the institutions of the Faith have now encircled the globe and are functioning in both the East and the West.

Bahá'u'lláh closes the Tablet of Aqdas with these soul-stirring words. In these passages are enshrined the tokens of God's bounty which He has vouchsafed to mankind, a bounty which is for every human being, and is bestowed upon him once he recognizes Bahá'u'lláh and turns to Him with humility and submissiveness:

> Say: Blessed the slumberer who is awakened by My Breeze. Blessed the lifeless one who is quickened through My reviving breaths. Blessed the eye that is solaced by gazing at My beauty. Blessed the wayfarer who directeth his steps towards the Tabernacle of My glory and majesty. Blessed the distressed one who seeketh refuge beneath the shadow of My canopy. Blessed the sore athirst who hasteneth to the soft-flowing waters of My loving-kindness. Blessed the insatiate soul who casteth away his selfish desires for love of Me and taketh his place at the banquet table which I have sent down from the heaven of divine bounty for My chosen ones. Blessed the abased one who layeth fast hold on the cord

of My glory; and the needy one who entereth beneath the shadow of the Tabernacle of My wealth. Blessed the ignorant one who seeketh the fountain of My knowledge; and the heedless one who cleaveth to the cord of My remembrance. Blessed the soul that hath been raised to life through My quickening breath and hath gained admittance into My heavenly Kingdom. Blessed the man whom the sweet savours of reunion with Me have stirred and caused to draw nigh unto the Dayspring of My Revelation. Blessed the ear that hath heard and the tongue that hath borne witness and the eye that hath seen and recognized the Lord Himself, in His great glory and majesty, invested with grandeur and dominion. Blessed are they that have attained His presence. Blessed the man who hath sought enlightenment from the Day-Star of My Word. Blessed he who hath attired his head with the diadem of My love. Blessed is he who hath heard of My grief and hath arisen to aid Me among My people. Blessed is he who hath laid down his life in My path and hath borne manifold hardships for the sake of My Name. Blessed the man who, assured of My Word, hath arisen from among the dead to celebrate My praise. Blessed is he that hath been enraptured by My wondrous melodies and hath rent the veils asunder through the potency of My might. Blessed is he who hath remained faithful to My Covenant, and whom the things of the world have not kept back from attaining My Court of holiness. Blessed is the man who hath detached himself from all else but Me, hath soared in the atmosphere of My love, hath gained admittance into My Kingdom, gazed upon My realms of glory, quaffed the living waters of My bounty, hath drunk his fill from the heavenly river of My loving providence, acquainted himself with My Cause, apprehended that which I concealed within the treasury of My Words, and hath shone forth from the horizon of divine knowledge engaged in My praise and glorification. Verily, he is of Me. Upon him rest My mercy, My loving-kindness, My bounty and My glory.[11]

Lawḥ-i-Maqṣúd

Notable among these later Tablets is the *Lawḥ-i-Maqṣúd** which was revealed in honour of a certain Mírzá Maqṣúd who was living in Syria at the time.

Most of Bahá'u'lláh's utterances in this Tablet are revealed in the words of His amanuenses.† In it He describes man as the 'supreme Talisman', claims that 'lack of a proper education' has deprived him 'of that which he doth inherently possess', regards man 'as a mine rich in gems of inestimable value', states that 'education, can, alone, cause it to reveal its treasures', defines a true man as one 'who, today, dedicateth himself to the service of the entire human race', declares that pride is not for him who loves his own country, 'but rather for him who loveth the whole world', counsels humanity to make endeavours for 'the rehabilitation of the world and the well-being of nations', proclaims to the peoples of the world that 'the tabernacle of unity hath been raised; regard ye not one another as strangers', likens all human beings to 'the fruits of one tree, and the leaves of one branch', discerns 'the signs of impending convulsions and chaos' within human society, reflects on the 'disturbances', 'wars' and 'unforeseen calamities' which have afflicted the peoples of the earth, advocates the 'imperative necessity for the holding of a vast, an all-embracing assemblage of men' which 'rulers and the Kings of the earth must needs attend', where they may consider 'such ways and means as will lay the foundations of the world's Great Peace amongst men', and foreshadows the outcome of reconciliation among the governments to be that 'the nations of the world will no longer require any armaments, except for the purpose of preserving the security of their realms and of maintaining internal order within their territories'.

In this Tablet Bahá'u'lláh further recommends the study of 'those branches of knowledge which are of use', and which

* Translated into English and published in *Tablets of Bahá'u'lláh*, pp. 161–78.

† see p. 23n.

benefit mankind, declares that any academic sudy which begins and ends in words, 'will never be of any worth', and gives as an example 'Persia's learned doctors' who study a philosophy which yields 'nothing but words'. He counsels moderation in all things, states that 'the heaven of divine wisdom is illumined with the two luminaries of consultation* and compassion', proclaims that 'the heaven of true understanding shineth resplendent with the light of two luminaries: tolerance and righteousness', and declares that 'the structure of world stability and order hath been reared upon, and will continue to be sustained by, the twin pillars of reward and punishment'.†

The Tablet of Maqṣúd contains many exhortations and counsels. The following words of Bahá'u'lláh may be said to summarize these:

> The Tongue of Wisdom proclaimeth: He that hath Me not is bereft of all things: Turn ye away from all that is on earth and seek none else but Me.[12]

Lawḥ-i-Siyyid Mihdíy-i-Dahají

This Tablet‡ was addressed to Siyyid Mihdíy-i-Dahají, who was one of the foremost teachers of the Faith during Bahá'u'lláh's Ministry. He was a proud and egotistical person whose ambition for leadership brought about his downfall after the ascension of Bahá'u'lláh. He joined hands with Mírzá Muḥammad-'Alí, the Arch-breaker of the Covenant of Bahá'u'lláh, arose against 'Abdu'l-Bahá, and brought to naught all the services he had rendered to the Cause in his earlier days. An account of his life and his violation of the Covenant is given in a previous volume.§

Siyyid Mihdí was the recipient of many Tablets from

* see vol. 3, pp. 317–18.

† For an explanation of the necessity of punishment see vol. 3, pp. 294–7.

‡ Translated into English and published in *Tablets of Bahá'u'lláh*, pp. 195–201.

§ see vol. 2.

Bahá'u'lláh. In this Tablet Bahá'u'lláh showers His bounties upon him, praises him for his travel teaching throughout the land and confirms one of His fundamental commandments when He states: 'To assist Me is to teach My Cause.' He moreover exhorts men to fear God and to 'sow not the seeds of dissension among men', and warns that 'those who perpetrate deeds that would create turmoil among the people have indeed strayed far from helping God and His Cause . . . '

There are many exhortations in this Tablet, some directed towards Siyyid Mihdí, others aimed at the community of the Most Great Name. We glean from among these only the commandment relating to teaching His Cause. Bahá'u'lláh, in this Tablet, repeats some of His counsels previously revealed for Áqá Muḥammad-i-Qá'iní in the Tablet of Ḥikmat when He explains the prerequisites for teaching the Faith effectively, and describes those conditions necessary for exerting influence upon people through the power of one's speech.* He also reveals invaluable advice concerning the power of the revealed Word in teaching the Cause, advice which has been carried out by many veteran teachers of the Faith and through which a great many souls have been led to the Cause of God. These are Bahá'u'lláh's assuring words:

> The sanctified souls should ponder and meditate in their hearts regarding the methods of teaching. From the texts of the wondrous, heavenly Scriptures they should memorize phrases and passages bearing on various instances, so that in the course of their speech they may recite divine verses whenever the occasion demandeth it, inasmuch as these holy verses are the most potent elixir, the greatest and mightiest talisman. So potent is their influence that the hearer will have no cause for vacillation. I swear by My life! This Revelation is endowed with such a power that it will act as the lodestone for all nations and kindreds of the earth.[13]

* see *Tablets of Bahá'u'lláh*, pp. 143, 198–9.

The following story by Ḥájí Mírzá Ḥaydar-'Alí confirms the power of the revealed Word. Ḥájí was introduced to a person who was opposed to the Faith and found it very difficult to be convinced of its truth. This is a summary of his account:

> A certain person who was a pious and devoted Muslim was introduced to me. No matter how much I spoke to him, he kept on insisting that he would never accept the Faith unless he was shown a miracle. In the end I was powerless to convince him of the truth of the Faith. So I said to him, 'There is an inherent ability within every soul by which it can distinguish the words of God from the words of man.' He agreed with me on this. I then said to him, 'I will now recite some words for you, so incline your inner ears to them and judge for yourself who is the Speaker.' I then chanted a Persian Tablet in which the overpowering majesty of the Words was clearly manifested. He had heard only a few verses when he lowered his head, prostrated himself on the ground, and said, 'These are the words of God, exalted be His glory. There are many miracles hidden in each word. I testify that these utterances unmistakably proclaim the advent of the Day of God . . . '
>
> He stayed with us for the whole night, during which he learnt about the teachings and the laws of the new Dispensation. This man became enraptured and set aglow with the fire of the love of God . . . [14]

17

'The Doors of Majesty . . . Were Flung Wide Open'

Nowhere were the evidences of the rising prestige of the Faith more evident than in the Holy Land itself where the sun of Bahá was shining in meridian splendour. The community of the Most Great Name in that land was enjoying the benefits of a freedom and prestige unprecedented in former times. The person of 'Abdu'l-Bahá, the Master, the guide and refuge of friend and foe alike, 'the stainless mirror of His light', and 'the perfect Exemplar of His teachings', was at this period at the pinnacle of public adoration and respect. Shoghi Effendi, the Guardian of the Bahá'í Faith, writes concerning this:

> 'Abdu'l-Bahá's visit to Beirut, at the invitation of Midhát Páshá, a former Grand Vizir of Turkey, occurring about this time; His association with the civil and ecclesiastical leaders of that city; His several interviews with the well-known Shaykh Muḥammad 'Abdú served to enhance immensely the growing prestige of the community and spread abroad the fame of its most distinguished member. The splendid welcome accorded him by the learned and highly esteemed Shaykh Yúsuf, the Muftí of Nazareth, who acted as host to the válís of Beirut, and who had despatched all the notables of the community several miles on the road to meet Him as He approached the town, accompanied by His brother and the Muftí of 'Akká, as well as the magnificent reception given by 'Abdu'l-Bahá to that same Shaykh Yúsuf when the latter visited Him in 'Akká, were such as to arouse the envy of those who, only a few years before, had treated Him and

His fellow-exiles with feelings compounded of condescension and scorn.[1]

Lawḥ-i-Arḍ-i-Bá

The visit of 'Abdu'l-Bahá to Beirut in 1879 at the invitation of the Governor of the Province of Syria was a significant event. It clearly demonstrated that the edict of the Sulṭán condemning Bahá'u'lláh and His companions to life imprisonment within the citadel of 'Akká had become irrelevant. It also enabled some outstanding personalities such as Shaykh Muḥammad 'Abdú', who later became the Grand Muftí of Egypt, to come into contact with the magnetic personality of 'Abdu'l-Bahá and become one of his ardent admirers. This great man was so fascinated by the Master's qualities and divine virtues that he wanted to travel with Him to 'Akká, a decision that 'Abdu'l-Bahá was able to cancel.

It was on this occasion of 'Abdu'l-Bahá's visit to Beirut that Bahá'u'lláh revealed the *Lawḥ-i-Arḍ-i-Bá* (Tablet of the Land of Bá, Beirut). Here is the full text of this glorious Tablet extolling the station of the Master, the Centre of the Covenant of Bahá'u'lláh.

> Praise be to Him Who hath honoured the Land of Bá through the presence of Him round Whom all names revolve. All the atoms of the earth have announced unto all created things that from behind the gate of the Prison-city there hath appeared and above its horizon there hath shone forth the Orb of the beauty of the great, the Most Mighty Branch of God – His ancient and immutable Mystery – proceeding on its way to another land. Sorrow, thereby, hath enveloped this Prison-city, whilst another land rejoiceth. Exalted, immeasurably exalted is our Lord, the Fashioner of the heavens and the Creator of all things, He through Whose sovereignty the doors of the prison were opened, thereby causing what was promised aforetime

in the Tablets to be fulfilled. He is verily potent over what He willeth, and in His grasp is the dominion of the entire creation. He is the All-Powerful, the All-Knowing, the All-Wise.

Blessed, doubly blessed, is the ground which His footsteps have trodden, the eye that hath been cheered by the beauty of His countenance, the ear that hath been honoured by hearkening to His call, the heart that hath tasted the sweetness of His love, the breast that hath dilated through His remembrance, the pen that hath voiced His praise, the scroll that hath borne the testimony of His writings. We beseech God – blessed and exalted be He – that He may honour us with meeting Him soon. He is, in truth, the All-Hearing, the All-Powerful, He Who is ready to answer.[2]

The Magnanimity of Bahá'u'lláh

The high esteem and veneration in which 'Abdu'l-Bahá was held throughout the Holy Land during this period was a reflection of the majesty of Bahá'u'lláh whom the population had come to regard as a person with superhuman powers and whom they referred to as the 'august leader'. Concerning the influence He exerted on the people of Palestine and the evidences of His spiritual power, Shoghi Effendi writes:

The drastic farmán of Sulṭán 'Abdu'l-'Azíz, though officially unrepealed, had by now become a dead letter. Though Bahá'u'lláh was still nominally a prisoner, 'the doors of majesty and true sovereignty were', in the words of 'Abdu'l-Bahá, 'flung wide open'. 'The rulers of Palestine', He moreover has written, 'envied His influence and power. Governors and mutisarrifs, generals and local officials, would humbly request the honor of attaining His presence – a request to which He seldom acceded . . . '

'Sulṭán 'Abdu'l-'Azíz', Bahá'u'lláh is reported by one of His fellow-exiles to have stated, 'banished Us to this country in the greatest abasement, and since his object was to destroy Us and humble Us, whenever the means of glory and ease presented themselves, We did not reject them.' 'Now, praise be to God,' He, moreover, as reported by Nabíl in his narrative, once remarked, 'it has reached the point when all the people of these regions are manifesting their submissiveness unto Us.' And again, as recorded in that same narrative: 'The Ottoman Sulṭán, without any justification, or reason, arose to oppress Us, and sent Us to the fortress of 'Akká. His imperial farmán decreed that none should associate with Us, and that We should become the object of the hatred of every one. The Hand of Divine power, therefore, swiftly avenged Us. It first loosed the winds of destruction upon his two irreplaceable ministers and confidants, 'Alí and Fu'ád, after which that Hand was stretched out to roll up the panoply of 'Azíz himself, and to seize him, as He only can seize, Who is the Mighty, the Strong.'

'His enemies', 'Abdu'l-Bahá, referring to this same theme, has written, 'intended that His imprisonment should completely destroy and annihilate the blessed Cause, but this prison was, in reality, of the greatest assistance, and became the means of its development.' ' . . . This illustrious Being,' He, moreover, has affirmed, 'uplifted His Cause in the Most Great Prison. From this Prison His light was shed abroad; His fame conquered the world, and the proclamation of His glory reached the East and the West.' 'His light at first had been a star; now it became a mighty sun.' 'Until our time,' He, moreover, has affirmed, 'no such thing has ever occurred.'

Little wonder that, in view of so remarkable a reversal in the circumstances attending the twenty-four years of His banishment to 'Akká, Bahá'u'lláh Himself should have penned these weighty words: 'The Almighty . . . hath transformed this Prison-House into the Most Exalted Paradise, the Heaven of Heavens.'[3]

During His stay in the Mansion of Bahjí, Bahá'u'lláh often visited 'Akká and, sometimes, its neighbouring villages. On all these occasions people spontaneously bowed before Him with the utmost reverence whenever He appeared in public.* On His visits to 'Akká He usually stayed at the House of 'Abbúd, and occasionally the homes of His brothers, Mírzá Músá entitled Áqáy-i-Kalím, or Mírzá Muḥammad-Qulí. In one of His Tablets[4] revealed in the home of Áqáy-i-Kalím situated in close proximity to the Súq-i-Abyaḍ (the White Market), Bahá'u'lláh states that on that occasion He had stayed eight days and nine nights in that house as a bounty on His part. During this period Bahá'u'lláh permitted all the believers to attain His presence. Each day and night these lovers of His Beauty sat in His presence spellbound by His utterances and were exhilarated by the outpouring of His loving favours. In this Tablet Bahá'u'lláh prays for His loved ones who had attained His presence in that house. He prays that their hearts may be illumined, their souls sanctified from all attachments save Him, and their steps made firm so that they may remain steadfast and arise to serve His Cause. He also showers His infinite bestowals and blessings upon Áqáy-i-Kalím who had served His Lord with the utmost devotion and love during those days.

Ḥájí Muḥammad-Ṭáhir-i-Málmírí has described the following episode in his memoirs:

> One evening when the Blessed Beauty was staying in the home of Jináb-i-Kalím, He was pacing up and down the courtyard and I was busy watering the small garden with a watering can. His blessed Person came to me, reached for my shawl† which was loosely tied around my waist, and said, 'This is loose, a Bábí ought to gird up his loins!' He then stood beside me for a short while and uttered words of loving-kindness to me.

---

* An example of this reverence is given in vol. 2, pp. 11–12.

† Persian men usually wore long garments over which they tied a wide shawl around their waist.

This is an example of how Bahá'u'lláh always made His loved ones feel easy in His presence.

When on a visit to 'Akká, Bahá'u'lláh occasionally visited the homes of His companions. This was a great honour that He bestowed on His loved ones. The same Ḥájí Muḥammad-Ṭáhir has recorded the following story:

> My residence, together with that of Nabíl-i-A'ẓam, was close to the home of Áqáy-i-Kalím which was situated in the Súq-i-Abyaḍ. Since I used to bid beads* quite frequently, one day Nabíl seized my prayer beads and hung them high up from the ceiling so that I could not reach them. That day I was staying in his room as his guest when the Blessed Beauty arrived and honoured us with His presence. He asked Nabíl in an amused tone, 'Whose prayer beads are those that you have imprisoned here?' Nabíl said, 'They belong to Áqá Ṭáhir . . . '

Remarks such as this on trivial matters always helped the believers to feel relaxed in Bahá'u'lláh's presence. Otherwise no one could have uttered one word when standing face to face with the One whom he knew to be the Supreme Manifestation of God. Bahá'u'lláh enjoyed humour; indeed, one of the attributes of God is 'Humorist'. Sometimes Bahá'u'lláh would make humorous remarks to His companions, some of whom were well able to reciprocate in their humble way. Notable among His companions who had a great sense of humour were Zaynu'l-Muqarrabín and Mishkín-Qalam.† There was also Mírzá Ja'far-i-Yazdí.

Ḥusayn-i-Áshchí‡ has recounted many stories about some of Bahá'u'lláh's humorous conversations with Mírzá Ja'far,

* It was a custom among the Persians to choose at random a number of beads, and by counting them n a certain manner determine which course of action would be best to follow in a given situation. (A.T.)

† For a brief account of their lives see vol. 1, pp. 25–6 and 26–8.

‡ He was a cook in the household of Bahá'u'lláh. For further information see vol. 2, pp. 169 and 404.

who was working as a servant in Bahá'u'lláh's household. He was an erudite and learned divine from Yazd, and had been an outstanding mujtahid (doctor of Islamic law) in that city. When He embraced the Cause of Bahá'u'lláh, He renounced his high office, went to Baghdád, discarded his priestly attire and became a servant in the household of Bahá'u'lláh. He accompanied Him in His exiles and was engaged in service until the end of his life.* The following is a summary of Ḥusayn-i-Áshchí's memoirs:

> The Blessed Beauty used to spend much of His time in the countryside . . . From the mansion of Bahjí He often went to the Mansion of Mazra'ih, to the garden of Junaynih† and the Garden of Riḍván. On these occasions He spoke to the believers with delightful humour . . . Mírzá Ja'far was a high-ranking mujtahid . . . but was working as a domestic servant . . . One day the Muftí of 'Akká, Shaykh 'Alíy-i-Mírí, attained the presence of Bahá'u'lláh in the Mansion of Bahjí and was seeking enlightenment on some religious subjects. Mírzá Ja'far was also there attending to his domestic work. Bahá'u'lláh called him in and said, 'Come and answer the questions of the Muftí.' He resolved the questions so well that the Muftí was surprised at the extent of his knowledge and learning . . . Bahá'u'lláh often made humorous remarks to Mírzá Ja'far and he usually responded wittily. One day He said to him jokingly, 'Jináb-i-Mujtahid (your excellency, the Mujtahid) do you wish me to reveal to you some of your bad qualities?' Mírzá Ja'far's prompt reply was, 'No thank you.' His response, full of wit and humour, delighted the heart of Bahá'u'lláh.

There is an interesting story about Mírzá Ja'far in the early days of the Faith in Yazd. Ḥájí Muḥammad-Ṭáhir-i-Málmírí has recorded this in his memoirs:

---

* For further information, and the story of his revival after death, see vol. 1, p. 290.

† Situated on the north side of 'Akká. (A.T.)

> Áqá Mírzá Ja'far was an erudite divine of Islám. In his youth, he taught at a theological school . . . He left the school altogether when he embraced the Cause and became a very steadfast believer. In those days, the Ancient Beauty was in Baghdád. Knowing that He was living an austere life in that city, Mírzá Ja'far wished to provide some funds for the relief of His blessed Person. In the end he came up with a plan. There were many vases and other ornaments made of copper in the mosques of Yazd. He used to go to a mosque at night, climb to the upper chambers, dismantle the ornamental copper vessels which were hanging from the ceiling, and take them home. Little by little he stole similar vessels from several mosques. In the end he gathered nearly half a ton of these copper items . . . He then transported them to Ardikán* to the home of a certain Ustád Káẓim, an ironmonger. There he cut the copper articles to pieces and eventually succeeded in selling the metal for seventy túmáns† in silver coins. He placed the silver inside a specially made leather cummerbund, tied it around his waist and set off on his journey on foot to Baghdád where he attained the presence of Bahá'u'lláh and presented the money to Him. The Blessed Beauty accepted the money from him, and bestowed upon him His blessings and favours. But He ordered him to accompany Mírzá Áqá Ján, Khádimu'lláh (the Servant of God), to the banks of the river and throw the money into its waters. Mírzá Ja'far became a servant of the household, and was among those companions who accompanied Bahá'u'lláh to Istanbul.

One of the exalted attributes of the Manifestation of God, distinguishing Him from the whole of the human race, is His utter detachment from the things of this world. Bahá'u'lláh had no regard whatsoever for the possession of material things. He has clearly stated in His Writings that this material world

* A town situated about 100 miles from Yazd. (A.T.)

† A very large sum of money in those days. (A.T.)

has no worth in His sight. In several Tablets He states that if this world had any value, He would have been occupying its highest thrones. In a Tablet revealed in 'Akká,[5] He states that the One who created this world has renounced it. For if it had any value He would not have allowed Himself to live in the most desolate of cities.

In another Tablet[6] revealed in the Holy Land He affirms that if His aim were to acquire earthly things, He could have taken possession of all that is on earth and no one could have questioned His authority to do so. He further states in the same Tablet that whenever He had accepted a gift from a believer, the basic reason had been to bestow His bounties and favours upon him. The mere acceptance of a gift endowed the soul of the individual with eternal blessings.

The believers sometimes sent articles such as carpets, clothing and similar items to Bahá'u'lláh, but He seldom used them for Himself. He usually gave all gifts away. One person who coveted them was His amanuensis, Mírzá Áqá Ján. Knowing that Bahá'u'lláh had no interest in keeping the believers' offerings for Himself, he longed to possess these gifts and Bahá'u'lláh sometimes gave them to him. Mírzá Áqá Ján did not realize that this was his test and the cause of his downfall. To be in close contact with Bahá'u'lláh, to serve Him day and night and to abide within such a sacred realm, required utter detachment from all earthly things. The desire for material benefits while serving in His holy presence was fatal.

God always tests man. The higher he is in the field of service, the greater are his tests. Mírzá Áqá Ján acted as a servant to Bahá'u'lláh and was the individual who was closest to Him. He was a materialistic and corrupt being who fell from grace during the latter part of Bahá'u'lláh's life, later violated His covenant and perished spiritually.*

When Bahá'u'lláh was in Adrianople a certain believer from Káshán by the name of Muḥammad-Báqir presented Him

* For more information see vol. 1.

with a small silk carpet. He wrote a Tablet,[7] thanked him for the gift and showered His bounties upon him. He told him that He had accepted the gift, but was now returning it to him as a favour on His part. He stated that He preferred to sit on the ground in that Remote Prison* than to sit on a silk carpet. This is a typical example of how Bahá'u'lláh would respond to gifts presented to Him.

One of the believers, a certain Mírzá Muḥammad-Qulí, presented Bahá'u'lláh with an overcoat. In a Tablet[8] Bahá'u'lláh informed him that He had worn the coat for one day as a bounty on His part.

Ḥájí Muḥammad 'Alíy-i-Afnán,† a cousin of the Báb, had sent a length of white flannel to 'Akká. According to a Tablet written in the handwriting of Mírzá Áqá Ján,[9] Bahá'u'lláh graciously accepted the gift from him and although since His departure from Baghdád He was in the habit of wearing coats made only of black flannel, He ordered a white one to be made as a token of His grace and favours towards the Afnán.

According to Ḥájí Muḥammad-Ṭáhir, Bahá'u'lláh would usually wear a long woollen upper garment and a woollen cloak; and in the summer, cotton garments.

These stories depicting some ordinary features of the life of Bahá'u'lláh, reveal His magnanimity and utter detachment from the things of this world. Sometimes Bahá'u'lláh ordered simple gifts to be sent to certain people. For instance, on one occasion Mírzá Áqá Ján wrote on the instructions of Bahá'u'lláh to the same Ḥájí Muḥammad-'Alíy-i-Afnán, who was living in Hong Kong, asking him to send some china dishes which were intended as a gift for 'Abbúd.[10] On another occasion Mírzá Áqá Ján was instructed to ask another of the Afnáns to send a few pairs of spectacles complete with cases for presentation to some of the authorities.[11]‡

---

* Adrianople.

† see *Memorials of the Faithful*, pp. 16–21.

‡ In those days there were no custom-made spectacles. A type which was commonly worn by people had a simple magnifying glass as a lens.

For his own personal use Bahá'u'lláh never ordered anything extravagant. The life of luxury to which He was accustomed in His youth had been denied Him since His imprisonment in the Síyáh-Chál of Ṭihrán when all His possessions had been confiscated. But He lived a life of austerity in a majesty such that, in the words of Edward Granville Browne of Cambridge University, He was 'the object of a devotion that kings might envy and emperors sigh for in vain'. His personal needs were simple and inexpensive. For instance, on one occasion when one of His companions, Ḥájí 'Alíy-i-Yazdí, was going to Istanbul on business, Bahá'u'lláh asked him to purchase a pair of shoes for Him. He gave him an old pair of His slippers for size. Ḥájí 'Alí later presented the slippers to the International Archives and they are now kept in the room of Bahá'u'lláh in the Mansion of Mazra'ih.

The Law of Ḥuqúqu'lláh

The greater part of the donations given to the Cause by the believers were spent at Bahá'u'lláh's behest in the promotion of the Faith and the care of the poor and needy of the community. He Himself and the members of His family, however, lived an austere life. There were many occasions when He was in great need, but did not accept financial help from the friends.

In the *Kitáb-i-Aqdas* (the Most Holy Book), Bahá'u'lláh revealed the law of Ḥuqúqu'lláh (the Right of God). It concerns those whose possessions reach a certain value. They are bidden by God to pay nineteen per cent of that value to the Centre of the Cause. In one of His Tablets, revealed in the words of His amanuensis,[12] Bahá'u'lláh states that when the full text of the *Kitáb-i-Aqdas* was completed He did not order its release for some time because it contained the law of Ḥuqúq, which has been ordained by God as a sign of His mercy and loving-kindness unto His servants. He explains that the reason for withholding the Book temporarily was His apprehensiveness lest some of the believers might not carry out this commandment or might come to wrong conclusions. The mere contemplation of this, He says, is unworthy of the Day of God. The very thought that some, in their immaturity, might possibly assume that the Ḥuqúq was intended for Bahá'u'lláh's personal use, must have been extremely painful to Him. The most cursory study of His life and teachings will amply demonstrate that He constantly exhorted His followers to detach themselves from earthly possessions and not to place their affections in the things of this world. In His Tablet to Napoleon III, Bahá'u'lláh admonishes the emperor in these words which clearly demonstrate how worthless is this material world in His sight:

> Exultest thou over the treasures thou dost possess, knowing they shall perish? Rejoicest thou in that thou rulest a span of earth, when the whole world, in the estimation of the people of Bahá, is worth as much as the black in the eye of a dead ant?[13]

In another Tablet Bahá'u'lláh makes a similar statement:

> By the righteousness of God! The world, its vanities and its glory, and whatever delights it can offer, are all, in the sight of God, as worthless as, nay even more contemptible than, dust and ashes. Would that the hearts of men could comprehend it. Wash yourselves thoroughly, O people of Bahá, from the defilement of the world, and of all that pertaineth unto it.[14]

The following passages gleaned from the Writings of Bahá'u'lláh portray His expectations from His followers:

> He is the true servant of God who, in this day, were he to pass through cities of silver and gold, would not deign to look upon them, and whose heart would remain pure and undefiled

from whatever things can be seen in this world, be they its goods or its treasures. I swear by the Sun of Truth! The breath of such a man is endowed with potency, and his words with attraction.

By Him Who shineth above the Day-Spring of sanctity! If the whole earth were to be converted into silver and gold, no man who can be said to have truly ascended into the heaven of faith and certitude would deign to regard it, much less to seize and keep it . . . They who dwell within the Tabernacle of God, and are established upon the seats of everlasting glory, will refuse, though they be dying of hunger, to stretch their hands, and seize unlawfully the property of their neighbor, however vile and worthless he may be. The purpose of the one true God in manifesting Himself is to summon all mankind to truthfulness and sincerity, to piety and trustworthiness, to resignation and submissiveness to the will of God, to forbearance and kindliness, to uprightness and wisdom. His object is to array every man with the mantle of a saintly character, and to adorn him with the ornament of holy and goodly deeds. Say, he is not to be numbered with the people of Bahá who followeth his mundane desires, or fixeth his heart on things of the earth. He is my true follower who, if he come to a valley of pure gold will pass straight through it aloof as a cloud, and will neither turn back, nor pause. Such a man is assuredly of Me. From his garment the Concourse on high can inhale the fragrance of sanctity.[15]

While Bahá'u'lláh was reluctant to send a copy of the *Kitáb-i-Aqdas* to Persia, some of the believers were requesting that the laws of the Faith be revealed for them. As a result of these requests, Bahá'u'lláh eventually sent a copy, but gave clear instructions that no one was to implement the law of the Ḥuqúq. For about five years after the revelation of the *Kitáb-i-Aqdas* this law was not put into execution. Then, as the Cause began to expand in Persia and neighbouring countries, there was a need for funds and those who were eligible to pay the Ḥuqúq did so with joy and gratitude.

This is the text of the law of Ḥuqúqu'lláh as revealed in the *Kitáb-i-Aqdas*:

> Should a person acquire one hundred mithqáls* of gold, nineteen mithqáls thereof belong unto God, the Creator of earth and heaven. Take heed, O people, lest ye deprive yourselves of this great bounty. We have prescribed this law unto you while We are wholly independent of you and of all that are in the heavens and on the earth. Indeed there lie concealed in this command, mysteries and benefits which are beyond the comprehension of anyone save God, the All-Knowing, the All-Informed. Say, through this injunction God desireth to purify your possessions and enable you to draw nigh unto such stations as none can attain, except those whom God may please. Verily, He is the Generous, the Gracious, the Bountiful.
>
> O people! Act not treacherously in the matter of Ḥuqúqu'lláh and dispose not of it, except by His leave. Thus hath it been ordained in His Epistles as well as in this glorious Tablet.
>
> Whoso dealeth dishonestly with God will in justice be exposed, and whoso fulfilleth the things he hath been commanded, divine blessings will descend upon him from the heaven of the bounty of his Lord, the Bestower, the Bountiful, the Most Generous, the Ancient of Days. Verily He desireth for you the things that are inscrutable to you at present, though the people themselves will readily discover them when their souls take their flight and the trappings of their earthly gaieties are rolled up. Thus warneth you the Author of the Preserved tablet.[16]

It must be noted that in the above passage Bahá'u'lláh has

* Each mithqál is equal to 3.6416666 grams.

merely set the rate of Ḥuqúq at nineteen per cent. It is not meant that the minimum amount subject to Ḥuqúq is one hundred mithqáls of gold; the minimum amount is the value of nineteen mithqáls of gold. Bahá'u'lláh Himself has clarified this point in the following statement:

> The minimum amount subject to Ḥuqúqu'lláh is reached when one's possessions are worth the number of Vaḥíd (19); that is, whenever one owneth 19 mithqáls of gold, or acquireth possessions attaining this value, after having deducted therefrom the yearly expenses, the Ḥuqúq becometh applicable and its payment is obligatory.[17]

As regards its application, Shoghi Effendi, the Guardian of the Faith, has stated through his secretary:

> Regarding the Ḥuqúqu'lláh . . . this is applied to one's merchandise, property and income. After deducting the necessary expenses, whatever is left as profit, and is an addition to one's capital, such a sum is subject to Ḥuqúq. When one has paid Ḥuqúq once on a particular sum, that sum is no longer subject to Ḥuqúq, unless it should pass from one person to another. One's residence, and the household furnishings are exempt from Ḥuqúq . . . Ḥuqúqu'lláh is paid to the Centre of the Cause.[18]

Bahá'u'lláh was very anxious that no one should ever feel forced to pay the Ḥuqúq. He instructed Ḥájí Abu'l-Ḥasan-i-Amín* the Trustee of the Ḥuqúq, and other eminent Bahá'ís, not to accept money from anybody unless they were sure that the individual wished to give with the utmost joy and devotion. He also forbade the soliciting of Ḥuqúq by the Trustees. In many of His Tablets Bahá'u'lláh has made such exhortations.

---

* see vol. 3, chapter 4.

To cite an example, the following is part of a Tablet revealed in honour of His Trustee Ḥájí Amín:

> O Abu'l-Ḥasan:
> May my Glory rest upon thee! Fix thy gaze upon the glory of the Cause. Speak forth that which will attract the hearts and the minds. To demand the Ḥuqúq is in no wise permissible. This command was revealed in the Book of God for various necessary matters ordained by God to be dependent upon material means. Therefore, if someone, with utmost pleasure and gladness, nay with insistence, wisheth to partake of this blessing, thou mayest accept. Otherwise, acceptance is not permissible.[19]

The following passage from the Writings of Bahá'u'lláh will shed further light on this subject:

> For a number of years Ḥuqúq was not accepted. How numerous the offerings that on reaching Our presence were returned to the donors, because they were not needed then. However, in recent years We have, in view of the exigencies of the times, accepted the payment of the Ḥuqúq, but have forbidden solicitation thereof. Everyone must have the utmost regard for the dignity of the Word of God and for the exaltation of His Cause. Were a person to offer all the treasures of the earth at the cost of debasing the honour of the Cause of God, were it even less than a grain of mustard, such an offering would not be permissible. All the world hath belonged and will always belong to God. If one spontaneously offereth Ḥuqúq with the utmost joy and radiance it will be acceptable, and not otherwise. The benefit of such deeds reverteth unto the individuals themselves. This measure hath been ordained in view of the necessity for material means, for 'averse is God from putting aught into effect except through its means'. Thus instructions were given to receive the Ḥuqúq.[20]

In one of His Tablets[21] Bahá'u'lláh states that there is no act more reprehensible than to beg for funds in the name of God.

A special responsibility concerning the Ḥuqúqu'lláh was placed upon the Hands of the Cause.* As we have already stated, Bahá'u'lláh always insisted that no one should be solicited to pay the Ḥuqúqu'lláh, and even that payment should not be accepted unless the individual was willing to observe the Ḥuqúq with the utmost joy. In His Tablets to the Hands, Bahá'u'lláh often gives the details of the numerous occasions on which He refused to accept donations from individuals as the Faith did not need financial assistance at that time. He urges them to uphold the standards of detachment, dignity and magnanimity which their Lord has always displayed.

In a Tablet to Ibn-i-Aṣdaq,[22] Bahá'u'lláh describes in the words of His amanuensis how at one time the King of the Martyrs† had felt that the means of subsistence for the Holy Family and the believers in the Holy Land were inadequate. He had dispatched therefore Jamál-i-Burújirdí to the province of Khurásán to solicit the friends for the payment of the Ḥuqúq. As soon as the news of this reached the Holy Land Bahá'u'lláh immediately issued strict intructions to withdraw from this action. The verses that were revealed by Him on that occasion forbidding Jamál to proceed on his mission were charged with supreme authority and might.

On receiving these instructions, Jamál, that egotistical teacher of the Faith,‡ was hurt. He wrote a letter to Mírzá Áqá Ján, Bahá'u'lláh's amanuensis, and complained that his services had never been accepted by, or pleasing to, Bahá'u'lláh. He indicated in this letter that a number of believers, all from Jewish background, had donated a certain sum of money with the utmost pleasure. If their contributions were to be refused, they would become disappointed. As a result of his petition

* see below, chs. 19 and 20.

† see above, ch. 5.

‡ He became a Covenant-breaker, see vol. 2.

Bahá'u'lláh ordered the acceptance of the sum, but at the same time made arrangements for all of it to be used in financing the teaching activities of a few chosen teachers of the Faith in Persia.

In the same Tablet Mírzá Áqá Ján gives further examples. When a few souls from Fárán* attained the presence of Bahá'u'lláh, they presented a sum of money to Him in payment of the Ḥuqúq. He graciously accepted their offering but then returned the full amount to them as a gift. He had done the same to many others and Mírzá Áqá Ján mentions the names of some of them in this Tablet. He further states that all throughout this period the means of livelihood in the Holy Land had been so inadequate that it had been necessary to borrow from time to time in order to enable the large number of pilgrims and believers to subsist. This Tablet was revealed a few months before the ascension of Bahá'u'lláh. Mírzá Áqá Ján mentions that a sum of money had been donated some time before by an individual believer through His Trustee, Ḥájí Amín, but up to the time of writing Bahá'u'lláh had not accepted it. However, it had not been returned either, because it could become a cause of embarrassment.

Another example of the magnanimity and detachment from earthly things manifested by Bahá'u'lláh comes to us through one of His Tablets to Mullá 'Alí-Akbar. A devoted servant of the Blessed Beauty by the name of 'Azím-i-Tafri<u>sh</u>í* had passed away in the Holy Land, and in his will had left all his savings to His Lord. But Bahá'u'lláh issued instructions for the money to be sent to 'Azím's heirs in Persia.

The concept that a portion of one's possessions is the right of God and belongs to Him may be appreciated by observing nature and examining certain physical laws. It has already been stated that the laws which exist in the physical world are also present in the spiritual worlds of God, and that religious

---

* They included Áqá Mír Muḥammad Big and his son <u>Sh</u>áh <u>Kh</u>alílu'lláh; for details see vol. 3, pp. 159–62.

teachings are the spiritual counterparts of physical laws. For instance, we may observe that the law of Ḥuqúqu'lláh finds its parallel in the vegetable kingdom. We observe that the blossoms, the flowers and the fruits do not originate from the tree. They are the hidden properties of the soil. The tree brings out all these potentialities which the earth possesses. The earth is the producer of everything and the entire substance of the tree comes from it. The earth produces the root, the trunk, the branches, the leaves and the fruits. It also provides all the nourishment for its growth and fruition.

Having established the fact that the tree owes its existence to the creative power of the earth, we note that each year the tree sheds it leaves upon the earth. It gives back to its creator, as a matter of course, a portion of its wealth. The fallen leaves do not benefit the earth. They act as a fertilizer and therefore their benefit reverts to the tree itself. This physical process is similar to the law of Ḥuqúqu'lláh, and, as Bahá'u'lláh has stated, 'the benefit of such deeds [payment of the Ḥuqúq] reverteth unto the individuals themselves'.

During Bahá'u'lláh's Ministry the law of Ḥuqúq was applicable to only a very small number of Bahá'ís. The great majority of the community were poor and not eligible to pay the Ḥuqúq. Often the Trustee of Bahá'u'lláh was unable to fully cover the expenses of the Bahá'í teachers and those in need. Of course, Ḥájí Amín, the Trustee, was not pleased about this. In one of His Tablets Bahá'u'lláh makes a sweet and humorous remark about His Trustee. He says: 'We must impose a fine upon Jináb-i-Amín! We have one treasurer and he is bankrupt! Gracious God, there is one treasury belonging to God, and that is empty of funds. Indeed, by virtue of its exalted station, such a treasury ought to be freed and sanctified from earthly things and not be confused with the treasuries of the world.'[23]

The Ḥuqúq should not be confused with the normal contributions of a believer to the International Funds. Although both are donated to the Centre of the Cause – today to the Universal

House of Justice – there is a great difference between the two. The Ḥuqúq in reality does not belong to the individual, as it is the right of God, whereas ordinary donations are given by the believer from his own resources and are motivated by a heartfelt desire to give of one's own substance for the promotion of the Cause of God.

18

Notable Teachers of the Faith

The revelation of so many Tablets by the Most Exalted Pen, progressively unveiling the glory of the Day of God during this latter part of Bahá'u'lláh's Ministry, infused such a spirit of devotion and self-sacrifice into the hearts of the faithful that as a result the community of the Most Great Name was endowed as never before with enormous potentialities sufficient to guarantee its expansion in future centuries to a point where it could encompass the whole of mankind. That community was now far more consolidated than in the days of Baghdád and Adrianople. The laws and teachings of the Faith had been clearly enunciated, its universality proclaimed, the many misrepresentations made by Mírzá Yaḥyá, which in former days had confused a number of believers, had been dispelled and the pre-eminent station of the Author of the Faith had been recognized. The believers throughout the length and breadth of Persia were now teaching the Cause with great wisdom and enabling the pure in heart to embrace it. In every locality could be found certain individuals who were on fire with the love of Bahá'u'lláh and endowed with the gift of understanding, who acted in the capacity of Bahá'í teachers and were entitled *muballigh* (teacher-proclaimer). They were the focal points for teaching on the local level. There were also a host of teachers of outstanding calibre who, by virtue of their knowledge and spirituality, were highly respected in the community. Under Bahá'u'lláh's constant guidance these souls travelled throughout all the regions of Persia and some of its neighbouring countries, diffusing the divine fragrances, enthusing, deepening and stimulating the believers. Notable among them were the four Hands of the Cause of God* appointed by

* For details see below, chs. 19–21.

Bahá'u'lláh in the latter part of His Ministry, together with Mírzá Abu'l-Faḍl, Ḥájí Mírzá Ḥaydar-'Alí, Nabíl-i-Akbar, Ḥájí Abu'l-Ḥasan-i-Amín and a few others.*

The outstanding feature of their successful teaching exploits was their detachment from the things of this world. Most of them earned their living by engaging in casual and modest work. For example, some time after being dismissed from his post as head of a theological college because he had embraced the Faith, and subsequent to his release from a long imprisonment, Mírzá Abu'l-Faḍl, the great Bahá'í scholar, used to earn his living as a scribe for illiterate people who wished to have letters written for them. Satisfied with very small earnings, enough to appease his hunger and pay for the expenses of a donkey to carry him around, Mírzá Abu'l-Faḍl travelled to all parts of Persia, to Turkistan, Syria and Egypt teaching the Cause of God, converting many seekers of Truth to the Faith, confirming and deepening souls in the verities of the Cause.

Mírzá Abu'l-Faḍl

When Mírzá Abu'l-Faḍl embarked on his travel-teaching activities, he was truly detached from all things. He had become like a shining mirror which had turned wholly towards Bahá'u'lláh and therefore he radiated the light of the Faith with such brilliance as to dazzle the eyes of those who came in contact with him. There are many stories about his teaching exploits and his attitude of utter dependence on God in his personal life. A few wealthy Bahá'ís wanted to deputize Mírzá Abu'l-Faḍl to teach the Cause on their behalf. Many wanted him to be free of the struggle to earn his daily pittance. But he declined their offer, while lovingly thanking them for it, pointing out that he always relied on God for his needs. In those days many poor people used to live on a piece of crisp bread at each meal. To make it a tastier dish they would indulge in the luxury of

* Brief accounts of the lives of these individuals are given in vols. 1, 2 and 3.

dipping each piece in a bowl of water before putting it in their mouths. This dish was known as 'crisp bread and water' and Mírzá Abu'l-Faḍl was well accustomed to it.

One of the devoted believers in Ṭihrán offered to pay all his travel expenses. This is a summary of the reply he wrote to him.

> . . . After my release from custody in Ṭihrán, I became assured that in this day, which is the Day of God, one's daily bread is provided through the power of the Almighty. So how can one accept the offer of deputization? In any case, up until now, God, the All-Possessing, the Most High, has not abandoned this servant. It is hoped that He will not do so during the remaining few days of his life. This servant does not consider himself to be worthy of serving this Most Great Cause. It is the Lord of Mankind who through His bounty has vouchsafed His assistance to this undeserving servant and enabled him to arise and serve His Cause. Of course, Jináb-i-Náyib and yourself, who have succeeded in assisting the teachers of the Cause, will be richly rewarded by God. However, this servant declines to accept your offer of funds . . .
>
> I have made it clear to all the friends that under no circumstances will I expect assistance from anybody except assistance in teaching work which necessitates that someone provide a place for meetings. While staying in these two cities [Hamadán and Kirmán<u>sh</u>áhán] I never approached any soul to give me, or even lend me, some money. And there have been times when the need has been so great that I had no choice but to sell some of my clothes, but I never mentioned this to anyone. If this servant could be spared from having to write replies to the many letters that he receives, he could earn a living by transcribing the Holy Writings . . . [1*]

* In the early days of the Faith the Bahá'í Writings were not available in printed form. It was the common practice of literate persons to produce a compilation of the Tablets or of certain Bahá'í books in handwriting for sale to the believers.

In another letter to the same person he writes:

> . . . Concerning the sum of money which Jináb-i-Náyib, upon him be the Glory of God, has offered for this servant, I am at a loss to know how to apologize to him. God, the Knower of all things, is my witness that in refusing to accept this I am in no way ill-disposed toward him. As long as I live, I am grateful for his kindness and that of others like him. In this day, the reward which the exalted Pen of God has inscribed upon the tablet of this world for those who have arisen to promote the Cause through the generous outpouring of their substance and the sacrifice of their lives, is such that the passage of time and the succession of centuries and ages shall never be able to erase it . . . Thanks be to God that this servant . . . has no attachments and is fully content to subsist on a piece of bread in any town or country. God knows that souls like unto this servant are taking their lives in their own hands. They are engaged in teaching the Cause of the Lord of Creation. Not a day passes that the enemies in various parts do not plot to take our lives or expel us from their midst. They demonstrate their animosity toward us by various means. There is not a safe haven anywhere for these servants, and no place can be found in any city where they can repose in peace without becoming a target for strife and sedition, unless we stop teaching and refrain from speaking about the Cause, and this is unthinkable . . .
>
> In a Tablet these exalted words have been revealed: 'O Abu'l-Faḍl, the All-Bountiful has been and will be with thee.' The revealer of these utterances is my witness that since these words were revealed I have never been found helpless. The bounties of the All-Glorious have, at all times, encompassed me, and the glances of His loving-kindness watched over me. At no time has He left me on my own. Sufficient witness is God unto me.[2]

On his teaching trips Mírzá Abu'l-Faḍl seldom stayed with any of the friends. He used to stay at a caravanserai and eat very simple food. But all his thoughts and deeds were concentrated towards teaching the Cause to the seekers of truth and deepening the believers in the knowledge of the Faith.

'Abdu'l-Bahá sent Mírzá Abu'l-Faḍl to the United States of America to teach the Faith and help the Bahá'ís to deepen their understanding of the teachings. He went there in 1901. Ali-Kuli Khan,* who translated for him, has written these words about his degree of reliance on God:

> Mírzá was almost continually in a state of prayer. His mornings, noons and evenings were taken up with devotions. Once I went to his door and found it locked. I rapped, there was no answer. We forced the door, and found that Mírzá had fainted away as he prayed, and that his jaws were locked together. The reason he prayed with such fervor, and such weeping, was his concept of the greatness of God and his own nothingness; his belief that his very existence, bestowed on him by Divine mercy, was a sin in this Day 'whereon naught can be seen except the splendors of the Light that shineth from the face of Thy Lord . . . ' I would say to him, 'You, a holy being, weeping like this. If you are a sinner, then what hope is there for the rest of us?' He would answer: 'The day will come when you, too, will know the degree of devotion worthy to serve as a language by which we can praise Bahá'u'lláh.'[3]

Prayer exerted the most potent influence upon his life. The remarkable qualities he displayed and the outstanding successes he achieved in the field of teaching were due to his complete attachment to God. A certain believer asked Mírzá Abu'l-Faḍl to outline for him the duties of a Bahá'í teacher and the conditions for success in teaching. He wrote these few lines in reply:

---

* A well-known Persian Bahá'í who served the Cause for many years in the United States; noted for his erudition and translations of the Bahá'í Writings into English.

> . . . Teachers of the Faith have varying methods when they travel-teach. This servant is of the opinion that a Bahá'í teacher ought to be freed from any encumbrance in his travels, be easy-going, patient, long-suffering, and detached in spirit. He should avoid becoming a cause of inconvenience for others, and never neglect to observe divine ordinances, the obligatory prayers and other chosen prayers; as He has revealed, 'The most exalted titles belong to God, so call on Him through them.'*
>
> The Bahá'í teacher should believe that the greatest means for the influence of his word and the exaltation of his soul is to tread the path of piety and the fear of God. Also, he should observe wisdom, which is like unto armour for the teacher and a stronghold and a protection for the Cause of God. It is in this way that through the assistance of the Almighty God his words may exert their influence upon his hearers, his deeds become victorious and his own end auspicious.[4]

The teaching exploits of Mírzá Abu'l-Faḍl are truly prodigious. He travelled throughout Persia, continually going from place to place for a period of three years. Then he continued this meritorious service outside Persia in 'I<u>sh</u>qábád, as well as Samarkand and Bu<u>kh</u>ára, both cities in Uzbikistán. During the Ministry of 'Abdu'l-Bahá he travelled to Syria, Egypt and the United States of America. In every place Mírzá Abu'l-Faḍl succeeded in bringing several souls under the shadow of the Cause of God, confirming them in their faith and deepening them in the understanding of the teachings. Many of them became true and renowned servants of the Faith.

Generally, when Bahá'í teachers in the early days of the Faith conversed with people about the Cause, they would employ three main methods of proving the authenticity of the claims of Bahá'u'lláh. One was based on rational and

* *Qur'án* 7: 180. (A.T.)

intellectual proofs, another on the contents and prophecies of the Holy Books of past Dispensations, and the third, which was employed only in certain cases, used the arguments of the other party to prove the case. This last method, which is not generally familiar to Westerners, is very interesting indeed. It was used only in cases when the individual had no intention of finding the truth but was intent upon conducting and winning an argument. Examples of this method, in the form of a dialogue, have been given in previous volumes.*

Mírzá Abu'l-Faḍl was a master of all three. There is no scope in this book to recount some of his fascinating discourses in which he lays bare the hidden mysteries of divine Revelation and brings forward irrefutable proofs of the coming of the Lord in the person of Bahá'u'lláh. His main teaching work was, of course, carried out among Muslims, but he also taught the Faith to the adherents of the Christian, the Jewish and Zoroastrian Faiths. The following dialogues are gleaned from the vast treasure-house of his teaching exploits, some related by himself in his own writings and some recounted by others.

In order to appreciate the first of these, which took place between himself and the Revd Dr Robert Bruce,† a British missionary in Iṣfahán, it is helpful to know that Mírzá Abu'l-Faḍl chose an unconventional method of countering this missionary, who was using his political influence and proudly boasting of his superior upbringing and education. It should be noted that Prince Ẓillu's-Sulṭán, the Governor of Iṣfahán, was under the influence of the British government whose support was vital in his ambitious plans. Under these circumstances it is natural that any British subject, and especially a high-ranking figure such as the Revd Bruce, should be a highly influential figure in Iṣfahán.

A certain believer arranged the meeting between Revd Bruce

---

* see vol. 3, pp. 40–44, and vol. 2, pp. 21–3.

† He was born in Ireland and graduated at Trinity College, Dublin.

and Mírzá Abu'l-Faḍl at a time when the people of Iṣfahán were ravaged by a famine, and poverty loomed over the city. The following is a summary of the unusual dialogue between the two, related by the late 'Ináyatu'lláh Suhráb, a devoted believer and a noteworthy Bahá'í teacher himself. The chronicler does not claim to have recorded the exact words that were exchanged, as his source of information was a verbal account. Nevertheless, it helps to portray what transpired at this unconventional encounter between one who wielded political and financial influence and one who was without either. After some preliminary discussions the following exchange took place:

> *Mírzá Abu'l-Faḍl*: Would it be possible for you please to tell me the extent of the funds involved in your work.
> *Revd Bruce*: So far I have donated about half a million túmáns for famine relief, and if it was necessary I could provide several times this amount.
> *Mírzá Abu'l-Faḍl*: What sort of political influence do you command?
> *Revd Bruce*: Well, my political power is such that should the fanatical Muslims close my church, I could direct the Governor of Iṣfahán, who is a son of the monarch, to open it with his own hands.
> *Mírzá Abu'l-Faḍl*: What are your educational qualifications?
> *Revd Bruce*: I am a graduate of a university and have grown up and lived in Britain which is foremost among the civilized countries of the world. From this you may guess the extent of my education and knowledge.
> *Mírzá Abu'l-Faḍl*: Having been richly endowed with such influence and knowledge, how many souls have you been able to convert to Christianity* since you have been in Iṣfahán?

* In spite of many enticements and the offer of some very attractive benefits, an insignificant number of people were converted from Islám to Christianity. Muslims would not take a step backwards to become Christians, in the same way that a Christian would not revert to becoming a Jew. (A. T.)

Revd Bruce: About thirty.

Mírzá Abu'l-Faḍl: Of these how many, do you think, are steadfast in their Christian faith and sincerely believe in it?

Revd Bruce (after a brief pause, thinking): I am certain about ten to fifteen of them are sincere in their faith.

Mírzá Abu'l-Faḍl: Of these ten to fifteen, how many will remain steadfast to the end and are willing to give their lives in the face of persecution and martyrdom?

Revd Bruce (after some pause): Perhaps two or three of them will remain steadfast till the end.

Mírzá Abu'l-Faḍl: If you permit me, I will now recount my position for you. Financially, I have no assets whatsoever. At times I even have nothing to subsist on. Sometimes my friends, who are also poor, insist on offering me a meal. My position with regard to political influence is as follows. Should people suspect that I am a Bahá'í they would undoubtedly put me to death in public, and those committing this crime would become the recipients of honours from the government. As to my knowledge, it is true that I have learnt religious subjects as are currently taught in Islamic schools. I am, nevertheless, born in and a product of a society steeped in ignorance and enveloped in darkness.

In spite of all these shortcomings, I have spoken to about one hundred people since my arrival in this city a month ago. Twenty-four souls among them have recognized the truth of this Faith and embraced it with such devotion and fervour that every one of them is ready to lay down his life in the path of God, as many other Bahá'ís have already done. Now, I want you to be fair in your judgement. Who, in this day, is assisted by the Holy Spirit, you or I?

The Reverend Dr Bruce had never expected that the dialogue conducted by Mírzá Abu'l-Faḍl would come so swiftly to an end and that he would find himself in such disarray. Discomfited, he asked for the meeting to be adjourned, and promised to continue the discussion at a later date.

The same Ali-Kuli Khan has recounted the following story about his conversation with another clergyman in the United States of America:

> Mírzá was a master of reasoning – he built a wall around people and trapped them so that they had either to accept his statements or acknowledge their ignorance. All kinds of scholars matched their minds with him here, but I never saw him defeated. He was deeply read in Church history, European theology and metaphysics, works on which he had studied in Arabic at Al-Azhar. I remember once a churchman came to him and violently attacked the Prophet Muḥammad. Mírzá said to him: 'Your leading authorities state that none of the Jewish or Roman historians of the First Century even mention Jesus, and many do not believe in the historicity of Christ. Certain Christians inserted a reference to Christ in the writings of Josephus, but the forgery was exposed. Others buried a tablet in China, which said that Christianity had been brought to that country in the First Century. This, too, was exposed. But as for the Prophet Muḥammad, He not only proclaimed the existence of a historical Christ, but He caused three hundred million people to believe in Him; to accept Him not only as a historical figure but also as the Spirit of God (Rúḥu'lláh). Was not Muḥammad, whom you condemn, a more successful Christian missionary than your own?'
>
> Mírzá never encouraged any talk which might lead to inharmony. Once, a friend came to him and said that another believer was doing harm to the Faith. Mírzá listened carefully. Then he told me to translate his answer word for word:
>
> 'Do you believe that Bahá'u'lláh is the promised Lord of Hosts?'
>
> 'Yes.'
>
> 'Well, if He is that Lord, these are the Hosts. What right have we to speak ill of the Hosts?' [5]

Mírzá Abu'l-Faḍl had another interview with Revd Bruce, this time in Tabríz. Unlike the account of the last dialogue, this one is recounted by Mírzá Abu'l-Faḍl himself:

> Early in the spring of this year (1887) I was staying in Tabríz when Mr Bruce, a learned divine of the honoured Christian community, who for years had been living in India and Persia and in latter years in Iṣfahán, arrived in Tabríz on his way to London. As he was known to me, I went to visit him in company with Jináb-i-Varqá and Áqá Khalíl-i-Tabrízí. After greeting each other, an American youth who was a Christian minister arrived and soon we were joined by Mustasháru'd-Dawlih, Mírzá Yúsuf Khán, who was a high-ranking government official. He was a man of good character and wisdom. As we sat around, a social atmosphere was created.
>
> Mr Bruce, referring to our meeting last year in Iṣfahán, said that he had been eager to find an opportunity to meet again and discuss three subjects which he considered to be the only things about which we disagreed. I said to him . . . that this was a good opportunity to discuss these matters as there was a meeting here in which men of culture and knowledge were present. I asked him to tell us what the three subjects were, so that I might explain them if I could.
>
> Mr Bruce said, 'The first question is this: You consider the Heavenly Father to be manifested in the form of a human temple, whereas we consider Him to be an Essence hidden from our eyes and unknowable by our intellect. He is exalted above any form or attribute.
>
> 'The second question: You consider the Old and the New Testament, as well as the *Qur'án*, to be Holy Books revealed by God. Whereas we believe that only the first two are the Words of God, the texts of which are free of interpolation and protected from change. Since the contents of the *Qur'án* differ from the former two, we consider it to be fallacious.
>
> 'The third question: We consider Christ to be a single

person, that is, Jesus. Whereas you consider Christ to be manifested in the form of many other persons.'

I said, 'I consider the criterion for considering these three questions ought to be the text of the Old and the New Testaments. Whatever these two Books testify will be acceptable to me and the basis for my argument. And now through the assistance of God, I would like to set forth the truth of our beliefs in the presence of these distinguished personages.'

He said, 'You are right, because in religious matters we do not consider anything authoritative and acceptable unless it conforms with the testimony of the Holy Books. We do not use intellectual and rational proofs in matters connected with faith and heavenly teachings.' He then asked for copies of the Old and the New Testament, which were brought in.

I said, 'Concerning the first question: It is clear and evident that the term "Heavenly Father" has been in use only among the Christian and Jewish peoples. Other nations, such as the Zoroastrians, Muslims, Hindus or Buddhists, do not use this phrase, and a great many of them have never heard of it. The origin of this term is in the Old Testament. From it, this term has entered into the New Testament which is born of the former Book. Therefore we must look at the testimony of the Old Testament concerning the "Heavenly Father", and be prepared to accept its description as authentic and not to follow the imaginations of the learned.' Mr. Bruce agreed with me on this point.

Then I asked him to read Chapter 9, verse 6 of Isaiah, which is as follows: 'For unto us a child is born, unto us a son is given; and the government shall be upon his shoulder: and his name shall be called Wonderful, Counsellor, the mighty God, the everlasting Father, the Prince of Peace.'

(Verse 7): 'of the increase of his government and peace there shall be no end, upon the throne of David, and upon his kingdom, to order it, and to establish it with judgement and with justice from henceforth even for ever. The zeal of the Lord of hosts will perform this.'

After these blessed verses were read out, I stated that these words testified that a son would be born who would save the Children of Israel from abasement and misery, and would be described by the following attributes: first, a 'Counsellor' who counsels the people; second, 'the mighty God' which means the Supreme Manifestation of God and the greatest Primal Word; third, 'the everlasting Father', through whom all human beings from the beginning till the end have been created and born of His sovereignty and omnipotence; fourth, 'the Prince of Peace', through whose Revelation the foundation of the oneness and unity of the human race would be laid, and the ills of discord and war which cause the destruction of the world and the degradation of the human race would be eliminated.

From this clear and explicit verse it is clear that the 'Heavenly Father' will appear in the form of the human temple, will be born of a mother and be known by the Greatest Name. It appears that in other passages of the Holy Books one may not be able to find a statement about the 'Heavenly Father' as explicit and evident as this one.

Mr Bruce, who was deeply immersed in thought, said, 'I have never heard such an exposition before.' Then he turned his attention to Edward, the American minister, and spoke a few words to him in English. Jináb-i-Áqá Khalíl, who knew English, conveyed to Jináb-i-Varqá the main points of the conversation between the two. Mr Bruce said, 'For a long time we have been giving the Old and the New Testament to the people of Islám. They do not grasp anything by studying them. But these people [the Bahá'ís] understand the meanings of heavenly Books so well. To be fair, they are right in the interpretation of the above verses in the Old Testament.'

Then this servant turned to Mr Bruce and said, 'Praise be to God, we have solved the first question and removed the differences between us. And now concerning the second question. . . [6]

Mírzá Abu'l-Faḍl sets out to prove the authenticity of the *Qur'án*, and begins to elucidate the subject. After one or two minutes of talking, the Revd Bruce interrupts him and brings the conversation to an abrupt end. Mírzá Abu'l-Faḍl writes about this:

> Mr Bruce, in a mood at once serious and light-hearted, hiding his inner disturbance with a smile characteristic of him, addressed me in these words:
>
> 'Truthfully and with sincerity I wish to make it clear that we know all that we ought to know about Muḥammad and the *Qur'án*. We can never submit to Him. Therefore, it is useless for you to speak to us on this question.'
>
> In reply, I said, 'Our purpose in coming here was not to enter into discussion with you, but rather to renew our acquaintance and fulfil our obligation to establish a loving relationship with you. The people of Bahá consider confict and dispute to be reprehensible behaviour. They regard love and amity as the most important feature in the life of man. It was because of your wish that we entered into discussion. We only responded to your questions.'
>
> Then Jináb-i-Varqá said to him, 'You were pleased with the answer to the first question. Surely there is no harm if you discuss the other questions too. Perchance you may find the answers to be to your satisfaction again.'
>
> But Mr Bruce said, 'As I have already stated, there is no point in continuing the discussion.' Thus our dialogue came to an end. We indulged in friendly conversation. He expressed an eagerness to take this servant with him to London. But I declined the offer so that I might serve this Most Great Cause.[7]

The travels of Mírzá Abu'l-Faḍl, both inside and outside Persia, undertaken for the promotion of the Faith, acted as a musk-laden breeze which wafted for almost three decades upon the newly-born community, refreshing its members and invigorating its growth. That he was a distinguished and exemplary instrument created by God to promote His Cause there can be no doubt. The example of his noble life is bound to inspire countless generations in future centuries and ages.

Ḥájí Mírzá Ḥaydar-'Alí

Another outstanding teacher of the Faith who travelled extensively throughout Persia during the Ministry of Bahá'u'lláh was the renowned Ḥájí Mírzá Ḥaydar-'Alí. He visited practically every locality in which a Bahá'í was living, and in many places where there were no Bahá'ís he succeeded in converting some souls to the Faith. One of his great achievements was that he had so thoroughly consecrated his life to the teaching work that no earthly power could ever distract him from his exalted goal of guiding the receptive souls to the Cause of God. No preoccupation, no material benefits, no pain or suffering or persecution could withhold him from serving His Lord. When he entered a town or village people who were endowed with spiritual vision sensed his presence and were drawn to him. Because he was detached from earthly things his heart was the well-spring of divine attributes. As a result of this, he radiated the power of the Faith to people, and his words sank deeply into their hearts. Some individuals who had been ill-disposed towards the Cause of God for years were favourably impressed by meeting him, and subdued at hearing a few of his words.

For example, when Ḥájí Mírzá Ḥaydar-'Alí was returning from the Holy Land to Persia, he stayed a few days in a small Kurdish town near the Persian border. There he came across a man named Karbilá'í Áqá Ján, who had been an enemy of the Faith for many years. Within a few days of associating with Ḥájí he recognized the truth of the Faith and became a new creation. His love for Bahá'u'lláh grew steadily and his enthusiasm knew no bounds. He surpassed many a veteran teacher of the Cause in his devotion to the Faith. Some time later, as a result of an armed rebellion by a certain religious leader, Karbilá'í Áqá Ján, who was a wealthy man, lost all his possessions and was forced to flee the town on foot. Destitution on the one hand and utter exhaustion on the other provoked in him a feeling of bitterness and despair. In this state of mind he raised his hands in supplication and addressed the Almighty in these simple words: 'Suppose we change places for a moment. I become God and you become Karbilá'í Áqá Ján. How would you have liked it if, as God, I had treated you in the same way you have treated Áqá Ján?'

No sooner were these words uttered than He who is the Knower of all things and the Hearer of our supplications responded to his plea. A short while later Karbilá'í Áqá Ján unexpectedly received a short Tablet from Bahá'u'lláh saying that He had heard His complaint in his prayer, and that God admitted that Áqá Ján was right! He assures him in this Tablet that God's assistance will be forthcoming. Soon he became prosperous and continued to serve the Cause of God till the end of his life.

In his teaching exploits Ḥájí Mírzá Ḥaydar-'Alí occasionally employed unusual tactics in order to open people's eyes and enable them to see the truth of the Cause of God. Here is the summary of a story told by Ḥájí himself; it happened in the city of Qum, which is a centre of the ecclesiastical hierarchy in Persia:

> They [two brothers who were Bahá'ís residing in Qum] informed me that there was a person who was a true believer in the Faith of Islám, who was God-fearing, honest and simple-minded, but very much attached to the clergy. They thought there was a chance that he might embrace the Faith of Bahá'u'lláh if I were to meet with him somewhere with a view to teaching him the Cause. We made the following arrangements:
>
> I was to retire to a scenic place in the countryside outside

> the city where I would be seen making tea and socializing with a friend. Then the two Bahá'í brothers* accompanied by their non-Bahá'í friend were to pass through the gardens in the area, and I was to greet and invite them to join me for a cup of tea. In the course of our conversation I could then bring up the subject of the Faith.
>
> We carried out this plan; they came and I spoke to him about the Faith. He was happy to converse with me, but when he realized who I was and what was my aim, he excused himself very politely and, with the utmost humility, said that the clergy had forbidden people to converse with the Bahá'ís . . . He demanded that we did not speak about religious subjects, otherwise he would have to leave us, and he suggested we might talk about other subjects.[8]

It is clear from the way that Ḥájí Mírzá Ḥaydar-'Alí conducted this discussion that he had recognized in this person a pure and simple soul who was capable of recognizing the truth of the Faith but who was deeply attached to the clergy and held them in high esteem. He therefore seems to have decided to do something to shake this person's confidence in the Persian clergy and show him their ugly side and true nature. He knew well that if this person were to take some searching questions about religion to the clergy, they would probably suspect him of being in contact with Bahá'ís and for this they could severely punish him, an act which could shatter his faith in the clergy.

This is how Ḥájí Mírzá Ḥaydar-'Alí continues the story:

> I said to him, 'I can appreciate that you consider it a sin to enter into conversation with me, but if I wanted to ask a question

* It was not possible under the circumstances prevailing at the time for Bahá'ís in general and these two brothers in particular to identify themselves as Bahá'ís, as it could have endangered their lives. It was, however, much easier for a person who was passing through a town, like Ḥájí Mírzá Ḥaydar-'Alí, to be presented as a Bahá'í and teach the Faith. For this reason the two brothers had to pretend to their friend that they were not Bahá'ís. (A.T.)

> from the clergy could you take it to them and bring back the answer?' He said, 'It depends on the nature of the question.' I said, 'The question is as follows: "What constitutes the proof of the authenticity of the glorious *Qur'án* and how can we be assured that the Book is a miracle?"' He said to me that if I wrote down the question he would be glad to take the letter and bring back the answer . . . And so this simple-minded and truthful person took my notes to the clergy.
>
> No sooner did these divines see the note than they beat the poor man very severely, cursed and denounced him as a Bahá'í and wanted to put him into prison. This cruel and inhuman treatment which was meted out to him, coupled with the inability of the divines to answer the question, opened the eyes of the person and caused him to embrace the Faith.[9]

In his vast travels in Persia, Ḥájí Mírzá Ḥaydar-'Alí taught the Faith to many souls. In the course of these journeys he encountered great opposition from the enemies, and many a time he was attacked physically. Some of the harrowing afflictions he endured in prison in the Sudan for several years is reflected in the story of his illustrious life recounted in a previous volume.* From the early days of the Ministry of Bahá'u'lláh until His ascension, and during the years of the Ministry of 'Abdu'l-Bahá, this man of God served the Cause with exemplary devotion and self-sacrifice and shed an imperishable lustre upon the annals of the Faith.

---

* see vol. 2.

19

The Role of the Hands of the Cause of God

Bahá'u'lláh has enjoined upon His followers to teach His Cause, and this commandment has always been carried out by every sincere and true Bahá'í. In the early days of the Faith the believers in Persia were devotedly engaged in awakening the souls, but each one played his part in accordance with his ability. Not everybody was able to speak about religion. The actual work of teaching, adducing proofs and confirming people was usually left to those who had the gift of knowledge and the understanding of religious subjects. As we have said, these individuals were known as *muballigh* (teacher). In every locality there were usually a few knowledgeable believers who were thus named and who were available to discuss the Faith in private meetings with people who had been contacted by individual Bahá'ís.

Often, teaching the Cause was carried out as team work. There were many who searched for receptive souls and were able to attract them to the Cause through prayer and perseverance, and eventually prepare them to attend a meeting in which a *muballigh* would speak to them about the Faith. There were others who would offer their homes for such meetings, and there were some who had to render other services to make these meetings possible. Wisdom was, and always is, an important aspect of teaching. The Bahá'í teachers first weighed up the capacity of the person, and then began teaching the Faith to him step by step with wisdom and prudence.*

These teachers of the Cause usually had a deep understanding of the Faith and were well versed in the Writings of

* see vol. 2, pp. 91–106.

Bahá'u'lláh and in the Holy Books of the past. Most of them were learned people, but there were some very successful teachers who were illiterate or had very little education. We have discussed in a previous volume* the difference between the ability to understand spiritual truth and the gift of knowledge. The former comes through having faith and being detached from earthly things, while the latter comes through learning. There have been some individuals who had great knowledge of the Faith, but did not understand its truth. On the other hand, there were many who possessed the two.

The outstanding qualities possessed by most teachers of the Cause in those days were a passionate love for Bahá'u'lláh which made them radiant souls, and a deep understanding of the Faith whether educated or not. In the absence of any institutions of the Faith such as local and national spiritual assemblies in the days of Bahá'u'lláh and 'Abdu'l-Bahá, a *muballigh* would play a significant part in deepening the friends in the knowledge of the Faith as well as helping and encouraging them to discharge their duties in the field of teaching.

As far back as 1881 Bahá'u'lláh in one of His Tablets[1] directed Ibn-i-Aṣdaq to make arrangements, in consultation with Mullá 'Alí-Akbar-i-Sháhmírzádí and another believer, for the appointment in every locality in Persia of a suitable resident Bahá'í teacher. He places great emphasis on this matter and regards it as the most important of all things. From the very early days, too, Bahá'u'lláh Himself directed a few outstanding and knowledgeable souls to travel continually throughout Persia and the neighbouring countries in the capacity of *muballigh* to teach the Faith in different towns and villages. Their main task was to speak to interested people in private meetings which were usually organized by local believers. These travelling teachers rendered an invaluable service: through their devotion, their knowledge, their spirituality and radiance they succeeded in helping the believers in their teaching work and

* see vol. 3, pp. 94–6.

brought a great many souls under the shadow of the Cause of God. This practice continued during the ministries of 'Abdu'l-Bahá and Shoghi Effendi, and as the numbers grew there were two categories of *muballigh*: the 'local' and the 'travelling'. When the national institutions of the Faith were established in Persia one of their important obligations was to ensure that in every locality there were some individuals who could function in the capacity of a *muballigh*.

Parallel with the duty of teaching the Faith is the principle of conducting the affairs of the community through the process of consultation which Bahá'u'lláh has ordained in His teachings. Before the establishment of the institutions of the Faith, important decisions, whether concerned with the local community or an individual, were often taken by consultation among a few teachers of the Faith and others who were older and more experienced Bahá'ís. As we have already stated, the practice of naming certain individuals as *muballigh* continued during the ministries of 'Abdu'l-Bahá and Shoghi Effendi. When the local spiritual assemblies were constituted in Persia during the ministry of the Guardian, he advised that the spiritual assembly in its decision-making process ought to pay special attention to the views of the *muballigh* in the area and try to implement his advice.

It seems that this process, which started at the time of Bahá'u'lláh and later was consolidated by the appointment of four Hands of the Cause by Him, was formally institutionalized during the ministry of Shoghi Effendi and later the Universal House of Justice. In the Formative Age of the Faith, which began with the ascension of 'Abdu'l-Bahá, the Hands of the Cause appointed* by Shoghi Effendi became an integral part of the institutions of the Administrative Order of Bahá'u'lláh. Similarly the Boards of Counsellors, appointed by the Universal House of Justice to perpetuate the main functions of the Hands of the Cause into the future, also constitute

* The first contingent of Hands of the Cause was appointed in 1951.

an institution of the Faith. This institution, together with its appointed arm known as Auxiliary Board Members and their assistants, seems to be carrying out the same functions which were once allotted to those teachers of the Faith entitled *muballigh* on the international, national and local levels. It must be stated, however, that there are today a great many teachers of the Faith, highly knowledgeable, devoted and active, who render notable service to the Cause but are not members of this institution, and therefore do not have certain responsibilities in relation to the Bahá'í community. These responsibilities, apart from teaching and encouraging the believers in their service to the Cause, include consultation with the local and national spiritual assemblies, responsibilities which are not unlike some of the functions of the *muballigh* in older days.

During the last few years of His life Bahá'u'lláh chose four of His devoted followers and designated them as Hands of the Cause of God. They were Ḥájí Mullá 'Alí-Akbar-i-Sháh-mírzádí, known as Ḥájí Ákhúnd; Mírzá Muḥammad-Taqí, known as Ibn-i-Abhar; Mírzá 'Alí-Muḥammad, known as Ibn-i-Aṣdaq; and Ḥájí Mírzá Ḥasan, surnamed Adíb. These appointments, so far as we know, did not take place at one time. Also, they did not take the form of announcing their names to the community or outlining their functions in one special Tablet. With the exception of Mírzá Ḥasan-i-Adíb, who embraced the Faith about three years before the ascension of Bahá'u'lláh, the other three Hands of the Cause were long-standing believers. They were the recipients of many Tablets in which, over the years, He showered upon them His blessings, guided their steps, praised their work and exalted their station in glowing terms. In these Tablets He often refers to them as 'the Chosen Ones', 'the loved ones', 'the detached souls', 'the pure in spirit' and similar designations.

Towards the end of His life He revealed a Tablet to each one of these souls, designating them as 'Hands of the Cause of God'. As far as we can gather, the first time He used the term 'Hand of the Cause' to refer to an individual with certain responsibilities was in a Tablet revealed in honour of Ibn-i-Aṣdaq on 19 Rajab 1304 (13 April 1887). Perhaps all three Hands of the Cause were appointed around the same time. There is a Tablet revealed in honour of Ibn-i-Abhar dated 24 Sha'bán 1306 (26 April 1889) which makes it clear that he had already been designated a Hand of the Cause. The present writer has not been able to find a definite date for the appointment of Ḥájí Mírzá Ḥasan-i-Adíb. He was the last appointee, as he only became a believer around 1889.

Perhaps it is true to say that for quite some time the believers did not appreciate the significance of the appellation 'Hand of the Cause' and the implications of designating certain individuals as such. One may think of two reasons for this. First, Bahá'u'lláh had often used the term 'Hands' in earlier Tablets such as the *Súriy-i-Haykal** and others without referring to any particular person; secondly, there was no apparent change in the activities of these souls after their appointment, since they continued to be always engaged in promoting the Cause and assisting the believers in their manifold activities. For instance, Bahá'u'lláh confirms in a Tablet[2] that from the early days of His arrival in 'Akká He had instructed Mullá 'Alí-Akbar to be engaged in the protection of the Cause. The friends began to understand the functions and duties of the Hands of the Cause gradually, as the years went by. This happened especially during the Ministry of 'Abdu'l-Bahá when He directed them to carry out certain duties as a body.

In order to appreciate the function of the Hands of the Cause, let us examine some basic principles of life and creation. In a Tablet[3] revealed in honour of His Trustee, Ḥájí Abu'l-Ḥasan-i-Amín, Bahá'u'lláh states that movement is caused by heat, and heat by the Word of God.† This is a profound statement, the first part of which is proved by science, the second taught by

* see vol. 3, chapter 7.

† For more information on this topic see above, pp. 43–4.

religion. This pronouncement is not only valid physically, but has deep spiritual significance as well. Religious enthusiasm and fervour are generated by the warmth of one's heart.

A believer can arise to serve the Cause with devotion only when his heart is warmed by the fire of the love of God. In simpler terms this means that when the love of Bahá'u'lláh enters the heart of a believer, he will feel exhilarated and uplifted. It is then that he will be motivated to serve Him. If service to the Cause is rendered without spiritual fire and love it will be ineffective in the end, even though at first it may appear to be successful. To serve without burning love within the heart results in frustration, despair and confusion. In this case the individual may experience great difficulties in his faith. Service rendered to the Cause, when motivated by a believer's love for Bahá'u'lláh, will become a means of drawing closer to Him, whereas service with an ulterior motive renders him egotistical and deprives him of true happiness.

We have learnt from the words of Bahá'u'lláh that the Word of God is the cause of producing the heat whereby creation has come into being. This is also true in a spiritual sense. Only the Word of God can light the flame of love in the heart of a believer, and then only provided the individual succeeds in severing his attachment from the things of this world. Those who attained the presence of Bahá'u'lláh experienced the power and majesty of the Word if they were pure in heart. Those who were not pure in heart did not receive this bounty, even though they were very close to His Person. The best example of this is provided by some of the sons and daughters of Bahá'u'lláh who were in attendance for years and yet were the remotest from Him in spirit.

There is nothing more potent than the Word of God in creating the fire of His love in the heart of a believer. Next to that is the influence which a true believer may exert on the heart of another through close association. So powerful is this influence that Bahá'u'lláh states in the *Hidden Words*:

ḤÁJÍ MULLÁ ʻALÍ-AKBAR-I-SHAHMÍRZÁDÍ

Hand of the Cause of God appointed by Bahá'u'lláh
Known as Ḥájí Ákhúnd

MÍRZÁ MUḤAMMAD-TAQÍ, IBN-I-ABHAR

Hand of the Cause of God appointed by Bahá'u'lláh

MÍRZÁ ʻALÍ-MUḤAMMAD, IBN-I-AṢDAQ

Hand of the Cause of God appointed by Bahá'u'lláh

MÍRZÁ ḤASAN-I-ADÍB

Hand of the Cause of God appointed by Bahá'u'lláh

> He that seeketh to commune with God, let him betake himself to the companionship of His loved ones; and he that desireth to hearken unto the word of God, let him give ear to the words of His chosen ones.[4]

This passage demonstrates the great contribution which the Hands of the Cause, themselves highly exhilarated by the love of their Lord, made towards enthusing and arousing the believers and enabling them thereby to draw nearer to Bahá'u'lláh. These devoted souls warmed the hearts of the friends by the fire of their faith which burnt brightly within them. To commune with these holy souls was to commune with God, and to hear their words was to hear the Word of God.

We can see, therefore, the vital role with which the Hands of the Cause were entrusted by Bahá'u'lláh. By virtue of the fire which raged within their hearts they were able to ignite others. Of course this role is not limited to the Hands. Any believer who is aglow with the love of God can impart the fire of his faith to others. The history of the Faith has recorded the names of many immortal teachers of the Cause who have been endowed with this quality.

Although Bahá'u'lláh appointed only four Hands of the Cause, He indicated that there were others whose rank He had not divulged. For example, Ḥájí Amín, the Trustee of Bahá'u'lláh, wrote Him a glowing report about some meritorious services rendered by one of the Afnáns in Yazd. In response, Bahá'u'lláh stated in a Tablet[5] that He knew there were some believers in that land who were accounted as Hands of the Cause in the sight of God, but through His wisdom He had not outwardly revealed their names, although in reality they were well known among the Concourse on high, the denizens of His Kingdom.

It becomes apparent from the study of the Writings of Bahá'u'lláh, that He gave the station of a Hand of the Cause to one other person. He was Áqá Siyyid Áqá, the eldest son of the illustrious Afnán, Áqá Mírzá Áqá entitled Núru'd-Dín.* In a Tablet[6] revealed in honour of Áqá Siyyid Áqá, Bahá'u'lláh confirms that through the bounty of God he is reckoned as an Afnán and a Hand of the Cause. Áqá Siyyid Áqá was a devoted believer, but somehow he was not involved in the work of the Hands. Maybe he could be considered as being in the category of those souls who rank spiritually among the Hands, but whose names, as indicated by Bahá'u'lláh, were not revealed in this life.

In another Tablet to one of the Afnáns[7] Bahá'u'lláh mentions that owing to the lack of capacity of the peoples of the world, the ranks and stations of believers have not been disclosed. In yet another Tablet[8] Bahá'u'lláh declares that any believer who has heard the call of God in this day, turned His whole being towards His Most Exalted Realm, and detached himself from every earthly thing, is reckoned as a Hand of the Cause among the people.

'Abdu'l-Bahá throws further light on this subject in His Writings. In answer to a question concerning the Hands of the Cause, 'Abdu'l-Bahá, as recorded by Mírzá Maḥmúd-i-Zarqání, the renowned chronicler of His journeys to Europe and America, is reported to have said these words:

> The Hands of the Cause are such blessed souls that the evidences of their sanctity and spirituality will be felt in the hearts of people. Their influence must be such that the souls may be carried away by their goodly character, their pure motives, their justice and fairness, that individuals may be enamoured of their praiseworthy character and their virtuous attributes, and that people may turn their faces towards them for their qualities and resplendent signs. 'Hand of the Cause' is not a title which can be given to anybody. Neither is it a position to be handed down to whomsoever may desire it . . . The more any soul becomes self-effacing, the more confirmed

* see below, pp. 350–1.

> will he be in the service of the Cause of God; and the more humble, the nearer will he be to Him.[9]

It must be made clear, however, that no one is qualified, nor has the right, to nominate a believer as a Hand of the Cause, except Bahá'u'lláh, 'Abdu'l-Bahá or Shoghi Effendi. 'Abdu'l-Bahá states in one of His Tablets[10] that the Hands of the Cause are those souls who have been appointed by the Most Exalted Pen, or who have been addressed by 'Abdu'l-Bahá with that designation.

The conclusion, therefore, is that Bahá'u'lláh appointed the four Hands of the Cause mentioned above, who functioned as Hands, held consultative meetings together, and became known in the community as occupying a position of spiritual leadership. During the Ministry of 'Abdu'l-Bahá these four could be seen to have created the nucleus of a sacred institution which was further developed and consolidated during the ministry of Shoghi Effendi, constituting one of the twin arms of the Administrative Order of Bahá'u'lláh. One of the four, Ibn-i-Aṣdaq, lived long enough to serve the Guardian during the opening years of the Formative Age. 'Abdu'l-Bahá did not appoint any Hands during His Ministry. He only referred to a few outstanding believers posthumously as having the station of the Hands of the Cause: they are Mullá Ṣádiq-i-Khurásání known as Ismu'lláhu'l-Aṣdaq,* Nabíl-i-Akbar,† 'Alí-Muḥammad-i-Varqá,‡ and Shaykh-Riḍáy-i-Yazdí.§ According to the provisions of 'Abdu'l-Bahá's Will and Testament Shoghi Effendi, the Guardian of the Faith, appointed some Hands of the Cause. During the last six years of his ministry he appointed thirty-two; he also appointed ten souls posthumously as Hands of the Cause.

---

* see vol. 3, pp. 62–3, 253–60, 266–7.

† see vols. 1 and 2.

‡ see above, ch. 4.

§ Since there are one or two others by the same name, it is not possible to identify him. However, some believe strongly that he is Mullá Muḥammad-i-Riḍáy-i-Muḥammad-Ábádí. For his life story see vol. 1, pp. 84–91.

In the same way as there are some souls whose spiritual qualities and exalted rank are concealed in this life, only to be revealed in the world beyond, the opposite is also true. In one of His Tablets[11] Bahá'u'lláh states that there are some people who become famous in this life and are prominent in the Kingdom of Names,* but in reality their inner beings are sunk in the abyss of evil passions and corrupt desires. Indeed, the history of the Bahá'í community is replete with stories of individuals such as these, individuals who were foremost among the teachers or administrators of the Faith and were renowned among the believers. But when confronted with tests,† they eventually revealed their true nature and perished spiritually at the end. The stories of a few such people who lived during the Ministries of Bahá'u'lláh and 'Abdu'l-Bahá have been described in previous volumes.‡ This condition, however, is not exclusive to the early days of the Faith. It exists today and will exist in the future also.

The greatest enemy of a believer and the most formidable barrier between him and God is self and evil passion. Should a person become a captive of his own base and appetitive nature he will be denuded of his spiritual qualities, and at the end will turn into a darkened self.

In several of His Tablets Bahá'u'lláh pays tribute to the devotion and self-sacrifice of the Hands of the Cause, describes their main functions as the diffusion of the divine fragrances and the protection of His Cause, and prays that they may be assisted by the Almighty to serve His Faith, to guide and enthuse the believers and at all times be ready to carry out His commandments. In a Tablet to Mullá 'Alí-Akbar[12] Bahá'u'lláh calls on the Hands to help the believers become aware of the laws and principles of the Faith and exert every effort to carry

---

* For an explanation of this term see vol. 2, pp. 39–43.

† For an explanation of the necessity and wisdom of tests see vol. 3, pp. 47–9.

‡ For example, the story of Jamál-i-Burújirdí and Siyyid Mihdíy-i-Dahají, and the Covenant-breakers in vol. 2.

them out. In a Tablet[13] He states that the Hands of His Cause circle around His Will, and do not speak except by His leave. He declares that through them the standards of the oneness of God have been raised among people and the banners of holiness unfurled in all regions. Bahá'u'lláh further testifies that the inmates of the highest Paradise, the denizens of His Kingdom, and beyond them the Tongue of Grandeur, bestow upon them their blessings and salutations.

In another Tablet[14] Bahá'u'lláh states that God has appointed the Hands of His Cause as guards and custodians of the stronghold of His Faith so that they can protect it from the onslaught of the unfaithful and the ignorant. He describes the Hands of the Cause as the lamps of guidance who stand guard at the entrance of His mighty edifice and prevent the ungodly from entering it. In several of His Tablets Bahá'u'lláh has revealed short prayers for the Hands of His Cause. One is revealed in the *Lawḥ-i-Dunyá** and has been translated into English:

> Light and glory, greeting and praise be upon the Hands of His Cause, through whom the light of fortitude hath shone forth and the truth hath been established that the authority to choose rests with God, the Powerful, the Mighty, the Unconstrained, through whom the ocean of bounty hath surged and the fragrance of the gracious favours of God, the Lord of mankind, hath been diffused. We beseech Him – Exalted is he – to shield them through the power of His hosts, to protect them through the potency of His dominion and to aid them through His indomitable strength which prevaileth over all created things. Sovereignty is God's, the Creator of the heavens and the Lord of the Kingdom of Names.[15]

In His Will and Testament 'Abdu'l-Bahá has summarized the duties of the Hands of the Cause in one passage:

* see below, ch. 22.

> The obligations of the Hands of the Cause of God are to diffuse the Divine Fragrances, to edify the souls of men, to promote learning, to improve the character of all men and to be, at all times and under all conditions, sanctified and detached from earthly things. They must manifest the fear of God by their conduct, their manners, their deeds and their words.

These statements extolling the station of the Hands of the Cause and delineating their functions must not be allowed to give rise to the view that in some ways the institution of the Hands, followed by that of the Counsellors, is carrying out the functions of priesthood as in other religions. The fact that Bahá'u'lláh has abolished priesthood is an ample testimony that this is not the case. The following statement by the Universal House of Justice clarifies this point:

> It should be apparent to the friends that, as Bahá'u'lláh Himself both abolished the priesthood and instituted the body of the Hands of the Cause, the Hands cannot be confused with a priesthood. There are basic differences between a priesthood and Bahá'í institutions, such as the Hands of the Cause and the Continental Boards of Counsellors. A priesthood is usually a profession, has sacramental functions and confers upon the individual occupant of the ecclesiastical office jurisdiction over the believers. In the Bahá'í Faith, there is no profession in any of its institutions, there are no sacraments and no individual has a sacramental function. Jurisdiction over communities and individuals is not vested in individuals. Even in the matter of teaching, the friends must realize that although a Hand of the Cause or a member of the Continental Board of Counsellors or indeed any other believer may be deeply learned in the Teachings so that one naturally gives weight to his exposition of them, no one, apart from the Master and the Guardian, is authorized to interpret the Sacred Writings.[16]

During His lifetime Bahá'u'lláh directed the Hands to consult among themselves and with other believers on issues which were vital for the growth and development of the Bahá'í community. For example, Ibn-i-Abhar, one of the Hands, had posed the question of the well-being and prosperity of the Bahá'ís of Persia. In a Tablet[17] revealed in 1889 Bahá'u'lláh in response states that one should adhere to any means which may become the cause of the exaltation of the Word of God, the elevation of the minds and souls, the upliftment of the station of man, and the achievement of those things which benefit humanity. He then asserts that the answer will come through consultation. He urges Ibn-i-Abhar and the other Hands to gather together and invite a few devoted souls who have attained the station of certitude in the Faith and are observing the teachings, to join them in consultation about the various affairs. The next step, Bahá'u'lláh advises, would be to rely on God's confirmations and carry out the decision reached. He assures them that if they do this, they will be inspired by Him to achieve that which is the cause of prosperity and salvation.

It seems that at a certain point in His Ministry Bahá'u'lláh, wishing to emphasize the importance of consultation in resolving various issues, sometimes deliberately declined to give guidance when asked for advice and instead urged the questioner to seek consultation on the subject. For instance, Ibn-i-Abhar once sought guidance from Bahá'u'lláh as to where he should reside in Persia. The answer was that first he ought to seek consultation with some souls who were well-assured and steadfast in the Faith, and then implement their decision.

In a Tablet[18] to His Trustee Ḥájí Amín, Bahá'u'lláh informs him that His Pen is ready to vouchsafe the bounties of God to any soul who may ask for a Tablet in his own name. He expresses willingness to do this so that the heedless ones may become informed and the fast-asleep be awakened. But the choice of names must be made through the consultation of the Hands. He states that He has given this commandment to the Hands so that the principle of consultation may be fully established and strengthened in this world. A few extracts from the Tablets of Bahá'u'lláh and 'Abdu'l-Bahá concerning the importance of consultation have been quoted in a previous volume.*

It is apparent from these statements that the consultative meetings of the Hands of the Cause in which the affairs of the community were consulted upon were in operation long before the establishment of local and national spiritual assemblies. Indeed, the consultative meeting of the Hands evolved into the Spiritual Assembly of Ṭihrán, the first assembly in the Bahá'í world. The consultative meeting of the Hands usually consisted of the Hands and those whom they invited to take part, but these were not always the same individuals. Discussions were mainly concerned with propagation of the Faith and its protection.

In 1899 'Abdu'l-Bahá instructed the Hands of the Cause to establish the first elected Spiritual Assembly of the Bahá'ís of Ṭihrán. The details were left to the Hands. Unlike the present system, in which the whole Bahá'í community in a town takes part in the election of the Spiritual Assembly, the Hands invited a number of well-known Bahá'ís of Ṭihrán to be the electors. These elected the members by secret ballot and the Hands were permanent members who actually issued credential papers for each elected member and invited them to serve on the Assembly.

It is interesting to note that one member of the Assembly, Mr Síyávash, was of Zoroastrian stock, and another, Mr Javáhirí, of Jewish background. This was a very significant development in the Bahá'í community, for in the early days the believers in Persia were not fully integrated. They were known as Bahá'ís of Muslim, Zoroastrian or Jewish backgrounds. The integration began at a slow pace during the time of the Master

* see vol. 3, pp. 317–18.

and gained momentum as intermarriages, though few at first, took place. Ibn-i-Abhar, one of the Hands of the Cause, gave his daughter in marriage to a Bahá'í youth of Jewish descent and this practice became universally acceptable among the Bahá'ís of Persia. During the Guardian's ministry every trace of division within the rank and file of the believers was eliminated. Today it is a difficult task to know who is from which background in the Bahá'í community.

It is obvious that every nation has its own prejudices. When people enter the Faith of God they are bound to bring with them various unacceptable practices to which they have been accustomed. But as the believers grow in the Faith and become more mature Bahá'ís, and especially when they enter into the arena of service to the Cause as teachers or administrators, they gradually become purged of their prejudices and are increasingly able to employ the teachings of Bahá'u'lláh in their individual as well as collective lives.

The Hands of the Cause, while serving on the Spiritual Assembly of Ṭihrán, reserved for themselves the right to cast two votes each during consultation. This practice continued for some years until 'Abdu'l-Bahá gave directions to change the system and to establish the principle of one vote for each person. Of course 'Abdu'l-Bahá had every confidence in the Hands, but He explained that if this practice were not stopped there could be great difficulties in the future. He gave the example of the time when influential people such as kings would enter the Faith. They could use this practice as a precedent and arrogate to themselves the right to cast multiple votes.

All communications to the Spiritual Assembly were effected through the Hands. At first all letters of the Spiritual Assembly were sent out under the signature of the Hands, and later a seal was made in four pieces and each piece kept by one of the Hands, who would put the seal of the Assembly on all communications. Gradually, the situation changed with the election of a chairman and a secretary. At last, at the

MEMBERS OF THE FIRST SPIRITUAL ASSEMBLY OF ṬIHRÁN

Seated, front row, from left: Ḥájí Mírzá ‘Abdu’lláh-Ṣaḥiḥ-Furúsh, Mírzá ‘Azízu’lláh Varqá, Áqá Dhakaríyyá Javáhirí (Jewish background); seated middle row, from left: three of the Hands of the Cause, Mírzá Ḥasan-i-Adíb, Mírza ‘Alí-Muḥammad Ibn-i-Aṣdaq, Ḥájí Mullá ‘Alí-Akbar (known as Ḥájí Ákhúnd), Ḥájí Mírzá Muḥammad-i-Vakílu’d-Dawlih (an Afnán); standing from left: ‘Alí-Muḥammad Khán-i-Áṣifu’l- Ḥukámá, Muḥammad Khán-i-Jadhbih, Mírzá Muhammad-Ḥusayn-i-Muhtadí, Mírzá Síyávash-i-Sefidvash (Zoroastrian background)

time when every person in the country was obliged to adopt a surname* and record it in the Registry office, 'Alí-Akbar-i-Muḥibb'us-Sulṭán, then secretary of the Spiritual Assembly, took the surname 'Rawhání' (Spiritual) and signed all communications under his surname which was considered very apt. The seal was also changed into one piece which was kept by the chairman.

* In the mid-1920s the government of Persia made it obligatory for every person to adopt a surname. Before that people did not have surnames.

Lives of the Hands of the Cause Appointed by Bahá'u'lláh

The stories of the four Hands of the Cause appointed by Bahá'u'lláh are among the most wonderful and uplifting testimonies of love for Him, of dedication to His Cause, of sufferings and imprisonments in His path, of utter self-effacement, of unrelenting whole-hearted service to the community, and of memorable achievements. A full account of their eventful lives is beyond the scope of this book,[1] but the following stories will at least provide an outline.

Ḥájí Mullá 'Alí-Akbar (Ḥájí Áḵẖúnd)

This great Apostle of Bahá'u'lláh came from the village of Shahmírzád in the province of Ḵẖurásán. As a youth he was so eager to acquire religious knowledge that he went to the city of Maṣẖhad where he received the usual religious education in various theological schools. But the more he searched for truth the less he found it in those circles. 'Abdu'l-Bahá describes this period of his life so eloquently:

> Yet another Hand of the Cause was the revered Mullá 'Alí-Akbar, upon him be the glory of God, the All-Glorious. Early in life, this illustrious man attended institutions of higher learning and labored diligently, by day and night, until he became thoroughly conversant with the learning of the day, with secular studies, philosophy, and religious jurisprudence. He frequented the gatherings of philosophers, mystics, and Ṣẖayḵẖís, thoughtfully traversing those areas of knowledge,

intuitive wisdom, and illumination; but he thirsted after the wellspring of truth, and hungered for the bread that comes down from Heaven. No matter how he strove to perfect himself in those regions of the mind, he was never satisfied; he never reached the goal of his desires; his lips stayed parched; he was confused, perplexed, and felt that he had wandered from his path. The reason was that in all those circles he had found no passion; no joy, no ecstasy; no faintest scent of love. And as he went deeper into the core of those manifold beliefs, he discovered that from the day of the Prophet Muḥammad's advent until our own times, innumerable sects have arisen: creeds differing among themselves; disparate opinions, divergent goals, uncounted roads and ways. And he found each one, under some plea or other, claiming to reveal spiritual truth; each one believing that it alone followed the true path – this although the Muḥammadic sea could rise in one great tide, and carry all those sects away to the ocean floor. 'No cry shalt thou hear from them, nor a whisper even.'*

Whoso ponders the lessons of history will learn that this sea has lifted up innumerable waves, yet in the end each has dissolved and vanished, like a shadow drifting by. The waves have perished, but the sea lives on. This is why 'Alí Qabl-i-Akbar could never quench his thirst, till the day when he stood on the shore of Truth and cried:

> Here is a sea with treasure to the brim;
> Its waves toss pearls under the great wind's thong.
> Throw off your robe and plunge, nor try to swim,
> Pride not yourself on swimming – dive headlong.[2]

He was about nineteen years of age when he came in contact with the Bábís of the time. Bahá'u'lláh was then in Ba<u>gh</u>dád, and a few copies of the *Kitáb-i-Íqán* were circulating among the believers. It appears that a perusal of that heavenly Book

* *Qur'án* 19:98.

in about the year 1861 ignited the fire of faith in his pure heart. This fire of the love of Bahá'u'lláh began to burn within him fiercely, and as time went on its heat could be felt by those who came in contact with him; indeed, he became the fulfilment of the words of Bahá'u'lláh revealed in a Tablet to Ibn-i-Aṣdaq describing the quality of a true Bahá'í:

> O Friends! You must all be so ablaze in this day with the fire of the love of God that the heat thereof may be manifest in all your veins, your limbs and members of your body, and the peoples of the world may be ignited by this heat and turn to the horizon of the Beloved.[3]

'Abdu'l-Bahá describes him as a fountain:

> Like a fountain, his heart welled and jetted forth; meaning and truth, like soft-flowing crystal waters, began to stream from his lips. At first, with humility, with spiritual poverty, he garnered the new light, and only then he proceeded to shed it abroad. For how well has it been said,
>
> Shall he the gift of life to others bear
> Who of life's gift has never had a share?
>
> A teacher must proceed in this way: he must first teach himself, and then others. If he himself still walks the path of carnal appetites and lusts, how can he guide another to the 'evident signs'* of God?[4]

Rank and fortune never came Mullá 'Alí-Akbar's way. Instead, sufferings and persecution were his lot from the early days of his conversion to the Faith. Soon after embracing the Cause of God he was forced out of the city of Ma<u>sh</u>had by the fanatical theological students. He returned to his native village and

* *Qur'án* 3:91.

began to teach the Cause there. Again the enemies became alarmed and attacked him in every way. Eventually he left his family and settled in Ṭihrán. Soon he became known as a Bahá'í there, and his teaching exploits evoked great opposition from the clergy. 'Abdu'l-Bahá writes of him in these words:

> This honored man was successful in converting a multitude. For the sake of God he cast all caution aside, as he hastened along the ways of love. He became as one frenzied, as a vagrant and one known to be mad. Because of his new Faith, he was mocked at in Ṭihrán by high and low. When he walked through the streets and bázárs, the people pointed their fingers at him, calling him a Bahá'í. Whenever trouble broke out, he was the one to be arrested first. He was always ready and waiting for this, since it never failed.[5]

The first time he was imprisoned was by order of Ḥájí Mullá 'Alíy-i-Kaní,* the highest religious dignitary of Ṭihrán. This is believed to have been around 1868. The Pen of Bahá'u'lláh addressed a Tablet[6] to this clergyman which is wrathful in its tone and highly condemnatory in its contents. He informs this proud and tyrannical high priest that the Prophet of Islám wept aloud in the highest paradise because of his wicked deeds. He sternly rebukes him for issuing death warrants for the believers, proclaims to him the greatness of His Cause, asserts that if all the powers of the earth were to be leagued against Him they would utterly fail to prevent the establishment of His Faith in the world, and warns that God lies in wait and is watchful of his doings. In other Tablets Bahá'u'lláh foreshadowed that God would soon strike him down in the same way as He did the 'Wolf' and the 'She-serpent',† and this what happened.

It is not known exactly how long Mullá 'Alí-Akbar was kept in this prison, but some years later in 1872 he was again

* For his involvement in the martyrdom of Badí' see vol. 3, p. 191.

† see above, ch. 6.

taken to prison by the orders of Kamrán Mírzá the Náyibu's-Salṭanih, the Governor of Ṭihrán.* This imprisonment, which lasted seven months, began only three days after his marriage to a certain Fáṭimih Khánum who became his devoted consort throughout his eventful life. It is reported that at the time of his marriage he was living in a dilapidated room and his earthly possessions consisted of a sheepskin and a kettle!

Mullá 'Alí-Akbar endured the hardships of imprisonment in a spirit of joy, of pride and of thankfulness to his Lord. He was kept in a narrow dark prison cell with a chain around his neck and stocks on his feet. He suffered greatly in this prison. In a Tablet[7] Bahá'u'lláh describes how the inmates of the highest Paradise have raised their voices and announced the glad-tidings that 'Alí-Akbar had entered the prison in the path of God. He showers upon his soul His blessings and His love, and denounces the actions of the oppressors. In another Tablet[8] He states that the Concourse on High have lamented for his sufferings, and urges him to become exhilarated with an abiding joy for he has endured severe hardships in the path of his Lord. Soon after his release from this prison he travelled to northern parts of Persia, where he was able to enthuse the believers and galvanize them into action. Bahá'u'lláh, in a Tablet[9] revealed after this journey, praises his work, states that God has chosen him for the service of His Cause, and asserts that the greatest service to His Threshold is that of uniting the souls and causing them to love each other. He directs him to be engaged in this type of activity at all times, and assures him of divine assistance in his life.

Mullá 'Alí-Akbar went on pilgrimage and attained the presence of his Lord for the first time in 1873. He basked in the sunshine of Bahá'u'lláh's unfailing love and bounties for about six months. Then he returned to Ṭihrán and resumed his devoted services to the Cause he loved so much. He was constantly teaching receptive souls, deepening the believers, and

* He was a son of Náṣiri'd-Dín Sháh, and an influential personality.

encouraging them with the utmost love to serve the Faith of God. Mullá 'Alí-Akbar was taken to prison six times altogether and spent about seven years bound with chains and fetters in the gloomy surroundings that were the Persian jails. 'Abdu'l-Bahá speaks of this in these words:

> Again and again he was bound with chains, jailed, and threatened with the sword. The photograph of this blessed individual, together with that of the great Amín, taken of them in their chains, will serve as an example to whoever has eyes to see. There they sit, those two distinguished men, hung with chains, shackled, yet composed, acquiescent, undisturbed.*
>
> Things came to such a pass that in the end whenever there was an uproar Mullá 'Alí would put on his turban, wrap himself in his 'abá and sit waiting, for his enemies to rouse and the farráshes to break in and the guards to carry him off to prison. But observe the power of God! In spite of all this, he was kept safe. 'The sign of a knower and lover is this, that you will find him dry in the sea.' That is how he was. His life hung by a thread from one moment to the next; the malevolent lay in wait for him; he was known everywhere as a Bahá'í – and still he was protected from all harm. He stayed dry in the depths of the sea, cool and safe in the heart of the fire, until the day he died.[10]

One of his imprisonments, which lasted about two years, was noteworthy in that Náyibu's-Salṭanih arrested a number of outstanding personalities among the Bahá'ís in 1882 and interrogated them extensively about the Faith.† Another imprisonment was around the year 1887 and finally his two-year imprisonment which began in 1891, the first part in the prison of Qazvín for about eighteen months in company with Ḥájí Amín and the remainder in the prison of Ṭihrán. It was on

* For this photograph see vol. 3, facing p. 61. (A.T.)

† For further details see below, pp. 404–5.

the occasion of their imprisonment in Qazvín that Bahá'u'lláh revealed the celebrated prayer* for the Hands of the Cause.

Soon after the martyrdom of Badí' a severe famine swept over Persia. Mullá 'Alí-Akbar begged Bahá'u'lláh for it to come to an end. We have already described Bahá'u'lláh's response in the previous volume. One of his great achievements was the transportation and protection of the remains of the Báb in Ṭihrán, a detailed account of which also appears in the previous volume.†

When Bahá'u'lláh revealed the *Kitáb-i-Aqdas* He withheld the publication of certain laws. These included the text of the Obligatory Prayers.‡ In one of His Tablets[11] Bahá'u'lláh orders His amanuensis, Mírzá Áqá Ján, to send a copy of the Obligatory Prayers to Persia as a favour to Mullá 'Alí-Akbar who had asked for them. He confirms that the Obligatory Prayers had been revealed a few years earlier. Mírzá Áqá Ján gives the date of this release as one and a half hours after sunset on 27 October 1887.

In numerous Tablets addressed to Mullá 'Alí-Akbar, Bahá'u'lláh urges him, as He does other Hands, to move around the community and instil into the minds of the believers the power of the Faith, to illumine their faces with the effulgent light of His Revelation and to ignite within their hearts the fire of the love of their Lord.

Mullá 'Alí-Akbar attained the presence of Bahá'u'lláh for the second time around the year 1888. When in His presence he would continually receive a share of the bounties of Bahá'u'lláh, and when away he used to write to Him regularly and receive various exalted Tablets. Once he wrote to Mírzá Áqá Ján, Bahá'u'lláh's amanuensis, and complained somewhat. When Bahá'u'lláh was informed He wrote that he had no right to complain, for so much spiritual food and imperishable

* see above, p. 305.
† see vol. 3, pp. 200–201, and Appendix I, for these two incidents.
‡ see vol. 3, pp. 348–51.

benefits had been showered upon him from the heaven of divine bounty that he would be unable to reckon them. Therefore he ought to thank, and thank and thank (Bahá'u'lláh repeats the word nine times!) his Lord for the blessings He has vouchsafed to him.[12]

It must be stated that one of the great services that all four Hands rendered to the Cause was the stewardship of the Bahá'í community after the ascension of Bahá'u'lláh. Through their loving care and vigilance they protected the believers from the onslaught of the Covenant-breakers, and enabled the faithful to remain steadfast in the Covenant.

'Abdu'l-Bahá pays a glowing tribute in this context to the memory of this great and godly man, who passed away in March 1910:

> After the ascension of Bahá'u'lláh, Mullá 'Alí continued on, loyal to the Testament of the Light of the World, staunch in the Covenant which he served and heralded. During the lifetime of the Manifestation, his yearning made him hasten to Bahá'u'lláh, Who received him with grace and favor, and showered blessings upon him. He returned, then, to Írán, where he devoted all his time to serving the Cause. Openly at odds with his tyrannical oppressors, no matter how often they threatened him, he defied them. He was never vanquished. Whatever he had to say, he said. He was one of the Hands of the Cause of God, steadfast, unshakeable, not to be moved.
>
> I loved him very much, for he was delightful to converse with, and as a companion second to none . . .
>
> His last resting-place is in Ṭihrán. Although his body lies under the earth, his pure spirit lives on, 'in the seat of truth, in the presence of the potent King.'* I long to visit the graves of the friends of God, could this be possible. These are the servants of the Blessed Beauty; in His path they were afflicted; they met with toil and sorrow; they sustained injuries and

* *Qur'án* 54–5.

suffered harm. Upon them be the glory of God, the All-Glorious. Unto them be salutation and praise. Upon them be God's tender mercy, and forgiveness.[13]

Mírzá 'Alí-Muḥammad (Ibn-i-Aṣdaq)

Mírzá 'Alí-Muḥammad was a son of one of the most illustrious of the believers, Mullá Sádiq-i-Khurásání, who was entitled by Bahá'u'lláh Ismu'lláhu'l-Aṣdaq* (The name of God, the most truthful). As he grew up it became clear that this son had inherited many of the outstanding qualities and virtues of his father. He became known among the believers as Ibn-i-Aṣdaq (The son of Aṣdaq). He had the great honour as a young boy of accompanying his father to Baghdád, where they both attained the presence of Bahá'u'lláh. In several interviews this youth came face to face with the Supreme Manifestation of God. These meetings left an abiding impression upon his soul and magnetized his whole being with the love of his newly-found Lord. While they were in Baghdád Bahá'u'lláh revealed a prayer[14] in which He supplicates God to feed the young boy with the milk of His bounty so that he may be enabled to raise the standards of victory in His Name and arise to serve His Cause when he is older. In this prayer Bahá'u'lláh describes him as one who in his tender years had travelled a long distance seeking to meet his Lord, and this he had achieved when he attained His presence.

Soon after his return home he tasted the agony of imprisonment and torture when, in the company of his illustrious father, he was consigned to the dungeon of Ṭihrán. A brief account of this episode is given in a previous volume.† As he grew up Ibn-i-Aṣdaq often accompanied his father on his teaching tours throughout Persia. Thus he became imbued with the spirit of service to the Cause of Bahá'u'lláh, and eventually developed a passionate love for Him, a love that knew no bounds.

* For a brief account of his noble life see vol. 3, p. 253–8.
† see vol. 3, pp. 266–7.

He was about thirty years of age when he sent a letter to the presence of Bahá'u'lláh and, among other things, begged Him to confer upon him a station wherein he might become completely detached from such realms as 'life and death', 'body and soul', 'existence and nothingness', 'reputation and honour'.

The gist of everything Ibn-i-Aṣdaq requested in this letter was the attainment of the station of 'utter self-sacrifice'; a plea for martyrdom, a state in which the individual in his love for his Beloved will offer up everything he possesses. It is an interesting thought that in one's quest for 'self-sacrifice' it is inappropriate for the soul to seek the station of utter nothingness and complete non-existence, for even these can become the means of attachment to oneself.

In response Bahá'u'lláh revealed a Tablet to Ibn-i-Aṣdaq.[15] This was in January 1880. In this Tablet He confers upon him infinite blessings and prays that he may become fully sanctified and detached from earthly things, that he may conduct himself in such wise as befits the Day of God, and that he may attain the station of the most great martyrdom. He states that service to the Cause is the greatest of all deeds, and that those who are the symbols of certitude ought to be engaged in teaching with the utmost wisdom. He further explains that martyrdom is not confined to the shedding of blood, as it is possible to live and yet be counted as a martyr in the sight of God. In this Tablet Bahá'u'lláh showers upon him His blessings, for he had offered up his all to his Lord.

Two years later Ibn-i-Aṣdaq again asked for martyrdom. Bahá'u'lláh assured him in a Tablet[16] that God had bestowed upon him the station of a martyr, and addressed him as Shahíd-ibn-i-Shahíd (martyr, son of the martyr). In this way both father and son, without physical martyrdom, were given this lofty station. Ibn-i-Aṣdaq attained the presence of Bahá'u'lláh once more in 'Akká. In a Tablet[17] Bahá'u'lláh asserts that on this visit his ears were blessed to hear the shrill voice of His exalted Pen,* his eyes to behold His Countenance, and his heart to turn to Him. He bids him illumine the hearts of men through the effulgent rays of His utterance, and brighten their eyes by the light of His Countenance. In every Tablet revealed in his honour by Bahá'u'lláh, one finds words of praise and appreciation for his devoted services, as well as counsels and exhortations for the living of a saintly life.

The life-style of Ibn-i-Aṣdaq was different from that of Mullá 'Alí-Akbar. He married a princess, a great-grand-daughter of Fatḥ-'Alí Sháh who was a devoted believer. This brought him close to people of high position and wealth and so he was able to teach those who could use their influence in assisting the oppressed community. He often used the phrase, 'one ought to hunt a lion, not a fox'. Ibn-i-Aṣdaq travelled extensively throughout the length and breadth of Persia, and Bahá'u'lláh always urged him to be engaged in this meritorious service. In a Tablet revealed in his honour, Bahá'u'lláh counsels him in these words:

> The movement itself from place to place, when undertaken for the sake of God, hath always exerted, and can now exert, its influence in the world.[18]

In another Tablet[19] Bahá'u'lláh exhorts Ibn-i-Aṣdaq to be as a flame of fire among the loved ones of God, so that every soul may sense the heat of the love of their Lord from him.

After the ascension of Bahá'u'lláh Ibn-i-Aṣdaq continued in his devoted services to the Cause. Along with the other Hands of the Cause, he promoted the Covenant of Bahá'u'lláh among the believers, instructed them in its significance and assisted them to remain steadfast in the face of the Covenant-breaking that occurred at that time. The range of his travels was extended during 'Abdu'l-Bahá's Ministry. He visited India and Burma, 'Ishqábád and even Europe where in 1919,

* see vol. 1, p. 35n.

accompanied by another believer, he personally presented a Tablet* addressed by 'Abdu'l-Bahá to the Central Organization for a Durable Peace at The Hague. He also attained the presence of the Master several times in his life.

Among his other outstanding services was that of helping to organize a teacher-training institute for Bahá'í women in Ṭihrán for the first time. He also delivered to the Sháh a treatise penned by the Master during the lifetime of Bahá'u'lláh and known as *Risáliy-i-Síyásíyyih* (Treatise on Politics). His contribution as a writer was no less significant. For instance, in 1919 he produced, with the assistance of other Hands of the Cause, a refutation of false accusations against the Faith published by Professor Edward Browne in his books. He also wrote various papers on the subject of the Covenant, in which he explained the station of 'Abdu'l-Bahá as the Centre of the Covenant and the authorized interpreter of Bahá'u'lláh's Writings, refuted the misrepresentations and false accusations of the Covenant-breakers and exposed their malicious intention to subvert the edifice of the Cause of God. He wrote this material during his last pilgrimage in the Holy Land and sent it to the friends in Ṭihrán. Ibn-i-Aṣdaq lived longer than all the other Hands, and passed away in Ṭihrán in 1928.

Mírzá Muḥammad-Taqí (Ibn-i-Abhar)

Mírzá Muḥammad-Taqí, addressed by Bahá'u'lláh as Ibn-i-Abhar (the son of Abhar) embraced the Cause through association with his father Mírzá Ibráhím-i-Abharí, who was one of the divines who became a believer in the early days of the Faith. After Bahá'u'lláh's declaration in Baghdád many Bábís were confused about the position of Mírzá Yaḥyá and his claims. Ibn-i-Abhar, then a young man, sought clarification from his father on this point. His father, who had already recognized the station of Bahá'u'lláh, advised his son to investigate

* Known as the 'Tablet to The Hague'.

the truth for himself by studying the *Bayán** carefully. The perusal of that Book enabled Ibn-i-Abhar to discover and believe that Bahá'u'lláh and no one else was the Promised One of the *Bayán*, and he joyously embraced His Cause. From that time onwards he grew spiritually and was transformed into a new creation by the potency of the Words of Bahá'u'lláh.

Ibn-i-Abhar went through a turbulent period soon after the death of his father in 1874. The details of the plots against him and the confiscation of all his possessions by his enemies are beyond the scope of this book. In 1876 he sent a letter to the presence of Bahá'u'lláh asking whether it was more meritorious to lay down one's life for the love of God or to teach the Cause with wisdom and the power of utterance. In a Tablet[20] Bahá'u'lláh counselled him that the latter was preferable. He states that after the martyrdom of Badí' He had advised the believers to act with prudence and care and not volunteer to give their lives. Martyrdom† in the path of God is undoubtedly the greatest bounty provided it takes place through circumstances beyond one's control. He urges Ibn-i-Abhar in this Tablet to engage himself in teaching the Cause with great wisdom.

Because of the opposition to him in his native village of Abhar, Ibn-i-Abhar moved to Zanján. There he succeeded in converting some souls to the Faith and also in reviving the faith of the many believers who had fallen prey to doubts raised by the Azalís. He created such a spirit of enthusiasm and devotion among the believers that the divines of the city of Zanján rose up against him and consigned him to prison. The conditions of prison life were extremely cruel, yet this godly man endured dire hardships in a spirit of resignation and forbearance. According to his own statement, his imprisonment lasted fourteen months and fifteen days.

---

* The Mother-Book of the Bábí Dispensation, revealed by the Báb.

† Bahá'u'lláh has ordained teaching the Cause to be as meritorious as giving one's life in His path. For further details see vol. 2, p. 94.

He attained the presence of Bahá'u'lláh about the year 1886. In a Tablet[21] revealed in his honour Bahá'u'lláh reminds him of the time he attained His presence when He showered his bounties upon him and enabled him to hearken to His sweet voice, a voice to which were attracted all created things. In the same Tablet Bahá'u'lláh directs Ibn-i-Abhar to pass through the cities, and even as a breeze that stirs at the break of dawn to shed upon whomsoever will turn to him the sweet savours of His loving-kindness and favours. This Ibn-i-Abhar did for the rest of his life. He chose Ṭihrán as his residence and travelled far and wide throughout Persia. His teaching exploits and loving care for the believers contributed in a large extent to the growth and consolidation of the Bahá'í community in that country. In one of His Tablets[22] Bahá'u'lláh states that Ibn-i-Abhar was created to extol God and magnify His name, to teach His Cause and to serve Him.

Early in 1891 the Persian government became suspicious of certain political activists and had them imprisoned. As was the usual practice, the authorities found it convenient to accuse the Bahá'ís of anti-government activities at the same time. Among those arrested were Ḥájí Abu'l-Ḥasan-i-Amín and Mullá 'Alí-Akbar, the Hand of the Cause, who were despatched to the prison of Qazvín.* Ibn-i-Abhar was consigned to the dungeon in Ṭihrán and kept in prison for about four years. During this period he was subjected to so much ill-treatment and torture that the full story, if written, would become very lengthy indeed. He took great pride in the fact that the same chains which had been once placed around Bahá'u'lláh's neck were put around his. A photograph† of him in chains, standing with poise and dignity while guarded by the gaolers reached the presence of 'Abdu'l-Bahá. He wrote this Tablet to Ibn-i-Abhar:

---

* see below, pp. 358–60.

† see p. 329.

He is God!
The Hand of the Cause of God, Jináb-i-Ibn-i-Abhar,
upon him be the Glory of God

> O thou who art steadfast in the Covenant,
>
> A few days ago I was glancing at some photographs of the friends. By chance I came across thy photograph. As I beheld thy person standing poised and in the utmost dignity with chains around thy neck, I was so affected that all sorrow was turned into joy and radiance, and I praised God that the world's Greatest Luminary hath nurtured and trained such servants who, while tied in chains and under the threat of the sword, shine forth in the utmost exultation and rapture. And this is but a token of the grace of thy Lord, the Merciful, the Compassionate.[23]

Because the food in prison was inadequate, a few Bahá'ís sent food to him regularly. Two Bahá'í women, who devoted their time and energy to serving him, posed as his sisters and brought food and other necessities for him every day. As there was no paper available for prisoners to write on, Ibn-i-Abhar used to write letters in very small characters on the wrappers of sugar cones,* tea or candles, and send them out with the two ladies. He even wrote some long letters in the same fashion for non-Bahá'ís in answer to their questions and proving the truth of the Message of Bahá'u'lláh for them. These letters were later compiled in their original form, producing a small book. In spite of all the hardships he underwent, he succeeded in teaching the Faith to a few people in the prison and enabled them to recognize the station of Bahá'u'lláh and embrace His Faith.

One form of torture usually inflicted upon victims in Persian prisons was the bastinado. The victim is made to lie

* In those days sugar was made in the form of large cones about 10 inches high and 5 inches in diameter, which were usually wrapped in thick blue paper. The cone had to be broken into small pieces.

on his back while his feet, inserted in a loop, are held up and the soles beaten with a cane or a whip. The soles of the feet were beaten so hard that the person could not move for days. At times Ibn-i-Abhar was subjected to this form of brutal flogging. On one occasion he was so badly injured that he decided not to appear before the ladies who usually brought food for him. Soon they found out what had happened, and the friends were plunged into deep sorrow. He then wrote the following letter to his loved ones, a letter which clearly demonstrates the spirit of utter sacrifice which dominated his whole being:

> May my life be sacrificed for your true loving-kindness and for the tears you have shed in the path of the Incomparable Friend. However, the situation did not justify weeping and lamenting. Because the first abode to which the wayfarer arrives in the path of love is that of renouncing life, possessions, rank and position. Was there ever an evening that I spent in your presence when you did not hear, the next morning, the reciting of the prayer, 'O Thou whose tests are a healing medicine unto such as are nigh unto Thee?' Now that this prayer has been answered, we must glorify God and render our thanks to Him.
>
> Would it be fitting for He who is the Ruler of all the nations and the Lord of all creation to accept tribulations in order that mankind might be freed from the fetters of prejudice, liberated from attachments to this mortal world and disentangled from animalistic evil passions, while this insignificant being, who considers himself as one of His servants, be exempt from similar sufferings?
>
> I swear by God, the Exalted, the Glorious, that while my legs from knee to toe were in great pain, my soul was communing with my Beloved in the utmost joy, and my inner being was engaged in conversing with the loved ones of God, His chosen ones and yourselves who are considered as leaves*

* Bahá'u'lláh designated women believers as 'leaves'.

> of the tree of the Cause. I did not pay any attention to the pain and suffering. For pain and bodily swellings will die down in a few days' time; only their mention will remain in this world but their bounty will last in the world of the spirit till eternity.
>
> Therefore this is an occasion for the utmost rejoicing, not for lamentation and weeping. I had asked the guards not to divulge my condition to you so that you might be spared sorrow and grief. And now I request you not to inform the rest of the friends, because some are tender-hearted and will become emotionally excited. There are others who are weak and may become perturbed . . .
>
> God knows that in order to hide this from you, I did not avail myself of meeting with you that day. The night before, I kept applying the yoke of an egg to my swollen feet so as to heal them. Now the pain has subsided. Please do not be sad, these hardships are not important. I was never caned in my school days. Instead, I receive beatings now in the path of the True Friend. But they have no effect upon the heart and the soul. The physical injuries are healed in a relatively short time . . . [24]

Ibn-i-Abhar was still in prison when the news of the ascension of Bahá'u'lláh reached him. He was heartbroken and filled with grief. For days he was unable to calm his emotions. He wrote a letter to 'Abdu'l-Bahá seeking His help in overcoming his heavyheartedness. 'Abdu'l-Bahá wrote a Tablet to him which brought great comfort and consolation in this bereavement. He advised Ibn-i-Abhar to read the *Qur'án* during his confinement; it was the only book available in the prison.

Soon after his release from prison in 1895, Ibn-i-Abhar travelled to the Holy Land and attained the presence of the Master. From there, 'Abdu'l-Bahá directed him to proceed to 'I<u>sh</u>qábád. During the Ministry of 'Abdu'l-Bahá, Ibn-i-Abhar travelled extensively throughout Persia, the Caucasus and India, visiting the Bahá'í communities, converting many souls

THE HAND OF THE CAUSE IBN-I-ABHAR IN CHAINS

A photograph taken in the prison of Ṭihrán

to the Faith, and meeting high-ranking officials in various localities. On his journey to India which took place in 1907 he was accompanied by two American Bahá'ís, Hooper Harris and Harlan Ober, and by Maḥmúd-i-Zarqání and his brother. They travelled to many parts of the sub-continent, and were able to further the achievements of the earlier teachers who had been despatched to that vast country during Bahá'u'lláh's and 'Abdu'l-Bahá's Ministries. It must also be noted that Ibn-i-Abhar travelled altogether eleven times to the Holy Land and attained the presence of the Master.

An interesting episode in the life of Ibn-i-Abhar is the story of his marriage to Munírih Khánum, the daughter of the Hand of the Cause Mullá 'Alí-Akbar. After the ascension of Bahá'u'lláh, Ibn-i-Abhar (who was then in prison) made a vow to devote his whole life to the service of the Cause. A certain Persian lady by the name of Fá'izih Khánum suggested to 'Abdu'l-Bahá in person that it was time Ibn-i-Abhar got married, and suggested the above-named Munírih Khánum. 'Abdu'l-Bahá asked one of His sons-in-law to approach Ibn-i-Abhar and convey to him the timeliness of his getting married. But Ibn-i-Abhar was adamantly opposed, saying that if he married he would become involved with obligations which would result in the breaking of his vow. At last 'Abdu'l-Bahá summoned Ibn-i-Abhar to His presence and directed him to return to Ṭihrán and marry the daughter of Mullá 'Alí-Akbar. Ibn-i-Abhar brought up the subject of the vow. 'Abdu'l-Bahá went close to him, nudged him with His shoulder and said, 'My good man! I am the Centre of the Covenant; when I say you will not break your vow by marrying, you will not!' 'Abdu'l-Bahá also sent a message to Mullá 'Alí-Akbar and informed him of the situation, saying that Fá'izih Khánum had persisted with her request several times.

When Ibn-i-Abhar arrived in Ṭihrán, 'Abdu'l-Bahá directed the Hand of the Cause Mírzá Ḥasan-i-Adíb to arrange the wedding within nine days of receiving His message. The

Master sent a sum of money for the marriage feast, and the Greatest Holy Leaf a simple dress for the bride.

Along with the other Hands of the Cause, Ibn-i-Abhar was a driving force for the establishment of the Spiritual Assembly of Ṭihrán. And as we have already stated, every one of the Hands contributed a great deal to the deepening of the friends in the important subject of the Covenant of Bahá'u'lláh. They also engendered such enthusiasm in the community that the believers greatly intensified their teaching activities, and as a result many souls, some of them highly educated and influential people, joined the ranks of the believers in Persia.

A special service rendered by Ibn-i-Abhar was the promotion of the education of women. He and his wife played an important part in the advancement of women in Persian society. In 1909 a special committee was formed for the liberation of women, and Ibn-i-Abhar and his wife were both members of this committee. Around the year 1910, an assembly formed exclusively of women was established, and became known as the Spiritual Assembly of the Bahá'í Women. The wives of Mullá 'Alí-Akbar and Ibn-i-Abhar were both members. This Assembly, which lasted for seven years, turned to the Spiritual Assembly of Ṭihrán, whose members were exclusively men, for guidance on basic issues. With the encouragement of Ibn-i-Abhar, his wife Munírih Khánum founded the first Bahá'í school for girls in Ṭihrán. Ibn-i-Abhar passed away in Ṭihrán in 1917.

Ḥájí Mírzá Ḥasan-i-Adíb

Mírzá Ḥasan-i-Adíb was a distinguished and learned man who combined the knowledge of Islamic theology, as a divine, with literary erudition. Before embracing the Faith he ranked high in the literary circles surrounding the royal family, and made important contributions to the production of various literary works. He was at one time installed as the Imám-Jum'ih (a high religious post) and a teacher at Dáru'l-Funún, the only school established on the pattern of a western educational institution. The school was usually attended by members of royalty and the sons of influential people. In recognition of his outstanding literary accomplishments he was given the title of Adíbu'l-'Ulamá (Literary man of the Ulama). He also taught religious subjects to a number of would-be divines.

Through various circumstances Mírzá Ḥasan met a believer who gave him a book of Bahá'í Writings and also introduced him to some well-known Bahá'í teachers. He came into particular contact with the renowned Nabíl-i-Akbar, and eventually saw the truth of the Faith, recognized the greatness of the Revelation of Bahá'u'lláh and acknowledged the awe-inspiring station of its Author. In the year 1889 he became a devoted believer; he was in his early forties at the time.

All his learning and erudition were now harnessed to the new powers which the Faith of Bahá'u'lláh had conferred upon him. Soon his heart became a wellspring of divine melodies. The soul-stirring poems he wrote proclaim the advent of the Day of God and, in offering up his all in the path of his Lord, serve as ample testimony to the intensity of his faith and the exaltation of his rank. No wonder that soon after his entering under the shadow of the Cause, Bahá'u'lláh designated this great spiritual being as one of the Hands of His Cause. Mírzá Ḥasan-i-Adíb did not have the bounty, as the other Hands had, of meeting Bahá'u'lláh. However, he had the honour and the privilege of attaining the presence of 'Abdu'l-Bahá.

During the Ministry of the Master, he dedicated all his being to the service of the Cause. He became a tower of strength for the believers and a great teacher of the Faith. His pen was no less active. He wrote several books on proofs of the Faith and its history. His poems were soul-stirring and the friends were inspired and uplifted by them. He had a major role in the formation of the Spiritual Assembly of Ṭihrán, and served on that body as its chairman.

Mírzá Ḥasan-i-Adíb was deeply interested in the education of Bahá'í youth. About the year 1904 a learned Bahá'í known as Ṣadru'ṣ-Ṣudúr had established the first teacher-training class for Bahá'í youth in Ṭihrán. It was a daily class which lasted for several years, and the students became well-versed in various aspects of the Faith and other religions. When Ṣadru's-Ṣudúr died about five years after the foundation of the youth class, Mírzá Ḥasan decided to teach in his place. Assisted by a few other knowledgeable Bahá'ís, he supervised the youth class for some time.

Another great achievement was the founding of the Tarbíyat Boys' School in Ṭihrán. Mírzá Ḥasan-i-Adíb played a significant part in creating this prestigious institution, which was considered for years the foremost educational establishment in the country. This school was also the forerunner of several other Bahá'í schools in various parts of Persia. The Tarbíyat Boys' School and the Girls' School by the same name, together with all the other Bahá'í schools in major cities, were closed down in December 1934 by order of the government for not heeding a warning by the Ministry of Education (headed by 'Alí-Aṣghar-i-Ḥikmat, a well-known Azalí) that the schools would officially be closed if they failed to remain open during Bahá'í holy days. Despite several representations by the National Spiritual Assembly, the authorities remained adamant and all the Bahá'í schools in Persia were closed down after closing on a Bahá'í holy day.

In 1903 'Abdu'l-Bahá directed Mírzá Ḥasan-i-Adíb to make a teaching trip to Iṣfahán. This journey took place at a time when a great upheaval was about to take place in Yazd through the machinations of the Mujtahid of Iṣfahán, Shaykh Muḥammad-Taqí (the Son of the Wolf). The presence of Mírzá Ḥasan in Iṣfahán put fuel to the fire; a serious upheaval took place in the city resulting in great sufferings for the Hand of the Cause. He at last succeeded in departing from the city without being noticed by the many guards whom the wicked mujtahid had especially posted in various quarters for the sole purpose of arresting him. From there Mírzá Ḥasan went to Ábádih and Shíráz, where he was able to teach the Cause to several people. Then he travelled to India, and eventually to the Holy Land where his soul was exhilarated by coming in contact with the Centre of the Covenant of Bahá'u'lláh. There his whole being was illumined with the effulgent rays of 'Abdu'l-Bahá's presence. He returned to Persia as a flame of fire ignited by the hand of the Master, and continued in his highly meritorious services until his death in 1919. His resting-place is in Ṭihrán, in common with the resting-places of the other three Hands of the Cause.

Tablets to the Hands of the Cause

The four Hands of the Cause were the recipients of a great many Tablets from Bahá'u'lláh. This is especially true in the case of the first three Hands, who were long-standing believers. For many years Bahá'u'lláh revealed Tablets in their names; through these He nurtured their souls and illumined their hearts and minds. Some of these Tablets are unusually lengthy and include sections addressed to many other individual believers.

Long before they were designated as Hands of the Cause, Mullá 'Alí-Akbar, Ibn-i-Aṣdaq and Ibn-i-Abhar used to carry out the same functions in deepening the friends' knowledge of the Faith, encouraging and supporting them in their teaching work and guiding their steps in their manifold activities. In the course of these services they used to write to Bahá'u'lláh and beseech His blessings for certain souls who were serving the Cause assiduously, and Bahá'u'lláh would respond by revealing Tablets in which He usually addressed each individual separately. Sometimes He would reveal several pages in honour of one individual. In this way the Tablets addressed to the Hands and indeed to other outstanding teachers of the Faith would often contain so many pages as to assume the size of a small book. So numerous are the Tablets revealed by Bahá'u'lláh in honour of the four individuals designated as Hands of the Cause, that a compilation of them would probably amount to one or two large volumes. Added to these are a vast number of Tablets which were sent to them by 'Abdu'l-Bahá. All we can do here is skim the surface and glean a few gems from such a vast treasury.

In one of His Tablets to Ibn-i-Aṣdaq, Bahá'u'lláh reveals

these celebrated Words on being informed that the friends in Ṭihrán had arranged to observe the commandment of the Mashriqu'l-Adhkár:*

> Blessed is the spot, and the house, and the place, and the city, and the heart, and the mountain, and the refuge, and the cave, and the valley, and the land, and the sea, and the island, and the meadow where mention of God hath been made, and His praise glorified.[1]

Bahá'u'lláh has portrayed a fascinating spectacle in the spiritual worlds of God where the holy souls and the Concourse on High are circling around any spot on this earth where the believers are engaged in praise and glorification of God. In one of His Tablets He reveals these thought-provoking words:

> By My life and My Cause! Round about whatever dwelling the friends of God may enter, and from which their cry shall rise as they praise and glorify the Lord, shall circle the souls of true believers and all the favoured angels. And should the door of the true eye be opened unto some, they shall witness the Supreme Concourse as it circleth and crieth: 'Blessed art thou, O house, for God hath made thee a resting-place for those He favoureth, and a lodging for those He holdeth dear, and a home for those in whom He hath placed His trust. Unto thee be His praise and His glory and His endless grace'.[2]

We may conclude, therefore, that one of the main reasons that Bahá'í gatherings are conducive to the spiritual upliftment and joy of the participants is the influence exerted by the company of God's chosen souls.

---

* Literally, the Dawning-Place of the mention of God, Bahá'í House of Worship. Bahá'u'lláh has ordained that the believers attend the Mashriqu'l-Adhkár before dawn for prayers. Although the friends did not have a House of Worship, they used to assemble at someone's house.

In His Tablets to the Hands of the Cause, Bahá'u'lláh has revealed a great many exhortations addressed to the Bahá'ís in general. These reiterate the basic teachings of the Faith such as love and unity among the believers, steadfastness in the Cause, teaching the Faith, detachment from earthly things, and many more. Since we have already covered these subjects in these volumes we mention only a few highlights here.

In a Tablet[3] to Mullá 'Alí-Akbar Bahá'u'lláh states that His Pen had been continually engaged during these days in revealing the meaning of the promotion of the Cause. This He did lest some foolish ones might commit an unseemly act which could become the cause of the cessation of divine bounties. Bahá'u'lláh then directs Mullá 'Alí-Akbar to urge the believers to become detached from the things of this world, to cleanse themselves from all unworthy and futile deeds, and turn their hearts and souls towards God. Only in this way can they be successful in promoting His Cause.

In another Tablet[4] to the same Hand of the Cause Bahá'u'lláh enjoins on His followers to adhere to such deeds as will bring about the exaltation of His Cause, reminds them that in this Dispensation conflict and contention are by no means permitted, and urges them to promote His Cause by the sword of wisdom and utterance and not by the sword of steel.

In a Tablet[5] to Ibn-i-Aṣdaq, Bahá'u'lláh addresses the people of Bahá and exhorts them to appreciate the great bounty of living in this Day, to adorn themselves with such holy deeds that the peoples of the world may inhale from them the fragrance of the beauty of God and recognize His characteristics from their behaviour. Writing about detachment in another Tablet[6] to the same Hand of the Cause, Bahá'u'lláh recalls the words of Christ when He said to His disciples that in the course of their missionary work they should shake off the very dust from their garments when they depart from a city.

In another Tablet[7] to Ibn-i-Aṣdaq, Bahá'u'lláh affirms that the effect of every pure deed carried out in this day will remain and be remembered for ever. In the same Tablet He mentions that everything is placed within the clutches of ultimate extinction except the Words that have been revealed by the Pen of the Most High.

In a Tablet[8] to Mullá 'Alí-Akbar Bahá'u'lláh mentions that if God's glances of favour were to be interrupted for one instant, every human being would become a heap of mouldering bones.

To Ibn-i-Aṣdaq[9] Bahá'u'lláh describes the greatness of His Revelation. He states that if anyone truly recognizes its grandeur, he will not be deflected from His Cause even if he were to be offered all the treasures of the world and all the good things that may be found therein. In the same Tablet He makes reference to three things in an interesting manner. He states that no one may be considered to be a human being unless he is adorned with the quality of justice and fairness; that there can be no real power except through unity; and that there can be no well-being and happiness except through consultation.

Referring to the perversity of people, and especially religious leaders, Bahá'u'lláh in a Tablet[10] to Mullá 'Alí-Akbar asserts that these unfortunate beings are unaware of the truth of the Cause of God. If only they could attain His presence during the time of revelation when the verses of God are being sent down, each one of them would be so carried away as to become humble and prostrate himself at the feet of his Lord.

In another Tablet[11] to Ibn-i-Aṣdaq, Bahá'u'lláh describes this perversity of the people, especially the Islamic clergy. He ascribes the cause of their deprivation and ignorance of the Faith of God to punishment for the deeds they had committed. He further invokes the wrath of God for those who rise up against His Cause and are determined to put out its light. He asserts the futility of their efforts and declares that in reality their inner beings deride their own selves for their foolish deeds.

In a Tablet[12] to Mullá 'Alí-Akbar Bahá'u'lláh proclaims

that every created thing bears witness to His steadfastness, His bounties and His mercy. Those who have heard His call and attained to His Faith are the people of Bahá and the companions of the Crimson Ark.* He announces that this is not the day for people to ask questions, to raise their voices, to deliver their own speeches or to make mention of themselves. It behoves them in this day to turn their ears to the most exalted Horizon and hearken to His voice. He informs them that whatever they possess will not benefit them, urges them to discard the material world and take the book of God in their hands in a spirit of resignation and submissiveness. These words of Bahá'u'lláh are very similar to His celebrated counsels in the *Hidden Words*:

> O Son of Dust! Blind thine eyes, that thou mayest behold My beauty; stop thine ears, that thou mayest hearken unto the sweet melody of My voice; empty thyself of all learning, that thou mayest partake of My knowledge; and sanctify thyself from riches, that thou mayest obtain a lasting share from the ocean of My eternal wealth. Blind thine eyes, that is, to all save My beauty; stop thine ears to all save My word; empty thyself of all learning save the knowledge of Me; that with a clear vision, a pure heart and an attentive ear thou mayest enter the court of My holiness.[13]

In these utterances Bahá'u'lláh is speaking as the Manifestation of God, upon whose Revelation the human world depends for its growth and development in the same way that life on this earth depends upon the sun. In one of His Tablets[14] to Mullá 'Alí-Akbar, Bahá'u'lláh affirms that should a person fully surrender himself to God and reach a stage of utter self-effacement in His path, such a soul will never become concerned with rank and position, or reputation and honour.

In His Tablets to the Hands of the Cause there are

* see *God Passes By*, p. 151.

innumerable references to teaching the Faith. In one of these[15] He states that there are many souls who have never entered a school, but who through the love of God have attained such an exalted position that the living waters of wisdom flow from their hearts and tongues. We have already referred to this subject in greater detail in previous volumes, and described the teaching achievements of some individuals who possessed the gift of true understanding and spiritual knowledge even though devoid of any learning and education.

In His Writings Bahá'u'lláh often speaks of wisdom in teaching. In a Tablet[16] to Mullá 'Alí-Akbar He explains that some individuals may accept the Faith on hearing a certain statement. They are also prone to reject it on hearing another. He urges the teachers of the Cause, therefore, when teaching a soul, to bring up those words through which the fire of the love of God may be enkindled in the heart. Should the seeker's heart become ignited with this fire, he will gradually learn about the Faith and become steadfast in it.

Innumerable passages in Bahá'u'lláh's Tablets to the Hands of the Cause contain similar exhortations and counsels, all revealing the high ideals and principles which constitute the foundation of the Cause of God. Numerous passages in these Tablets also reveal the glory of the Revelation of Bahá'u'lláh, laud its greatness, and unveil in unmistakable terms the awe-inspiring station of its Author. Another feature of these Tablets is the outpouring of loving-kindness, admiration, encouragement, prayer, and praise upon the Hands of the Cause, expressed with such tenderness and warmth as no pen but His own can describe. Also, Bahá'u'lláh had issued many and varying instructions to His chosen instruments, all aimed at fostering the infant Faith of God, protecting its precious foundations, furthering its interests, promoting its teachings and strengthening the faith of its adherents.

The Commandment to Act with Wisdom

In Most of His Tablets to the Hands of the Cause, Bahá'u'lláh speaks of wisdom. For instance, in a Tablet[17] to Ibn-i-Aṣdaq He states that even teaching the Cause, the most important of all deeds, is dependent upon the exercise of wisdom. First comes the observance of wisdom, then the utterance of words. By wisdom is meant taking any praiseworthy action through which the Cause of God may be promoted. Lack of wisdom is to take actions which owing to circumstances result in harming the Faith, even though they may be carried out with the best possible motive. The commandment of Bahá'u'lláh to act with wisdom is valid for all time. Indeed, as the Cause of God continues to grow the forces of opposition will array themselves against it in proportion to its growth. In this battle against the forces of darkness, wisdom applied by the individual believer as well as by the institutions of the Faith plays a major part in the protection and promotion of the Cause of God.

Bahá'u'lláh has urged the Hands of the Cause to be vigilant and help the friends to avoid taking any action which might adversely affect the interests of the Faith. We cite two examples. In a previous volume* we have described how some time after the *Kitáb-i-Aqdas* was revealed Bahá'u'lláh allowed Jamál-i-Burújirdí† to copy certain parts of it and take them with him to Persia. At some point Jamál advocated the establishment of the local Houses of Justice enjoined in the *Kitáb-i-Aqdas*. The Hand of the Cause Mullá 'Alí-Akbar sought guidance from Bahá'u'lláh on this issue. In a Tablet[18] to him Bahá'u'lláh responded by stating that the application of any of His laws was conditional upon the exercise of wisdom. He explained that the establishment of this institution was not timely, because should the enemies of the Cause discover it, they would create a commotion, the elected members would

* see vol. 3, p. 280.
† see vol. 2 and above, pp. 152, 199, 269.

become targets and their lives would be in great danger. He envisaged that these institutions would be formed at a later time when conditions became more favourable. Furthermore, He affirmed that because of the immaturity and perversity of the public, and for the protection of the believers, He had not required them to implement most of the laws of the *Kitáb-i-Aqdas*. The main reason for the dispatch of a copy to Persia was that a record of the laws might be kept in the hands of the friends.

Another example in the exercise of prudence and wisdom may be found in a Tablet[19] to the same Mullá 'Alí-Akbar. This concerns the printing of Bahá'u'lláh's Writings, for which he had asked permission. While stating that this matter ought to be resolved through consultation, Bahá'u'lláh advised caution and prudence. He explained that it was not wise at that time to print books, because should a large number of books become available, the enemies of the Cause (who were waiting for an excuse) could be provoked into bringing about an upheaval in that land. Bahá'u'lláh intimates that it was for the same reason that He had stopped the dissemination of the *Kitáb-i-Íqán* which had been printed some twenty years before.

Bahá'u'lláh and 'Abdu'l-Bahá have counselled the believers to exercise wisdom in the promotion of the Cause, but wisdom must not be interpreted as fear and lack of enthusiasm for the Faith. Mullá 'Alí-Akbar was once advised by his fellow Hands of the Cause to conceal himself from the enemies during the month of Muḥarram when the emotions of the mob are deeply stirred by the clergy. This is a month of mourning for Shí'ah Islám, commemorating the martyrdom of Imám Ḥusayn, and people usually become very wild. Mullá 'Alí-Akbar, who was always an easy target for attack, is reported to have smiled and said these words in reply:

> It is true that in the Holy Tablets we are commanded to observe wisdom. By wisdom is not meant to be fearful or to have no

reliance upon God. It means to act with thoroughness, and to conduct oneself with truthfulness, benevolence and patience; it means to sow the seeds of the teachings of God in the pure and goodly soil of the hearts. It does not mean fear or hiding.

When I was a child, I fell into a river and was carried down the stream for a few miles. People were sure that I was drowned, but somehow I was thrown on the bank almost lifeless, and in the end I recovered. God saved me. On another occasion, I fell twice on a mountain, from a height of about one hundred metres. I survived, for it was meant that I should live. Besides, I have been captured many times, and from periods of six months up to three years I have been imprisoned, chained and fettered. On each of these occasions there was no hope of freedom. And yet many souls who were not as famous as I, but were worthy to lay down their lives in the path of God, have been martyred. But so far I have not. If it is the will of God, and if this incomparable bounty of laying down my life becomes mine, imagine what a great gift that would be! Furthermore, is it possible or conceivable to be able to run away from God's decree? On the contrary one has to speed up towards Him.[20]

Ḥájí Mírzá Ḥaydar-'Alí, the chronicler of this story, concludes by saying, 'Mullá 'Alí-Akbar spoke so convincingly that those present felt ashamed, and recognized that their advice to him indicated a lack of understanding of reliance upon God on their part.'

How Tablets were Delivered to their Recipients

Bahá'u'lláh's Tablets were usually revealed in honour of known individual Bahá'ís, whose names were inscribed in them. However, sometimes the name of the intended recipient was not given, or sometimes it would be given in abbreviated form. In such a case the individual might receive the Tablet intended for him in an unusual way. For example, in a previous volume* we noted that Bahá'u'lláh revealed a Tablet without a name but intended for Ḥájí Muḥammad-Ṭáhir-i-Málmírí when he was only a child, and he received this Tablet in a mysterious way almost twenty years later. Sometimes Bahá'u'lláh used to send a few Tablets without names to a well-known Bahá'í, asking him to give each to any one of the believers he felt moved to give them to. Those who received a Tablet in this way discovered that Bahá'u'lláh had indeed intended it for them. Bahá'u'lláh, in a Tablet[21] revealed in honour of the Hand of the Cause Ibn-i-Aṣdaq and written in the words of His amanuensis, issued certain instructions as how to deliver nine Tablets without names to nine individuals whose names were supplied in a separate list without indicating which Tablet belonged to whom. The reason for not inscribing the names of the recipients on the Tablets, was to protect the believers from the enemies, who were anxious to know the identity of the members of the Bahá'í community. The instructions of Bahá'u'lláh, as conveyed by His amanuensis, were for Ibn-i-Aṣdaq first to carry out certain devotions, then to position the Tablets in a high place, and while turning his heart to Bahá'u'lláh to reach for one, write on it whichever of the nine names came to mind, and deliver it to him. It is also indicated by Bahá'u'lláh's amanuensis that more Tablets would be sent to Ibn-i-Aṣdaq for distribution in the same fashion.

As it was the will of Bahá'u'lláh for each individual to receive the very Tablet which was intended for him, this method of spiritual communication, which He Himself had authorized, became truly effective. Each recipient clearly saw that the contents of his Tablet fit precisely his own personal circumstances and answered his questions.

This is not surprising to the followers of Bahá'u'lláh, for they believe that every major development that takes place in this Dispensation is guided by His Will. Nothing is impossible

* vol. 1, pp. 38–40.

of achievement if the Will of God becomes the motivating influence. It is the Will of God which enables nature to create life and to bring about an abundance of miracles – the miracle of a tiny seed turning into a mighty tree, producing branches, leaves, blossoms and fruits; the miracle of a single cell in the womb of a mother, multiplying in an orderly fashion, becoming at the end a perfect human being; the miracles of the atom, of the universe and of every other created thing. All these happen through the Will of God.

The miracle of religions is no less remarkable. A religion comes into being as a seemingly insignificant movement at first, but through the power of God and His Will it flourishes and creates a civilization of its own. It is the miracle of the ascendancy of the Will of God which enables the Founders of all religions to triumph over their adversaries, and causes Their word to become creative. In an address to His disciples the Báb, referring to the power of God, said:

> . . . fix your gaze upon the invincible power of the Lord, your God, the Almighty. Has He not, in past days, caused Abraham, in spite of His seeming helplessness, to triumph over the forces of Nimrod? Has He not enabled Moses, whose staff was His only companion, to vanquish Pharaoh and his hosts? Has He not established the ascendancy of Jesus, poor and lowly as He was in the eyes of men, over the combined forces of the Jewish people? Has He not subjected the barbarous and militant tribes of Arabia to the holy and transforming discipline of Muḥammad, His Prophet? Arise in His name, put your trust wholly in Him, and be assured of ultimate victory.[22]

Today Bahá'u'lláh has promised that He will infallibly guide the Universal House of Justice. It is nothing but the realization of the Will of God which makes it possible for the members of the House of Justice to be guided by Him in their decisions. The distribution of Tablets without names to their intended recipients mentioned above is another example of the guidance of God which He bestows, at times, upon whomsoever He wills. It is interesting to note that Ibn-i-Aṣdaq was not the only person who delivered Bahá'u'lláh's Tablets in this fashion; others too were occasionally asked to distribute unaddressed Tablets to certain believers. For example, soon after His arrival in 'Akká Bahá'u'lláh sent a number of Tablets to Raḍa'r-Rúh and asked him to hand each one to whichever believer should come to his mind. Shaykh Salmán is another example: we have given an account of this in a previous volume.* All this is not more amazing or incredible than the miracle of a babe, Moses, placed in a casket and delivered to the waters of the Nile for its protection!

On some occasions 'Abdu'l-Bahá also sent unaddressed Tablets to some individuals and gave special instructions as to the manner of choosing the recipients. The following account by Ḥájí Mírzá Ḥaydar-'Alí is very illuminating indeed:

> I went to Ábádih.† Each one of the believers in Ábádih and the neighbouring villages, may my life be sacrificed for them all, is like a mountain in his steadfastness and as a shining lamp in his love and servitude. I attained their presence in their gatherings. These meetings became the sources of illumination, the dawning-places of the mention of God where the angels descended and the faithful assembled numbering one hundred or more. We met every day in the morning, at noon and in the evening. The sweet savours of devotion, self-sacrifice and detachment from all worldly things were wafted in those gatherings.
>
> While in Ábádih I received eighty-one Tablets in the handwriting of 'Him Whom God hath purposed' ['Abdu'l-Bahá]. I was instructed to take out nineteen, and, without

* see vol. 1, p. 113.

† A small town in the province of Fárs, well-known as the burial place of the heads of the martyrs of Nayríz. See *The Dawn-Breakers*, pp. 644–5.

reading them, to, inscribe on each Tablet the name of one of the believers of Ábádih whom I happened to meet, and then hand the Tablet to him. I was to do the same with the remainder for the believers of Yazd, Bavánát and Iṣfahán. Again, without reading them, I was to write on each the name of a person of my choice, then either hand it to him in person or send it to him. I did all of this. Every person who had the honour to receive a Tablet in this way testified that 'Abdu'l-Bahá had clearly described his thoughts, his ideas, his inner feelings, and had answered his questions and wishes.

There was an Englishman, the head of the Telegraph office in Ábádih. He was present in the gathering. He said, 'I cannot imagine that any human being who walks on this earth can ever know the inner feelings and the thoughts of the people or to inform them of their future. I have been associating with these devoted souls and have come to know their character, their manners, and their way of life, which are accurately referred to in these Holy Tablets written in their honour. Now I can see 'Abdu'l-Bahá's spiritual power, which is supreme and encompasses all things. I was a witness to all this. I was here when you opened each envelope, and I saw that since you were not allowed to, you did not read the Tablets before inscribing a name on each and handing it over.'

Praise be to God, this Englishman became a steadfast and enthusiastic believer.[23]

The Englishman mentioned by Ḥájí Mírzá Ḥaydar-'Alí is William J. Patchin, a young official who had been befriended by the believers of Ábádih who taught him the Faith. Notable among those who helped him to recognize the truth of the Cause of God was a devoted and influential believer, Mírzá Aṭá'u'lláh entitled Saráju'l-Ḥukamá. He was the first believer in Ábádih and one who served the Faith with distinction. He succeeded in erecting a suitable building on the burial site of the heads of the martyrs of Nayríz, which was designated by

'Abdu'l-Bahá as Ḥadiqatu'r-Raḥmán (Garden of the Merciful). As to William Patchin, a brief account was written in memory of him by Dr Susan Moody, one of the earliest American pioneers to Persia:

> Mr William J. Patchin aged 28 years, a native of London, England, died at Ṭihrán, Persia, Dec. 31, 1910. He lived the Bahá'í life and was constantly serving the Cause. He had resigned his position with Indo-European Telegraph Co. that he might go to Egypt to see 'Abdu'l-Bahá, when he was suddenly summoned to the Supreme.[24]

WILLIAM PATCHIN

An English believer in Ábádih,
with Saráju'l-Ḥukamá (right) and his young son

22

'For the Advancement of the World'

Lawḥ-i-Dunyá

Áqá Mírzá Áqáy-i-Afnán (Núru'd-Dín)

This Tablet* was revealed in 1891 in honour of Áqá Mírzá Áqáy-Afnán, entitled Núru'd-Dín. His mother was a sister of Khadíjih Bagum, the wife of the Báb,† and Áqá Mírzá Áqá was born two years before His Declaration. In a Tablet to His wife revealed in the prison of Máh-Kú the Báb assures her that when Áqá Mírzá Áqá reaches the age of maturity he will be her helper and protector. These prophetic words of the Báb were fulfilled, for Áqá Mírzá Áqá dedicated his life to the service of his beloved aunt, whom he revered and served with unbounded devotion. Khadíjih Bagum lovingly taught him the Faith and at the age of thirteen Áqá Mírzá Áqá recognized the truth of the Mission of the Báb. It was through his efforts that Ḥájí Mírzá Siyyid Muḥammad, the eldest maternal uncle of the Báb, went to meet Bahá'u'lláh in Baghdád and as a result became the recipient of the *Kitáb-i-Íqán* which assured him of the truth of the Báb's Revelation.

Soon after His Declaration near Baghdád‡ Bahá'u'lláh sent Nabíl-i-A'ẓam to Persia to announce the momentous news to the Bábís. Nabíl went to the home of Áqá Mírzá Áqá, and announced the joyful tidings to the believers in Shíráz. Áqá Mírzá Áqá immediately gave his allegiance to Bahá'u'lláh and

---

* The full text revealed in Persian has been translated into English and is published in *Tablets of Bahá'u'lláh*, pp. 83–97.

† For some details of her noble life see vol. 2, pp. 382–7.

‡ For details see vol. 1, pp. 153–9.

considered himself a humble servant at His threshold. On one occasion the wife of the Báb, who was seated behind a curtain, heard Nabíl inform the friends that the Blessed Beauty was the Promised One of the Bayán, 'Him Whom God shall make Manifest'. No sooner did that noble woman hear this announcement than she put her forehead to the ground in adoration of her newly-found Lord and is reported to have whispered to her nephew: 'offer at His sacred threshold my most humble devotion.' Thus the bonds of love and adoration which had united these two became strengthened through their immediate response to the Cause they had both spontaneously espoused.

From the early days Áqá Mírzá Áqá became the recipient of many favours and bounties from Bahá'u'lláh. The custodianship of the House of the Báb, which was conferred upon the wife of the Báb and her sister, also included him and his descendants.* In 1879 Áqá Mírzá Áqá moved to India and established a trading business in Bombay. A few years later, in 1887, he travelled to Egypt and Beirut where he stayed for some time in the home of his maternal uncle Ḥájí Mírzá Siyyid Ḥasan, known as Afnán-i-Kabír (the Great Afnán).† In Beirut he and his eldest son Áqá Siyyid Áqá‡ received permission to visit Bahá'u'lláh. They both attained His presence for the first time on the anniversary of the Báb's Declaration which that year coincided with 20 January 1888.§ Bahá'u'lláh bestowed unbounded blessings upon them. He is reported to have honoured them by ordering His servant to place a fur-lined overcoat on the shoulders of each as they were sitting in His presence.¶

* For details see Appendix II.

† see below, pp. 430–3.

‡ see above, p. 302.

§ In the East the Declaration of the Báb is celebrated according to the lunar calendar. Since there are eleven days' difference between the lunar and the solar calendars, the dates are different each year.

¶ In the absence of central heating a room was usually heated by charcoal burning in a small brazier. It was a mark of respect to place a fur coat or similar clothing around the shoulders of an honoured guest to keep him warm.

ÁQÁ MÍRZÁ ÁQÁ

Entitled Núru'd-Dín, he was the nephew of Khadíjih Bagum, the wife of the Báb. He is seen holding the Tablet bearing the seal of Bahá'u'lláh in which his family are nominated custodians of the House of the Báb in Shíráz

With Bahá'u'lláh's approval Áqá Mírzá Áqá and his eldest son proceeded to Port Said and established a business there. Each year he was permitted to go to the Holy Land where he attained the presence of Bahá'u'lláh. He went in 1889, 1890 and 1891. His last visit was the most memorable as he stayed for nine months and was accompanied by his family; they preceded him to Haifa and arrived on 17 July 1891 when Bahá'u'lláh was staying at the foot of Mount Carmel on his last visit to that spot. The party consisted of Áqá Mírzá Áqá's wife, four of their sons, and their only daughter. Áqá Mírzá Áqá himself joined his family fifteen days later when his eldest son returned to Port Said.

One of his sons Ḥájí Mírzá Ḥabíbu'lláh, who was then fifteen years of age, has recorded in his memoirs some interesting anecdotes of their pilgrimage. The following are extracts from his notes summarized and translated:

> When the ship reached Haifa the very thought of prostrating ourselves at His threshold and attaining His presence which the Prophets and His chosen ones had wished to attain invoked such eagerness and excitement in our hearts that with tears streaming down our cheeks, we were transported into a different world. We arrived at a spot where the souls of all the Manifestations of God were circumambulating day and night around His Blessed Person. My eldest brother, Áqá Siyyid Áqá, who had previously attained the presence of Bahá'u'lláh, taught us how to conduct ourselves in that holy presence with absolute humility, servitude and utter self-effacement . . .
>
> I remember clearly that the sun had not yet fully risen, the air was fresh and vivifying as we were led to His Blessed tent which was pitched at the foot of Mount Carmel* . . . Our wish was truly fulfilled when our guide pushed the curtain aside

* The location where Bahá'u'lláh pitched His tent has been preserved and is owned by the Bahá'í World Centre. (A.T.)

and we beheld the most holy Figure of the Blessed Beauty standing in the middle of the room.*

On our right sat Mírzá Áqá Ján in front of a samovar. Bahá'u'lláh ordered tea for us and then the Tongue of Grandeur addressed us in these words, 'O flowers of the rose-garden of Jináb-i-Afnán,† you are welcome. Your journey from Shíráz was very difficult. The will of God and the efforts of Jináb-i-Afnán enabled you to attain to this Most Holy Threshold . . . '

The house next door to that of the Blessed Beauty was rented for us, and we stayed in this close proximity of His luminous Person. Attaining His presence and meeting with the early believers made us forget everything else. It is impossible to describe the sweetness of life and the joy of our souls in those days.

Fifteen days had passed when my eldest brother returned to Port Said and my father arrived. My father was the recipient of much blessing and bounty from Bahá'u'lláh. It was around that time that the news of the martyrdom of the seven martyrs of Yazd‡ reached there . . .

The weather in Haifa and 'Akká was now improving. Autumn was setting in. The Blessed Beauty returned to the Mansion of Bahjí. A small house close to the Mansion was provided for us . . . From our house we could see the room of Bahá'u'lláh. When we arose at dawn for our devotions, we could often see His room lighted and His Blessed Person pacing up and down revealing verses, and Mírzá Áqá Ján taking down His words . . . In those days Mírzá Yúsuf Khán-i-Vujdání and Siyyid Asadu'lláh-i-Qumí were tutors to the Aghṣán.§ The Blessed Beauty instructed the three of us, Ḥájí Mírzá Buzurg, Ḥájí Mírzá Díyá and myself, to attend their lessons. The late Mishkín Qalam taught us calligraphy and

* Bahá'u'lláh at that time stayed in a house not far from the tent. (A.T.)

† Áqá Mírzá Áqá. (A.T.)

‡ see below, pp. 369–73. (A.T.)

§ Literally, 'Branches'. A designation used by Bahá'u'lláh to refer to His male descendants. (A.T.)

one of the rooms on the ground floor of the Mansion was set aside as our classroom.

One day before sunrise a servant of Bahá'u'lláh's household informed us that His Blessed Person would be coming to our house. On hearing this news tears of joy flowed from our eyes. With infinite joy we hastened to Him. He was coming toward our house with great majesty and grandeur. We all prostrated ourselves and kissed His feet. Upon each one of us He showered His bounties. He entered our home and conferred upon us everlasting honour. I brought a cup of tea for Him. He drank half of it and gave me the rest. He also gave me a black rosary made of olive wood which He was holding in His hands. I kissed His hands. I loved that rosary as my own life and have left it in the archives of the House of the Báb in Shíráz.

As I have already mentioned, we could see the room of the Blessed Beauty from our house. I saw Him several times at the hour of dawn or in the early morning engaged in revealing verses of God. Often His Blessed Person was uttering words and Mírzá Áqá Ján was sitting in His presence. Usually Mírzá Áqá Ján had several pens* cut to a fine nib, with paper and ink ready at his side. The outpouring of the Word of God was swift, and billowed as a surging sea.

Mírzá Áqá Ján wrote as quickly as he could. The speed was such that sometimes his pen jumped out of his hand. He then would take another pen. And on some occasions he was unable to cope with the speed of Revelation . . .

The festival on the first day of Muḥarram 1309 (7th August 1891)† was celebrated by the Blessed Perfection. He had summoned all the friends to attend. Since my father was

* Pens were made of bamboo reeds and had to be cut to make a nib for them. For more information see vol. 1, p. 35. (A.T.)

† The birth of the Báb occurred on the 1st of Muḥarram, AH 1235, according to the lunar calendar. The birth of Bahá'u'lláh occurred on the second day of the same month, AH 1233. These two days Bahá'u'lláh has ordained to be considered as one festival. (A.T.)

a heavily built man and suffered from rheumatism he could not sit on the floor, and the Blessed Perfection said, 'Bring a chair for the Afnán.' One of the servants brought a chair for him. He then said, 'Bring chairs for his sons also.' So all of us sat on chairs.* All the resident believers and pilgrims were present. That day the utterances of His Blessed Person centred around the theme of the divisions which had occurred in past religions . . . He then Himself distributed some sweetmeats to all present. At the end He said, 'This is a day on which the exalted Herald was born, and illumined the whole world with the brightness of His light. This is the time of rejoicing.'† And then He dismissed all from His presence. After this the believers could be seen standing in small groups close to the Mansion near the pine trees, repeating the words of the Blessed Perfection to each other so as to commit them to memory.

The next day, the 2nd of Muḥarram, which was the anniversary of the birthday of the One who is the Creator of the world and the Lord of mankind [Bahá'u'lláh], all the pilgrims and resident Bahá'ís were summoned to His holy presence. That day He spoke about the greatness of His Revelation, the power of the Most Exalted Pen, the circumstances of His exile and His arrival at the Most Great Prison. He then spoke in great detail about the oppression and the persecution on the part of the tyrant enemies and divines . . . He stated that in spite of all the sufferings inflicted upon them by the government and the Sháh, the friends do not cease to demonstrate their allegiance to the Cause. They disregard wisdom and caution‡ and they are not to be blamed for this, because

* In the East it was not customary at the time to sit on chairs. (A.T.)

† These are not the exact words of Bahá'u'lláh, but the recollections of the chronicler. (A.T.)

‡ The caution referred to above relates to the celebration of the birth of the Báb and Bahá'u'lláh on consecutive days of the month of Muḥarram. Because this month is the month of mourning for Shí'ah Islám, Bahá'u'lláh had advised His followers to exercise great caution in celebrating these festivals lest their enthusiasm and rejoicing upset the Muslims and inflame further their animosity towards the Faith. (A.T.)

two great festivals have been combined together. He gave us the glad-tidings that the future of the Cause throughout the world would be very brilliant . . . When His utterances ended He distributed sweetmeats and we were dismissed from His presence.

One evening we were informed that the Beloved of the World [Bahá'u'lláh] intended to visit the Garden of Junaynih and had directed that all the pilgrims and resident Bahá'ís accompany Him in the morning. That night we could not sleep because we were so excited . . . that we should have the bounty of being in His holy presence for several hours the next day. At the hour of dawn we faced His blessed room and engaged in prayers and devotions. Before sunrise we all assembled outside the gate of the Mansion. It took about one hour until His Blessed Person came downstairs and mounted a white donkey . . . All the believers followed Him on foot to the garden. One of the local believers, Ḥájí Khávar, was a tall man. He walked alongside Bahá'u'lláh and held an umbrella over His head as a protection against the heat of the sun. The air was refreshing as we arrived in the garden . . . His Blessed Person was extremely happy that day and each one of the friends received his share of the bounties from His presence. We had lunch in the garden, then we assembled together and attained His presence.

It was at that time that 'Abdu'l-Bahá arrived from 'Akká. The Blessed Beauty said, 'The Master is coming, hasten to attend Him' . . . On those days Bahá'u'lláh used to sow the seeds of loyalty and servitude toward 'Him whom God hath purposed' ['Abdu'l-Bahá] in the hearts of the believers and explained the lofty station and the hidden reality of the Master to all.

Attended by everyone, 'Abdu'l-Bahá came with great humility into the presence of the Blessed Beauty. Then the Tongue of Grandeur uttered words to this effect, 'From morning until now this garden was not very pleasant, but

> now with the presence of the Master it has become truly most delightful.' Then, turning to the Master, He remarked, 'You should have come in the morning.' 'Abdu'l-Bahá responded, 'The Governor of 'Akká and some residents had requested to meet with Me. Therefore I had to receive and entertain them.' Bahá'u'lláh, with a smiling face, said, 'The Master is our shield. Everybody here lives in the utmost comfort and peace. Association with the outside people such as these is very, very difficult. It is the Master who stands up to everything, and prepares the means of comfort for all the friends. May God protect Him from the evil of the envious and the hostile.'*

Áqá Mírzá Áqá and his family basked in the sunshine of Bahá'u'lláh's presence for nine months. When the time came to depart they were all plunged into deepest sorrow. But Bahá'u'lláh showered His blessings upon them and they left His presence. On the day of their departure Maryam Sulṭán Bagum, the beloved wife of Áqá Mírzá Áqá, attained the presence of Bahá'u'lláh to pay her last homage to Him. She is reported to have kissed the hands of Bahá'u'lláh and made a wish that He might give her the ring He was wearing on His finger as a token of blessing for her family. She did not, however, express her wish. She then went to say farewell to the Greatest Holy Leaf, the daughter of Bahá'u'lláh. While she was there, one of the maids of the household brought Bahá'u'lláh's ring and said to Maryam Sulṭán Bagum, 'The Blessed Beauty has given this for you.'

Circumstances of the Revelation of the *Lawḥ-i-Dunyá*

The *Lawḥ-i-Dunyá* was revealed in Haifa, and a copy handed by Bahá'u'lláh to Ḥájí Mírzá Buzurg, the son of Áqá Mírzá

* These are not to be taken as the exact words of Bahá'u'lláh or 'Abdu'l-Bahá. (A.T.)

Áqá in whose honour it was revealed. This Tablet dates from the time when the Hand of the Cause of God Mullá 'Alí-Akbar and the Trustee of Bahá'u'lláh, Ḥájí Abu'l-Ḥasan-i-Amín* were both imprisoned in Qazvín. Bahá'u'lláh bestows His bounties upon the two in the opening paragraph of this Tablet:

> Praise and thanksgiving beseem the Lord of manifest dominion Who hath adorned this mighty Prison with the presence of their honours 'Alí Akbar and Amín, and hath illumined it with the light of certitude, constancy and assurance. The glory of God and the glory of all that are in the heavens and on the earth be upon them.
>
> Light and glory, greeting and praise be upon the Hands of His Cause, through whom the light of fortitude hath shone forth and the truth hath been established that the authority to choose rests with God, the Powerful, the Mighty, the Unconstrained, through whom the ocean of bounty hath surged and the fragrance of the gracious favours of God, the Lord of mankind, hath been diffused. We beseech Him – Exalted is he – to shield them through the power of His hosts, to protect them through the potency of His dominion and to aid them through His indomitable strength which prevaileth over all created things. Sovereignty is God's, the Creator of the heavens and the Lord of the Kingdom of Names.[1]

The 'mighty Prison' is the prison of Qazvín. As already mentioned earlier (p. 325) a group of political agitators were imprisoned by the Persian government in 1891. Three eminent Bahá'ís, Ibn-i-Abhar, Mullá 'Alí-Akbar and Ḥájí Amín were also cast into prison at the same time in order to appease the enemies of the Cause, by order of Kámrán Mírzá the Náyibu's-Salṭanih, the Governor of Ṭihrán. The last two were put in chains and taken to the prison of Qazvín where they remained

* Ḥájí Amín was posthumously designated a Hand of the Cause of God by Shoghi Effendi, the Guardian of the Faith.

for eighteen months in chains and fetters;* afterwards they were transferred to the prison of Ṭihrán. Mullá 'Alí-Akbar was released after six months while Ḥájí Amín's imprisonment was prolonged further; he was released after the ascension of Bahá'u'lláh.

Bahá'u'lláh's Counsels to His Followers

In the Tablet of Dunyá Bahá'u'lláh reiterates some of His choicest exhortations and counsels:

> Every man of insight will, in this day, readily admit that the counsels which the Pen of this Wronged One hath revealed constitute the supreme animating power for the advancement of the world and the exaltation of its peoples. Arise, O people, and, by the power of God's might, resolve to gain the victory over your own selves, that haply the whole earth may be freed and sanctified from its servitude to the gods of its idle fancies – gods that have inflicted such loss upon, and are responsible for the misery of their wretched worshippers. These idols form the obstacle that impedeth man in his efforts to advance in the path of perfection. We cherish the hope that the Hand of divine power may lend its assistance to mankind and deliver it from its state of grievous abasement . . .
>
> Every verse which this Pen hath revealed is a bright and shining portal that discloseth the glories of a saintly and pious life, of pure and stainless deeds. The summons and the message which We gave were never intended to reach one land or one people only. Mankind in its entirety must firmly adhere to whatsoever hath been revealed and vouchsafed unto it. Then and only then will it attain unto true liberty. The whole earth is illuminated with the resplendent glory of God's Revelation.[2]

* They were photographed wearing these chains, see vol. 3, facing p. 61.

Because the 'Most Great Spirit' of God speaks to mankind through Bahá'u'lláh, we find that every word revealed by Him is an exhortation to goodly deeds; for this reason it is impossible to find a single word in any of His Writings from which the odour of mischief may be inhaled. God never advocates wrongdoing. Indeed, one of the best ways by which the truth of the Revelation of Bahá'u'lláh may be ascertained is for the seeker to study the teachings and counsels of the Most Exalted Pen. In doing so, he will find nothing but praiseworthy exhortations and divine guidance.

In the *Lawḥ-i-Dunyá* Bahá'u'lláh addresses His followers in these words, 'O people of God! Do not busy yourselves in your own concerns; let your thoughts be fixed upon that which will rehabilitate the fortunes of mankind and sanctify the hearts and souls of men.' He states that this can be achieved 'through a virtuous life and a goodly behaviour', reminds the believers that what ensures 'the triumph of this Cause' is a 'saintly character', forbids His loved ones 'to engage in contention or conflict', exhorts them 'to righteous deeds and praiseworthy character', admonishes them 'to observe courtesy' which He describes as 'the prince of virtues', and counsels them in these words:

> O people of Justice! Be as brilliant as the light and as splendid as the fire that blazed in the Burning Bush. The brightness of the fire of your love will no doubt fuse and unify the contending peoples and kindreds of the earth, whilst the fierceness of the flame of enmity and hatred cannot but result in strife and ruin. We beseech God that He may shield His creatures from the evil designs of His enemies. He verily hath power over all things.[3]

One of the distinguishing features of this great Revelation, which was not possible to achieve in previous Dispensations is the establishment of unity among people. Disunity has been and still is the hallmark of the old order. The Revelation of Bahá'u'lláh has vouchsafed to humanity the priceless gift of unity. These words are revealed in the *Lawḥ-i-Dunyá*:

> We have erewhile declared – and Our Word is the truth – : 'Consort with the followers of all religions in a spirit of friendliness and fellowship.' Whatsoever hath led the children of men to shun one another, and hath caused dissensions and divisions amongst them, hath, through the revelation of these words, been nullified and abolished. From the heaven of God's Will, and for the purpose of ennobling the world of being and of elevating the minds and souls of men, hath been sent down that which is the most effective instrument for the education of the whole human race . . . of old it hath been revealed: 'Love of one's country is an element of the Faith of God.' The Tongue of Grandeur hath, however, in the day of His manifestation proclaimed: 'It is not his to boast who loveth his country, but it is his who loveth the world.' Through the power released by these exalted words He hath lent a fresh impulse and set a new direction to the birds of men's hearts, and hath obliterated every trace of restriction and limitation from God's holy Book.[4]

In many of His Tablets Bahá'u'lláh has admonished His loved ones to protect themselves against the influence exerted by the wicked and the ungodly. 'Eschew all fellowship with the ungodly'[5] is Bahá'u'lláh's counsel in His *Hidden Words*. In the *Lawḥ-i-Dunyá* Bahá'u'lláh clearly defines who the ungodly are. 'The Evil One', He states, 'is he that hindereth the rise and obstructeth the spiritual progress of the children of men.'[6]

One of the most wonderful counsels revealed by the Pen of the Most High is the following in the *Lawḥ-i-Dunyá*.

> We have ere this uttered these sublime words: Let them that bear allegiance to this Wronged One be even as a raining

> cloud in moments of charity and benevolence and as a blazing fire in restraining their base and appetitive natures.[7]

In this Tablet Bahá'u'lláh promulgates some of His Teachings aimed at the reconstruction of human society. These mostly reiterate teachings previously revealed, such as the establishment of an international language, promotion of fellowship among all peoples, and the education of children. He attaches great importance to agriculture, recommends the establishment of constitutional government, condemns the actions of the 'unbelievers and the faithless' – an allusion to the enemies of the Faith in Persia – who 'have set their minds' on 'the shedding of blood', 'the burning of books', 'the shunning of the followers of other religions' and 'the extermination of other communities and groups'. He reproaches the Shí'ah sect of Islám for their 'foul imprecations' when they 'invoke the word *Mal'ún* (accursed) – uttered with a guttural sound of the letter *ayn*'.* He beseeches God, however, to 'guide aright' these people, and 'to purge them of unseemly conduct'.

He further expresses astonishment at the people of Persia, for it was reported to Him that 'a certain person went to the seat of the imperial throne in Persia and succeeded in winning the good grace of some of the nobility by his ingratiating behaviour'. This is a reference to Siyyid Jamálu'd-Din-i-Afghání, a brief outline of whose notorious activities is given elsewhere in this book.†

In the *Lawḥ-i-Dunyá* Bahá'u'lláh calls on the ministers of the House of Justice 'to promote the Lesser Peace . . . '

---

* Cursing is a common practice among the Persians, especially among the clergy who pride themselves in pronouncing a person to be *Mal'ún* (accursed) with a guttural sound of the letter 'U'. By doing so, not only has the clergy put a curse on someone, but by pronouncing the letter 'U' with a guttural sound he proudly puts himself in the category of a scholar of the Arabic language. Thus he makes a great impression upon the untutored multitude who never know how to use a guttural sound and are lost in admiration for one who does.

† see below, pp. 428–9.

Although the Universal House of Justice is not yet fully known to mankind, it has found it timely to initiate this process. It has taken the initial steps in the promotion of the Lesser Peace by issuing an open letter entitled *The Promise of World Peace* and addressed to the peoples of the world. It points out the obstacles in the path of peace, delineates the features of a lasting peace, affirms the inevitability of its establishment, outlines the way for its achievement and pledges unremitting support for its promotion by the Bahá'í community throughout the world.

In the *Lawḥ-i-Dunyá* Bahá'u'lláh again pays tribute to those men of learning who are detached from the things of this world and engaged in the guidance of other souls. He bestows His blessings upon them in these words:

> O people of God! Righteous men of learning who dedicate themselves to the guidance of others and are freed and well guarded from the promptings of a base and covetous nature are, in the sight of Him Who is the Desire of the world, stars of the heaven of true knowledge. It is essential to treat them with deference. They are indeed fountains of soft-flowing water, stars that shine resplendent, fruits of the blessed Tree, exponents of celestial power, and oceans of heavenly wisdom. Happy is he that followeth them. Verily such a soul is numbered in the Book of God, the Lord of the mighty Throne, among those with whom it shall be well.[8]

Ḥájí Muḥammad-Riḍáy-i-Iṣfahání

There is a passage in this Tablet which may not be apparent to some as being a reference to the martyrdom of Ḥájí Muḥammad-Riḍáy-i-Iṣfahání. Bahá'u'lláh describes this episode with great feeling:

> Day and night this Wronged One yieldeth thanks and praise

> unto the Lord of men, for it is witnessed that the words of counsel and exhortation We uttered have proved effective and that this people hath evinced such character and conduct as are acceptable in Our sight. This is affirmed by virtue of the event which hath truly cheered the eye of the world, and is none other than the intercession of the friends with the high authorities in favour of their enemies.[9]

Ḥájí Muḥammad-Riḍá was originally from the province of Khurásán, but lived in Iṣfahán and worked as a merchant. He was a devoted believer and a very active teacher of the Cause. Because of his teaching activities he was put in prison, but was released after some time. He then left Iṣfahán and eventually went to 'Akká and attained the presence of Bahá'u'lláh. Coming into contact with the Person of Bahá'u'lláh was the cause of igniting within his heart the fire of love and devotion for his Lord. He begged Him to accept him as a martyr and enable him to lay down his life in His path. Bahá'u'lláh is reported to have told him that it was not necessary, as many souls had already sacrificed their lives in His path. But Ḥájí Muḥammad-Riḍá was so intoxicated with the wine of Bahá'u'lláh's presence that he wanted to give his all to his Beloved. So he repeated his plea. This time the Blessed Beauty remained silent and he took it as a sign of consent. Later he asked Bahá'u'lláh to assign for him a city to reside in. He was bidden to proceed to 'Ishqábád. He lived there for several years and was engaged in teaching the Cause among the Muslim population.

On 1 July 1889 Ḥájí Muḥammad-Riḍá received a Tablet[10] from Bahá'u'lláh in which He praises him for his devoted services, bestows His blessings upon him for his steadfastness and devotion to the Cause, and assures him that all his deeds and aspirations are manifest before Him. He further states that a grievous upheaval has occurred in the city of Ishqábád and describes it as the attack of a serpent upon one who is the recipient of the bounties of His Lord.

Although the identity of the believer who was the target is not disclosed by Bahá'u'lláh, He prays for Ḥájí Muḥammad-Riḍá that God may give strength to his body and assurance to his heart. This Tablet arrived at a time when Ḥájí Muḥammad-Riḍá had invited all the believers of 'Ishqábád to a feast. When it was read out to the friends, Mírzá Abu'l-Faḍl explained that although no upheaval had taken place so far in 'Ishqábád, since Bahá'u'lláh has used the past tense and clearly indicated that one of the believers had been struck down by the enemies, it was an absolute certainty that this upheaval was inevitable. It would happen soon and only one person would be martyred. Ḥájí Muḥammad-Riḍá said to the friends that he believed that he was the believer whose martyrdom Bahá'u'lláh had foretold in this Tablet. And this happened two months later.

Incensed by the remarkable progress of the Faith in 'Ishqábád, the Shí'ah Muslim community had been secretly planning to assassinate a number of believers. Although their plan did not materialize, they succeeded in murdering Ḥájí Muḥammad-Riḍá. Two men armed with daggers attacked him in the bazaar and stabbed him to death. This was on the morning of 8 September 1889. It is reported that they stabbed him thirty-two times amid the jubilation of a great number of people who had gathered to watch him die. Some of the believers attributed the prayers revealed by Bahá'u'lláh in the Tablet he had received, which beseeched God to give strength to his body, as an indication of the agonizing and torturous way in which he was to be martyred. The murderers were so bloodthirsty that they were seen licking their daggers which were dripping with blood, until the Russian police arrived and took them into custody.

On discovering the plot, which had been intended to kill a number of prominent Bahá'ís, the believers sent a petition to General Komaroff, the Governor-General of Transcaspia, and appealed for protection. This was granted to them and in this way the enemies' plans were frustrated. A prolonged

ḤÁJÍ MUḤAMMAD-RIḌÁ

Martyr of the Faith in ‘Ishqábád in 1889

investigation was conducted in the law courts where, in the presence of spectators, many Bahá'ís and non-Bahá'ís were questioned. At the end the court delivered the verdict of guilty and sentence was pronounced. The two murderers were to be executed by hanging, and a few men accessory to the crime were to be exiled to Siberia. This was the first time in the history of the Faith that those responsible for killing a Bahá'í had been brought to justice. The verdict infuriated the Shí'ah clergy in Persia, who were in the habit of decorating the murderers of the Bahá'ís. They made desperate attempts to free the criminals, but did not succeed in influencing the Russian government.

In the meantime, while the prisoners were behind bars awaiting their execution, a number of their relatives accompanied by a few leading merchants visited some prominent Bahá'ís and begged them to intercede with the government for the commuting of the death sentence. The Bahá'ís held a meeting, consulted and decided to take action. Mírzá Abu'l-Faḍl and another believer made representations to the Governor on behalf of the Bahá'í community and interceded with the government, in the first place to absolve the murderers of their crime, and if not possible to mitigate their sentences. The Governor was deeply impressed by the attitude of the Bahá'ís and their willingness to forgive the assassins.

This request was passed on to the Czar, who approved the commuting of the sentences. But the decision was kept a secret and only revealed dramatically at the last moment. On the execution day gallows were erected and graves dug. The prisoners dressed in white robes and ready for execution were brought out of the prison and led to the scaffold. When the moment arrived a government official, in the presence of great multitudes, read out a proclamation announcing that as a result of the intercession of the Bahá'ís with the government requesting pardon for their enemies, His Majesty the Czar had commuted the sentences of the two murderers to life imprisonment in

Siberia, and halved the sentences of the others.

This act of intercession on behalf of their enemies was acclaimed by Bahá'u'lláh as a princely deed. It brought great satisfaction to His heart that through His counsels and exhortations for well-nigh forty years, the believers had at last risen to such heights of faith as to intercede for the release of those who were their deadly enemies.

The Tyrant of Yazd

In the *Lawḥ-i-Dunyá* Bahá'u'lláh states:

> The tyrant of the land of Yá [Yazd], committed that which hath caused the Concourse on High to shed tears of blood.[11]

He was Prince Maḥmúd Mírzá the Jalálu'd-Dawlih, Governor of Yazd. Bahá'u'lláh is referring to the martyrdom on his orders of seven believers known as the first seven martyrs of Yazd. This heinous crime took place on 19 May 1891; the news reached Bahá'u'lláh when He was staying in Haifa. He withheld the Revelation of His words for nine days, and during this period no one was admitted into His presence. The first Tablet which was revealed after this lapse of nine days was the *Lawḥ-i-Dunyá*. The details of the martyrdom of these seven is given in the *Táríkh-i-Shuhadáy-i-Yazd* (the History of the Martyrs of Yazd), and Shoghi Effendi in his masterly fashion has summarized it as follows:

> In Yazd, at the instigation of the mujtahid of that city, and by order of the callous Maḥmúd Mírzá, the Jalálu'd-Dawlih, the governor, a son of Ẓillu's-Sulṭán, seven were done to death in a single day in horrible circumstances. The first of these, a twenty-seven year old youth, 'Alí-Aṣghar, was strangled, his body delivered into the hands of some Jews who, forcing the dead man's six companions to come with them, dragged

the corpse through the streets, surrounded by a mob of people and soldiers beating drums and blowing trumpets, after which, arriving near the Telegraph office, they beheaded the eighty-five year old Mullá Mihdí and dragged him in the same manner to another quarter of the city, where, in view of a great throng of onlookers, frenzied by the throbbing strains of the music, they executed Áqá 'Alí in like manner. Proceeding thence to the house of the local mujtahid, and carrying with them the four remaining companions, they cut the throat of Mullá 'Alíy-i-Sabzivárí, who had been addressing the crowd and glorying in his imminent martyrdom, hacked his body to pieces with a spade, while he was still alive, and pounded his skull to a pulp with stones. In another quarter, near the Mihríz gate, they slew Muḥammad-Báqir, and afterwards, in the Maydán-i-Khán, as the music grew wilder and drowned the yells of the people, they beheaded the survivors who remained, two brothers in their early twenties, 'Alí-Aṣghar and Muḥammad-Ḥasan. The stomach of the latter was ripped open and his heart and liver plucked out, after which his head was impaled on a spear, carried aloft, to the accompaniment of music, through the streets of the city, and suspended on a mulberry tree, and stoned by a great concourse of people. His body was cast before the door of his mother's house, into which women deliberately entered to dance and make merry. Even pieces of their flesh were carried away to be used as a medicament. Finally, the head of Muḥammad-Ḥasan was attached to the lower part of his body and, together with those of the other martyrs, was borne to the outskirts of the city and so viciously pelted with stones that the skulls were broken, whereupon they compelled the Jews to carry the remains and throw them into a pit in the plain of Salsabíl. A holiday was declared by the governor for the people, all the shops were closed by his order, the city was illuminated at night, and festivities proclaimed the consummation of one of the most barbarous acts perpetrated in modern times.[12]

Some years later in 1903 a great massacre of the Bahá'ís took place in Yazd during the governorship of the same Jalálu'd-Dawlih. He tried hard to avert the catastrophe but his soldiers and officials failed to suppress the convulsions caused by the clergy. He lost control for a few days and many Bahá'ís in the city and neighbouring townships and villages were martyred in the most horrible circumstances. When 'Abdu'l-Bahá was in London, Jalálu'd-Dawlih, then living in exile, came in a state of dejection to see Him. Apparently penitent for his past crimes, he threw himself at 'Abdu'l-Bahá's feet, but the Master, who did not wish to see him humiliated, immediately made him feel at ease in His presence.

Tablet to *The Times*

The seven martyrs were executed less than a month after the imprisonment of Mullá 'Alí-Akbar and Ḥájí Amín to which we have referred previously. Bahá'u'lláh wrote a Tablet in which He describes the two events. Because He addresses *The Times* of London in this Tablet, it is referred to as the 'Tablet to *The Times*'. In the opening paragraph Bahá'u'lláh states that the martyrdom of the seven and the imprisonment of the two have created the most joyous jubilation among the Concourse on High. He describes in glowing terms the festive mood among the inmates of the highest paradise as they rejoice and celebrate with exceeding gladness the victory of the triumphant martyrs over their adversaries. Neither the onslaught of the bloodthirsty tyrant nor the fury of the beastly oppressor had succeeded in dampening their faith and enthusiasm or extinguishing the fire of the love of their Lord within their hearts. Their steadfastness in the face of such brutal treatment had endowed the Faith with enormous potentialities.

In this Tablet Bahá'u'lláh describes the circumstances of the martyrdom of the seven in detail, and recounts the story of each. Of Mullá 'Alíy-i-Sabzavárí, one of the seven, Bahá'u'lláh says that this great man of God proclaimed the Cause of God at the very moment of martyrdom, and testified to its truth with his own life-blood. Just before he was beheaded, he cried aloud to the teeming multitudes who had assembled around him, these soul-stirring words: 'At the time of his martyrdom on the plane of Karbilá, Imám Ḥusayn, the Prince of Martyrs, called out to those around him: "Is there any one capable of helping, to help me." And I say to you: Is there any one capable of beholding, to behold me!'* Bahá'u'lláh showers His praise and blessings upon him for these words.

This Tablet is significant for its portrayal of the sufferings and persecutions which the people of Persia inflicted upon the believers. Only a small part of this Tablet to *The Times* has so far been translated into English:

> O 'Times', O thou endowed with the power of utterance! O dawning place of news! Spend an hour with the oppressed of Írán, and witness how the exemplars of justice and equity are sorely tried beneath the sword of tyrants. Infants have been deprived of milk, and women and children have fallen captive to the lawless. The blood of God's lovers hath dyed the earth red, and the sighs of His near ones have set the universe ablaze.
>
> O assemblage of rulers, ye are the manifestations of power and might, and the fountainheads of the glory, greatness and authority of God Himself. Gaze upon the plight of the wronged ones. O daysprings of justice, the fierce gales of rancour and hatred have extinguished the lamps of virtue and piety. At dawn, the gentle breeze of divine compassion hath wafted over charred and cast-out bodies, whispering these exalted words: 'Woe, woe unto you, O people of Írán! Ye have spilled the blood of your own friends and yet remain

* In the original Arabic the two sayings sound almost the same. The only difference between the two is that the letter 's' in *Náṣir* (helper) is changed into 'z' in *Náẓir* (beholder).

in ignorance of what ye have done. Should ye become aware of the deeds ye have perpetrated, ye would flee to the desert and bewail your crimes and tyranny.'

O misguided ones, what sin have the little children committed? Hath anyone, in these days, had pity on the dependants of the oppressed? A report hath reached Us that the followers of the Spirit (Christ) – may the peace of God and His mercy be upon Him – secretly sent them provisions and befriended them out of utmost sympathy. We beseech God, the Eternal Truth, to confirm all in accomplishing that which is pleasing to Him.

O newspapers published throughout the cities and countries of the world! Have ye heard the groan of the downtrodden, and have their cries of anguish reached your ears? Or have these remained concealed? It is hoped that ye will investigate the truth of what hath occurred and vindicate it . . . [13]

The Charter for the World Centre

Lawḥ-i-Karmil

This well-known Tablet* in Arabic was revealed by Bahá'u'lláh on Mount Carmel and is one of the most momentous revealed during His Ministry. The first time Bahá'u'lláh visited Haifa was in 1868 when the Austrian Lloyd steamer arrived there in the morning of 31 August. Haifa was then a small town. Bahá'u'lláh disembarked from the ship, stayed a few hours on shore and then sailed to the prison-city of 'Akká. About fifteen years later, when He had moved His residence to the Mansion of Bahjí, Bahá'u'lláh paid a short visit to Haifa and stayed in a house in the German colony. As we have mentioned in a previous volume,† a number of German Templers, expecting the return of Christ, went to the Holy Land and built houses at the foot of Mount Carmel, but none recognized Him when He appeared among them. Bahá'u'lláh even lived in their houses and revealed a Tablet for their chief, yet they remained deprived of the knowledge of the advent of the Day of God. The third visit took place in 1890 when He again stayed in the German colony; and the fourth visit, about a year before His ascension, took place in 1891 when He spent about three months in that area.

It is believed to be on this occasion that Bahá'u'lláh went to the Cave of Elijah on Mount Carmel. Centuries before, a Christian order had built a monastery over it in the expectation that Christ, returning in the glory of the Father, would bless

---

* Translated into English by Shoghi Effendi, *Gleanings from the Writings of Bahá'u'lláh*, XI.

† see vol. 3, pp. 28–31.

it with His presence. It is not surprising that, like the German Templers, none of the monks who were present at the time recognized the station of Bahá'u'lláh when He visited that place. Bahá'u'lláh pitched His Tent in close proximity to the monastery and there revealed the Tablet of Carmel. It is well known that in the future a Mas͟hriqu'l-Ad͟hkár (Bahá'í House of Worship) will be built on that site.

This Tablet contains significant allusions to the establishment of the World Centre of the Faith and is considered its charter. Before the revelation of this Tablet there was apparently nothing in Bahá'u'lláh's Writings concerning the international Seat of His world-encircling order. From the moment He blessed the mountain of God with His footsteps, mysterious forces were released for the creation of the spiritual and administrative centre of the Faith, a centre from which the world-vivifying energies latent within His Revelation will flow to mankind.

In the Tablet of Carmel Bahá'u'lláh enters into a dialogue with the mountain, Carmel. This is not unusual; in other Tablets He has similarly addressed certain cities or locations – for instance, His address to the Land of Ṭá (Ṭihrán),* or His dialogue with Jerusalem as revealed in the *Lawḥ-i-Aqdas*.† The dialogue in the Tablet of Carmel is at once beautiful, profound and moving. The sublime picture that Bahá'u'lláh has portrayed begins with Himself as He directs His footsteps towards Carmel; the first act in this divine scene is when the voices of 'all created things' are heard addressing Carmel. Then comes Carmel's jubilant words in thanksgiving to its Lord and finally Bahá'u'lláh's response. The opening paragraph of this Tablet raises the curtain of this exalted spectacle.

> All glory be to this Day, the Day in which the fragrances of mercy have been wafted over all created things, a Day so blest

* see vol. 1, pp. 46–9.

† see *Tablets of Bahá'u'lláh*, pp. 9–17.

> that past ages and centuries can never hope to rival it, a Day in which the countenance of the Ancient of Days hath turned towards His holy seat. Thereupon the voices of all created things, and beyond them those of the Concourse on High, were heard calling aloud: 'Haste thee, O Carmel, for lo, the light of the countenance of God, the Ruler of the Kingdom of Names and Fashioner of the heavens, hath been lifted upon thee.'[1]

How fascinating is the concept of the voices informing Carmel of Bahá'u'lláh's arrival there, and how beautiful are the words, 'Haste thee, O Carmel, for lo, the light of the countenance of God, the Ruler of the Kingdom of Names and Fashioner of heavens, hath been lifted upon thee.' In this passage Bahá'u'lláh extols the glory of His Revelation and clearly indicates that by His presence there, He has chosen Mount Carmel as 'His holy seat'. The seat is a visible sign, an outward centre of His innermost majesty and dominion.

Of course, the voices of 'all created things' mentioned in the above passage are not heard physically by anyone, let alone when addressing a mountain. This is a spiritual phenomenon which only the Manifestation of God has access to. However, it is interesting to note that on countless occasions Bahá'u'lláh has stated that all created things such as the atoms of the earth, the drops of the ocean, the rocks and the trees have been exhilarated through the vibrating influence of His Revelation. For example, in the *Lawḥ-i-Aqdas* He testifies that 'every stone and every tree shouteth aloud: "The Lord is come in His great glory".'[2]

In another Tablet[3] He expresses astonishment that whereas the mineral world is vibrating through the breath of God's utterances in this day, the generality of mankind has remained unaffected. When Bahá'u'lláh was sailing from Gallipoli to 'Akká He indicated in a Tablet[4] that because the Lord was sailing the drops of the sea were exhilarated in such wise that

He heard from each drop what no ear could ever hear. We as human beings are not in a position to see or hear such expressions from lifeless objects. We can do no better than to admit our inability to grasp these statements from a physical point of view, but to try to understand their spiritual significance.

On the other hand, all things in the universe are somehow related to each other, and every created thing, even an atom, must have some relationship with its creator. But how that relationship works we shall never know. Science has already proved that many things are happening around us which the human body has no way of sensing. For example, the human senses are incapable of detecting electromagnetic waves, yet we are immersed within them. Lately scientists have discovered that trees communicate with each other, but how this is done they have not yet found out. They have proved this by letting a swarm of insects attack one tree. They have noticed that as a result all other trees within a large area change their chemistry in readiness for a similar attack. Our senses are incapable of detecting such a communication.

If this is so, can we not believe that as attested by Bahá'u'lláh there was a certain reaction by the drops of the sea as He, embodying the Most Great Spirit of God, moved over them? Or can we not say that Mt. Carmel expressed, in a language that its Creator alone could understand, a feeling of exhilaration as Bahá'u'lláh walked over it? But who knows the answer to these questions? Whatever these statements may signify to each believer, let us remember that Bahá'u'lláh has repeatedly mentioned them in His Writings. It is not right to look upon God and His creation through one's limited and narrow vision. Who knows the mysterious workings of God in this vast universe? Who knows in what manner all created things respond to their Creator?

A simple and an enlightened approach to the study of the Tablet of Carmel is to consider the dialogue between the voice of the mountain and that of Bahá'u'lláh as a way of expressing

God's plan in the language of imagery. That plan was to erect upon that mountain the majestic seat of His spiritual and temporal sovereignty. In this dialogue the mountain of God addresses Bahá'u'lláh in this fashion:

> Seized with transports of joy, and raising high her voice, she thus exclaimed: 'May my life be a sacrifice to Thee, inasmuch as Thou hast fixed Thy gaze upon me, hast bestowed upon me Thy bounty, and hast directed towards me Thy steps. Separation from Thee, O Thou Source of everlasting life, hath well nigh consumed me, and my remoteness from Thy presence hath burned away my soul. All praise be to Thee for having enabled me to hearken to Thy call, for having honoured me with Thy footsteps, and for having quickened my soul through the vitalizing fragrance of Thy Day and the shrilling voice of Thy Pen, a voice Thou didst ordain as Thy trumpet-call amidst Thy people. And when the hour at which Thy resistless Faith was to be made manifest did strike, Thou didst breathe a breath of Thy spirit into Thy Pen, and lo, the entire creation shook to its very foundations, unveiling to mankind such mysteries as lay hidden within the treasuries of Him Who is the Possessor of all created things.'[5]

The literal significance of these words is that before Bahá'u'lláh's visit which blessed the spot with His footsteps, Mt. Carmel was a desolate wilderness, a heap of rocks and rubble. 'Separation from Thee, O Thou Source of everlasting life, hath well nigh consumed me, and my remoteness from Thy presence hath burned away my soul.' And Bahá'u'lláh's response changes the scene of desolation into that of joy and luxuriance: 'Rejoice, for God hath in this Day established upon thee His throne . . . give thanks unto Him in as much as He . . . hath turned Thy sorrow into gladness . . . ' are the reassuring words of Bahá'u'lláh. How clearly these words re-echo the vision of Isaiah:

> The wilderness and the solitary place shall be glad for them; and the desert shall rejoice, and blossom as the rose. It shall blossom abundantly, and rejoice even with joy and singing: the glory of Lebanon shall be given unto it, the excellency of Carmel and Sharon, they shall see the glory of the Lord, and the excellency of our God.[6]

In these statements by Bahá'u'lláh there is no ambiguity as to where the international Seat of His Faith was to be established. From the moment this Tablet was revealed, Mt. Carmel was destined to flourish and become the World Centre of a World Faith, the early stages of which have already come into being. Bahá'u'lláh addresses Carmel in these words:

> No sooner had her voice reached that most exalted Spot than We made reply: 'Render thanks unto Thy Lord, O Carmel. The fire of thy separation from Me was fast consuming thee, when the ocean of My presence surged before thy face, cheering thine eyes and those of all creation, and filling with delight all things visible and invisible. Rejoice, for God hath in this Day established upon thee His throne, hath made thee the dawning-place of His signs and the dayspring of the evidences of His Revelation. Well is it with him that circleth around thee, that proclaimeth the revelation of thy glory, and recounteth that which the bounty of the Lord thy God hath showered upon thee. Seize thou the Chalice of Immortality in the name of thy Lord, the All-Glorious, and give thanks unto Him, inasmuch as He, in token of His mercy unto thee, hath turned thy sorrow into gladness, and transmuted thy grief into blissful joy. He, verily, loveth the spot which hath been made the seat of His throne, which His footsteps have trodden, which hath been honoured by His presence, from which He raised His call, and upon which He shed His tears.[7]

Although the voice of Bahá'u'lláh in this Tablet is directed to Carmel, and many of the passages concern the building of the World Centre of the Faith, in reality He is also addressing His followers. Indeed, there are many meanings concealed in this Tablet which the believers may be able to grasp by turning to Bahá'u'lláh in an attitude of prayer and meditation. It is not proper for us to embark upon interpretations of the many passages which are pregnant with divine wisdom and which foreshadow great events. Every individual believer has to deepen himself in the knowledge of the Faith and through prayer and study of the Writings discover the significances which are concealed therein. Each soul is entitled to discover his own interpretation, which must, however, remain personal; his findings will never be authoritative unless they conform to the interpretations of the Master and the Guardian of the Faith.

The following are the concluding passages of the Tablet of Carmel:

> 'Call out to Zion, O Carmel, and announce the joyful tidings: He that was hidden from mortal eyes is come! His all-conquering sovereignty is manifest; His all-encompassing splendour is revealed. Beware lest thou hesitate or halt. Hasten forth and circumambulate the City of God that hath descended from heaven, the celestial Kaaba round which have circled in adoration the favoured of God, the pure in heart, and the company of the most exalted angels. Oh, how I long to announce unto every spot on the surface of the earth, and to carry to each one of its cities, the glad-tidings of this Revelation – a Revelation to which the heart of Sinai hath been attracted, and in whose name the Burning Bush is calling: "Unto God, the Lord of Lords, belong the kingdoms of earth and heaven." Verily this is the Day in which both land and sea rejoice at this announcement, the Day for which have been laid up those things which God, through a bounty beyond the ken of mortal mind or heart, hath destined for revelation. Ere long will God

sail His Ark upon thee, and will manifest the people of Bahá who have been mentioned in the Book of Names.'

Sanctified be the Lord of all mankind, at the mention of Whose name all the atoms of the earth have been made to vibrate, and the Tongue of Grandeur hath been moved to disclose that which had been wrapt in His knowledge and lay concealed within the treasury of His might. He, verily, through the potency of His name, the Mighty, the All-Powerful, the Most High, is the ruler of all that is in the heavens and all that is on earth.[8]

The first part of the above passage, 'Call out to Zion, O Carmel, and announce the joyful tidings: He that was hidden from mortal eyes is come!' may be regarded as a commandment of Bahá'u'lláh to proclaim His Cause to mankind.

The longing of Bahá'u'lláh 'to announce unto every spot on the surface of the earth, and to carry to each one of its cities, the glad-tidings of this Revelation . . . ' may be said to have been fulfilled initially by 'Abdu'l-Bahá with the issuing of the Tablets of the Divine Plan. These Tablets, fourteen in all, which constituted the charter for the teaching of the Faith, were addressed by 'Abdu'l-Bahá to the Bahá'ís of North America. He delineated a world-encircling plan of teaching, the initial stages of which were later incorporated by Shoghi Effendi into a series of national plans which were followed by a world plan known as the Ten Year Crusade. The implementation of the latter was particularly responsible for carrying the Message of Bahá'u'lláh to almost every part of the world. This process will continue until such time as these utterances of Bahá'u'lláh revealed in the *Lawḥ-i-Dunyá* are fulfilled:

How vast is the tabernacle of the Cause of God! It hath overshadowed all the peoples and kindreds of the earth, and will, ere long, gather together the whole of mankind beneath its shelter.[9]

The most significant part of the Tablet of Carmel is the following:

> Hasten forth and circumambulate the City of God that hath descended from heaven, the celestial Kaaba round which have circled in adoration the favoured of God.[10]

Shoghi Effendi has interpreted the meaning of the 'City of God, the celestial Kaaba' as the Shrine of the Báb on Mt. Carmel. The forces which were released by Bahá'u'lláh for the implementation of the mighty enterprise involving the transfer of the remains of the Báb and the building of His Shrine became effective almost immediately after the revelation of this Tablet. Bahá'u'lláh one day went to the heart of the mountain where a clump of cypress trees was growing in a circle. His tent was pitched in the centre, and 'Abdu'l-Bahá was present in His service. Shoghi Effendi has described this event in these words:

> In that same year Bahá'u'lláh's tent, the 'Tabernacle of Glory', was raised on Mt. Carmel, 'the Hill of God and His Vineyard', the home of Elijah, extolled by Isaiah as the 'mountain of the Lord', to which 'all nations shall flow'.[11]

An eye-witness has explained that while Bahá'u'lláh was facing the East and 'Abdu'l-Bahá the West, the Tongue of Grandeur issued instructions to the Master to arrange the transportation of the remains of the Báb from Persia to the Holy Land and their interment in a mausoleum below the clump of cypress trees at a spot which He indicated with His hand. Thus the initial step for this holy enterprise was undertaken by Bahá'u'lláh Himself.

It took almost eight years before 'Abdu'l-Bahá was able to arrange the transfer of the remains of the Báb. The casket containing the sacred remains arrived in 'Akká on 31 January

1899. Ten years later on Naw-Rúz* 1909 'Abdu'l-Bahá, with His own hands and in the presence of believers from East and West, placed the wooden casket inside a marble sarcophagus which was lowered into the vault built especially for it inside one of the six rooms constructed by 'Abdu'l-Bahá for this purpose.† In a Tablet He conveyed this good news to the believers in these words:

> The most joyful tidings is this, that the holy, the luminous body of the Báb . . . after having for sixty years been transferred from place to place, by reason of the ascendancy of the enemy, and from fear of the malevolent, and having known neither rest nor tranquillity has, through the mercy of the Abhá Beauty, been ceremoniously deposited, on the day of Naw-Rúz, within the sacred casket, in the exalted Shrine on Mt. Carmel . . . By a strange coincidence, on that same day of Naw-Rúz a cablegram was received from Chicago, announcing that the believers in each of the American centers had elected a delegate and sent to that city . . . and definitely decided on the site and construction of the Mas͟hriqu'l-Ad͟hkár.[12]

In 1948 preparations were begun by Shoghi Effendi for the building of the superstructure of the Shrine of the Báb. In the course of its construction in 1951 he gave this description in a message to the American believers:

> I cannot at this juncture overemphasize the sacredness of that holy dust embosomed in the heart of the Vineyard of God, or overrate the unimaginable potencies of this mighty institution founded sixty years ago, through the operation of the Will of, and the definite selection made by, the Founder of our Faith, on the occasion of His historic visit to that holy mountain, nor can I lay too much stress on the role which this institution, to

* Bahá'í New Year, 21 March.

† For more details see vol. 3, Appendix I.

> which the construction of the superstructure of this edifice is bound to lend an unprecedented impetus, is destined to play in the unfoldment of the World Administrative Center of the Faith of Bahá'u'lláh and in the efflorescence of its highest institutions constituting the embryo of its future World Order.
>
> For, just as in the realm of the spirit, the reality of the Báb has been hailed by the Author of the Bahá'í Revelation as 'The Point round Whom the realities of the Prophets and Messengers revolve', so, on this visible plane, His sacred remains constitute the heart and center of what may be regarded as nine concentric circles,* paralleling thereby, and adding further emphasis to the central position accorded by the Founder of our Faith to One 'from Whom God hath caused to proceed the knowledge of all that was and shall be', 'the Primal Point from which have been generated all created things'.[13]

By 1953 the superstructure of the Shrine of the Báb was completed by Shoghi Effendi. And now, 'the city of God . . . the celestial Kaaba, round which have circled in adoration the favoured of God, the pure in heart, and the company of the most exalted angels,' stands majestically in the bosom of God's mountain.

In his cable to the Bahá'í world Shoghi Effendi described the Shrine as the 'QUEEN OF CARMEL ENTHRONED GOD'S MOUNTAIN, CROWNED GLOWING GOLD, ROBED SHIMMERING WHITE, GIRDLED EMERALD GREEN, ENCHANTING EVERY EYE, FROM AIR, SEA, PLAIN, HILL'.[14]

Another significant passage in the Tablet of Carmel is the following:

> Ere long will God sail His Ark upon thee, and will manifest the people of Bahá who have been mentioned in the Book of Names.[15]

---

* For further details see *Citadel of Faith*, pp. 95–6. (A. T.)

In the Bahá'í Writings the term 'Ark' is often used to signify the Cause of God, or the Covenant, and Bahá'u'lláh, the Holy Mariner. For example, the Báb in the Qayyúmu'l-Asmá has lauded the community of the Most Great Name, the Bahá'ís, as the companions of the Crimson-coloured Ark. But the 'Ark' in the Tablet of Carmel, according to Shoghi Effendi signifies the Ark of the Law of God. He explains that the sailing of the Ark upon Mount Carmel is an allusion to the establishment of the Universal House of Justice, the supreme legislative body of the Faith from which the law of God will flow to all mankind. Shoghi Effendi also refers to the members of the House of Justice as occupants of the Ark mentioned in the Tablet of Carmel. The Universal House of Justice is the main organ of the international Administrative Centre of the Faith, while there are other institutions which form part of this centre.

Again, the Prophets of Israel foresaw these events thousands of years ago, as in this quotation from Isaiah:

> And it shall come to pass in the last days, that the mountain of the Lord's house shall be established in the top of the mountains, and shall be exalted above the hills; and all nations shall flow unto it. And many people shall go and say, Come ye, and let us go up to the mountain of the Lord, to the house of the God of Jacob; and he will teach us of his ways, and we will walk in his paths: for out of Zion shall go forth the law, and the word of the Lord from Jerusalem. And he shall judge among the nations, and shall rebuke many people: and they shall beat their swords into plowshares, and their spears into pruning-hooks: nation shall not lift up sword against nation, neither shall they learn war anymore.[16]

The first step taken by Shoghi Effendi in creating the world Administrative Centre was the acquisition of land on Mt. Carmel in close proximity to the Shrine of the Báb, and the interment of the remains of the Greatest Holy Leaf, the daughter of Bahá'u'lláh, the noblest woman in the Bahá'í Dispensation, in that consecrated spot. This was followed by the transfer of the remains of the Purest Branch, 'created of the light of Bahá', the martyred son of Bahá'u'lláh, offered up by his Father as a 'ransom for the unification of the human race', together with those of his mother, the saintly Navváb, and their burial in the same surroundings.

The next step taken by Shoghi Effendi was the creation of an arc surrounding these resting-places and facing the Qiblih* of the people of Bahá. The various institutions of the Administrative Centre, including the Universal House of Justice, were to be housed in several edifices erected around this arc. The initial step in the construction of this Administrative Centre was taken when the International Archives Building was built; it was completed by Shoghi Effendi in 1957. Since then the Seat of the Universal House of Justice has been constructed, and it is now planned to erect other edifices to house the remaining institutions and thus complete the Bahá'í World Administrative Centre.† The establishment of the Throne of God mentioned in the Tablet of Carmel, as interpreted by Shoghi Effendi, is none other than the establishment of the World Centre on Mount Carmel. He writes:

> The conjunction of these three resting-places, under the shadow of the Báb's own Tomb, embosomed in the heart of Carmel, facing the snow-white city across the bay of 'Akká, the Qiblih of the Bahá'í world, set in a garden of exquisite beauty, reinforces, if we would correctly estimate its significance, the spiritual potencies of a spot, designated by Bahá'u'lláh Himself the seat of God's throne. It marks, too, a further milestone in the road leading eventually to the establishment of that permanent world Administrative Centre of

---

* The Point of Adoration, the Shrine of Bahá'u'lláh.

† Since the original publication of this volume, the Centre for the Study of the Texts, the International Teaching Centre, and the Terraces of the Shrine of the Báb have been completed. (Ed.)

SITE OF THE FUTURE MASHRIQU'L-ADHKÁR ON MOUNT CARMEL

Marked by an obelisk, the site is near 'the Spot hallowed by the footsteps of Bahá'u'lláh' when He revealed the Tablet of Carmel

THE GROVE OF CYPRESS TREES

Here Bahá'u'lláh indicated to 'Abdu'l-Bahá the site of the Shrine of the Báb

THE BAHÁ'Í WORLD CENTRE

This aerial view shows, right to left, the Shrine of the Báb and the Terraces, the International Archives Building, the Centre for the Study of the Texts, the Seat of the Universal House of Justice and the International Teaching Centre Building. The arc and the monument gardens may also be seen

> the future Bahá'í Commonwealth, destined never to be separated from, and to function in the proximity of, the Spiritual Centre of that Faith, in a land already revered and held sacred alike by the adherents of three of the world's outstanding religious systems.[17]

The Spiritual Centre on Mt. Carmel is the Shrine of the Báb, 'the spot round which the Concourse on high circle in adoration'. The Administrative Centre is under the shadow of that sacred Shrine. The combination of the Spiritual and Administrative Centres constitute the Bahá'í World Centre on Mt. Carmel.

In former religions the spiritual and administrative centres have been separated from each other. In Christianity, for example, the administration of religion was moved away from the Holy Land which was its birthplace and spiritual home. This happened in Islám too: the seat of the Caliphate, the temporal ruling body, was established far away from Mecca. This separation of the spiritual and administrative centres in former religions may be regarded as a reflection of the disunity among their followers, divided as they were into many sects and denominations. One of the distinguishing features of the Revelation of Bahá'u'lláh is that the Spiritual and Administrative Centres of the Faith are united and permanently established on the Mountain of God. The authority for this comes from Bahá'u'lláh in His Tablet of Carmel and it is He Who has released the spiritual forces for its realization. The progressive unfoldment of the international institutions of the Cause in the Holy Land demonstrates their inseparability from their spiritual centre. The unity of the two is symbolic of the unity of the Bahá'í community throughout the world, a unity which is destined to embrace the whole of mankind and the establishment of which within human society remains the main aim and purpose of Bahá'u'lláh's Revelation for this age.

In one of his communications to the Bahá'í world, Shoghi Effendi projects his vision of the future development of the

World Centre of the Faith, unveiling vistas of unimaginable glory in store for mankind:

> The raising of this Edifice* will in turn herald the construction, in the course of successive epochs of the Formative Age of the Faith, of several other structures, which will serve as the administrative seats of such divinely appointed institutions as the Guardianship, the Hands of the Cause, and the Universal House of Justice. These Edifices will, in the shape of a far-flung arc, and following a harmonizing style of architecture, surround the resting-places of the Greatest Holy Leaf, ranking as foremost among the members of her sex in the Bahá'í Dispensation, of her Brother, offered up as a ransom by Bahá'u'lláh for the quickening of the world and its unification, and of their Mother, proclaimed by Him to be His chosen 'consort in all the worlds of God.' The ultimate completion of this stupendous undertaking will mark the culmination of the development of a world-wide divinely-appointed Administrative Order whose beginnings may be traced as far back as the concluding years of the Heroic Age of the Faith.
>
> This vast and irresistible process, unexampled in the spiritual history of mankind, and which will synchronize with two no less significant developments – the establishment of the Lesser Peace and the evolution of Bahá'í national and local institutions – the one outside and the other within the Bahá'í world – will attain its final consummation, in the Golden Age of the Faith, through the raising of the standard of the Most Great Peace, and the emergence, in the plenitude of its power and glory, of the focal Center of the agencies constituting the World Order of Bahá'u'lláh. The final establishment of this seat of the future Bahá'í World Commonwealth will signalize at once the proclamation of the sovereignty of the Founder of our Faith and the advent of the Kingdom of the Father repeatedly lauded and promised by Jesus Christ.

* Bahá'í International Archives Building. (A.T.)

This World Order will, in turn, in the course of successive Dispensations of the Bahá'í Cycle, yield its fairest fruit through the birth and flowering of a civilization, divinely inspired, unique in its features, world-embracing in its scope, and fundamentally spiritual in its character – a civilization destined as it unfolds to derive its initial impulse from the spirit animating the very institutions which, in their embryonic state, are now stirring in the womb of the present Formative Age of the Faith.[18]

24

Epistle to the Son of the Wolf

Shaykh Muḥammad-Taqí, the Son of the Wolf

This momentous Epistle was revealed by Bahá'u'lláh in the last year of His earthly life. It is addressed to Shaykh Muḥammad-Taqí, known as Áqá Najafí, a son of Shaykh Muḥammad-Báqir who was stigmatized by Him as 'Wolf'.* After the death of his father in 1883, Áqá Najafí succeeded him as a leading mujtahid of Iṣfahán. He was an inveterate enemy and formidable opponent of the Cause of Bahá'u'lláh, a vicious and evil-minded clergyman who fulfilled the famous saying: 'The child is the secret of his sire.' He well merited the title 'Son of the Wolf'.

In his younger days he collaborated with his father in pursuing the policy of murdering the Bahá'ís. He was the one who rolled up his sleeves on the occasion of the martyrdom of the King and the Beloved of the Martyrs and announced his readiness to carry out their execution personally should the official executioner refuse to co-operate. Once he assumed office it was through his instigation and on his direct orders that the great upheavals against the Bahá'ís occurred in Iṣfahán and neighbouring townships. It was by his command that several believers were put to death, and in 1903 he was the chief instigator of the upheaval of Yazd, the bloodiest massacre of the Bahá'ís since the bloodbath of Ṭihrán in 1852.

To such a man, who was perpetrating the most heinous crimes against His followers in Persia, Bahá'u'lláh addressed this weighty Epistle. The opening paragraph is in praise of God, and the second, in praise of Bahá'u'lláh as the 'Supreme Mediator', 'the Most Exalted Pen', 'the dawning-place' of

* see above, ch. 6.

God's 'most excellent names', and 'the dayspring of His most exalted attributes'. Having unequivocally announced His own station to Áqá Najafí, Bahá'u'lláh in the next paragraph proclaims to him that 'the ear of man hath been created that it may hearken unto the Divine Voice of this Day', counsels him first to 'purify' his soul 'with the waters of renunciation', to 'crown' his head with 'the crown of the fear of God' and then to arise from his seat, turn his face in the direction of Bahá'u'lláh's abode and recite a prayer which is revealed especially for him.

From the manner in which Áqá Najafí continued his opposition to the Faith after receiving this Epistle, we can guess the extent of his anger on reading the first three paragraphs. The perusal of the lengthy prayer which followed must have enraged him further. Although the revelation of this prayer, and indeed the whole Epistle, is a genuine attempt by Bahá'u'lláh to lead his misguided soul to God, the prayer nevertheless serves as the best descriptive material for depicting the infamous life of Áqá Najafí. Among some beautiful passages we find condemnatory statements such as these, in which Áqá Najafí is counselled by Bahá'u'lláh to recite in a prayerful attitude and beg God's forgiveness for his wicked deeds:

> 'I testify, O my God, and my King, that Thou hast created me to remember Thee, to glorify Thee, and to aid Thy Cause. And yet, I have aided Thine enemies . . . '
>
> 'Alas, alas, for my waywardness, and my shame, and my sinfulness, and my wrong-doing . . . alas, alas! and again alas, alas! for my wretchedness and the grievousness of my transgressions! Thou didst call me into being, O my God, to exalt Thy Word, and to manifest Thy Cause. My heedlessness, however, hath deterred me and compassed me about, in such wise that I have arisen to blot out Thy signs, and to shed the blood of Thy loved ones . . .
>
> 'O Lord, my Lord! and again, O Lord, my Lord! and yet again, O Lord, my Lord! I bear witness that by reason of mine

iniquity the fruits of the tree of Thy justice have fallen, and through the fire of my rebelliousness the hearts of such of Thy creatures as enjoy near access to Thee were consumed, and the souls of the sincere among Thy servants have melted. O wretched, wretched that I am! O the cruelties, the glaring cruelties, I inflicted! Woe is me, woe is me, for my remoteness from Thee, and for my waywardness, and mine ignorance, and my baseness, and my repudiation of Thee, and my protests against Thee! . . .

'Alas, alas! My turning away from Thee hath burnt up the veil of mine integrity, and my denial of Thee hath rent asunder the covering cast over mine honor. O would that I were beneath the depths of the earth, so that my evil deeds would remain unknown to Thy servants! Thou seest the sinner, O my Lord, who hath turned towards the dawning-place of Thy forgiveness and Thy bounty, and the mountain of iniquity that hath sought the heaven of Thy mercy and pardon. Alas, alas! My mighty sins have prevented me from approaching the court of Thy mercy, and my monstrous deeds have caused me to stray far from the sanctuary of Thy presence. Indeed, I am he that hath failed in duty towards Thee, and hath broken Thy Covenant and Thy Testament, and committed that which hath made the dwellers of the cities of Thy justice, and the dawning-places of Thy grace in Thy realms, to lament. I testify, O my God, that I have put away Thy commandments, and clung to the dictates of my passions, and have cast away the statutes of Thy Book, and seized the book of mine own desire. O misery, misery! As mine iniquities waxed greater and greater, Thy forbearance towards me augmented, and as the fire of my rebelliousness grew fiercer, the more did Thy forgiveness and Thy grace seek to smother up its flame. By the power of Thy might! O Thou Who art the desire of the world and the Best-Beloved of the nations! Thy long-suffering hath puffed me up, and Thy patience hath emboldened me . . .

' . . . Thou hast given me a tongue wherewith to remember

and praise Thee, and yet it uttereth that which hath caused the souls of such of Thy chosen ones as are nigh unto Thee to melt . . .

'. . . Thou hast given me eyes to witness Thy signs, and to behold Thy verses, and to contemplate the revelations of Thine handiwork, but I have rejected Thy will, and have committed what hath caused the faithful among Thy creatures and the detached amidst Thy servants to groan. Thou hast given me ears that I may incline them unto Thy praise and Thy celebration . . .

'. . . And yet, alas, alas, I have forsaken Thy Cause, and have commanded Thy servants to blaspheme against Thy trusted ones and Thy loved ones, and have acted, before the throne of Thy justice, in such wise that those that have recognized Thy unity and are wholly devoted to Thee among the dwellers of Thy realm mourned with a sore lamentation . . .

'. . . Alas, alas! Thou hast ordained that every pulpit be set apart for Thy mention, and for the glorification of Thy Word, and the revelation of Thy Cause, but I have ascended it to proclaim the violation of Thy Covenant, and have spoken unto Thy servants such words as have caused the dwellers of the Tabernacles of Thy majesty and the denizens of the Cities of Thy wisdom to lament . . .

'. . . By Thy glory! I know not for which sin to beg Thy forgiveness and implore Thy pardon, nor from which of mine iniquities to turn aside unto the Court of Thy bounteousness and the Sanctuary of Thy favor. Such are my sins and trespasses that no man can number them, nor pen describe them . . . [1]

No one but God can address a man in this way and lay bare before him his sinfulness and transgressions. Never for one moment did Áqá Najafí look upon himself in the light of this prayer while on this earth. But no doubt he has been able to see his true self in the world beyond, like every other soul, and discover how grievously he erred in his earthly life.

A noticeable feature throughout the *Epistle to the Son of the Wolf* is Bahá'u'lláh's loving exhortation. There is no revenge in God's domain. Although He is addressing one of His bitterest enemies, God's loving compassion can be seen at work. While condemning his wicked deeds, He prays that he may change his ways. While sometimes appearing wrathful, He is never vindictive in His remarks. While denouncing his machinations, He is never extreme in His words. His dispassionate exposition of His teachings, His explicit description of the circumstances of His Revelation, His profound arguments setting forth the proofs of the validity of His Mission, His challenging remarks addressed to His adversaries, are all interwoven with passages reflecting His compassion, His exalted counsels, and His unbounded love for His servants, whether friend or foe.

The Re-revelation of Tablets

In His Tablets Bahá'u'lláh occasionally quotes passages from Writings He has previously revealed. But the *Epistle to the Son of the Wolf* is different, in that it contains a great many quotations from His earlier Tablets. It includes an anthology of His Writings, chosen by Himself. We have already described in previous volumes* the manner in which Bahá'u'lláh revealed His Writings and the speed with which His amanuensis was empowered by Him to write down His words. Whereas any compiler will copy the required source material for his quotations, the Revealer of the Word of God does not follow this pattern. It is inconceivable to imagine that when He wished to quote from a previous Tablet, Bahá'u'lláh would stop the flow of His Revelation and direct His amanuensis to insert a certain part of a Tablet as a quotation. It must be remembered that Bahá'u'lláh revealed about fifteen thousand Tablets during the forty years of His Ministry. Most of these were not easily accessible at the time, and none of them were indexed so as to

* see vol. 1, ch. 3.

enable one to retrieve a desired passage from among so many pages. For Bahá'u'lláh's amanuensis or anyone else to try to find part of a Tablet in those days would be very much like looking for a needle in a haystack.

On the other hand, divine revelation, as witnessed by many of Bahá'u'lláh's disciples, was accompanied by the release of enormous powers which emanated from His person, manifesting the majesty of God and His awe-inspiring glory as verses of God poured down like copious rain. To suddenly stop this heavenly outpouring and busy oneself with the cumbersome task of looking for a passage among so many pages, would not only have been inconsistent with the dignity and majesty of the Revealer of the Word of God, but would also degrade him to the position of a human author.

Every quotation one finds in the *Epistle to the Son of the Wolf* was re-revealed by Bahá'u'lláh at the time. This is one of the evidences of the power of God, that His Mouthpiece can utter the same words which had been revealed to Him some years before. Not only was this true in relation to His own Writings, but, as mentioned previously,* He quoted passages from the Writings of the Báb without having access to His Works. Of course this knowledge is not limited to Books of Scripture but extends to everything. In the Tablet of Ḥikmat Bahá'u'lláh confirms this to Nabíl-i-Akbar in these words:

> Thou knowest full well that We perused not the books which men possess and We acquired not the learning current amongst them, and yet whenever We desire to quote the sayings of the learned and of the wise, presently there will appear before the face of thy Lord in the form of a tablet all that which hath appeared in the world and is revealed in the Holy Books and Scriptures. Thus do We set down in writing that which the eye perceiveth. Verily His knowledge encompasseth the earth and the heavens.

* see above, p. 50.

> This is a Tablet wherein the Pen of the Unseen hath inscribed the knowledge of all that hath been and shall be – a knowledge that none other but My wondrous Tongue can interpret.[2]

A careful examination of the quotations in the *Epistle to the Son of the Wolf* shows that the quotations and the original texts are almost exactly the same. Very rarely they may differ in one or two words, usually an adverb, a preposition or an adjective, but the meaning remains the same. The reason for this is that a certain word has been re-revealed differently. The discrepancy is more noticeable in the original language, for the translation into English is not affected by the change of an adverb or a preposition.

To cite an example: in the *Epistle to the Son of the Wolf*, Bahá'u'lláh quotes the 'second leaf of the Most Exalted Paradise' from His Tablet known as *Kalimát-i-Firdawsíyyih*. The phrase 'Pen of the Most High' in the original Tablet is re-revealed in the *Epistle to the Son of the Wolf* as 'Pen of the Divine Expounder',* but the rest of the quotation remains the same as in its original form.

Bahá'u'lláh's Presentation of His Teachings

A deep study of the *Epistle to the Son of the Wolf* requires some knowledge of Islamic subjects. A detailed study of these is beyond the scope of this book, but some brief notes are given in Appendix III, and the English edition also has a useful glossary. Some historical events too need explanation, but most of these have already been described in this and former volumes; references will be given to these where necessary.

Throughout the Epistle Bahá'u'lláh addresses Áqá Najafí as the 'Shaykh'. He proclaims to him the advent of the Day of God, identifies Himself as God's Supreme Manifestation and describes the verities enshrined in His Revelation. He describes

* see *Tablets of Bahá'u'lláh*, p. 63, and *Epistle to the Son of the Wolf*, p. 28.

His Mission clearly, introducing Himself to the Shaykh when he states:

> This Wronged One hath frequented no school, neither hath He attended the controversies of the learned. By My Life! Not of Mine own volition have I revealed Myself, but God, of His own choosing, hath manifested Me.[3]

He then quotes some verses He had revealed in the *Lawḥ-i-Sulṭán*[*] addressed to Náṣiri'd-Dín Sháh, beginning with this celebrated passage:

> O King! I was but a man like others, asleep upon My couch, when lo, the breezes of the All-Glorious were wafted over Me, and taught Me the knowledge of all that hath been. This thing is not from Me, but from One who is Almighty and All-Knowing.[4†]

In this Epistle Bahá'u'lláh outlines some of His basic teachings such as love, unity, and similar principles which constitute the cornerstones of His Faith. Most of the utterances expressing these teachings are gleaned by Himself from His previously revealed Writings. He probably uses this method in order to assure the Shaykh that these teachings are not newly formulated but have been promulgated from the very beginning of His Revelation, and that for several decades the believers have been exhorted to carry them out. These are some of the teachings which, among many more, He presents to the Shaykh:

> The Divine Messengers have been sent down . . . for the purpose of promoting the knowledge of God, and for furthering unity and fellowship amongst men . . .[5]

---

* For details of the *Lawḥ-i-Sulṭán* see vol. 2, pp. 337–57, and vol. 3, ch. 9.

† For an interpretation of this passage by 'Abdu'l-Bahá see vol. 2, pp. 346–7.

Justice and equity are twin Guardians that watch over men . . .[6]

That the diverse communities of the earth, and the manifold systems of religious belief, should never be allowed to foster the feelings of animosity among men, is, in this Day, the essence of the Faith of God and His religion . . .[7]

Religious fanaticism and hatred are a world-devouring fire, whose violence none can quench . . .[8]

Ye are the fruits of one tree and the leaves of one branch. Deal ye with one another with the utmost love and harmony, with friendliness and fellowship . . .[9]

So powerful is the light of unity that it can illuminate the whole earth . . .[10]

Consort with all men, O people of Bahá, in a spirit of friendliness and fellowship . . .[11]

A kindly tongue is the lodestone of the hearts of men . . .[12]

O ye friends of God in His cities and His loved ones in His lands! This Wronged One enjoineth on you honesty and piety . . .[13]

We enjoin the servants of God and His handmaidens to be pure and to fear God, that they may shake off the slumber of their corrupt desires, and turn toward God . . .[14]

Revile ye not one another. We, verily, have come to unite and weld together all that dwell on earth . . .[15]

Lay fast hold on whatever will profit you, and profit the

peoples of the world. Thus commandeth you the King of Eternity, Who is manifest in His Most Great Name . . . [16]

In this Revelation the hosts which can render it victorious are the hosts of praiseworthy deeds and upright character . . . [17]

Verily I say: The fear of God hath ever been a sure defence and a safe stronghold for all the peoples of the world . . . [18]

We, verily, have chosen courtesy, and made it the true mark of such as are nigh unto Him. Courtesy, is, in truth, a raiment which fitteth all men, whether young or old . . . [19]

Purge your hearts from love of the world, and your tongues from calumny, and your limbs from whatsoever may withhold you from drawing nigh unto God . . . [20]

This Wronged One hath, at all times, summoned the peoples of the world unto that which will exalt them, and draw them nigh unto God . . . [21]

Say: O people of God! Adorn your temples with the ornament of trustworthiness and piety. Help then, your Lord with the hosts of goodly deeds and a praiseworthy character.[22]

These are just a few of Bahá'u'lláh's exhortations, constituting the essence of His spiritual teachings, which He has set forth in the *Epistle to the Son of the Wolf* for the Shaykh. He also quotes for him a celebrated passage revealed as an admonishment to His son, Badí'u'lláh,* a passage which may be regarded as a charter of moral conduct for an individual:

---

* After the ascension of Bahá'u'lláh he broke the Covenant and rose up against 'Abdu'l-Bahá. For more information see the *Will and Testament of 'Abdu'l-Bahá*. The present author intends to give an account of his misdeeds in the forthcoming volumes entitled *The Covenant of Bahá'u'lláh* (now published).

Be generous in prosperity, and thankful in adversity. Be worthy of the trust of thy neighbor, and look upon him with a bright and friendly face. Be a treasure to the poor, an admonisher to the rich, an answerer of the cry of the needy, a preserver of the sanctity of thy pledge. Be fair in thy judgment, and guarded in thy speech. Be unjust to no man, and show all meekness to all men. Be as a lamp unto them that walk in darkness, a joy to the sorrowful, a sea for the thirsty, a haven for the distressed, an upholder and defender of the victim of oppression. Let integrity and uprightness distinguish all thine acts. Be a home for the stranger, a balm to the suffering, a tower of strength for the fugitive. Be eyes to the blind, and a guiding light unto the feet of the erring. Be an ornament to the countenance of truth, a crown to the brow of fidelity, a pillar of the temple of righteousness, a breath of life to the body of mankind, an ensign of the hosts of justice, a luminary above the horizon of virtue, a dew to the soil of the human heart, an ark on the ocean of knowledge a sun in the heaven of bounty, a gem on the diadem of wisdom, a shining light in the firmament of thy generation, a fruit upon the tree of humility.[23]

'Shed not the blood of anyone'

Another category of teachings which features prominently in the *Epistle to the Son of the Wolf* is that which forbids contention, strife, religious hostility, warfare, and all acts from which a trace of mischief or sedition may be detected. The reason for Bahá'u'lláh's emphasis on this topic becomes apparent in the light of history. During the Bábí Dispensation the followers of the Báb defended themselves heroically against the onslaught of their enemies. The upheavals of Mázindarán, Nayríz and Zanján* are typical examples. Since they took up arms and defended themselves so valiantly, the Bábís were highly feared by the Persian populace. This sense of fear was heightened by

* For details see *The Dawn-Breakers*.

the attempt on the life of Náṣiri'd-Dín Sháh by a few irresponsible Bábís in 1850.

From the early days of His Ministry Bahá'u'lláh admonished the followers of the Báb to abandon the practice of the use of force, to put their swords in their sheaths and never bring them out again. 'In the Book of God, the Mighty, the Great,' Bahá'u'lláh admonishes His loved ones, 'Ye have been forbidden to engage in contention and conflict.' He exhorted His followers not to resist their enemies by force, and if the occasion demanded it, to give their lives willingly in the path of God rather than to kill. Concerning this transformation, Bahá'u'lláh writes in the *Epistle to the Son of the Wolf*:

> Day and night, while confined in that dungeon,* We meditated upon the deeds, the condition, and the conduct of the Bábís, wondering what could have led a people so high-minded, so noble, and of such intelligence, to perpetrate such an audacious and outrageous act against the person of His Majesty. This Wronged One, thereupon, decided to arise, after His release from prison, and undertake, with the utmost vigor, the task of regenerating this people . . .
>
> After Our arrival,† We revealed, as a copious rain, by the aid of God and His Divine Grace and mercy, Our verses, and sent them to various parts of the world. We exhorted all men, and particularly this people, through Our wise counsels and loving admonitions, and forbade them to engage in sedition, quarrels, disputes and conflict. As a result of this, and by the grace of God, waywardness and folly were changed into piety and understanding, and weapons converted into instruments of peace.[24]

In spite of this complete transformation, the people of Persia did not differentiate between the Bábís and the Bahá'ís. They

* Síyáh-Chál of Ṭihrán, see vol. 1, pp. 8–11. (A. T.)

† In 'Iráq. (A.T.)

insisted on regarding the followers of Bahá'u'lláh as Bábís and in associating them with violence. It is for this reason that throughout this Epistle Bahá'u'lláh quotes passages such as these:

> Beware lest ye shed the blood of anyone. Unsheathe the sword of your tongue from the scabbard of utterance, for therewith ye can conquer the citadels of men's hearts . . . [25]

> O people! Spread not disorder in the land, and shed not the blood of anyone . . . [26]

> The sword of the virtuous character and upright conduct is sharper than the blades of steel . . . [27]

Not only were the public given wrong impressions about the conduct of the believers: Náṣiri'd-Din Sháh himself is said to have been afraid throughout his reign even of coming face to face with a Bahá'í. This fear was somewhat understandable, because he always remembered the attempt on his life.

For example, in 1882 a number of believers were imprisoned in Ṭihrán by the orders of Náyibu's-Salṭanih, the Governor of Ṭihrán, who was a son of the Sháh. Among the prisoners were the Hand of the Cause Mullá 'Alí-Akbar,* Mírzá Abu'l-Faḍl† and Mullá Muḥammad-Riḍáy-i-Yazdí.‡ Their imprisonment lasted two years, and the Governor, who appeared to be very tolerant, used to invite the learned among the prisoners to explain various aspects of the Faith to him. In several sessions, which lasted for hours, these souls were able to prove the validity of the claims of Bahá'u'lláh and describe His teachings. The knowledge of Mírzá Abu'l-Faḍl, the audacity of Mullá Riḍá and the spiritual qualities of Mullá 'Alí-Akbar combined

---

* see above, pp. 312–20.

† For his life story see vol. 3, pp. 91–107, and vol. 3, Appendix II.

‡ For an account of his life see vol. 1, pp. 84–91.

together and resulted in an unprecedented proclamation of the teachings of the Faith in high circles. A detailed account of their brilliant discussions is beyond the scope of this book.

When Náṣiri'd-Dín S͟háh became aware of this, he is reported to have intimated to his son, the Náyibu's-Salṭanih, that he desired to meet Mullá 'Alí-Akbar but feared to come face to face with the prisoner. The Náyibu's-Salṭanih assured his father that there was no danger involved. But the S͟háh would not take the risk. Mullá 'Alí-Akbar was consequently brought into a room; the S͟háh looked from behind a window at the dignified and composed person of Mullá 'Alí-Akbar in chains and fetters, majestically seated on a chair. The S͟háh was so impressed that he ordered his photographer to take a photograph of him in that condition (see page 407).

It was because of the S͟háh's mistrust that Bahá'u'lláh revealed passages such as these, to dissociate the conduct of the Bahá'ís from the conduct of those of the past and assure him and the S͟hayk͟h of their loyalty and truthfulness:

> Night and day hath this Wronged One been occupied in that which would unite the hearts, and edify the souls of men. The events that have happened in Persia during the early years have truly saddened the well-favored and sincere ones. Each year witnessed a fresh massacre, pillage, plunder, and shedding of blood. At one time there appeared in Zanján that which caused the greatest consternation; at another in Nayríz, and at yet another in Ṭabarsí, and finally there occurred the episode of the Land of Ṭá (Ṭihrán). From that time onwards this Wronged One, assisted by the One True God – exalted be His glory – acquainted this oppressed people with the things which beseemed them. All have sanctified themselves from the things which they and others possess, and have clung unto, and fixed their eyes upon that which pertaineth unto God.
>
> It is now incumbent upon His Majesty the S͟háh – may God, exalted be He, protect him – to deal with this people

with loving-kindness and mercy. This Wronged One pledgeth Himself, before the Divine Kaaba, that, apart from truthfulness and trustworthiness, this people will show forth nothing that can in any way conflict with the world-adorning views of His Majesty.[28]

In another passage He states:

O Shaykh! It is incumbent upon the divines to unite with His Majesty, the Sháh – may God assist him – and to cleave day and night unto that which will exalt the station of both the government and the nation. This people are assiduously occupied in enlightening the souls of men and in rehabilitating their condition. Unto this testifieth that which hath been sent down by the Most Sublime Pen in this lucid Tablet.[29]

And again He demonstrates the spiritual character of the Bahá'ís and their readiness to give their lives rather than hurting their enemies:

O Shaykh! This people have passed beyond the narrow straits of names, and pitched their tents upon the shores of the sea of renunciation. They would willingly lay down a myriad lives, rather than breathe the word desired by their enemies. They have clung to that which pleaseth God, and are wholly detached and freed from the things which pertain unto men. They have preferred to have their heads cut off rather than utter one unseemly word. Ponder this in thine heart. Methinks they have quaffed their fill of the ocean of renunciation. The life of the present world hath failed to withhold them from suffering martyrdom in the path of God.

In Mázindarán a vast number of the servants of God were exterminated. The Governor, under the influence of calumniators, robbed a great many of all that they possessed. Among the charges he laid against them was that they had been laying

THE HAND OF THE CAUSE OF GOD ḤÁJÍ ÁKHÚND IN CHAINS AND STOCKS

This photograph was taken at the request of Náṣiri'd-Dín Sháh

> up arms, whereas upon investigation it was found out that they had nothing but an unloaded rifle! Gracious God! This people need no weapons of destruction, inasmuch as they have girded themselves to reconstruct the world. Their hosts are the hosts of goodly deeds, and their arms the arms of upright conduct, and their commander the fear of God. Blessed that one that judgeth with fairness.[30]

The reader may be helped to appreciate the significance of the term 'narrow straits of names' used above by referring to the subject of the 'Kingdom of Names' discussed in volume 2.*

'The aim . . . is to quench the flame of hate'

In order to highlight the transformation which had taken place since the days of the Bábí upheavals, Bahá'u'lláh cites the examples of a few of the Bahá'í martyrs who had put up no resistance even under the threat of death. He addresses the Shaykh in these words:

> O Shaykh! Time and again have I declared, and now yet again I affirm, that for two score years We have, through the grace of God and by His irresistible and potent will, extended such aid to His Majesty the Sháh – may God assist him – as the exponents of justice and of equity would regard as incontestable and absolute . . .
>
> Previous to these forty years controversies and conflicts continually prevailed and agitated the servants of God. But since then, aided by the hosts of wisdom, of utterance, of exhortations and understanding, they have all seized and taken fast hold of the firm cord of patience and of the shining hem of fortitude, in such wise that this wronged people endured steadfastly whatever befell them, and committed everything unto God, and this notwithstanding that in Mázindarán and

* pp. 39–43.

> at Ra<u>sh</u>t a great many have been most hideously tormented. Among them was his honor, Ḥájí Naṣír, who, unquestionably, was a brilliant light that shone forth above the horizon of resignation. After he had suffered martyrdom, they plucked out his eyes and cut off his nose, and inflicted on him such indignities that strangers wept and lamented, and secretly raised funds to support his wife and children.[31]

Ḥájí Naṣír was a devoted believer in whose honour Bahá'u'lláh revealed the Tablet of Naṣír. Part of this important Tablet has been translated by Shoghi Effendi into English, and a brief account of his life and martyrdom as well as a description of this well-known Tablet is given in a previous volume.*

Bahá'u'lláh also refers to the martyrdom of the 'twin shining lights', the King and Beloved of Martyrs:†

> O <u>Sh</u>ay<u>kh</u>! My Pen is abashed to recount what actually took place. In the land of Ṣád (Iṣfahán) the fire of tyranny burned with such a hot flame that every fair-minded person groaned aloud. By thy life! The cities of knowledge and of understanding wept with such a weeping that the souls of the pious and of the God-fearing were melted. The twin shining lights, Ḥasan and Ḥusayn (the King of Martyrs and the Beloved of Martyrs) offered up spontaneously their lives in that city. Neither fortune, nor wealth, nor glory, could deter them! God knoweth the things which befell them and yet the people are, for the most part, unaware! [32]

Bahá'u'lláh further cites the example of other martyrs for the <u>Sh</u>ay<u>kh</u>:

> Before them one named Káẓim and they who were with him, and after them, his honor A<u>sh</u>raf, all quaffed the draught of

* see vol. 2, pp. 245–59.
† see above, ch. 5.

> martyrdom with the utmost fervor and longing, and hastened unto the Supreme Companion.[33]

By Káẓim is meant Mullá Káẓim from Talkhunchih, a village in the neighbourhood of Iṣfahán. He was a learned divine well respected by the people of Iṣfahán. He became a believer in AH 1288 (AD 1871–2) and began to teach the Faith to his people, some of whom became believers. The news spread and he was forced to leave his native village. For a time he lived in Iṣfahán where he succeeded in bringing a number of people under the shadow of the Cause. This news reached the powerful mujtahid of the city, the inveterate enemy of the Cause Shaykh Muḥammad-Báqir (the Wolf), who immediately wrote his death sentence. By this time, however, Mullá Káẓim had relinquished his clerical attire and was working as a labourer in a public bath in the city. He succeeded in slipping out of Iṣfahán back to his own village. Then followed a period of comings and goings to Iṣfahán, Shíráz and Ṭihrán. At last he was arrested in his native village and sent to Iṣfahán where he was put in prison. Prince Mas'úd Mírzá the Ẓillu's-Sulṭán summoned Mullá Káẓim to his presence, and when he refused to recant his Faith the Prince implemented the death sentence and ordered his execution. This was in 1877.

The execution took place in a large public square, the famous Maydán-i-Sháh, where great crowds had assembled to watch. Having refused to recant his Faith and be freed, Mullá Káẓim was beheaded by the executioner. Shaykh Muḥammad-Báqir ordered his corpse to be hung upside-down from a pole situated on the executioner's platform. The rope from which he was suspended broke and his body fell down from a great height. His smashed body was again suspended and the Shaykh announced that anyone who threw a stone at the corpse would assuredly secure a place for himself in paradise. A frenzied crowd carried out the attack. For two days men and women could be seen walking long distances carrying stones. Even pregnant women who could hardly walk took part in this shameful crime. When the body was deserted at night some men even gouged out the eyes and cut off the fingers, the nose, the lips and the ears.

On the morning of the third day Shaykh Muḥammad-Báqir arrived on the scene. Not satisfied with the savage indignities which had been heaped upon the victim, he ordered the corpse to be lowered to the ground for a horseman to gallop over it. And when every part of the corpse was broken, it was delivered to the flames and the charred bones were thrown into a disused well.

As to Ashraf mentioned in the passage cited above, he was a native of Najafábád, but since he lived in Ábádih for some time he became known as Mírzá Ashraf of Ábádih. He was a great teacher of the Faith who enabled many souls to embrace the Cause of God. He travelled to India, stayed for some time in Bombay and eventually went to live in Iṣfahán. He had such a radiant personality that people were drawn to him for his spiritual qualities, his piety and his knowledge.

It was in 1888 when Ẓillu's-Sulṭán discovered that one of his secretaries, together with a young servant, were attracted to the Faith and were studying the *Kitáb-i-Íqán*. The Prince was filled with rage when he discovered that it was Mírzá Ashraf who had been teaching the Faith to these two. He arrested Ashraf and put him in prison. A few days later the Prince invited a number of divines including Áqá Najafí (the Son of the Wolf) to interrogate Mírzá Ashraf in his presence. With great eloquence and conviction Ashraf in a loud voice, which could be heard outside the room, declared his beliefs and proved the validity of the Faith he had embraced. Confounded and utterly helpless to refute his arguments in support of the Faith, the divines used their usual weapon of denunciation. Áqá Najafí wrote Ashraf's death sentence and delivered it into the hands of the Prince who ordered his execution.

Mírzá Ashraf was executed on 23 October 1888 by hanging in the same public square as Mullá Káẓim. By order of Áqá

Najafí, his body was trampled underfoot, savagely mutilated by the mob, delivered to the flames and then thrown into a ditch and a wall pulled down over it. These barbarous acts of killing were typical of the way in which a great many Bahá'í martyrs met their deaths in a spirit of resignation and reliance upon God.

In the *Epistle to the Son of the Wolf* Bahá'u'lláh cites the names of a few other martyrs. He mentions Badí', who delivered Bahá'u'lláh's Tablet to the Sháh, gives a brief account of the martyrdom of Áqá Najaf-'Alí, calls to mind the stories of Mírzá Muṣṭafá, of Abá Baṣír and Ashraf-i-Zanjání, of Abá Badí' (the father of Badí'), and of Siyyid Ismá'íl. The stories of these martyrs are recounted in previous volumes.* In the *Epistle to the Son of the Wolf* Bahá'u'lláh marvels at the

> splendour and glory which the light of renunciation, shining from the upper chamber of the heart of Mullá 'Alí-Ján, hath shed. He was so carried away by the breezes of the Most Sublime Word and by the power of the Pen of Glory that to him the field of martyrdom equalled, nay outrivalled, the haunts of earthly delights.[34]

Mullá 'Alí-Ján was a native of Mázindarán and was born in the year 1846. In his youth he displayed a passion for acquiring religious knowledge. He therefore studied Islamic theology and became well-versed in the *Qur'án* and the traditions of Islám. One day he came across some traditions extolling the merits of the city of 'Akká. He was puzzled by this, and no one among the divines could explain to him the significance of these traditions. He searched for an answer until he came across a well-known Bahá'í who taught him the Faith. Embracing the Cause of Bahá'u'lláh endowed Mullá 'Alí-Ján with new vision, and his religious passion found an outlet in

* see in order mentioned above: vol. 3, ch. 9; vol. 2, pp. 222–3; vol. 2, pp. 60–61; vol. 2, pp. 223–30; vol. 2, pp. 128–36; vol. 1, pp. 101–3.

the teaching field. With exemplary devotion and enthusiasm he taught the Faith to many souls; he even took the unusual step of proclaiming the Faith from the pulpits of the mosques. This resulted in great numbers entering the Faith in different villages.

Then began a period of great opposition. The divines clamoured for his death, and he was sent to Ṭihrán where he was imprisoned. Eventually, with the approval of Náṣiri'd-Dín Sh̲áh, on 29 June 1883 he was escorted by a band of soldiers beating drums and blowing trumpets to a public square in Ṭihrán and executed. Shoghi Effendi has summarized the story of his martyrdom in these words:

> Mullá 'Alí Ján was conducted on foot from Mázindarán to Ṭihrán, the hardships of that journey being so severe that his neck was wounded and his body swollen from the waist to the feet. On the day of his martyrdom he asked for water, performed his ablutions, recited his prayers, bestowed a considerable gift of money on his executioner, and was still in the act of prayer when his throat was slit by a dagger, after which his corpse was spat upon, covered with mud, left exposed for three days, and finally hewn to pieces.[35]

Another example cited in the *Epistle to the Son of the Wolf* of the Bahá'ís showing compassion and extending forgiveness to their enemies is the story of the martyrdom of Ḥájí Muḥammad-Riḍá in 'Is̲h̲qábád, a moving episode which has already been related elsewhere in this book.*

By referring to these heart-rending stories of the martyrs, Bahá'u'lláh highlights the most important aim of His Cause, namely to blot out every trace of enmity and hatred from the hearts of men and unite mankind through the power of His Revelation. He testifies to this exalted aim in His Will and Testament, the Book of the Covenant:

* see above, pp. 364–9.

> The aim of this Wronged One in sustaining woes and tribulations, in revealing the Holy Verses and in demonstrating proofs hath been naught but to quench the flame of hate and enmity, that the horizon of the hearts of men may be illumined with the light of concord and attain real peace and tranquillity . . .[36]

In the *Epistle to the Son of the Wolf* Bahá'u'lláh cites for the Shaykh long passages from His Tablets to the kings and rulers of His time, Tablets through which He had proclaimed His Mission, unveiled the nature of His Revelation, elucidated its fundamental verities, described some of His universal teachings, issued His exhortations, and summoned the most potent among the crowned heads of the world to embrace His Cause. Parts of these Tablets addressed to Náṣiri'd-Dín Sháh (known as the *Lawḥ-i-Sulṭán*), to Napoleon III, to the Czar of Russia and Queen Victoria are re-revealed in this mighty Epistle. These Tablets have already been referred to in some detail in previous volumes.*

Another subject which comes up in various parts of the *Epistle to the Son of the Wolf* is the suffering inflicted upon Bahá'u'lláh from the early days of the Báb's Ministry. Quoting a passage from His Tablet to Queen Victoria Bahá'u'lláh remarks:

> Consider these days in which He Who is the Ancient Beauty hath come in the Most Great Name, that He may quicken the world and unite its peoples. They, however, rose up against Him with sharpened swords, and committed that which caused the Faithful Spirit to lament, until in the end they imprisoned Him in the most desolate of cities, and broke the grasp of the faithful upon the hem of His robe . . .

---

* For the *Lawḥ-i-Sulṭán* see vol. 2, ch. 16, and vol. 3, ch. 9. For the Tablet to Napoleon III see vol. 2, pp. 368–9, and vol. 3, pp. 110–15. For the Tablet to Czar Alexander II see vol. 3, pp. 118–23. For the Tablet to Queen Victoria see vol. 3, pp. 123–8.

> . . . At all times He was at the mercy of the wicked doers. At one time they cast Him into prison, at another they banished Him, and at yet another hurried Him from land to land. Thus have they pronounced judgment against Us, and God, truly, is aware of what I say.[37]

In a passage addressed to the Shaykh Bahá'u'lláh recounts some of the ordeals He was subjected to in the earlier days in Persia.

> O Shaykh! That which hath touched this Wronged One is beyond compare or equal. We have borne it all with the utmost willingness and resignation, so that the souls of men may be edified, and the Word of God be exalted. While confined in the prison of the Land of Mím (Mázindarán) We were one day delivered into the hands of the divines. Thou canst well imagine what befell Us. Shouldst thou at sometime happen to visit the dungeon of His Majesty the Sháh, ask the director and chief jailer to show thee those two chains, one of which is known as Qará-Guhar, and the other as Salásil. I swear by the Day-Star of Justice that for four months this Wronged One was tormented and chained by one or the other of them. 'My grief exceedeth all the woes to which Jacob gave vent, and all the afflictions of Job are but a part of My sorrows!'[38]

In mentioning 'the prison of the Land of Mím', Bahá'u'lláh is referring to the incident in Ámul where He was bastinadoed and imprisoned for a short while.* The 'dungeon of His majesty the Sháh' is the Síyáh-Chál of Ṭihrán.† The verse at the end of the above passage comes from the famous Arab poet, Ibn-i-Fáriḍ, in his celebrated ode the *Qaṣídiy-i-Tá'íyyih*. Bahá'u'lláh wrote His own *Qaṣídiy-i-Varqá'íyyih* in a rhyme and metre identical with the former, and He quotes this verse from Ibn-i-Fáriḍ in

* For details see *The Dawn-Breakers*, pp. 368–76, and above, p. 155.

† see vol. 1, p. 9.

His *Qaṣídih.* The circumstances of its revelation are described in a former volume.*

In another passage Bahá'u'lláh describes His afflictions in these words:

> The one true God well knoweth, and all the company of His trusted ones testify, that this Wronged One hath, at all times, been faced with dire peril. But for the tribulations that have touched Me in the path of God, life would have held no sweetness for Me, and My existence would have profited Me nothing. For them who are endued with discernment, and whose eyes are fixed upon the Sublime Vision, it is no secret that I have been, most of the days of My life, even as a slave, sitting under a sword hanging on a thread, knowing not whether it would fall soon or late upon him. And yet, notwithstanding all this We render thanks unto God, the Lord of the worlds.[39]

* see vol. 1, pp. 62–4.

25

Epistle to the Son of the Wolf (continued)

The Machinations of the Azalís in Constantinople

The sufferings Bahá'u'lláh endured through the acts of His enemies, though very severe, were insignificant when compared with the manifold acts of treachery and misrepresentation perpetrated by the followers of Mírzá Yaḥyá, or the shameful behaviour of those who were reckoned among His own followers but who dishonoured His Name through their misdeeds. These men of evil inflicted far greater sufferings upon Him than His enemies who persecuted Him physically. In one of His Tablets He testifies to this:

> I sorrow not for the burden of My imprisonment. Neither do I grieve over My abasement, or the tribulation I suffer at the hands of Mine enemies. By My life! They are My glory, a glory wherewith God hath adorned His own Self. Would that ye knew it! . . .
>
> My sorrows are for those who have involved themselves in their corrupt passions, and claim to be associated with the Faith of God, the Gracious, the All-Praised.[1]

In several parts of the *Epistle to the Son of the Wolf* Bahá'u'lláh refers to the machinations of the followers of Mírzá Yaḥyá who together with a few so-called Bahá'ís unfaithful to Him created a series of disgraceful scandals in Constantinople (Istanbul) with the aim of tarnishing the good name of the Faith. Their shameful activities, which continued for about a decade, brought great pain and suffering to the heart of Bahá'u'lláh. The following is a reference in the *Epistle to the Son of the Wolf* to this episode.

> Gracious God! This is the day whereon the wise should seek the advice of this Wronged One, and ask Him Who is the Truth what things are conducive to the glory and tranquillity of men. And yet, all are earnestly striving to put out this glorious and shining light, and are diligently seeking either to establish Our guilt, or to voice their protest against Us. Matters have come to such a pass, that the conduct of this Wronged One hath, in every way, been grossly misrepresented, and in a manner which it would be unseemly to mention. One of Our friends hath reported that among the residents of the Great City (Constantinople) he had heard with the greatest regret someone state that, each year, a sum of fifty thousand tumans was being despatched from his native land to 'Akká! It hath not, however, been made clear who had disbursed the sum, nor through whose hands it had passed!
>
> Briefly, this Wronged One hath, in the face of all that hath befallen Him at their hands, and all that hath been said of Him, endured patiently, and held His peace, inasmuch as it is Our purpose, through the loving providence of God – exalted be His glory – and His surpassing mercy, to abolish, through the force of Our utterance, all disputes, war, and bloodshed, from the face of the earth. Under all conditions We have, in spite of what they have said, endured with seemly patience, and have left them to God.[2]

In another passage He refers to this episode again:

> O Shaykh! We have time and again stated that for a number of years We have extended Our aid unto His Majesty the Sháh. For years no untoward incident hath occurred in Persia. The reins of the stirrers of sedition among various sects were

> held firmly in the grasp of power. None hath transgressed his limits. By God! This people have never been, nor are they now, inclined to mischief. Their hearts are illumined with the light of the fear of God, and adorned with the adornment of His love. Their concern hath ever been and now is for the betterment of the world. Their purpose is to obliterate differences, and quench the flame of hatred and enmity, so that the whole earth may come to be viewed as one country. On the other hand, the officials of the Persian Embassy in the Great City (Constantinople) are energetically and assiduously seeking to exterminate these wronged ones. They desire one thing, and God desireth another. Consider now what hath befallen the trusted ones of God in every land. At one time they have been accused of theft and larceny; at another they have been calumniated in a manner without parallel in this world.[3]

He further states:

> God alone – exalted be His glory – is cognizant of the things which befell this Wronged One. Every day bringeth a fresh report of stories current against Us at the Embassy in Constantinople. Gracious God! The sole aim of their machinations is to bring about the extermination of this servant. They are, however, oblivious of the fact that abasement in the path of God is My true glory. In the newspapers the following hath been recorded: 'Touching the fraudulent dealings of some of the exiles of 'Akká, and the excesses committed by them against several people, etc . . . .' Unto them who are the exponents of justice and the daysprings of equity the intention of the writer is evident and his purpose clear. Briefly, he arose and inflicted upon Me divers tribulations, and treated Me with injustice and cruelty. By God! This Wronged One would not barter this place of exile for the Most Sublime Habitation. In the estimation of men of insight whatsoever befalleth in the

> path of God is manifest glory and a supreme attainment . . .
> Such abasement hath been inflicted that each day they spread fresh calumnies.[4]

The background to all this is as follows: from the early days of the Faith the city of Constantinople had been a centre of Bahá'í activity. It all began with the exile of Bahá'u'lláh to that city. When Bahá'u'lláh went to Adrianople, He made arrangements for one or two faithful believers to remain in Constantinople to act as a channel of communication between Him and His followers. Constantinople being the capital of the Ottoman empire and an important centre for trade and business, other individuals soon arrived, some of whom were faithful believers and some followers of Mírzá Yaḥyá or trouble-makers. In this way Constantinople became a nest of conspiracy and intrigue against the Faith of Bahá'u'lláh.

The situation grew worse as the years went by, and the campaign of hostility and vilification reached such proportions as to become a cause of distress to Bahá'u'lláh during the last ten years of His life.

Two prominent followers of Mírzá Yaḥyá in Constantinople were a certain Shaykh Muḥammad-i-Yazdí and Muḥammad 'Alíy-i-Tabrízí. In one of His Tablets[5] Bahá'u'lláh describes the former as the most wicked of all men. The latter was expelled from the Holy Land by Bahá'u'lláh because of gross misconduct and shameful behaviour. He went to Constantinople and joined hands with the former, and together they used every possible means at their disposal to undermine the unity of the Bahá'ís and to destroy the good name of the Faith.

Around the year 1880 some prominent members of the Afnán family, including Ḥájí Mírzá Muḥammad-'Alí and his brother Ḥájí Mírzá Muḥammad-Taqí,* maternal cousins of the Báb, decided to establish a trading company in Constantinople. They already had several such establishments in various parts

---

* see above, pp. 125–29.

of Asia and Egypt. They obtained permission from Bahá'u'lláh for the project and invited a very experienced Bahá'í merchant of Qazvín to join them in this enterprise. He was Shaykh Muḥammad-'Alí, entitled by Bahá'u'lláh Nabíl ibn-i-Nabíl (Nabíl son of Nabíl). He was the younger brother of Shaykh Káẓim-i-Samandar,* one of the Apostles of Bahá'u'lláh. Nabíl was an enthusiastic, devoted and pious believer. When Bahá'u'lláh issued permission, Nabíl went to Constantinople and started a business there which quickly became successful. This was in 1882. He applied standards of honesty and fairness in all his business transactions and soon became known as one of the most trustworthy merchants in the city. This aroused the jealousy and antagonism of the Azalís who began a campaign of vilification and slander against Nabíl in high circles. At first their activities were trivial and unimportant, until a new figure arrived on the scene. This was a certain Muḥammad-'Alíy-i-Iṣfahání, a so-called Bahá'í who was a trouble-maker and had been sent from 'Akká to Constantinople by Bahá'u'lláh. He was a small tradesman and had settled in the city before the arrival of Nabíl. The full story of the conspiracy and mischief which ensued over the years is given in full by Mírzá 'Abdu'l-Ḥusayn-i-Samandar, a nephew of Nabíl who was personally a witness to it all. It is a complex story and only a summary of it is given here.

From the start Muḥammad-'Alí, the mischief-maker, began causing difficulties for the Afnán's trading establishment. Eventually, in order to contain him, Nabíl, with the approval of the Afnáns, invited Muḥammad-'Alí to become a partner in the business. For some years the affairs of the company went smoothly, and Muḥammad-'Alí became the recipient of huge profits. However, during these years he involved himself secretly with the Azalís, especially his namesake Muḥammad-'Alíy-i-Tabrízí and Shaykh Muḥammad-i-Yazdí. Hand in hand with the Azalís, Muḥammad-'Alí began a campaign of

* see vol. 3, pp. 88–91.

defamation against the followers of Bahá'u'lláh. Their lies and calumnies reached such proportions that Nabíl could no longer bear them. One evening he attempted suicide by throwing himself into the sea, but he was rescued in the nick of time.

During this time another believer, Abu'l-Qásim-i-Náẓir, arrived on his way to 'I<u>sh</u>qábád. Muḥammad-'Alíy-i-Iṣfahání befriended Náẓir and persuaded him to postpone his journey. Soon after his attempted suicide, Nabíl was invited by Bahá'u'lláh to go to 'Akká. This was in the spring of 1889. In the meantime Muḥammad-'Alíy-i-Iṣfahání stole four hundred pounds in cash from the coffers of the trading house and accused Náẓir of stealing it. This accusation he circulated throughout the city, and with the help of the Azalís brought a case against Náẓir to the Persian Ambassador who, after questioning, relieved him of the charges. He then brought the case to the Ottoman court which declared the innocence of Náẓir once again.

Being defeated, Muḥammad-'Alí found no other option but to attack the Faith. Supported by the Azalís, he published a statement in the newspaper *A<u>kh</u>tar* in which he falsely accused Ḥájí Mírzá Siyyid Ḥasan,* known as the Afnán-i-Kabír, of having robbed him of his profits, imputed to him dishonesty and deceitfulness, announced that he was severing relations with the trading house, warned people to beware of the treachery of the Bahá'ís and hinted that some of the Writings of Bahá'u'lláh had been responsible for the whole affair.

This was not, however, the end of the story. Although the company had by then been wound up by Mírzá Muḥsin-i-Afnán (the son of the Afnán-i-Kabír) and the son of Samandar, and both men had returned to the Holy Land, it was necessary to refute the misrepresentations of Muḥammad-'Alí. Three people were sent by Bahá'u'lláh to clear up the affair. These were Siyyid Aḥmad-i-Afnán (another son of Afnán-i-Kabír), Ḥájí Amín and Náẓir. Later it was necessary for Nabíl to join

* He was a brother of the wife of the Báb, see below, pp. 429–33.

them as well. This was the autumn of 1889. Their mission was successful insofar as Nabíl was able to prove in the Ottoman court the falsity of the claims of Muḥammad-'Alí and the innocence of the Bahá'ís. A document was signed by the leading merchants of the city, testifying that Muḥammad-'Alí had lied all the way through and that he owed the Afnáns a considerable sum of money. However, the mission failed to force Muḥammad-'Alí to pay his debts to the Bahá'ís.

In the meantime Muḥammad-'Alí and his infamous associates intensified their campaign of slander and calumny against the Bahá'ís. Nabíl, who was to return to Persia on the orders of Bahá'u'lláh, was, alas, engulfed again in the mesh of their conspiracy and intrigues. He could not endure this any more. This time he succeeded in putting an end to his own life by poisoning himself. Bahá'u'lláh describes his fate in *Epistle to the Son of the Wolf*:

> In this connection it is necessary to mention the following occurrence, that haply men may take fast hold of the cord of justice and truthfulness. Ḥájí Shaykh Muḥammad 'Alí – upon him be the glory of God, the Ever-Abiding – was a merchant of high repute, well-known unto most of the inhabitants of the Great City (Constantinople). Not long ago, when the Persian Embassy in Constantinople was secretly engaged in stirring up mischief, it was noticed that this believing and sincere soul was greatly distressed. Finally, one night he threw himself into the sea, but was rescued by some passers-by who chanced to come upon him at that moment. His act was widely commented upon and given varied interpretations by different people. Following this, one night he repaired to a mosque, and, as reported by the guardian of that place, kept vigil the whole night, and was occupied until the morning in offering, ardently and with tearful eyes, his prayers and supplications. Upon hearing him suddenly cease his devotions, the guardian went to him, and found that he had already surrendered his

soul. An empty bottle was found by his side, indicating that he had poisoned himself. Briefly, the guardian, while greatly astonished, broke the news to the people. It was found out that he had left two testaments. In the first he recognized and confessed the unity of God, that His Exalted Being had neither peer nor equal, and that His Essence was exalted above all praise, all glorification and description. He also testified to the Revelation of the Prophets and the holy ones, and recognized what had been written down in the Books of God, the Lord of all men. On another page, in which he had set down a prayer, he wrote these words in conclusion: 'This servant and the loved ones of God are perplexed. On the one hand the Pen of the Most High hath forbidden all men to engage in sedition, contention or conflict, and on the other that same Pen hath sent down these most sublime words: "Should anyone, in the presence of the Manifestation, discover an evil intention on the part of any soul, he must not oppose him, but must leave him to God." Considering that on the one hand this binding command is clear and firmly established, and that on the other calumnies, beyond human strength to bear or endure, have been uttered, this servant hath chosen to commit this most grievous sin. I turn suppliantly unto the ocean of God's bounty and the heaven of Divine mercy, and hope that He will blot out with the pen of His grace and bounteousness the misdeeds of this servant. Though my transgressions be manifold, and unnumbered my evil-doings, yet do I cleave tenaciously to the cord of His bounty, and cling unto the hem of His generosity. God is witness, and they that are nigh unto His Threshold know full well, that this servant could not bear to hear the tales related by the perfidious. I, therefore, have committed this act. If He chastise me, He verily is to be praised for what He doeth; and if He forgive me, His behest shall be obeyed.'

Ponder, now, O Shaykh, the influence of the word of God, that haply thou mayest turn from the left hand of idle fancy unto the right hand of certitude . . . We beseech God – blessed

> and glorified be He – to forgive the aforementioned person (Ḥájí Shaykh Muḥammad 'Alí), and change his evil deeds into good ones. He, verily, is the All-Powerful, the Almighty, the All-Bounteous.[6]

After the death of Nabíl, Ḥájí Amín and Náẓir left Constantinople, but Siyyid Aḥmad-i-Afnán remained there, and when it became necessary for him to go to 'Ishqábád, Bahá'u'lláh sent 'Azízu'lláh-i-Jadhdháb,* a dedicated believer and a capable businessman, to relieve the Afnán, take over the management of his affairs in Constantinople and expedite the departure of Siyyid Aḥmad-i-Afnán to the Holy Land and then to 'Ishqábád.

The night before Siyyid Aḥmad's departure for 'Akká, Muḥammad-'Alí came up with another of his lies. He announced that a servant of the Afnán had broken into his premises and stolen a large sum of money. He circulated the allegation far and wide, saying that the stolen money was being taken to 'Akká. Jadhdháb proved to the Persian Consul that the whole episode was a mere fabrication. In this way the perfidy and dishonourable conduct of this unscrupulous man from Iṣfahán, who was a tool in the hands of the Azalís, were once again revealed for all to see.

In a Tablet[7] revealed in October 1890 (18 Safar 1308) Bahá'u'lláh states that on several occasions the Azalís have stolen some money and accused the believers directly and Himself indirectly of being the perpetrators of the crime. He cites the example of Náẓir, and then Siyyid Aḥmad-i-Afnán, the latter being accused of stealing ninety pounds in cash together with valuable papers and taking them to 'Akká. Bahá'u'lláh in this Tablet asserts that all these calumnies originated from Mírzá Yaḥyá in Cyprus and were then made effective through the machinations of Shaykh Muḥammad-i-Yazdí.

Two of the chief instigators of the mischief were Shaykh Aḥmad-i-Rúḥí and Áqá Khán-i-Kirmání. Both men were from

* see vol. 3, pp. 168–73.

the province of Kirmán. They collaborated for many years to discredit Bahá'u'lláh. They arrived in Constantinople in about 1888 and soon went on a visit to Cyprus to meet their leader Mírzá Yaḥyá. This visit resulted in the marriage of the two to his daughters, marriages which soon broke up.

Mírzá Áqá Khán and Shaykh Aḥmad were both highly intelligent, erudite and talented writers. They were the elite in the group of Azalís in Constantinople. In many of His Tablets Bahá'u'lláh has condemned these two as the embodiments of evil and the source of all sedition. Long before their activities against the Faith were noticed, Bahá'u'lláh had remarked in the *Kitáb-i-Aqdas* the existence of the foreboders of evil in the land of Kirmán, stated that there existed an undercover situation displeasing to God which was hidden from the eyes of men, and promised that God would raise up men 'endued with mighty valour' in that city who would make mention of Him. No one could guess who the perpetrator of evil was until Shaykh Aḥmad embarked upon his notorious activities against the Faith. Later, in several of Bahá'u'lláh's Tablets, it was made clear that the ominous remarks in the *Kitáb-i-Aqdas* referred to Shaykh Aḥmad-i-Rúhí. He was the son of Mullá Ja'far-i-Kirmání, an Azalí and an inveterate enemy of Bahá'u'lláh.

In a Tablet[8] revealed in 1880 Bahá'u'lláh, in the words of His amanuensis, describes how in earlier times Shaykh Aḥmad used to consider himself a believer while committing vile and contemptible deeds. When his wretched conduct became public knowledge he sent several letters to Bahá'u'lláh through a certain believer, repenting of his actions and expressing deep regret. In these letters he demonstrated such submissiveness and loyalty that a reader might become convinced of his sincerity. In another Tablet[9] revealed around the same time, Mírzá Áqá Ján states that Bahá'u'lláh responded to his letters by saying that God would forgive him provided he remained steadfast in the Cause. Yet notwithstanding all this he broke his own promises, joined hands with Mírzá Yaḥyá, distributed false accusations against the Faith and caused great pain and suffering for Bahá'u'lláh. He thus brought about the fulfilment of the warnings of Bahá'u'lláh in the *Kitáb-i-Aqdas* concerning the 'land of Kirmán'.

As to his accomplice, Mírzá Áqá Khán, he used to befriend the believers in Constantinople, and through them he gained a good deal of information about Bahá'u'lláh and the activities of the Bahá'ís in various parts. He even asked permission to visit Bahá'u'lláh and, when he did, it was obvious that his intentions were dishonourable. In one of His Tablets[10] 'Abdu'l-Bahá recalls that when Mírzá Áqá Khán went to 'Akká he indicated that his intention in coming was to ask some questions so as to find the truth. Bahá'u'lláh intimated that Áqá Khán's aim was otherwise and that soon he would show his true colours. Áqá Khán did not ask any questions while in 'Akká, but on his return to Constantinople he published an account saying that he was not satisfied with the answers, whereas Mírzá Yaḥyá had already resolved his questions.

In one of His Tablets[11] referring to Mírzá Áqá Khán Bahá'u'lláh states that when a person rejects the proofs of the truth of the Cause which are demonstrated to him, he will receive his punishment. As we shall see, this perfidious man was executed in a most brutal fashion about four years after the ascension of Bahá'u'lláh.

One of the weapons in the hand of Áqá Khán was the Persian newspaper *Akhtar* published in Constantinople. At some point he gained control of the newspaper and for several years published false and injurious statements about the Faith, its Author and the believers, such as the accusation against Afnán-i-Kabír described above (p. 422). This is the same newspaper mentioned by Bahá'u'lláh in *Epistle to the Son of the Wolf* (see above, p. 419). He refers again to this newspaper when he states:

> . . . Briefly, they have incited a great many such as *Akhtar* and others, and are busying themselves in spreading calumnies. It is clear and evident that they will surround with their

> swords of hatred and their shafts of enmity the one whom they knew to be an outcast among men and to have been banished from one country to another. This is not the first time that such iniquity hath been perpetrated, nor the first goblet that hath been dshed to the ground, nor the first veil that hath been rent in twain in the path of God, the Lord of the worlds. This Wronged One, however, remained calm and silent in the Most Great Prison, busying Himself with His own affairs, and completely detached from all else but God. Iniquity waxed so grievous that the pens of the world are powerless to record it.[12]

Shaykh Aḥmad and Mírzá Áqá Khán found another outlet in Constantinople to further their sinister designs. This was the Pan-Islamic movement led by Jamálu'd-Dín-i-Afghání, a deceitful person who was intent upon dethroning Náṣiri'd-Dín Sháh of Persia. Inwardly he was against the Bábís, but he was playing politics, and so the three men had no difficulty in pooling their talents and resources to make mischief everywhere. This union suited the two Azalís very well, because they too were pursuing the policy of overthrowing the government of Persia, which was the policy of Mírzá Yaḥyá and his supporters. The intrigues and conspiracies created by these three knew no bounds. Jamálu'd-Dín wrote an account against the Faith in an Arabic encyclopaedia published in Beirut about which Bahá'u'lláh states in the *Lawḥ-i-Dunyá* that 'the well-informed and the learned were astonished'. Jamálu'd-Dín then went to Paris and published a newspaper by the name *'Urvatu'l-Vuthqá* (The Sure Handle). Being a two-faced man, he used to send a copy to the Master on a weekly basis as a friendly gesture, and offered to publish any statement that the Master might wish to make, an offer which was totally ignored.

In 1896 one of Jamálu'd-Dín's supporters in Persia succeeded in assassinating Náṣiri'd-Dín Sháh. From then on events moved very fast. Three men, including Shaykh Aḥmad and Mírzá Áqá Khán, were sent back to Persia by order of the Sulṭán of Turkey, and were mercilessly beheaded in Tabríz by order of the Crown Prince, Muḥammad-'Alí Mírzá, for committing acts of treason against their country. Thus the machinations of the Azalís in Constantinople received their death blow. Jamálu'd-Dín escaped the net and died a year later.

Ḥájí Mírzá Siyyid Ḥasan (Afnán-i-Kabír)

The sufferings and pain that this lengthy episode, stretching over almost a decade, inflicted upon Bahá'u'lláh is evident from the contents of many of His Tablets. For instance, the accusations against Afnán-i-Kabír described above are mentioned by Bahá'u'lláh in the following passages from *Epistle to the Son of the Wolf*:

> . . . In the Great City (Constantinople) they have roused a considerable number of people to oppose this Wronged One. Things have come to such a pass that the officials in that city have acted in a manner which hath brought shame to both the government and the people. A distinguished siyyid, whose well-known integrity, acceptable conduct, and commercial reputation, were recognized by the majority of fair-minded men, and who was regarded by all as a highly honored merchant, once visited Beirut. In view of his friendship for this Wronged One they telegraphed the Persian Dragoman informing him that this siyyid, assisted by his servant, had stolen a sum of money and other things and gone to 'Akká. Their design in this matter was to dishonor this Wronged One . . . This Wronged One, however, beseemeth the one true God to graciously assist every one in that which beseemeth these days.[13]

And in another instance He states:

> Moreover, many are now engaged in spreading lies and calumnies, and have no other intention than to instill distrust into

> the hearts and souls of men. As soon as some one leaveth the Great City (Constantinople) to visit this land, they at once telegraph and proclaim that he hath stolen money and fled to 'Akká. A highly accomplished, learned and distinguished man visited, in his declining years, the Holy Land, seeking peace and retirement, and about him they have written such things as have caused them who are devoted to God and are nigh unto Him to sigh.[14]

The 'distinguished Siyyid' and 'highly accomplished, learned and distinguished man' mentioned in these passages are both references to Ḥájí Mírzá Siyyid Ḥasan known as the Afnán-i-Kabír, a brother of the wife of the Báb. He was also a paternal cousin of the mother of the Báb. He was very much attracted to the person of the Báb, and became a believer in Yazd through the teaching efforts of Ḥájí Muḥammad-Ibráhím, entitled by Bahá'u'lláh '*Muballigh*' (Bahá'í teacher). It was to this teacher of the Cause that Bahá'u'lláh revealed the Tablet quoted in the Tablet of Ishráqát (*Tablets of Bahá'u'lláh*, pp. 117–19) and in the *Epistle to the Son of the Wolf*, pp. 131–4.

Afnán-i-Kabír was a pillar of strength to his sister Khadíjih Bagum, the wife of the Báb, during her days of loneliness and bereavement. Later in life he rejoiced when one of his sons Siyyid 'Alí was given the honour of marrying Fúrúghíyyih, a daughter of Bahá'u'lláh. But he did not live to see the downfall of these two who became Covenant-breakers and perished spiritually.* The Afnán had a great love for Bahá'u'lláh and in the latter part of his life he was permitted to go to the Holy Land and spend the rest of his days there. He lived very close to the Mansion of Bahjí, and passed away about a year after the ascension of Bahá'u'lláh. 'Abdu'l-Bahá has paid tribute to him in *Memorials of the Faithful*. This is part of the short biography by the Master:

* see vol. 2, pp. 386–7.

SHAYKH MUḤAMMAD-‘ALÍ, KNOWN AS NABÍL SON OF NABÍL

A devoted believer from Qazvín, he became a victim of the attacks by the Azalís in Constantinople

ḤÁJÍ MÍRZÁ SIYYID ḤASAN, AFNÁN-I-KABÍR

'The Great Afnán', a brother of the wife of the Báb

Among the most eminent of those who left their homeland to join Bahá'u'lláh was Mírzá Ḥasan, the great Afnán, who during the latter days won the honor of emigrating and of receiving the favor and companionship of his Lord. The Afnán, related to the Báb, was specifically named by the Supreme Pen as an offshoot of the Holy Tree. When still a small child, he received his portion of bounty from the Báb, and showed forth an extraordinary attachment to that dazzling Beauty. Not yet adolescent, he frequented the society of the learned, and began to study sciences and arts. He reflected day and night on the most abstruse of spiritual questions, and gazed in wonderment at the mighty signs of God as written in the Book of Life. He became thoroughly versed even in such material sciences as mathematics, geometry, and geography; in brief, he was well grounded in many fields, thoroughly conversant with the thought of ancient and modern times.

A merchant by profession, he spent only a short period of the day and evening at his business, devoting most of his time to discussion and research. He was truly erudite, a great credit to the Cause of God amongst leading men of learning. With a few concise phrases, he could solve perplexing questions. His speech was laconic, but in itself a kind of miracle.[15]

The Supreme Manifestation of God

One of the major themes of the *Epistle to the Son of the Wolf* is the unveiling of Bahá'u'lláh's station as the Supreme Manifestation of God. In the early days when He was cast into the darksome dungeon of Ṭihrán which witnessed the birth of His Revelation, Bahá'u'lláh alluded in His *Ras͟hh-i-'Amá*, a celebrated ode,* to the advent of the Day of God. From that time on He announced these glad-tidings in innumerable Tablets, and as the sun of His Revelation mounted to its zenith, He unceasingly proclaimed this theme to mankind and identified

* For further information see vol. 1, pp. 45–6.

Himself as the Revealer of the Most Great Spirit of God whose advent had been promised by the Prophets of the past.

It is because of the immensity of this claim that the enemies of the Faith had misrepresented His statements and accused Him of claiming to be the Essence of Divinity itself. Bahá'u'lláh refutes this in the *Epistle to the Son of the Wolf*. Addressing the Shaykh He states:

> Either thou or someone else hath said: 'Let the Súrih of Tawḥíd be translated, so that all may know and be fully persuaded that the one true God begetteth not, nor is He begotten. Moreover, the Bábís believe in his (Bahá'u'lláh's) Divinity and Godhood.'[16]

The Súrih of Tawḥíd is one of the shortest chapters of the *Qur'án* and proclaims the unity of God:

> Say, God is one God; the eternal God: He begetteth not, neither is He begotten and there is not anyone like unto Him.[17]

Bahá'u'lláh explains the meaning of divinity in great detail, demonstrates that the appearance of the Lord has been prophesied by the Prophets of old, quotes from the sayings of the Prophet of Islám and the Holy Imáms passages in support of His argument,* and poses questions such as this for the Shaykh to resolve:

> What explanation can they give concerning that which the Seal of the Prophets (Muḥammad) . . . hath said: 'Ye verily, shall behold your Lord as ye behold the full moon on its fourteenth night'?[18]

Bahá'u'lláh further states:

---

* see *Epistle to the Son of the Wolf*, pp. 41–4.

> Men have failed to perceive Our purpose in the references We have made to Divinity and Godhood. Were they to apprehend it, they would arise from their places, and cry out: 'We, verily, ask pardon of God!' The Seal of the Prophets – may the souls of all else but Him be offered up for His sake – saith: 'Manifold are Our relationships with God. At one time, We are He Himself, and He is We Ourself. At another He is that He is, and We are that We are.'[19]

Bahá'u'lláh in this Epistle unveils the glory of His station to the Shaykh and through him to all mankind. He imparts the glad-tidings that the Day promised by the Prophets of old, when mankind shall behold the face of God and attain His presence, is now come. We cite below a few out of several prophecies which Bahá'u'lláh quotes in the *Epistle to the Son of the Wolf*.*

From the *Qur'án*: 'To him who hopeth to attain the presence of God, the set time of God will surely come. And He is the Hearer, the Knower.'[20]

From Isaiah: 'Get thee up into the high mountain, O Zion, that bringest good tidings; lift up Thy Voice with strength, O Jerusalem, that bringeth good tidings. Lift it up, be not afraid; say unto the cities of Judah: "Behold your God! Behold the Lord God will come with strong hand, and His arm shall rule for Him".'[21]

From Amos: 'Prepare to meet Thy God, O Israel, for, lo, He that formeth the mountains and createth the wind, and declareth unto man what is his thought, that maketh the morning darkness,† and treadeth upon the high places of the earth, the Lord, the God of Hosts, is His Name.'[22]

From the Writings of the Báb:‡ 'In the year nine [AH 1269,

---

* For these prophecies see *Epistle to the Son of the Wolf*, pp. 115–19, 140–47, 151–60.

† To 'make the morning darkness' is an allusion to Mírzá Yaḥyá, who was entitled Ṣubḥ-i-Azal (Morn of Eternity). (A.T.)

‡ For more information about the utterances of the Báb concerning the Revelation of Bahá'u'lláh, see vol. 1, ch. 18, and above, pp. 132–4.

AD 1852–3] ye will attain unto the Presence of God.' 'He, verily, is the One Who, under all conditions, proclaimeth, "I, in very truth, am God!"'[23]

In many of His Tablets Bahá'u'lláh has explained the meaning of the presence of God in this day, and while claiming to represent Him on this earth, He unequivocally dissociates Himself from the Divine Being. We observe that on the one hand, Bahá'u'lláh proclaims, "I verily am God', and on the other, He declares to the Shaykh, 'This Servant, this Wronged One, is abashed to claim for Himself any existence whatever, how much more those exalted grades of being!' This apparent contradiction and the true station of Bahá'u'lláh have both been explained in this* and previous volumes in great detail.

Once again in the *Epistle to the Son of the Wolf* Bahá'u'lláh explains this important subject:

> In all the Divine Books the promise of the Divine Presence hath been explicitly recorded. By this Presence is meant the Presence of Him Who is the Day-spring of the signs, and the Dawning-Place of the clear tokens, and the Manifestation of the Excellent Names, and the Source of the attributes, of the true God, exalted be His glory. God in His Essence and in His own Self hath ever been unseen, inaccessible, and unknowable. By Presence, therefore, is meant the Presence of the One Who is His Viceregent amongst men. He, moreover, hath never had, nor hath He, any peer or likeness. For were He to have any peer or likeness, how could it then be demonstrated that His being is exalted above, and His essence sanctified from, all comparison and likeness?[24]

Bahá'u'lláh's Summons to the Shaykh

Throughout the *Epistle to the Son of the Wolf* Bahá'u'lláh admonishes the Shaykh to heed His message and examine

* see above, pp. 130–45.

His Cause. In a language at once moving and compassionate, He urges one of the greatest enemies of His Faith, this bloodthirsty mujtahid, to mend his ways and turn to his God. The following passages gleaned from this mighty Epistle testify to God's loving-kindness and mercy, which are shown even to His bitterest enemy:

> O Shaykh! We have learned that thou hast turned away from Us, and protested against Us, in such wise that thou hast bidden the people to curse Me, and decreed that the blood of the servants of God be shed . . .[25]

> O Shaykh! Verily, I say, the seal of the Choice Wine* hath, in the name of Him Who is the Self-Subsisting, been broken; withhold not thyself therefrom.[26]

> O Shaykh! I swear by the Sun of Truth Which hath risen and shineth above the horizon of this Prison! The betterment of the world hath been the sole aim of this Wronged One.[27]

> O Shaykh! No breeze can compare with the breezes of Divine Revelation, whilst the Word which is uttered by God shineth and flasheth as the sun amidst the books of men.[28]

> O Shaykh! Every time God the True One – exalted be His glory – revealed Himself in the person of His Manifestation, He came unto men with the standard of 'He doeth what He willeth, and ordaineth what He pleaseth.' None hath the right to ask why or wherefore, and he that doth so, hath indeed turned aside from God, the Lord of Lords.[29]

> O Shaykh! That which hath touched this Wronged One is beyond compare or equal. We have borne it all with the

* see Appendix III.

utmost willingness and resignation, so that the souls of men may be edified, and the Word of God be exalted.[30]

O Shaykh! We had seized the reins of authority by the power of God and His Divine might, as He alone can seize, Who is the Mighty, the Strong. None had the power to stir up mischief or sedition. Now, however, as they have failed to appreciate this loving-kindness and these bounties, they have been, and will be, afflicted with the retribution which their acts must entail.[31]

In other passages Bahá'u'lláh summons the Shaykh to embrace His Cause and arise to promote it among the peoples of the world. No one except the Supreme Manifestation of God can address a wicked enemy in these words:

O Shaykh! This Wronged One beseecheth God – blessed and glorified by He – to make thee the one who will open the door of justice, and reveal through thee His Cause among His servants. He, verily, is the All-Powerful, the Almighty, the All-Bounteous.[32]

And again He says:

O Shaykh! Seek thou the shore of the Most Great Ocean, and enter, then, the Crimson Ark* which God hath ordained in the Qayyúm-i-Asmá† for the people of Bahá. Verily, it passeth over land and sea. He that entereth therein is saved, and he that turneth aside perisheth. Shouldst thou enter therein and attain unto it, set thy face towards the Kaaba of God, the Help in Peril, the Self-Subsisting, and say: 'O my God! I beseech Thee by Thy most glorious light, and all Thy lights are verily glorious.'‡ Thereupon, will the doors of the Kingdom be flung

* see Appendix III.

† see Appendix III.

‡ This short prayer is part of a special prayer in Islám, in which the Greatest Name (Bahá) is featured. For more details see vol. 1, p. 117.

> wide before thy face, and thou wilt behold what eyes have never beheld, and hear what ears have never heard.[33]

In several passages Bahá'u'lláh invites the Shaykh to attain His presence and witness for himself the revelation of the verses of God which are sent down upon Him. In one of these passages He thus addresses the Shaykh:

> O Shaykh! Ponder upon the things which have been mentioned, perchance thou mayest quaff the Sealed Wine through the power of the name of Him Who is the Self-Subsisting, and obtain that which no one is capable of comprehending. Gird up the loins of endeavor, and direct thyself towards the Most Sublime Kingdom, that haply thou mayest perceive, as they descend upon Me, the breaths of Revelation and inspiration, and attain thereunto. Verily, I say: The Cause of God hath never had, nor hath it now, any peer or equal. Rend asunder the veils of idle fancies. He, in truth, will reinforce thee, and assist thee, as a token of His grace. He, verily, is the Strong, the All-Subduing, the Almighty. While there is yet time, and the blessed Lote-Tree is still calling aloud amongst men, suffer not thyself to be deprived. Place thy trust in God, and commit thine affairs unto Him, and enter then the Most Great Prison, that thou mayest hear what no ear hath ever heard, and gaze on that which no eye hath ever seen. After such an exposition, can there remain any room for doubt? Nay, by God, Who standeth over His Cause![34]

Although the *Epistle to the Son of the Wolf* was addressed to Shaykh Muḥammad-Taqí, many of Bahá'u'lláh's utterances in it are directed towards humanity in general, and some to particular individuals. In addition to the references to historical events and the presentation and expounding of His teachings, considerable space is given to the unfaithfulness of Mírzá Yaḥyá and his followers, who are referred to as the 'People of the Bayán'; the machinations of Siyyid Muḥammad-i-Iṣfahání; the activities of Mírzá Hádíy-i-Dawlat-Ábádí and several others. An attempt to elaborate on all these subjects would fill a large volume in itself, and in fact they have already been considered in this and the preceding volumes of this series. To assist the reader in the study of this last major work of Bahá'u'lláh, some notes are given as Appendix III of this volume.

26

The Ascension of Bahá'u'lláh

The ascension of Bahá'u'lláh* on 29 May 1892 brought to a close the outpouring of a most momentous and transcendental Revelation, pre-eminent among all the Revelations of the past. For well-nigh forty years this earth had been made the 'footstool' of its God, and 'been chosen as the seat of His mighty throne'. The day of God, whose advent 'all the Prophets and Chosen Ones and the holy ones' had 'wished to witness', had been ushered in. The 'everlasting Father', the 'mighty God', who was to appear in the form of a human temple, as prophesied by Isaiah and other Prophets, had manifested Himself. 'The purpose underlying all creation' which as testified by Bahá'u'lláh was 'the revelation of this most sublime, this most holy Day', had been realized. In the course of four decades this earth had been immersed in an ocean of Revelation, releasing thereby enormous spiritual energies for the regeneration of mankind, energies that are sufficient to bring about in the fullness of time the birth of the Bahá'í civilization which is itself destined to usher in an age when the human race will have achieved such a nobility of character as to make this world appear as a reflection of the Kingdom.

With the ascension of Bahá'u'lláh the revelation of the verses of God came to an end and the bounty of the release of spiritual energies ceased, never to reappear before the lapse of at least a full millennium. The truth of these words revealed by Him in Baghdád were fully realized after His ascension:

O Son of Spirit! The time cometh, when the nightingale of

* The term 'ascension' as commonly used by Bahá'ís signifies the passing of Bahá'u'lláh, the ascension of His Spirit to the worlds beyond.

> holiness will no longer unfold the inner mysteries and ye will all be bereft of the celestial melody and of the voice from on high.[1]

The ascension of Bahá'u'lláh took place in the Mansion of Bahjí, and it caused indescribable consternation among His followers. Nabíl-i-A'ẓam, a true lover of the Blessed Beauty and one of His devoted Apostles, has left to posterity a moving description of this calamitous event. The following is a summary translation of his account:

> As attested by the Most Great Branch,* nine months before this most grievous event – His ascension – Bahá'u'lláh had voiced His desire to depart from this world. During these nine months, from the tone of His exhortations and remarks to those friends who attained His presence it became increasingly apparent that the end of His earthly life was approaching. He seemed to be arranging the affairs with a sense of urgency. But He never spoke openly about the approaching end of His life.
>
> On the eve of Sunday, the eleventh of the month of Shavvál 1309 AH (8 May 1892), fifty days after Naw-Rúz, He contracted a fever, though He did not mention it to anyone. The following morning a number of the friends attained His presence. Late in the afternoon the fever was intensified. In the evening only one of the companions who had an urgent demand was admitted to His presence. On Monday (the second day of His illness) only one of the friends was admitted. On Tuesday this helpless servant was given the honour of an audience with His blessed Person. At noon He summoned me to His presence alone and spoke to me for about half an hour, sometimes seated and sometimes pacing up and down.

* During Bahá'u'lláh's Ministry 'Abdu'l-Bahá was known by several titles, including Áqá (Master) and the Most Great Branch. The designation 'Abdu'l-Bahá (Servant of Bahá) was adopted by Himself after the ascension of His Father. (A.T.)

He vouchsafed unto me His infinite bounties and His exalted utterances reached the acme of perfection.

I wish I had known that this was going to be my last audience with Him, so that I could have clung to the hem of His holy vesture and begged Him to accept me as a sacrifice in His path, to relieve me from the vanity of this world and admit me into the realm of everlasting joy. Alas! Alas! what had been pre-ordained did come to pass.

In the afternoon of that day Ḥájí Níyáz [a well-known believer] arrived from Egypt and, along with some others, was permitted to attain the presence of Bahá'u'lláh. Till sunset a number of the friends were admitted into His presence in groups. The following day the door of union with Him was closed to the face of the believers, no one was able to attain His presence, and an atmosphere of gloom and sorrow descended upon the hearts of His forlorn lovers. This situation remained unchanged for a few days, until Monday (the ninth day) which proved to be the day of grief for the friends. On that day the Most Great Branch left the presence of Bahá'u'lláh and went to the Pilgrim House. He conveyed Bahá'u'lláh's greetings to all, and said that the Ancient Beauty had stated: 'All the friends must remain patient and steadfast, and arise for the promotion of the Cause of God. They should not become perturbed, because I shall always be with them, and will remember and care for them.' On hearing these piercing words the hearts of the believers were crying out with grief, for the tone of 'Abdu'l-Bahá's remarks indicated that the end of the earthly life of the One who was the Lord of all creation was fast approaching. The friends were thrown into such turmoil and dismay that they were about to expire.

This being so, the bounties of the Incomparable Beloved were vouchsafed unto all, and the following day, Tuesday (the tenth day), was turned into a joyful day. The day-star of delight and blissfulness shone forth and the Most Great Branch conveyed at the hour of dawn the joyful news of the well-being of His blessed Person. Happy and smiling, He arrived at the Pilgrim House, and like unto a musk-laden breeze which had wafted from the abode of the Beloved, or as the holy Spirit of the Mercy of the Lord, He awoke the friends one by one, bade them arise, drink their morning tea with the utmost joy, and offer thanksgiving to God, for, Praise be to His Most Exalted and Glorious Being, perfect health had returned to His blessed Person, and the signs of the most great favours were manifested in His countenance. Truly, on that day the joy and happiness of the friends, those who circled around the throne of the Beauty of their Lord, were such that all the inhabitants of 'Akká and indeed the people of Syria were influenced and affected by their condition. All the people both low and high were congratulating each other as in a day of festival.

The reason for this was that on the same day that Bahá'u'lláh contracted the fever, the government rounded up about one thousand farmers and poor people, clad them in military uniforms and held them against their will as conscripts. They were receiving military training to be dispatched to far-off lands in a few days' time. The tents of these oppressed people were near the grounds of the Mansion of Bahjí, and the cries of their weeping and lamenting and those of their families could be heard by day and by night. However, in the morning of the 'day of joy', a royal telegram was unexpectedly received ordering the release of the conscripts. This news was rapturously received by the people who were filled with delight. The Most Great Branch on that day distributed food among the conscripts, the poor, the inmates of prison and the orphans. Consequently the people of 'Akká and outside were heartily offering thanks to Bahá'u'lláh for His loving favours and gifts. No one among the inhabitants of Syria could remember having seen a day as blissful as that day.

That same day the Most Great Branch went to 'Akká, visited every Bahá'í household and conveyed to every single believer, man and woman alike, loving greetings from the Blessed Beauty. On Sunday (the fifteenth day) afternoon, all the friends who were present at the Mansion, together with pilgrims and resident Bahá'ís, were summoned to Bahá'u'lláh's presence. The entire body of the friends, weeping and grief-stricken, attained His presence as He lay in bed leaning against one of his sons.*

The Tongue of Grandeur [Bahá'u'lláh] gently and affectionately addressed them all saying: 'I am well pleased with you all, you have rendered many services, and been very assiduous in your labours. You have come here every morning and evening. May God assist you to remain united. May He aid you to exalt the Cause of the Lord of being.'† This was the last audience with Him. The birds of the hearts of His lovers were addressed from on high: 'Verily the door of union is closed to all who are in heaven and on earth . . . '

On the eve of Saturday (twenty-first day after contracting fever), the 2nd of Dhi'l-Qa'dih 1309 AH (29 May 1892) . . . 13th of the month of 'Aẓamat 49, Bahá'í Era . . . seventy days after Naw-Rúz, while there was no sign of fever, the will of the King of Eternity to leave the prison of 'Akká and to ascend to His 'other dominions whereon the eyes of the people of names have never fallen', mentioned in the Tablet of Ru'yá† revealed . . . nineteen years previously, was at long last realized. Methinks, the spiritual commotion set up in the world of dust had caused all the worlds of God to tremble.‡ Eight hours after sunset on that darksome night when the heavens wept over the earth, what had been revealed in the *Kitáb-i-Aqdas*§ was finally realized. My inner and outer tongue are powerless to portray the condition we were in . . . In the midst of the prevailing confusion, a multitude of the inhabitants of 'Akká and

* Not 'Abdu'l-Bahá, as is stated in Ayyám-i-Tis'ih.

† The passage quoting Bahá'u'lláh's words is a translation by Shoghi Effendi. (A.T.)

‡ see vol. 3, pp. 223–4. (A. T.)

§ For these verses see vol. 3, pp. 371–2. (A.T.)

of the neighbouring villages, that had thronged the fields surrounding the Mansion, could be seen weeping, beating upon their heads, and crying aloud their grief . . . *

For a full week after that great calamity, a great number of mourners, the rich, the poor, the orphans and the oppressed partook of the food that was generously dispensed by the bereaved family . . . From the second day of the ascension of the Ever-Living, the Self-Subsistent Lord to His Most Holy and exalted Dominions on high, men of learning and poets, both Muslim and Christian, began to send telegrams of condolence to the presence of the Most Great Branch. They sent poems eloquently extolling the virtues and lamenting the loss of the Beloved . . . [2]

Shoghi Effendi describes some of the events after the ascension of Bahá'u'lláh in these words:

The news of His ascension was instantly communicated to Sulṭán 'Abdu'l-Ḥamíd in a telegram which began with the words 'the Sun of Bahá has set' and in which the monarch was advised of the intention of interring the sacred remains within the precincts of the Mansion, an arrangement to which he readily assented. Bahá'u'lláh was accordingly laid to rest in the northernmost room of the house which served as a dwelling-place for His son-in-law, the most northerly of the three houses lying to the west of, and adjacent to, the Mansion. His interment took place shortly after sunset, on the very day of His ascension . . . Notables, among whom were numbered Shí'ahs, Sunnís, Christians, Jews and Druzes, as well as poets, 'ulamás and government officials, all joined in lamenting the loss, and in magnifying the virtues and greatness of Bahá'u'lláh, many of them paying to Him their written tributes, in verse and in prose, in both Arabic and Turkish. From cities as far afield as Damascus, Aleppo, Beirut and Cairo similar tributes were

* This sentence from Nabíl is Shoghi Effendi's translation. (A.T.)

received. These glowing testimonials were, without exception, submitted to 'Abdu'l-Bahá, Who now represented the Cause of the departed Leader, and Whose praises were often mingled in these eulogies with the homage paid to His Father.

And yet these effusive manifestations of sorrow and expressions of praise and of admiration, which the ascension of Bahá'u'lláh had spontaneously evoked among the unbelievers in the Holy Land and the adjoining countries, were but a drop when compared with the ocean of grief and the innumerable evidences of unbounded devotion which, at the hour of the setting of the Sun of Truth, poured forth from the hearts of the countless thousands who had espoused His Cause, and were determined to carry aloft its banner in Persia, India, Russia, 'Iráq, Turkey, Palestine, Egypt and Syria.[3]

Nabíl, his heart burning with the fire of bereavement, paid this last tribute to His Lord and wrote these lines as a supplication to Him:

O Thou the King of creation and the Ruler of this world and the world to come! Both in Thy presence and in Thy absence, Thou hast been the cause of the tranquillity of the hearts of men and the advancement of the nations. From the moment Thou didst mount Thy throne at the hour of dawn on the 2nd of Muḥarram 1233 (12 November 1817) until Thy ascension to the Realms of Eternity, eight hours after sunset on the 2nd of Dhi'l-Qa'dih 1309 (29 May 1892) a period of seventy-seven years less two months according to the lunar calendar . . . Thou wert at all times, at day and at night, each month and each year, the cause of the exaltation of mankind. No needy suppliant who had set his heart toward Thee was turned back from the door of Thy generosity without vouchsafing unto him supreme felicity and goodly gifts, and no sorrowful destitute was sent out of Thy All-glorious presence except that Thou didst bestow upon him blissful joy and ample hope. And

> now far be it from Thee not to relieve me from my dreadful woes, and lead me to the abode of a never-ending felicity. Thou art God and there is no God save Thee.[4]

Nabíl, who was asked by 'Abdu'l-Bahá to select from the Writings of Bahá'u'lláh those passages which constitute the text of the Tablet of Visitation, which nowadays is usually recited in the Shrine of Bahá'u'lláh and the Báb, was inconsolable after the ascension of his Lord. To the ordeal of separation from his Beloved was added soon afterwards a far more grievous blow – the violation of the Covenant by 'Abdu'l-Bahá's brothers; which although it had not been made public at that time was clearly discernible to those who were close to the Holy Family. Nabíl could no longer bear the agony of those cruel and tempestuous days. He took his own life by drowning himself in the sea a few months after the ascension of Bahá'u'lláh.*

During His illness Bahá'u'lláh summoned the members of His family to His bedside, bade His last farewell to them and assured them that in a special document entrusted to 'Abdu'l-Bahá He had clearly directed their steps in the service of the Cause. The document referred to was His Will and Testament, designated by Himself '*Kitáb-i-'Ahdí*' (The Book of My Covenant).† On the morning of the ninth day after the ascension, in the presence of nine witnesses chosen from amongst members of His family and friends, this document in Bahá'u'lláh's own handwriting was read aloud by Áqá Riḍáy-i-Qannád,‡ and in the afternoon of the same day it was read again by Majdu'd-Dín§ in the Holy Tomb in the presence of a

* see vol. 1, pp. 205–6.

† The full text of the *Kitáb-i-'Ahdí*, or, as it is usually called, the *Kitáb-i-'Ahd* (Book of the Covenant), is translated into English and published in *Tablets of Bahá'u'lláh*, pp. 219–23.

‡ see vol. 1, pp. 288–9, and *Memorials of the Faithful*, pp. 39–41.

§ The son of Mírzá Músá, Áqáy-i-Kalím, the faithful brother of Bahá'u'lláh. However, Majdu'd-Din violated the Covenant and was one of 'Abdu'l-Bahá's formidable adversaries.

large number of friends. There was now no shadow of doubt as who the Centre of the Covenant was. But alas, the fire of jealousy which had been smouldering in the hearts of 'Abdu'l-Bahá's unfaithful brothers over a long period of time now burst into flame. This, coupled with the lust for leadership of Mírzá Muḥammad-'Alí, the Arch-breaker of the Covenant of Bahá'u'lláh, created a severe crisis in the fortunes of the Faith.

The signs of the violation of the Covenant appeared on the actual day of the ascension. The body of Bahá'u'lláh was awaiting interment when His sons secretly launched their treacherous schemes to rob the Centre of the Covenant of His legitimate successorship which was explicitly conferred upon Him by Bahá'u'lláh Himself. A detailed account of this breaking of the Covenant is beyond the scope of this book. It is, however, the hope of the present author to produce, God willing, one or two volumes on the Covenant of Bahá'u'lláh as a sequel to the four volumes of *The Revelation of Bahá'u'lláh*. The study of the *Kitáb-i-'Ahd* with all its implications will also be carried out in these forthcoming volumes.

With the ascension of Bahá'u'lláh the most momentous and the most fertile period in the history of religion was terminated. The spiritual energies for the advancement of humanity were so intense that even during His own Ministry, a mere forty years, their creative power began to exert their influence not only upon the Bahá'í community but also outside it. In the course of the most turbulent years of His Ministry, we may observe with feelings of awe and wonder how a series of miraculous and highly significant achievements take place, all due to the outpouring of His Revelation.

The rapid and revolutionizing change in the conduct of the Bábí community while Bahá'u'lláh was in 'Iráq; the revelation of the *Kitáb-i-Íqán*, the key to the understanding of all religions; the rising prestige of Bahá'u'lláh and the community He represented in the eyes of the public both in 'Iráq and Adrianople; the public proclamation of His Faith to the Kings and leaders of the world; the steadily declining influence of Mírzá Yaḥyá; the banishment of Bahá'u'lláh to the Holy Land in fulfilment of the prophecies of past religions; the offering up of the life of His beloved son, the Purest Branch, as a sacrifice so that the servants of God 'may be quickened, and all that dwell on earth be united'; His miraculous release from the barracks of 'Akká; the gradual recognition of His divine qualities and superhuman powers by the inhabitants of 'Akká; the revelation of the *Kitáb-i-Aqdas* and formulation of the laws described by Him as 'the highest means for the maintenance of order in the world and the security of its peoples'; the arrival of many pilgrims to attain His presence, resulting in widening their vision of the Faith and galvanizing them into a new creation; the heroic self-sacrifice of many martyrs shedding a great lustre on the annals of the Faith; the departure of Bahá'u'lláh from the prison-city and the transfer of His residence to the Mansion of Mazra'ih, thus making the edict of the Sulṭán for life imprisonment a dead letter; the unsolicited and genuine marks of honour shown to Bahá'u'lláh by the rulers of Palestine, the high-ranking government officials and outstanding men of culture; the steadily mounting prestige of 'Abdu'l-Bahá, the outpouring of whose love and compassion upon high and low alike made Him the acknowledged father of the poor, a counsellor to the authorities and a source of knowledge for the learned; the enormous expansion of the community in Persia; the conversion of many outstanding men of learning to the Faith; the conversion of Jewish and Zoroastrian people; the expansion of the Faith outside Persia to more than ten countries in Asia and Africa; the conversion of Buddhists to the Faith in India and Burma; the building up of the vibrant community in 'Ishqábád and the preparations for the erection of a House of Worship there; the transfer of Bahá'u'lláh's residence to the Mansion of Bahjí, described by Him as 'the most sublime vision of mankind'; the enormous extension in the range of Bahá'u'lláh's Writings and the Revelation of principles and precepts of the Faith, which

ENTRANCE TO THE SHRINE OF BAHÁ'U'LLÁH AT BAHJÍ

together with the laws of the *Kitáb-i-Aqdas* constitute the warp and woof of the fabric of His future World Order; the appointment of the Hands of the Cause of God, forerunners of one of the arms of the Administrative Order of His Faith; the constant movement of travel teachers throughout Persia and adjoining countries; the revelation of the Tablet of Carmel, the charter for the building of the Spiritual and Administrative Centre of the Faith on God's holy mountain; and finally one of the most momentous acts of His Ministry, the establishment of a mighty Covenant with His followers bequeathing to posterity the gift of 'a day that shall not be followed by night' – these are some of the achievements of the Ministry of Bahá'u'lláh. They are but a prelude to the emergence in the fullness of time of a slowly maturing divine civilization embracing the whole of mankind. The following words of 'Abdu'l-Bahá portray the state of the Cause in its present infancy and its coming of age in the future:

> One of the great events which is to occur in the Day of the manifestation of that incomparable Branch is the hoisting of the Standard of God among all nations. By this is meant that all nations and kindreds will be gathered together under the shadow of this Divine Banner, which is no other than the Lordly Branch itself, and will become a single nation. Religious and sectarian antagonism, the hostility of races and peoples, and differences among nations, will be eliminated. All men will adhere to one religion, will have one common faith, will be blended into one race and become a single people. All will dwell in one common fatherland, which is the planet itself.[5]

He has moreover explained:

> Now, in the world of being, the Hand of Divine power hath firmly laid the foundations of this all-highest bounty, and this

wondrous gift. Whatsoever is latent in the innermost of this holy Cycle shall gradually appear and be made manifest, for now is but the beginning of its growth, and the dayspring of the revelation of its signs. Ere the close of this century and of this age, it shall be made clear and evident how wondrous was that spring-tide, and how heavenly was that gift.[6]

The People of 'Ád and Thamúd; Húd; Ṣáliḥ and the She-Camel

These names mentioned in the *Lawḥ-i-Burhán* (Chapter 6 above) appear in various chapters of the *Qur'án*. Húd and Ṣáliḥ were prophets of God who appeared before Abraham, but they are not mentioned in the Old or the New Testament. The people of 'Ád and Thamúd inhabited a large tract of country in Southern Arabia. Tradition has it that 'Ád was a fourth-generation descendant of Noah. His people, who are said to be of a tall race, were idolators and aggressive people. In the *Qur'án* it is stated that the People of both 'Ád and Thamúd were fine builders, gifted with intelligence and skills, but that they were guided by the Evil One, Satan.

God chose Húd to be a prophet to the people of 'Ád. He too is said to be a fourth-generation descendant of Noah, and therefore a cousin of 'Ád. Húd proclaimed to his people that God had chosen him as a prophet, and preached to them the one true God and the destruction of their idols. But they rejected him and only a few became his followers. When the people did not respond to his preaching, he warned them of an impending calamity. This took place, and all perished except Húd and his followers. The nature of this calamity is given in the *Qur'án*:

> . . . and Ad were destroyed by a roaring and furious wind; which God caused to assail them for seven nights and eight days successively: thou mightest have seen people, during the same, lying prostrate, as though they had been the roots of hollow palm-trees, and couldst thou have seen any of them remaining?[1]

According to tradition Húd is buried in Hadhramaut, in the south of the Arabian peninsula.

The people of Thamúd were the successors to the culture and civilization of 'Ád. Tradition has it that they were a younger branch of the same tribe and lived in the same regions of the Arabian peninsula. Thamúd himself is also said to be a descendant of Noah. The people of Thamúd were skilful in carving stone. They are reputed to have made buildings out of solid rock. Like the people of 'Ád, they were idolators. According to the *Qur'án*, God had bestowed upon them skills: they had plenty of cornfields and date farms, but they were unholy, oppressive and unkind to the poor.

Then God sent Ṣáliḥ to them as a prophet. He was one of the people of Thamúd. Like Húd, he exhorted people to believe in God and stop worshipping idols. He argued with them for a long time, but they said that they could not find in him the signs of prophethood. Thereupon God brought forth a she-camel as a sign. Tradition has it that the she-camel came out of a rock. Ṣáliḥ asked the people to take care of the she-camel and to drink of her milk, but they did not. And when she came to drink of their water, which was scarce in that land and therefore vital to their existence, they raised great objections and eventually they hamstrung the she-camel and killed her.

Ṣáliḥ repeatedly warned the people that if they did not respond to his message they would be struck by a calamity and would be seized by God with a grievous punishment. When the sign from God, the she-camel, had no effect on the people and the animal was killed, an earthquake wiped them out, all except Ṣáliḥ and his followers, who were saved. The *Qur'án* describes this episode in this way:

> Then they hamstrung the she-camel, and insolently defied the order of their Lord, saying: 'O Ṣáliḥ I bring about thy threats, if thou art an apostle.'

> So the earthquake took them unawares, and they lay prostrate in their homes in the morning.[2]

The versions we have given in these pages are based on the verses of the *Qur'án*.* However, there are further details derived from various traditions other than the *Qur'án*, but these seem to be unreal and pure fantasy.

The stories of Húd and Ṣáliḥ are somewhat similar to the story of Noah, the flood and the Ark. They are all symbolic. In the Bahá'í Writings we find explained the significance of such terms as Noah's Ark, the flood, the she-camel and other incidents. For example, 'Abdu'l-Bahá in a Tablet[3] explains that the she-camel was symbolic of the holy spirit of Ṣáliḥ, and the milk was symbolic of the spiritual food which his spirit offered to the people. The significance of the she-camel being hamstrung is the suffering inflicted by the wicked people on that holy soul, Ṣáliḥ. The spring of water which the people denied to the she-camel signifies life on this earth. The people were so attached to earthly things that they could not recognize the gifts of God to them, and so they rose up in opposition to Ṣáliḥ, and when he departed from their midst they became deprived of his spiritual influence. His absence was the calamity which caused them to be deprived of the bounties of God and consequently they perished spiritually.

There is a chapter in the *Qur'án* known as the Súrah of Húd. It tells the story of all the Prophets including Húd and Ṣáliḥ. It describes how they were all denied, opposed and persecuted by their own people. Bahá'u'lláh refers to this in the *Kitáb-i-Íqán*:

> To them that are possessed of true understanding and insight the Súrah of Húd surely sufficeth. Ponder a while those holy words in your heart, and with utter detachment, strive to grasp their meaning. Examine the wondrous behaviour of the

* For more information see *Qur'án* 7, 11, 17, 26, 29, 51, 69.

> Prophets, and recall the defamations and denials uttered by the children of negation and falsehood, perchance you may cause the bird of the human heart to wing its flight away from the abodes of heedlessness and doubt unto the nest of faith and certainty, and drink deep from the pure waters of ancient wisdom, and partake of the fruit of the tree of divine knowledge.[4]

He also dwells briefly upon the story of Húd and Ṣáliḥ in these words:

> And after Noah the light of the countenance of Húd shone forth above the horizon of creation. For well-nigh seven hundred years, according to the sayings of men, He exhorted the people to turn their faces and draw nearer unto the Riḍván of the divine presence. What showers of afflictions rained upon Him, until at last His adjurations bore the fruit of increased rebelliousness, and His assiduous endeavours resulted in the wilful blindness of His people. 'And their unbelief shall only increase for the unbelievers their own perdition.'*
>
> And after Him there appeared from the Riḍván of the Eternal, the Invisible, the holy person of Ṣáliḥ, Who again summoned the people to the river of everlasting life. For over a hundred years He admonished them to hold fast unto the commandments of God and eschew that which is forbidden. His admonitions, however, yielded no fruit, and His pleading proved of no avail. Several times He retired and lived in seclusion. All this, although that eternal Beauty was summoning the people to no other than the city of God. Even as it is revealed: 'And unto the tribe of <u>Th</u>amúd We sent their brother Ṣáliḥ. 'O my people,' said He, 'Worship God, ye have none other God beside Him . . . .'They made reply: 'O Ṣáliḥ, our hopes were fixed on thee until now; forbiddest thou us to worship that which our fathers worshipped? Truly we

* *Qur'án* 35:9.

misdoubt that whereunto thou callest us as suspicious.'* All this proved fruitless, until at last there went up a great cry, and all fell into utter perdition.[5]

* *Qur'án* 11:61 and 11:62.

APPENDIX II

The House of the Báb in Shíráz

In a Tablet revealed in 'Akká Bahá'u'lláh granted custodianship of the House of the Báb, the centre of formal pilgrimage* and the holiest place in Persia, to the wife of the Báb and her sister Zahrá Bagum. This Custodianship, He states, is to be passed on to the descendants of the latter and his descendants. Zahrá Bagum had one son, Áqá Mírzá Áqá entitled Núru'd-Din, who was the recipient of the *Lawḥ-i-Dunyá* (see Chapter 22 above).

The House of the Báb has had a turbulent history. It was originally bought by the father of the Báb. While his father was alive the Báb spent his childhood days in that House, but when his father died He went to live with His maternal uncle Ḥájí Mírzá Siyyid 'Alí. Later when He married Khadíjih Bagum they lived in this House, and His Declaration took place in the upper chamber of the House. When the Báb left Shíráz His wife and mother continued to live there. But the news of His martyrdom dealt such a blow to these two souls that His mother went to live in Karbilá in order to be near the holy shrines of Islám, while His wife, who could no longer bear to live in that House, went to stay in the home of that same uncle, Ḥájí Mírzá Siyyid 'Alí, who had been martyred in Ṭihrán.

After this the House was let for some years to some individuals who were not believers and proved to be dishonest people. After some years, not only had the House fallen into disrepair, but the occupants claimed ownership. Áqá Mírzá Áqá eventually succeeded in regaining ownership by providing alternative accommodation for these people. He then carried out some necessary repairs and made arrangements for certain Bahá'ís

* see vol. 2, p. 240.

to live in the House. In the meantime the House was damaged by earth tremors and had to be repaired again.

Early in 1872 when Munírih Khánum, who was later to become the consort of 'Abdu'l-Bahá, was on her way to 'Akká, Khadíjih Bagum, the wife of the Báb, asked her to seek permission from Bahá'u'lláh for the repair of the House and the transference of her residence to it. Bahá'u'lláh approved the request and issued instructions that the repairs must be carried out in accordance with the wishes of Khadíjih Bagum. Áqá Mírzá Áqá was instructed by her to demolish two rooms, to widen the courtyard and change the place of the pool.* The reason for these changes was that the thought of living in the House of the Báb in its original form brought such painful memories to her mind as to plunge her into the deepest grief and sorrow. The changes were made, and Khadíjih Bagum lived in the House until the end of her life in 1882. After her passing Bahá'u'lláh gave permission for Zahrá Bagum (the sister of the wife of the Báb) and her son Áqá Mírzá Áqá to transfer their residence to the House and be its custodians.

It was in 1905 that 'Abdu'l-Bahá wrote a Tablet to Áqá Mírzá Áqá and instructed him to restore the House of the Báb to its original form. He emphasized the importance of rebuilding the two rooms and the courtyard to the exact size and shape as in the earlier days. He asked for a drawing to be sent to Him, and when He received it He approved it and urged Áqá Mírzá Áqá to proceed immediately with the project. Again He stressed the need for great accuracy in measurements, so that the rooms which were to be rebuilt would be an exact replica of the old ones. He also urged the utmost speed in the execution of this important undertaking.

Áqá Mírzá Áqá was quite familiar with the position of the two rooms. He excavated the area until the original foundations of the rooms were sighted. Within two months the building

---

* In the absence of water mains, it was customary to have a small pool of water reserved for domestic use. The water would be taken from a well.

work was completed and the doors and windows installed. However, the interior decoration had hardly been finished when Áqá Mírzá Áqá passed away to the world beyond. It was then that the believers understood the wisdom of 'Abdu'l-Bahá in emphasizing speed and instructing Áqá Mírzá Áqá to carry out the work with a sense of urgency. 'Abdu'l-Bahá knew that his days were numbered, and he was the only person who knew the full details of the original construction.

The House of the Báb has been a target for attacks by the enemies of the Faith in Persia throughout the years. Considerable damage was done to the House in 1955 when a large crowd incited by the Muslim clergy demolished a portion of it. The damaged parts were soon repaired and the House was restored to its original form. (In their battle against the forces of truth, the perverse usually resort to physical force and false accusations. These are the two weapons at their disposal, and these two unfailingly bring about their own downfall at the end.)

Incensed by the vast expansion of the Bahá'í community in all the continents of the globe, and unable to arrest the onward march of the Faith throughout the world, a vigilant and inveterate enemy once again put on the armour of violence and among many other atrocities struck at the House of the Báb. This time, in 1980, that noble edifice was razed to the ground. But the Cause of God will be victorious in the end, for none of these cowardly deeds can frustrate the creative power of the Word of God. That House has been ordained as a centre of pilgrimage in Persia and so it shall be.

APPENDIX III

Notes for the Study of *Epistle to the Son of the Wolf*

In the diversity of its topics, in the profundity of its arguments, in the sublimity of its style, in the compelling force of its challenges, and in the hidden significances of its allusions, this book assumes a very special position among the Writings of the Author of the Faith. The study of such a work requires some background knowledge of history and religious terminology.

These notes are intended to provide a brief explanation of some of the terms used in *Epistle to the Son of the Wolf*. Since many of its themes have already been discussed in the four volumes of *The Revelation of Bahá'u'lláh*, references are given mainly to these volumes. To enlarge the scope of information, references to other works are supplied where necessary. The page numbers shown in the left-hand column are from *Epistle to the Son of the Wolf* (ESW), Wilmette, Bahá'í Publishing Trust, 1962 edition; vols. 1, 2, 3, refer to *The Revelation of Bahá'u'lláh*, while 'above, p. 000', refers to the page number in this present volume.

page

11 '*This Wronged One hath frequented no school*', see vol. 1, pp. 19, 20, 22, 62–3.

11 '*Tablet, addressed to His Majesty the Sháh*', see vol. 2, pp. 338–56; vol. 3, pp. 174–91.

13 The Tablet quoted was revealed in honour of Ḥájí Mírzá Ḥaydar-'Alí.

14 '*The war that hath involved the two Nations . . .*' The two

nations are Persia and Russia. During the reign of Fatḥ-'Alí Sh͟áh (1797–1834), the clergy declared holy war and Persia was the loser. It resulted in the successive disastrous treaties of Gulistán (1813) and Turkomanchay (1826).

15 '*Book of Fáṭimih*', see vol. 1, pp. 71–2.

16 These passages from the *Hidden Words* allude to the waywardness of the divines. See vol. 2, p. 350.

17 '*Willingly will I obey the judge . . .* ', a quotation from an ode by Ibn-i-Fáriḍ (AH 576–632), the famous Egyptian poet who was a leading Súfí.

17 Ḥill and Ḥaram: see ESW, p. 187.

17 Kaaba: see ESW, p. 188.

18 '*The seal of the Choice Wine hath . . . been broken.*' The reference to choice wine, sealed, may be found in the *Qur'án* (see 83:22–6). The significance of 'sealed' is that the true meanings of the Words of God in former Dispensations were not disclosed until the advent of Bahá'u'lláh (see vol. 1, pp. 160–61, on this prophecy of Daniel). The unsealing of the Choice Wine signifies the revelation of the Word of God in this age, disclosing to mankind new teachings and new laws. Bahá'u'lláh declares in the *Kitáb-i-Aqdas*, 'Think not that We have revealed unto you a mere code of laws. Nay rather We have unsealed the Choice Wine with the fingers of might and power.'

19 '*fisherman*', a reference to Peter, the Disciple of Christ.

19 'Abú-D͟har, the Shepherd', see ESW, p. 183.

19 '*He Who was wholly unversed . . .* ' This passage recalls the story mentioned in the *Kitáb-i-Aqdas* concerning Ja'far, 'the sifter of Wheat', see *The Dawn-Breakers*, p. 99.

19 '*whilst the acknowledged exponent . . . of . . . sciences . . .* ' This refers to Sh͟ayk͟h Muḥammad-Ḥasan-i-Najafí, the leading mujtahid of Persia and a great enemy of the Cause of the Báb and Bahá'u'lláh.

20–21 '*The attempt upon the life of His Majesty . . . to the dungeon . . .*' See *God Passes By*, pp. 61–72, and vol. 1, pp. 7–11.

32 '. . . *a knowledge which, when applied, will largely, though not wholly eliminate fear.*' This knowledge has not been expounded by Bahá'u'lláh.

32 '*Crimson Book*' usually refers to the *Kitáb-i-'Ahd*, Bahá'u'lláh's Will and Testament. In this instance He writes, '*A word . . . recorded . . . in the Crimson Book which is capable of fully disclosing that force which is hid in men . . .*' This passage may be a reference to this verse in the *Kitáb-i-'Ahd*: 'O Ye My Branches! A mighty force, a consummate power lieth concealed in the world of being . . . '

41 Siyyid of Findirisk, Abú-Naṣr, and Abú-'Alí Síná: see ESW, pp. 192 and 183.

45 Tablet to Napoleon III: see *The Promised Day Is Come*, also vol. 2, pp. 368–9, and vol. 3, pp. 109–15.

56 '*Tablet . . . to the Czar of Russia*', see *The Promised Day Is Come*, also vol. 3, pp. 118–23.

59 '*Tablet of Her Majesty, the Queen*', see *The Promised Day Is Come*, also vol. 3, pp. 123–8.

68 '*A highly accomplished . . . man.*' This is Ḥájí Mírzá Siyyid Ḥasan, the Afnán-i-Kabír, see above, p. 429–33.

68 '*Mírzá Ḥusayn Khán, Mushíru'd-Dawlih.*' Persian ambassador to Constantinople, see vol. 2, vol. 3, pp. 218–19.

68 '*Prince Shujá'u'd-Dawlih, accompanied by Mírzá Ṣafá'*, see vol. 2, pp. 55–8.

68 '*Kamál Páshá*', see vol. 2, pp. 3, 56.

70 '*Siyyid Muḥammad*', Muḥammad-i-Iṣfahání, the Anti-Christ of the Bahá'í Revelation, see vols. 1, 2, 3.

72 '*Ḥájí Naṣír*', see above, p. 409.

72 '*The twin shining lights, Ḥasan and Ḥusayn*', see above, Chapter 5.

72 '*one named Káẓim*', see above, pp. 409–11.

72 '*his honour Ashraf*', see above, pp. 409, 411–12.

73 '*Sardár 'Azíz Khán*', Governor of Ádhirbáyján, see vol. 2, p. 61.

73 '*Mírzá Muṣṭafá*', see vol. 2, pp. 60–61.

73 ‘*his honour Badí‘*’, see vol. 3, Chapter 9.

73 ‘*his honour Najaf-‘Alí*’, see vol. 2, pp. 222–3.

73 ‘*Mullá ‘Alí-Ján*’, see above, pp. 412–13.

73 ‘*Abá-Baṣír and Siyyid Ashraf-i-Zanjání*’, see vol. 2, pp. 223–32.

75 ‘*The father of Badí‘*’, Ḥájí ‘Abdu’l-Majíd-i-Níshápúrí, Abá Badí‘, see vol. 2, pp. 128–36.

75 ‘*his honour Siyyid Ismá‘íl*’, see vol. 1, pp. 101–3.

76 ‘*he that was chosen to be slain was but one person*’, a reference to the sacrifice of Abraham.

76 ‘*Balál, the Ethiopian*’, ‘*sín*’ and ‘*shín*’, see ESW, p. 184.

77 ‘*prison of the Land of Mím*’, a reference to Bahá’u’lláh’s imprisonment in Ámul. See *The Dawn-Breakers*, pp. 368–76.

77 ‘*Qará-Guhar*’ and ‘*Salásil*’, see vol. 1, p. 9.

77 ‘*Ḥájí Muḥammad-Riḍá*’, see above, pp. 364–7.

79 ‘*Lawḥ-i-Burhán*’, see above, Chapter 6.

86 ‘*Mírzá Hádí Dawlat-Ábádí*’ who ‘ascended the pulpits and spoke words which ill befitted him’, see above, pp. 183–6.

86 ‘*Ṣád-i-Iṣfahání*’, Mírzá Murtiḍá the Ṣadru’l-’Ulamá, a clergyman of low intelligence who became a Bábí and fell under the spell of Siyyid Muḥammad-i-Iṣfahání.

88 For the upheavals of Zanján, Nayríz and Ṭabarsí see *The Dawn-Breakers*.

94 ‘*One of My Branches (sons) . . .* ’, a reference to Mírzá Badí‘u’lláh who later became a Covenant-breaker. See *The Will and Testament of ‘Abdu’l-Bahá*.

106 ‘*In the Great City (Constantinople) they have roused a considerable number of people to oppose this Wronged One . . .*’, see above, pp. 429 et seq.

107 ‘*Luqmán*’, see ESW, p. 189.

108 ‘*Akhtar*’, a newspaper published in Istanbul. See above, pp. 422, 427.

108 ‘*Ḥájí Shaykh Muḥammad-‘Alí*’, Nabíl son of Nabíl. See above, pp. 421–5.

111 ‘*Imám Ṣádiq*’, Ja‘far-i-Ṣádiq, the sixth Imám of Shí‘ah Islám.

111	'*Imám 'Alí*' the first Imám of S͟hí'ah Islám.
112	'*Abí-'Abdi'lláh*', a reference to Imám Ṣádiq.
112	'*Mufaḍḍal*', '*Abu Ja'far-i-Ṭúsí*', and '*Jábir*' (p. 113): compilers of ḥadít͟h (Traditions of Islám) handed down from the sixth Imám.
114	'*The Lote-Tree beyond which there is no passing . . .*' This originates from the Arabic word 'Sadratu'l-Muntahá'. It is the symbol of the Manifestation of God, to which no one has access.
115–19	'*Divine Presence*', see above, p. 436, and vol. 2, pp. 16–18.
120	'*. . . The Prince of the World*', a reference to the Báb.
120	'*S͟hayk͟h-i-Ahsá'í (S͟hayk͟h Aḥmad)*', the founder of the S͟hayk͟hí sect. See *The Dawn-Breakers*.
122	'*. . . Our loved ones have been arrested in the land of Ṭá (Ṭihrán) . . .*' This is a reference to the imprisonment of the Hands of the Cause, Ḥájí Mullá 'Alí-Akbar and Ḥájí Amín, in the prison of Qazvín in 1891. See above, pp. 359. This date provides also a clue to the period in which the *Epistle to the Son of the Wolf* was revealed.
123	'*officials of the Persian Embassy in the Great City*', see above, p. 419.
125	'*Touching the fraudulent dealings . . .*' see above, pp. 419 et seq.
128	'*O people of S͟hín (S͟híráz)! Have ye forgotten My loving-kindness . . .*' This is a reference to the Revelation of the Báb in S͟híráz.
130	'*The heedless ones have hamstrung Thy white She-Camel . . .*', see Appendix I.
131	'*Wings that are besmirched with mire can never soar.*' See *Gleanings*, CLIII.
131–4	'*. . . These perspicuous verses have . . . been sent down from the Kingdom of Divine knowledge . . .*' For the origin of this Tablet see above, pp. 161–2.
135–9	'*Qayyúm-i-Asmá*', the Báb's commentary on the Súrih of Joseph, described by Bahá'u'lláh as 'the first, the greatest,

and mightiest of all books' in the Bábí Dispensation. Its first chapter was revealed on the evening of 22 May 1844 in the presence of Mullá Ḥusayn. See vol. 1, pp. 280, 293, 302.

135–9 '*Crimson Ark*', mentioned in the Qayyúm-i-Asmá, its occupants are the people of Bahá. See *God Passes By*, p. 23.

136 Tablet concerning trustworthiness, see above, pp. 17–18.

137 '*Kamál Pá<u>sh</u>á visited this Wronged One.*' See vol. 2, pp. 3, 56.

138 '*At present, a new language and a new script have been devised.*' This is possibly a reference to Esperanto which was invented about four years before Bahá'u'lláh wrote this Epistle.

141–3 Words of the Báb concerning the greatness of the Revelation of Bahá'u'lláh, see vol. 1, Chapter 18, and above, pp. 132–4.

142 '*his honour, 'Aẓím*', Mullá 'Alí, a well-known disciple of the Báb. See *The Dawn-Breakers*, under 'Aẓím' in index.

148 '*Lawḥ-i-Ra'ís*', and '*Lawḥ-i-Fu'ád*', see vol. 3.

149 '*Land of Ṭá (Ṭihrán)*', see vol. 1, pp. 46–9.

150 '*Neither is there a thing green or sere, but it is noted in a distinct writing.*' *Qur'án* 6:59. See vol. 3, pp. 245–6.

151–63 Passages from the Báb concerning the Revelation of Bahá'u'lláh, see vol. 1, Chapter 18, and vol. 2, pp. 370–81.

153–5 '*Him Whom God shall make manifest*', the Promised One of the Bayán who was to manifest Himself after the Báb, i.e. Bahá'u'lláh. See vol. 1, Chapter 18.

156 '*mirrors*'. The Báb had bestowed the designation 'mirror' upon a few of His followers. See vol. 2, pp. 376–7.

158 '*<u>Dh</u>i'l-Jaw<u>sh</u>an, and Ibn-i-Anas and Aṣbaḥí*', see ESW, pp. 185, 187.

160 '*O Mirror of My generosity*', a reference to Ḥájí Siyyid Javád-i-Karbilá'í, a devoted follower of the Báb and Bahá'u'lláh. See vol. 1, pp. 221–4, vol. 2, pp. 376–7, and vol. 3, pp. 279–80.

163–77 '*Hádí*', Hádíy-i-Dawlat-Ábádí, who had publicly recanted his faith in the Báb, yet was installed as the successor to Mírzá Yaḥyá. See ESW, p. 86, and above, pp. 183–6.

164 '*Siyyid Muḥammad*', as above, note to ESW, p. 70.

164 '*he joined Mírzá Yaḥyá*', Bahá'u'lláh's half-brother, the breaker of the Covenant of the Báb. See vol. 1, chapter 15, and also vols. 2 and 3.

164 '*Mawlavís*', an order of whirling dervishes.

166 '*Mírzá Músá*', a faithful brother of Bahá'u'lláh and one of His apostles. See vols. 1, 2 and 3.

168 '*The authorship of the Kitáb-i-Íqán . . .* ' The followers of Mírzá Yaḥyá had shamefully circulated the rumour that the author of this Book was Mírzá Yaḥyá. See vol. 2, pp. 66–70.

169 '*Ḥasan-i-Mázindarání*', a paternal cousin of Bahá'u'lláh and a faithful believer. See vol. 1, p. 50n, and vol. 3, pp. 68, 209n, 216–17.

169 '*. . . one of the sisters of this Wronged One . . .* ', a reference to Sháh Sulṭán Khánum known as Khánum Buzurg, who became a follower of Mírzá Yaḥyá. See vol. 1, p. 50, and vol. 2, p. 206.

169–70 '*Mírzá Riḍá-Qulí*', a half-brother of Bahá'u'lláh. See vol. 1, p. 12, and vol. 3, pp. 218–19.

170 '*Mírzá Muḥammad-Ḥasan's daughter*', Shahr-Bánú, see vol. 2, pp. 205–6. Her father was a faithful half-brother of Bahá'u'lláh.

170 '*Farmán-Farmá and Ḥisamu's-Salṭanih*', both princes and paternal uncles of Náṣiri'd-Dín Sháh.

173 '*Siyyid Ḥusayn*', a native of Yazd, one of the Letters of the Living who was a companion of the Báb in Máh-Kú and Chihríq and served Him as His amanuensis till His martyrdom. See *The Dawn-Breakers*, under 'Ḥusayn-i-Yazdí, Siyyid', in the index.

173 '*Mírzá Aḥmad*', a reference to Mullá 'Abdu'l Karím-i-Qazvíní, a trusted disciple of the Báb. See *The Dawn-Breakers*, pp. 504–5, *God Passes By*, p. 51, and vol. 1, pp. 53–4.

173 '*he . . . who was continually surrounded by five of the handmaidens of God.*' This is an allusion to Mírzá Yaḥyá who practised polygamy. He had married eleven wives and was known to be a person who lusted after women.

174 '*Mullá Báqir*', a native of Tabríz and a Letter of the Living. See vol. 2, pp. 146–7.

174–7 '*Dayyán*', a reference to Mírzá Asadu'lláh of Khuy, an outstanding disciple of the Báb who was murdered on the orders of Mírzá Yaḥyá. See vol. 1, pp. 249–52.

176 '*Mírzá 'Alí-Akbar*', a paternal cousin of the Báb who was murdered in Baghdád on the orders of Mírzá Yaḥyá. See vol. 1, pp. 251.

176 '*Abu'l-Qásim-i-Káshí*', one of the disciples of the Báb who had attained His presence in Káshán. He went to Baghdád, recognized the station of Bahá'u'lláh and became an ardent lover of the Blessed Beauty. He was murdered in Baghdád on the orders of Mírzá Yaḥyá.

176 '*Siyyid Ibráhím*', entitled by the Báb as Khalíl. He was a native of Tabríz, a learned divine of the Shaykhí sect, a disciple of the Báb who attained His presence in Ádhirbáyján and received several Tablets from Him. He attained the presence of Bahá'u'lláh in Baghdád. Mírzá Yaḥyá endeavoured to have him killed, but did not succeed. See vol. 1, p. 250.

177 ' . . . *that which had been done, affecting the honour of the Báb, which hath truly overwhelmed all lands with sorrow.*' This is a reference to Mírzá Yaḥyá's marriage with the second wife of the Báb. See vol. 1, pp. 248–9.

178–81 For an explanation of the Islamic terms and names in these pages see ESW glossary.

Bibliography

'Abdu'l-Bahá. *Memorials of the Faithful*. Translated from the original Persian text and annotated by Marzieh Gail. Wilmette, Illinois: Bahá'í Publishing Trust, 1971.

— *Selections from the Writings of 'Abdu'l-Bahá*. Compiled by the Research Department of the Universal House of Justice; translated by a Committee at the Bahá'í World Centre and by Marzieh Gail. Haifa: Bahá'í World Centre, 1978.

— *Some Answered Questions*. Collected and Translated from the Persian by Laura Clifford Barney. Newly Revised by a Committee at the Bahá'í World Centre. Haifa: Bahá'í World Centre, 2014.

Abu'l-Faḍl, Mírzá. *Kitábu'l-Fará'id*. An apologia. Cairo, undated. Written in AH 1315 (AD 1897).

Alá'í 'Abdu'l-'Alí. *Mu'assisiy-i-Ayádíy-i-Amru'lláh* (The Institution of The Hands of the Cause of God). Ṭihrán: Bahá'í Publishing Trust, BE 130 (AD 1973).

Bahá'í Meetings; The Nineteen Day Feast. Extracts from the Writings of Bahá'u'lláh, 'Abdu'l-Bahá, Shoghi Effendi and the Universal House of Justice. Compiled by the Research Department of the Universal House of Justice. Wilmette, Illinois: Bahá'í Publishing Trust, 1980. (Published in the UK under the title *Seeking the Light of the Kingdom*.)

Bahá'í World, The. An International Record.
Vol. VIII. 1938–40. Wilmette, Illinois: Bahá'í Publishing Committee, 1942.
Vol. IX. 1940–44. Wilmette, Illinois: Bahá'í Publishing Committee, 1945.
Vol. XII. 1950–54. Wilmette, Illinois: Bahá'í Publishing Trust, 1956.

Bahá'í World Faith. Selected Writings of Bahá'u'lláh and 'Abdu'l-Bahá. Wilmette, Illinois: Bahá'í Publishing Committee, 1943.

BAHÁ'U'LLÁH. *Áthár-i-Qalam-i-A'lá* (The Traces of the Supreme Pen). A compilation of the Writings of Bahá'u'lláh. Ṭihrán: Bahá'í Publishing Trust. Vol. 1, BE 120 (AD 1963); Vol. 4, BE 125 (AD 1968).

— *Epistle to the Son of the Wolf.* Translated by Shoghi Effendi. Wilmette, Illinois: Bahá'í Publishing Trust, rev. edn 1953.

— *Gleanings from the Writings of Bahá'u'lláh.* Translated by Shoghi Effendi. Wilmette, Illinois: Bahá'í Publishing Trust, 1935; rev. edn 1952. London: Bahá'í Publishing Trust, 1949.

— *The Hidden Words.* Translated by Shoghi Effendi with the assistance of some English friends. First published in England 1932. London: Bahá'í Publishing Trust, 1949. Wilmette, Illinois: Bahá'í Publishing Trust, rev. edn 1954.

— *Iqtidárát.* A compilation of the Tablets of Bahá'u'lláh. AH 1310 (AD 1892–3).

— *Ishráqát* (A compilation of the Tablets of Bahá'u'lláh). India: AH 1310 (AD 1892–3).

— *Kitáb-i-Aqdas.* Extracts translated by Shoghi Effendi in *Synopsis and Codification of the Kitáb-i-Aqdas, the Most Holy Book of Bahá'u'lláh.* Haifa: Bahá'í World Centre, 1973.

— *Kitáb-i-Íqán. The Book of Certitude.* Translated by Shoghi Effendi. Wilmette, Illinois: Bahá'í Publishing Trust, rev. edn 1974.

— *Prayers and Meditations by Bahá'u'lláh.* Translated by Shoghi Effendi. Wilmette, Illinois: Bahá'í Publishing Trust, 6th RP 1974.

— *The Seven Valleys and the Four Valleys.* Translated by Marzieh Gail and All-Kuli Khan. Wilmette, Illinois: Bahá'í Publishing Trust, rev. edn 1978.

— *Tablets of Bahá'u'lláh revealed after the Kitáb-i-Aqdas.* Compiled by the Research Department of the Universal House of Justice and translated by Habíb Taherzadeh with the assistance of a Committee at the Bahá'í World Centre. Haifa: Bahá'í World Centre, 1978.

BLOMFIELD, LADY (Sitárih Khánum). *The Chosen Highway.* London: Bahá'í Publishing Trust, 1940. Wilmette, Illinois: Bahá'í Publishing Trust, 1967. RP Oxford: George Ronald, 2007.

FÁDIL-I-MÁZINDARÁNÍ, ASADU'LLÁH, MÍRZÁ. *Amr Va Khalq* (Revelation and Creation). Ṭihrán: Bahá'í Publishing Trust. Vol. 1, BE 122 (AD 1965); Vol. 3, BE 128 (AD 1971); Vol. 4, BE 131 (AD 1974).

— *Asráru'l-Á<u>th</u>ár.* A glossary of Bahá'í terms. Ṭihrán: Bahá'í Publishing Trust, 5 Vols., BE 124–9 (AD 1967–72).

FAIZI, MUḤAMMAD-'ALÍ. *<u>Kh</u>ánidán-i-Afnán* (The Afnán Family). Ṭihrán, BE 127 (AD 1970).

ḤAYDAR-'ALÍ, ḤÁJÍ MÍRZÁ. *Bihjatu'ṣ-Ṣudúr.* Reminiscences and autobiography. Bombay: 1913.

HOFMAN, DAVID. *A Life of George Townshend.* Oxford: George Ronald, 1983.

Ḥuqúq'u'lláh. Extracts from the Writings of Bahá'u'lláh, 'Abdu'l-Bahá, Shoghi Effendi and the Universal House of Justice. Compiled by the Research Department of the Universal House of Justice. London: Bahá'í Publishing Trust, 1987.

I<u>SH</u>RÁQ <u>KH</u>ÁVARÍ, 'ABDU'L-ḤAMÍD. *Núrayn-i-Nayyirayn.* An account of the lives of the King and Beloved of Martyrs and some others martyred in Iṣfahán, including Tablets related to them. Ṭihrán, Bahá'í Publishing Trust, BE 123 (AD 1966).

— *Risáliy-i-Ayyám-i-Tis'ih.* The history of the nine Bahá'í Holy Days together with a compilation of relevant Tablets. Ṭihrán: Bahá'í Publishing Trust, BE 103 (AD 1946); 3rd RP BE 121 (AD 1964).

Koran, The. Translated by George Sale. London: Frederick Warne & Co., undated.

Má'idiy-i-Ásamání. A compilation of Bahá'í Writings. Compiled by 'Abdu'l-Ḥamíd Ishráq <u>Kh</u>ávarí. 9 vols. and one index volume. Ṭihrán: Bahá'í Publishing Trust, BE 129 (AD 1972).

MAXWELL, MAY. *An Early Pilgrimage.* Oxford: George Ronald, 1969.

MEHRÁB<u>KH</u>ÁNÍ, RÚḤU'LLÁH. *<u>Sh</u>arḥ-i-Aḥvál-i-Mírzá 'Abu'l-Faḍl-i-Gulpáygání* (Biography of Mírzá Abu'l-Faḍl of Gulpáygán). Iran: BE 131 (AD 1975).

MU'AYYAD, DR HABÍB. *<u>Kh</u>áṭirát-i-Ḥabíb* (Memoirs of Habíb). Ṭihrán: 1961.

NABÍL-I-A'ẒAM (Muḥammad-i-Zarandí). *The Dawn-Breakers.* Nabíl's Narrative of the Early Days of the Bahá'í Revelation. Wilmette, Illinois: Bahá'í Publishing Trust, 1932.

Nafaḥát-i-Quds. A short compilation of Tablets of Bahá'u'lláh and 'Abdu'l-Bahá. New Delhi: Bahá'í Publishing Trust, n.d.

National Archives Committee of the National Spiritual Assembly of the Bahá'ís of Iran. Series of unpublished compilations of the Writings of Bahá'u'lláh. Nos. 15, 18, 19, 22, 23, 27, 28, 31, 32, 38, 41, 73.

Qur'án, see *Koran*.

Samandar, Shaykh Káẓim. *Táríkh-i-Samandar* (The History of Samandar). Ṭihrán: Bahá'í Publishing Trust, BE 131 (AD 1974).

Shoghi Effendi. *The Advent of Divine Justice*. First published 1939. Wilmette, Illinois: Bahá'í Publishing Trust, rev. edn 1963.

— *Citadel of Faith: Messages to America* 1947–1957. Wilmette, Illinois: Bahá'í Publishing Trust, RP 1980.

— *Dawn of a New Day: Messages to India* 1923–1957. New Delhi: Bahá'í Publishing Trust, 1970.

— *God Passes By*. Wilmette, Illinois: Bahá'í Publishing Trust, 1944.

— *Letters from the Guardian to Australia and New Zealand:* 1923–1957. National Spiritual Assembly of the Bahá'ís of Australia, 1970.

— *Messages to the Bahá'í World:* 1950–1957. Wilmette, Illinois: Bahá'í Publishing Trust, 1971.

— *The Promised Day is Come*. First published 1941. Wilmette, Illinois: Bahá'í Publishing Trust, rev. edn 1961.

— *The World Order of Bahá'u'lláh*. First published 1938. Wilmette, Illinois: Bahá'í Publishing Trust, rev. edn 1955.

Sulaymání, 'Azízu'lláh. *Masábiḥ-i-Hidáyat*. Biography of some of the early Bahá'ís. Ṭihrán: Bahá'í Publishing Trust, Vol. 5, BE 118 (AD 1961); Vol. 7, BE 129 (AD 1972); Vol. 8, BE 130 (AD 1973).

Trustworthiness. Extracts from the Writings of Bahá'u'lláh, 'Abdu'l-Bahá and Shoghi Effendi. Compiled by the Research Department of the Universal House of Justice. London: Bahá'í Publishing Trust, 1987.

Women. Extracts from the Writings of Bahá'u'lláh, 'Abdu'l-Bahá, Shoghi Effendi and the Universal House of Justice. Compiled by the Research Department of the Universal House of Justice. London, Wilmette: Bahá'í Publishing Trust, 1986.

ZARQÁNÍ, MÍRZÁ MAḤMÚD-I-. *Kitáb-i-Badáyi'u'l-Á<u>th</u>ár.* Diary of 'Abdu'l-Bahá's travels in Europe and America, written by His secretary. Bombay: Vol. I, 1914: Vol. II, 1921.

ZAYNU'L-MUQARRABÍN. Unpublished compilation of the Writings of Bahá'u'lláh.

REFERENCES

Full details of authors and titles are given in the Bibliography.

1: BAHÁ'U'LLÁH AT THE MANSION OF MAZRA'IH

1. Blomfield, *Chosen Highway*, pp. 100–101.
2. *Bihjatu's-Ṣudúr*, pp. 251–2.

2: THE GARDEN OF RIḌVÁN

1. Psalms 46:4 and 5.
2. Isaiah 33:21.
3. The story of Ḥájí Yahúdá was given to the present writer by his nephew Mr Nusrat'u'lláh Majzub.
4. Blomfield, *Chosen Highway*, p. 97.
5. *Tablets of Bahá'u'lláh*, pp. 121–2.
6. *Má'idiy-i-Ásamání*, vol. 4, p. 25. This English translation is published in *Trustworthiness*, compilation by the Research Department of the Universal House of Justice, p. 3, no. 12.
7. *Tablets of Bahá'u'lláh*, p. 37.
8. ibid. pp. 120–21.
9. ibid. p. 121.
10. Unpublished compilation, National Archives Committee, no. 28, p. 58.
11. The story of Ḥájí Muḥammad's travel to Jaddih was given to the present writer by his son, Mr Azíz Yazdí.
12. *Má'idiy-i-Ásamání*, vol. 9, pp. 106–7. This English translation, *Trustworthiness*, p. 13, no. 47.
13. *Má'idiy-i-Ásamání*, vol. 9, p. 96. This English translation, *Trustworthiness*, p. 14, no. 48.
14. *Gleanings*, CXIV.
15. *Tablets of Bahá'u'lláh*, p. 63.
16. Maxwell, *An Early Pilgrimage*, pp. 32–4.
17. *Kháṭirát-i-Ḥabíb*, vol. 1, pp. 458–9.

3: *LAWḤ-I-ḤIKMAT*

1. *Memorials of the Faithful*, pp. 4–5.
2. *Tablets of Bahá'u'lláh*, pp. 137–8.
3. ibid. p. 138.
4. *Á͟thár-i-Qalam-i-A'lá*, vol. 5, pp. 110–11.
5. *Qur'án* 15:99.
6. Unpublished compilation, National Archives Committee, no. 38, p. 251.
7. *Tablets of Bahá'u'lláh*, pp. 138–9.
8. Letter dated 4 November 1931.
9. *Tablets of Bahá'u'lláh*, pp. 139–40.
10. ibid.
11. *Á͟thár-i-Qalam-i-A'lá*, vol. 7, p. 113.
12. *Tablets of Bahá'u'lláh*, p. 140.
13. *Some Answered Questions*, ch. 80, pp. 323–4.
14. ibid. p. 281.
15. *Gleanings*, LXXXI, p. 157.
16. *Tablets of Bahá'u'lláh*, p. 140.
17. ibid.
18. Readers are referred to a scholarly article in Persian by Dr Vahíd Ra'fatí, published in *'Andalíb*, no. 19.
19. *Má'idiy-i-Ásamání*, vol. 4, p. 24.
20. John 1:1.
21. Isaiah 55:10–11.
22. *Tablets of Bahá'u'lláh*, p. 141.
23. ibid. pp. 140–41.
24. *Some Answered Questions*, ch. 53, pp. 235–6.
25. *Tablets of Bahá'u'lláh*, p. 142.
26. *Mu'assisiy-i-Ayádíy-i-Amru'lláh*, vol. 2, pp. 64–7.
27. *Qur'án* 10:94.
28. *Epistle to the Son of the Wolf*, pp. 165, 167.
29. *Tablets of Bahá'u'lláh*, pp. 148–9.
30. ibid. p. 143.

4: VARQÁ, APOSTLE OF BAHÁ'U'LLÁH

1. *Memorials of the Faithful*, pp. 85–6.
2. Related by Varqá's son, the Hand of the Cause of God Valíyy'u-'lláh Varqá, to the Hand of the Cause of God D͟hikru'lláh K͟hadem.

3. *Qur'án* 22:5.
4. *Hidden Words*, Persian no. 59.
5. *Bihjatu'ṣ-Ṣudúr*, p. 413.
6. Unpublished compilation, National Archives Committee, no. 19, p. 279.
7. *Hidden Words*, Arabic no. 42.
8. Bahá'u'lláh, quoted by Shoghi Effendi, *The Advent of Divine Justice*, p. 65.
9. Unpublished compilation, National Archives Committee, no. 19, pp. 303–4.
10. Unpublished compilation, National Archives Committee, no. 32, p. 317.
11. *Iqtidárát*, p. 301.
12. *Hidden Words*, Arabic no. 59.
13. ibid. Persian no. 27.
14. ibid. Persian no. 26.
15. *Epistle to the Son of the Wolf*, p. 2.
16. *Tablets of Bahá'u'lláh*, p. 219.
17. *Áthár-i-Qalam-i-A'lá*, vol. 2, pp. 48–9.
18. Unpublished; dated 29 Rabí'u'l-Avval 1304 (26 December 1886).
19. Unpublished compilation, National Archives Committee, no. 19, p. 338.
20. *Gleanings*, LXI.
21. *Tablets of Bahá'u'lláh*, p. 84.

5: THE KING AND BELOVED OF THE MARTYRS

1. *Núrayn-i-Nayyirayn*, p. 147.
2. ibid. pp. 131–2.
3. ibid. p. 135.
4. *Hidden Words*, Persian no. 53.
5. *Núrayn-i-Nayyirayn*, p. 136.
6. *Iqtidárát*, p. 27.
7. *Gleanings*, CXLII, pp. 308–9.
8. ibid. C, p. 204.
9. *Núrayn-i-Nayyirayn*, p. 139.
10. ibid. pp. 146–7.
11. ibid. pp. 169–70.
12. ibid. pp. 185–6.
13. ibid. p. 151.

14. Unpublished compilation, National Archives Committee, no. 28, p. 517.

6: A DIVINE REBUKE: *LAWḤ-I-BURHÁN*

1. *Tablets of Bahá'u'lláh*, p. 207.
2. ibid. p. 205.
3. ibid. p. 207.
4. ibid. p. 209.
5. ibid. p. 210.
6. ibid. p. 213.
7. ibid. p. 205.
8. ibid. p. 207–8.
9. ibid. p. 208–9.
10. ibid. p. 214.
11. ibid. p. 215.
12. ibid. p. 214.
13. ibid. pp. 215–16.
14. ibid. p. 211.
15. ibid. p. 213.
16. Quoted by Shoghi Effendi, *The Promised Day Is Come*, p. 19.
17. Unpublished compilation, National Archives Committee, no. 28, P. 364.
18. *Tablets of Bahá'u'lláh*, pp. 61–2.
19. *Synopsis*, p. 26.
20. *God Passes By*, pp. 232–3.

7: THE MANSION OF BAHJÍ

1. *God Passes By*, p. 193.
2. *Á<u>th</u>ár-i-Qalam-i-A'lá*, vol. 5, p. 135.
3. *Maṣábih-i-Hidáyat*, vol. 5, pp. 456–7.
4. *Asráru'l-Á<u>th</u>ár*, vol. 4, p. 52.
5. *Á<u>th</u>ár-i-Qalam-i-A'lá*, vol. 1, p. 302.
6. Unpublished compilation, National Archives Committee, no. 73, p. 338.
7. *Má'idiy-i-Ásamání*, vol. 8, pp. 147–8.
8. Unpublished compilation, National Archives Committee, no. 15, p. 1.
9. *God Passes By*, p. 216.

8: THE DAY OF GOD: *TAJALLÍYÁT*

1. *Tablets of Bahá'u'lláh*, p. 49.
2. *God Passes By*, p. 300.
3. Bahá'u'lláh, quoted by Shoghi Effendi, *The Advent of Divine Justice*, p. 64.
4. ibid. p. 65.
5. ibid. p. 67.
6. ibid. p. 66.
7. ibid.
8. Bahá'u'lláh, quoted by Shoghi Effendi, 'The Dispensation of Bahá'u'lláh', in *The World Order of Bahá'u'lláh*, pp. 106–7.
9. ibid. p. 104.
10. *Tablets of Bahá'u'lláh*, p. 53.
11. Unpublished compilation, National Archives Committee, no. 41, p. 4.
12. 'The Dispensation of Bahá'u'lláh', in *The World Order of Bahá'u'lláh*, pp. 112–13.
13. Quoted by Shoghi Effendi, ibid. p. 113.
14. ibid.
15. *Prayers and Meditations*, no. 176.
16. ibid. no. 183.
17. *Má'idiy-i-Ásamání*, vol. 9, p. 24.
18. *Amr Va Khalq*, vol. 1 , p. 71.
19. *Bahá'í World Faith*, pp. 342–3.
20. Quoted by Shoghi Effendi, 'The Dispensation of Bahá'u'lláh', in *The World Order of Bahá'u'lláh*, p. 109.
21. Quoted by Shoghi Effendi, *The Advent of Divine Justice*, p. 65.
22. Quoted by Shoghi Effendi, 'The Dispensation of Bahá'u'lláh', in *The World Order of Bahá'u'lláh*, p. 104.
23. ibid. p. 113.
24. *Letters from the Guardian to Australia and New Zealand*, p. 41.
25. *Bihjatu'ṣ-Ṣudúr*, pp. 72–3.
26. *Tablets of Bahá'u'lláh*, p. 47.
27. *Synopsis*, p. 27, also in *Gleanings*, LXX.
28. *Tablets of Bahá'u'lláh*, p. 50.
29. ibid. p. 51.
30. *Ishráqát*, p. 196.

9: SPLENDOURS OF THE REVELATION: *ISHRÁQÁT*

1. *Má'idiy-i-Ásamání*, vol. 2, pp. 74–5.
2. *Tablets of Bahá'u'lláh*, p. 103.
3. ibid. p. 105.
4. ibid. pp. 106–7.
5. ibid. p. 108.
6. *Kitábu'l-Fará'id*, pp. 492–3. An edited version of a translation made by Dr Kházeh Fanánápazir.
7. *Tablets of Bahá'u'lláh*, p. 107.
8. ibid. pp. 117–18.
9. Daniel 12:8–9.
10. *Qur'án* 7:34.
11. *Gleanings*, LXI.
12. Unpublished compilation, National Archives Committee, no. 41, p. 331.
13. *Áthár-i-Qalam-i-A'lá*, vol. 5, pp. 113.
14. ibid. vol. 4, p. 19.
15. *Gleanings*, CIII.
16. *Tablets of Bahá'u'lláh*, p. 129.
17. *Nafaḥát-i-Quds*, pp. 5–8.

10: GLAD-TIDINGS TO ALL PEOPLES: *BISHÁRÁT*

1. Unpublished compilation, National Archives Committee, no. 27, p. 491.
2. *Tablets of Bahá'u'lláh*, p. 22.
3. *Má'idiy-i-Ásamání*, vol. 4, p. 33.
4. *Tablets of Bahá'u'lláh*, p. 24.
5. ibid. p. 26.
6. ibid. p. 24.
7. Quoted by A. Sulaymání, *Maṣábih-i-Hidáyat*, vol. 1, p. 488.
8. *Má'idiy-i-Ásamání*, vol. 2, p. 105.
9. ibid. p. 88.
10. *Dawn of a New Day*, pp. 77–8.
11. *Tablets of Bahá'u'lláh*, p. 28.

11: TRUTHS OF THE CAUSE: *ṬARÁZÁT*

1. *Tablets of Bahá'u'lláh*, p. 33.
2. *Kháṭirát-i-Ḥabíb*, vol. 1, p. 81.

3. ibid. p. 449.
4. *Tablets of Bahá'u'lláh*, p. 33.
5. Unpublished compilation, National Archives Committee, no. 41, p. 241.
6. *Tablets of Bahá'u'lláh*, p. 35.
7. ibid. p. 42.
8. ibid.
9. ibid. p. 79.
10. ibid. p. 42.

12: THE LIGHT OF FAITH REACHES INDIA AND BURMA

1. *Táríkh-i-Samandar*, p. 213.
2. *Maṣábih-i-Hidáyat*, vol. 8, pp. 134–6.
3. *Memorials of the Faithful*, p. 136.
4. ibid. pp. 136–7.
5. ibid. pp. 137–8.
6. Zarqání, *Badáyi'u'l-Áthár*, vol. 2. p. 158.

13: THE MEANING OF UNITY

1. Quoted in a letter from the Universal House of Justice to the Persian Bahá'ís, 10 February 1980.
2. *Tablets of Bahá'u'lláh*, p. 143.
3. *Áthár-i-Qalam-i-A'lá*, vol. 8, p. 57.
4. *Ishráqát*, p. 230.
5. Unpublished compilation, National Archives Committee, no. 18, p. 382.
6. *Má'idiy-i-Ásamání*, vol. 9, p. 129.
7. *Tablets of Bahá'u'lláh*, p. 64.
8. *Gleanings*, CXXXII.
9. Lawḥ-i-Maqṣúd, *Tablets of Bahá'u'lláh*, p. 164.
10. *Gleanings*, CXXXI.
11. ibid. CXI.
12. ibid. XCIII.
13. *Qur'án* 4:33.
14. *Women* (comp.), p. 1.
15. ibid. p. 2.
16. ibid.
17. ibid. pp. 2–3.

18. *Selections*, p. 302.
19. ibid. pp. 79–80.

14: *SÚRIY-I-VAFÁ*

1. *Tablets of Bahá'u'lláh*, pp. 187–8; also *Gleanings* LXXIX.
2. ibid. p. 185.
3. ibid. p. 182.
4. ibid. p. 186.
5. ibid. pp. 184–5.
6. *Kitáb-i-Íqán*, p. 223.
7. See *The Dawn-Breakers*, pp. 256–65.
8. *Tablets of Bahá'u'lláh*, pp. 183, 184, 185 passim.
9. ibid. p. 189.
10. ibid. p. 190.
11. ibid. p. 188.
12. *Synopsis*, p. 22.

15: *KALIMÁT-I-FIRDAWSÍYYIH*

1. *Tablets of Bahá'u'lláh*, p. 64.
2. Long Obligatory Prayer, *Prayers and Meditations*, no. 183.
3. Quoted by May Maxwell, *An Early Pilgrimage*, p. 40.
4. *Tablets of Bahá'u'lláh*, pp. 61–2.
5. ibid. pp. 78–9.
6. Unpublished compilation, National Archives Committee, no. 28, p. 292.
7. *Á<u>th</u>ár-i-Qalam-i-A'lá*, vol. 5, p. 63.
8. ibid. vol. I, p. 309.
9. *Tablets of Bahá'u'lláh*, pp. 74–5.
10. ibid. p. 75.
11. ibid. pp. 75–6.
12. ibid. p. 61.
13. Dated AH 1339.
14. *Tablets of Bahá'u'lláh*, p. 69.
15. Quoted by Lady Blomfield, The *Chosen Highway*, p. 184.
16. *Tablets of Bahá'u'lláh*, pp. 59–60.

16: OTHER OUTSTANDING TABLETS

1. *Tablets of Bahá'u'lláh*, p. 11.

2. ibid. pp. 9–10.
3. ibid. p. 14.
4. Quoted by Shoghi Effendi, *The Promised Day is Come*, pp. 104–5.
5. ibid. p. 105.
6. *Tablets of Bahá'u'lláh*, p. 13.
7. Quoted by David Hofman, *A Life of George Townshend*, p. 49.
8. *Tablets of Bahá'u'lláh*, p. 13.
9. Quoted by Shoghi Effendi, 'America and the Most Great Peace', *The World Order of Bahá'u'lláh*, pp. 74–5.
10. *Citadel of Faith*, p. 130.
11. *Tablets of Bahá'u'lláh*, pp. 16–17.
12. ibid. p. 169.
13. ibid. p. 200.
14. *Bihjatu'ṣ-Ṣudúr*, p. 184.

17: 'THE DOORS OF MAJESTY . . . WERE FLUNG WIDE OPEN'

1. *God Passes By*, p. 193.
2. *Tablets of Bahá'u'lláh*, pp. 227–8.
3. *God Passes By*, pp. 193, 195–6.
4. Unpublished compilation in the handwriting of Zaynu'l-Muqarrabín.
5. *Á<u>th</u>ár-i-Qalam-i-A'lá*, vol. 1, p. 310.
6. *Iqtidárát*, p. 292.
7. Unpublished compilation, National Archives Committee, no. 18, p. 24.
8. ibid. p. 546.
9. ibid. no. 31, p. 168.
10. ibid. p. 169.
11. ibid. p. 205.
12. *Á<u>th</u>ár-i-Qalam-i-A'lá*, vol. 7, p. 236.
13. *Epistle to the Son of the Wolf*, p. 56.
14. Quoted by Shoghi Effendi, *The Advent of Divine Justice*, p. 25.
15. ibid. pp. 19–20, 26.
16. *Ḥuqúq'u'lláh*, no. 10.
17. ibid. no. 18.
18. ibid. no. 80.
19. ibid. no. 9.
20. ibid. no. 27.
21. *Iqtidárát*, p. 292.

22. Unpublished compilation, National Archives Committee, no. 27, pp. 206–7.
23. Unpublished compilation, National Archives Committee, no. 28, p. 482. Translation by the author, approved at the Bahá'í World Centre.

18: NOTABLE TEACHERS OF THE FAITH

1. Quoted by R. Mehrábkhání, *Sharḥ-i-Aḥvál-i-Mírzá Abu'l-Faḍl-i-Gulpáygání*, pp. 88–9.
2. ibid. pp. 89–91.
3. *Bahá'í World*, vol. IX, pp. 857–8.
4. Quoted by Mehrábkhání, op. cit. p. 94. The quotation from the *Qur'án* is from Súrih 7, v. 180.
5. *Bahá'í World*, vol. IX, p. 859.
6. Quoted by Mehrábkhání, op. cit. pp. 119–24.
7. ibid.
8. *Bihjatu'ṣ-Ṣudúr*, pp. 219–20.
9. ibid. p. 220.

19: THE ROLE OF THE HANDS OF THE CAUSE OF GOD

1. Unpublished compilation, National Archives Committee, no. 27, p. 281.
2. ibid. no. 22, p. 9.
3. *Iqtidárát*, p. 249.
4. *Hidden Words*, Persian no. 56.
5. Unpublished compilation, National Archives Committee, no. 15, p. 96.
6. *Khánidán-i-Afnán*, p. 221.
7. Unpublished compilation, National Archives Committee, no. 23, p. 273.
8. *Áthár-i-Qalam-i-A'lá*, vol. 6, p. 327.
9. Cited in *Má'idiy-i-Ásamání*, vol. 2, p. 13.
10. ibid.
11. ibid. vol. 7, p. 36.
12. Unpublished compilation, National Archives Committee, no. 15, p. 385.
13. *Mu'assisiy-i-Ayádíy-i-Amru'lláh*, p. 11.
14. ibid. p. 12.
15. *Tablets of Bahá'u'lláh*, p. 83.
16. Letter dated 19 May 1969 to a National Spiritual Assembly.

17. *Mu'assisiy-i-Ayádíy-i-Amru'lláh*, p. 425.
18. Unpublished compilation, National Archives Committee, no. 15, p. 71.

20: LIVES OF THE HANDS OF THE CAUSE APPOINTED BY BAHÁ'U'LLÁH

1. A good deal of research on their lives has been carried out by the learned scholar of the Faith, Dr Shápúr Rássekh, and published in Persia in the Bahá'í periodical *Ahang-i-Badí'*, Nos. 3–5 (BE 107) and Nos. 7–12 (BE 129). The author is indebted to Dr Rássekh for much of the material in this chapter.
2. *Memorials of the Faithful*, pp. 9–10.
3. Unpublished compilation, National Archives Committee, no. 27, p. 394.
4. *Memorials of the Faithful*, p. 10.
5. ibid. pp. 10–11.
6. *Má'idiy-i-Ásamání*, vol. 4, p. 360.
7. *Mu'assisiy-i-Ayádíy-i-Amru'lláh*, p. 391.
8. Unpublished compilation, National Archives Committee, no. 19, p. 421.
9. *Mu'assisiy-i-Ayádíy-i-Amru'lláh*, pp. 394–5.
10. *Memorials of the Faithful*, p. 11.
11. Unpublished compilation, National Archives Committee, no. 15, p. 435.
12. ibid. p. 414.
13. *Memorials of the Faithful*, pp. 11–12.
14. *Mu'assisiy-i-Ayádíy-i-Amru'lláh*, p. 466.
15. Unpublished compilation, National Archives Committee, no. 27, p. 351.
16. ibid. p. 314.
17. ibid. p. 222.
18. Shoghi Effendi in *The Advent of Divine Justice*, p. 70.
19. Unpublished compilation, National Archives Committee, no. 27, p. 178.
20. *Mu'assisiy-i-Ayádíy-i-Amru'lláh*, p. 422.
21. ibid. p. 424.
22. ibid. p. 442.
23. Tablet inscribed on the photograph of Ibn-i-Abhar.
24. *Mu'assisiy-i-Ayádíy-i-Amru'lláh*, pp. 430–31.

21: TABLETS TO THE HANDS OF THE CAUSE

1. Unpublished compilation, National Archives Committee, no. 27, p. 354. Shoghi Effendi's English translation is well-known to Bahá'ís and appears on the title-page of *Bahá'í Prayers* (Wilmette, Illinois: Bahá'í Publishing Trust, 1982).
2. *Bahá'í Meetings*, p. 21.
3. Unpublished compilation, National Archives Committee, no. 28, p. 157.
4. ibid. p. 190.
5. ibid. no. 27, p. 394.
6. ibid. p. 419.
7. ibid. pp. 379–80.
8. ibid. no. 28, p. 3.
9. ibid. no. 27, p. 297.
10. ibid. no. 28, pp. 7–8.
11. ibid. no. 27, p. 226.
12. ibid. no. 15, p. 395.
13. *Hidden Words*, Persian no. 11.
14. Unpublished compilation, National Archives Committee, no. 28, p. 190.
15. ibid. no. 27, p. 230.
16. ibid. no. 28, p. 191.
17. ibid. no. 27, p. 264.
18. ibid. no. 28, p. 179.
19. ibid. no. 15, pp. 423–4.
20. Quoted by Ḥájí Mírzá Ḥaydar-'Alí, *Bihjatu'ṣ-Ṣudúr*, pp. 426–7.
21. Unpublished compilation, National Archives Committee, no. 27, p. 314.
22. Quoted by Nabíl-i-A'ẓam, *The Dawn-Breakers*, p. 94.
23. *Bihjatu'ṣ-Ṣudúr*, pp. 316–17.
24. *Bahá'í News* (later *Star of the West*), 1910, vol. I, no. 18. The author is grateful to Mr. Rahbar Agah for supplying the photograph of Saráju'l-Ḥukamá and William Patchin on page 327.

22: 'FOR THE ADVANCEMENT OF THE WORLD': *LAWḤ-I-DUNYÁ*

1. *Tablets of Bahá'u'lláh*, p. 83.
2. ibid. pp. 86, 89.
3. ibid. p. 88.

4. ibid. pp. 87–8.
5. Persian no. 3.
6. *Tablets of Bahá'u'lláh*, p. 87.
7. ibid. p. 94.
8. ibid. pp. 96–7.
9. ibid. pp. 90–91.
10. Ustád 'Alí-Akbar-i-Banná, unpublished history of 'Ishqábád.
11. *Tablets of Bahá'u'lláh*, p. 85.
12. *God Passes By*, pp. 201–2.
13. *Má'idiy-i-Ásamání*, vol. 4, pp. 129–30. The extract printed here has been authorized by the Universal House of Justice.

23: THE CHARTER FOR THE WORLD CENTRE: *LAWḤ-I-KARMIL*

1. *Gleanings*, XI.
2. *Tablets of Bahá'u'lláh*, p. 13.
3. Unpublished compilation, National Archives Committee, no. 19, pp. 262–3.
4. ibid. no. 73, p. 363.
5. *Gleanings*, XI.
6. Isaiah 35:1–2.
7. *Gleanings*, XI.
8. ibid.
9. *Tablets of Bahá'u'lláh*, p. 84.
10. *Gleanings*, XI.
11. *God Passes By*, p. 194.
12. Quoted by Shoghi Effendi, *God Passes By*, p. 276.
13. *Citadel of Faith*, p. 95.
14. Bahá'í World, vol. XII, p. 239.
15. *Gleanings*, XI.
16. Isaiah 2:2–4.
17. *God Passes By*, p. 348.
18. *Messages to the Bahá'í World*, pp. 74–5.

24: *EPISTLE TO THE SON OF THE WOLF*

1. *Epistle to the Son of the Wolf*, pp. 3–8.
2. *Tablets of Bahá'u'lláh*, pp. 148–9.
3. *Epistle to the Son of the Wolf*, p. 11.
4. ibid.

5. ibid. p. 12.
6. ibid. p. 13.
7. ibid.
8. ibid. p. 14.
9. ibid.
10. ibid.
11. ibid. p. 15.
12. ibid.
13. ibid. p. 23.
14. ibid.
15. ibid. p. 24.
16. ibid.
17. ibid. p. 26.
18. ibid. p. 27.
19. ibid. p. 50.
20. ibid. p. 54.
21. ibid. p. 137.
22. ibid. p. 135.
23. ibid. pp. 93–4.
24. ibid. pp. 21–2.
25. ibid. p. 25.
26. ibid.
27. ibid. p. 29.
28. ibid. pp. 88–9.
29. ibid. p. 137.
30. ibid. p. 74.
31. ibid. pp. 71–2.
32. ibid. p. 72.
33. ibid.
34. ibid. p. 73.
35. *God Passes By*, p. 201.
36. *Tablets of Bahá'u'lláh*, p. 219.
37. *Epistle to the Son of the Wolf*, pp. 63–4.
38. ibid. pp. 76–7.
39. ibid. p. 94.

25: *EPISTLE TO THE SON OF THE WOLF* (continued)

1. *Gleanings*, XLVI.
2. *Epistle to the Son of the Wolf*, pp. 33–5.

3. ibid. pp. 122–3.
4. ibid. pp. 125–6.
5. Unpublished compilation, National Archives Committee, no. 19, p. 455.
6. *Epistle to the Son of the Wolf*, pp. 108–10.
7. Unpublished compilation, National Archives Committee, no. 15, pp. 404–5.
8. ibid. no. 27, pp. 343–4.
9. ibid. no. 31, p. 32.
10. *Má'idiy-i-Ásamání*, vol. 5, pp. 18–19.
11. *Asráru'l-Á<u>th</u>ár*, vol. 1, p. 21.
12. *Epistle to the Son of the Wolf*, p. 108.
13. ibid. p. 106.
14. ibid. pp. 67–8.
15. *Memorials of the Faithful*, pp. 21–2.
16. *Epistle to the Son of the Wolf*, p. 41.
17. *Qur'án*, 112.
18. *Epistle to the Son of the Wolf*, pp. 41–2.
19. ibid. p. 43.
20. ibid. p. 116.
21. ibid. pp. 144–5.
22. ibid. pp. 145–6.
23. ibid. pp. 141, 142.
24. *Epistle to the Son of the Wolf*, pp. 118–19.
25. ibid. p. 17.
26. ibid. p. 18.
27. ibid. p. 36.
28. ibid. p. 42.
29. ibid. p. 67.
30. ibid. p. 76.
31. ibid. pp. 105–6.
32. ibid. p. 96.
33. ibid. pp. 139–40.
34. ibid. pp. 113–14.

26: THE ASCENSION OF BAHÁ'U'LLÁH

1. *Hidden Words*, Persian no. 15.
2. Ishráq <u>Kh</u>ávarí, *Ayyám-i-Tis'ih*, pp. 399–406.
3. *God Passes By*, pp. 222–3.

4. Ishráq Kháavarí, *Ayyám-i-Tis'ih*, pp. 404–5.
5. Quoted by Shoghi Effendi, 'The Unfoldment of World Civilization', *The World Order of Bahá'u'lláh*, pp. 204–5.
6. ibid. p. 205.

APPENDIX I: THE PEOPLE OF 'ÁD AND THAMÚD; HUD; ṢÁLIḤ AND THE SHE-CAMEL

1. *Qur'án*, 69:6.
2. *Qur'án*, 7:77–8.
3. *Má'idiy-i-Ásamání*, vol. 2, pp. 99–100.
4. *Kitáb-i-Íqán*, pp. 5–6.
5. ibid. pp. 9–10.

Index

Abá Badí‘ (Ḥájí ‘Abdu’l-Majíd-i-Níshápúrí), 416, 465
Abá Baṣír, 416, 465
Ábádih, 334, 346, 411
‘Abbúd, 262
‘Abbúd, House of, 34, 111, 257
‘Abdu’l-‘Azíz, Sulṭán, 28, 99, 109, 110, 254, 255, 450
‘Abdu’l-Bahá, 185-6, 387, 401n.
and Abu’l-Faḍl, 37
and Abu’l-Qásim, 29
Ascension of, 246-7
and Ascension of Bahá’u’lláh, 442-53
on attributes, 209
and Bahá’u’lláh in the Garden of Junaynih, 357
and Bahjí, 1, 5, 111, 112
at Beirut, 253
Centre of the Covenant, 150, 330, 449
on Christ, 160
describes Covenant-breaking, 86
describes Ḥájí Mullá ‘Alí-Akbar, 312-3, 314, 316-7, 319
and Dr Habíb Mu’ayyad, 32
on emanation and incarnation, 42
establishes first elected Assembly of Ṭihrán, 308
on equality of men and women, 214
on faith, 229
on future, 452-3
and Garden of Riḍván, 11, 14
guidance to teachers, 314
on a *ḥadíth*, 41n.
and Ḥájí Muḥammad-i-Yazdí, 23
and Hands of the Cause, 51, 295, 303, 304, 305, 308
on history, 48-9
on importance of the West, 245-6
on imprisonment of Bahá’u’lláh, 256
infallibility of, 157
and interpretation of Scripture, 154, 295, 380, 399n., 456
interprets the ‘Ishráqát, 154
Jalálu’d-Dawlih meets, 371
and Jamálu’d-Din, 428
life in ‘Akká, 1-6
makes arrangements for pilgrims, 2
and marriage of Ibn-i-Abhar, 330
and Mashriqu’l-Adhkár of ‘Ishqábád, 127
Master of ‘Akká, 2
on nature of God, 42-3, 46-7, 137-8
on nuclear energy, 237
permission for pilgrimage sought from, 92
praises Nabíl-i-Akbar, 34-5
prayer for King of Martyrs, 87
prestige of, 253-5, 450
prophecies concerning Mount Carmel, 179-80
schools built during ministry of, 127n.
sends message to Amínu’s-Sulṭán, 197-8
sends teachers to India, 193, 195
sends unaddressed Tablets, 345-6
shields Bahá’u’lláh from outside world, 1-2, 4-6, 357
and Shrine of the Báb, 381-3
on Spiritual Assemblies, 308
station of, 60, 254-5, 323, 357-8
stories attributed to, 179
and Sulaymán Khán, 193, 195, 198-9

Tablet to Covenant-breakers, 153
Tablet on creation, 41, 43, 46-7
Tablet to Ibn-i-Abhar, 326
Tablet to Mírzá Áqá Khán, 236
Tablets on trustworthiness, 27-8
Tablet to Ustád 'Alí-Akbar, 127, 128, 130
and *Tablets of the Divine Plan*, 381
titles of, 442n.
Townshend's poem to, 244-5
travel teachers during the ministry of, 293, 323, 328-9, 333
tribute to Afnán-i-Kabír, 430-1
tribute to Ḥájí Mullá Mihdíy-i-'Aṭrí, 55-6
Ṭúbá Khánum's reminiscences of, 2-4, 13-14
on unity, 2-4
Ustád 'Ali-Akbar meets, 127
and Varqá and his children, 62
Will and Testament of, 303, 305, 401n.
on wisdom, 342
writes Tablets, 347
Ẓillu's-Sulṭán meets, 106
mentioned, 16, 77, 90, 97, 234, 290, 292, 332, 347-8, 460
'Abdu'l-Ḥamíd, Sulṭán, 446
'Abdu'l-Ḥusayn-i-Samandar, Mírzá, 421
'Abdu'l Karím-i-Qazvíní, Mullá (Mírzá Aḥmad), 468
'Abdu'l-Majíd-i-Marághi'í, 89-90
'Abdu'l-Majíd-i-Níshápúrí, Ḥájí (Abá Badí'), 465
'Abdu'l-Majíd-i-Shírází, 48
'Abdu'lláh-i-Núrí, Mírzá, 59
'Abdu'lláh Páshá, 1
'Abdu'r-Raḥím-i-Qannád, 23-4
Abhá Kingdom, 35, 237
Abhar, 324
Abraham (Ibráhím), 32, 345, 454, 465
Abú-'Alí Síná, 464
Abú-Dhar, 463
Abú-Naṣr, 464
Abu'l-Faḍl, Mírzá, 14, 104, 158-9, 274-87, 366
on certitude, 37
dialogues of, 278-87
an example, 37
imprisonment of, 404
simple life of, 274-77
teaching work of, 274-87
travels of, 187, 274-87
Abu'l-Ḥasan-i-Amín, Ḥájí (Ḥájí Amín), 16n., 195, 267-8, 270, 271, 274, 295, 301, 317, 317, 325, 359, 360, 371, 422, 425, 466
Abu'l-Qásim, (the gardener), 28-33
Abu'l-Qásim-i-Faráhání, Mírzá (Qá'im-Maqám), 233-4, 237
Abu'l-Qásim-i-Káshí, 468
Abu'l-Qásim-i-Khurásání, Mírzá (caretaker at the Shrine of Bahá'u'lláh), 31n.
Abu'l-Qásim-i-Náẓir, 422, 425
'Ád, 101, 454-6
Adam, 141
Ádhirbáyján, 88, 152-3, 196, 221, 465, 469
Adíb, *see* Ḥájí Mírzá Ḥasan
Adíbu'l-'Ulamá, *see* Ḥasan-i-Adíb, Ḥájí Mírzá
Administrative Order, 247, 293-4, 303, 452
Adrianople, 1, 5, 7, 85, 113, 121, 161, 246, 261, 273, 420, 449
Afghanistan, 193
Afnán-i-Kabír (Ḥájí Mírzá Siyyid Ḥasan), *illus. 432*; 351, 422, 427, 429-33, 455
Afnáns, 53, 77, 124-5, 263, 302
establish trading company in Istanbul, 420-2
in India, 188-91
take counsel on community affairs, 124n.
Africa, 246, 450
Agah, Rahbar, 486
Aghṣán, 10, 354
Agriculture, 363
Aḥmad, Mírzá (Mullá 'Abdu'l Karím-i-Qazvíní), 468
Aḥmad, Tablet of, 148

Aḥmad-i-Afnán, Siyyid, 422, 425-6
Aḥmad Effendi, 24
Aḥmad-i-Ruḥí, Shaykh, 426-7
Akhtar (newspaper), 422, 427, 465
Ákhúnd, Ḥájí, *see* 'Alí-Akbar-i-Sháhmírzádí, Hand of the Cause Ḥájí Mullá
'Akká
  'Abdu'l-Bahá's life in, 1-6, 47
  Bahá'u'lláh's exile to, 7, 81, 256, 295, 374, 376
  Bahá'u'lláh's life in, 1-2, 109-10, 255-6
  Governor of, 7, 358
  Holy Family in, 111
  'Master of', *see* 'Abdu'l-Bahá
  Muftí of, 253
  Navváb remains in, 1, 111
  Nabíl-i-Akbar at, 34
  pilgrims to, 8, 12, 34, 89-90, 91, 125, 188, 229
  Shaykh Yúsuf visits, 253
  Siyyid Asadu'lláh's pilgrimage to, 201
  Sulaymán Khán in, 188, 191, 195, 199
  traditions regarding, 412
  mentioned, 9, 11, 14, 26, 32, 54, 61, 108, 112, 121, 179, 216, 259n., 322, 346, 365, 386, 418, 425, 427, 429, 430, 444, 445, 450, 460
'Alá'u'd-Dawlih, Governor of Zanján, 64
Alchemy, 238
Aleppo, 446
Alexander the Great, 48
Alexandria, 23, 24
'Alí (minister of Sulṭán 'Abdu'l-'Azíz), 256
'Alí, Áqá (martyr of Yazd), 370
'Alí, Ḥájí Mírzá Siyyid, 459
'Alí, Imám, 221, 466
'Alí, Mullá ('Aẓím), 467
'Alí, Shaykh, 24
'Alí, Siyyid, 16
'Alí, Siyyid (son-in-law of Bahá'u'lláh), 430
'Alí-Akbar, Mírzá, 468
'Alí-Akbar-i-Banná, Ustád, *illus. 126*; 31, 123-30
'Alí-Akbar-i-Muḥibb'us-Sulṭán (Rawḥání), 311
'Alí-Akbar-i-Sháhmírzádí, Hand of the Cause Ḥájí Mullá (Ḥájí Ákhúnd), *illus. 407*, 14n, 195, 294, 292, 294
  daughter of, 330, 331
  imprisonment of, 316, 325, 359, 360, 371, 405, 466
  life of, 312-34
  and Náṣiri'd-Dín Sháh, 405
  Tablets to, 335-46
  wife of, 331
'Alí-Aṣghar (first martyr of Yazd), 369
'Alí-Aṣghar (sixth martyr of Yazd), 370
'Alí-Aṣghar-i-Ḥikmát, 333
'Alí-Aṣghar-i-Khán, the Amínu's-Sulṭán, 195
'Alíy-i-Basṭamí, Mullá, 220
'Alí-Ján, Mullá, 412, 465
'Alíy-i-Káni, Ḥájí Mullá, 315
Ali-Kuli Khan, 277, 282
'Alíy-i-Mírí, Shaykh, Muftí of 'Akká, 259
'Alí-Muḥammad, Mírzá, *see* Ibn-i-Aṣdaq
'Alí-Muḥammad-i-Varqá, 18, 303
'Alíy-i-Sabzivárí, Mullá (martyr of Yazd), 370, 371
'Alíy-i-Sayyáh (disciple of the Báb and Bahá'u'lláh), 106n.
'Alíy-i-Yazdí, Ḥájí, 263
'Alíy-i-Yazdí, Siyyid, 23-5
America, 246-7, 277, 278, 282, 302, 381
Amín, Ḥájí, *see* Abu'l-Ḥasan, Ḥájí
Amínu's-Sulṭán, *see* 'Alí-Aṣghar Khán
Amos, 435
Amr va Khalq, 48
Ámul, 156, 415, 465
'Andalíb, Tablet to, 88
'Angel of Carmel', *see* Ḥaydar-'Alí, Ḥájí Mírzá

Animals
animal nature of humans, 149
kingdom of, 209
Anti-Christ, *see* Muḥammad-i-Iṣfahání
Apostle, the, *see* Muḥammad
Áqá Ján, Mírzá (Khádimu'lláh), 8, 9, 24, 77, 110, 111, 120, 261-2, 269-70, 318, 354, 426
downfall of, 261
records revelation, 130, 231, 354, 355
Áqáy-i-Kalím, *see* Músá, Mírzá
Áqá Khán, Mírzá (Qá'im Maqámí), 235-6
Áqá Khán-i-Kirmání, Mírzá, 426-7
Áqá Mírzá Áqáy-i-Afnán (Núru'd-Din), *illus. 352*; 8, 302, 350-68, 459-31
Áqá Siyyid Áqá, 302, 351-3
Arabia, 25, 219, 345, 454, 455
Arabic, 49, 168, 240, 282, 363n., 372n., 446
Arák, 235, 237
Arawaka, Viscount, 238
Archbishops, 243
Archives, Bahá'í International, *illus. 387*; 263, 386
Ardabíl, 196
Ardikán, 260
Ark, 381, 385
Crimson, 339, 385, 438, 467
Armaments, 183, 249
Arts, 123n., 144, 151, 170, 182, 433
Asadu'lláh, Mírzá (Dayyán), 469
Asadu'lláh, Siyyid, 201
Asadu'lláh-i-Qumí, Siyyid, 14, 195-7, 235-6, 354
Ashraf, Mírzá, 184-5
Ashraf, Mírzá, (of Ábádih), 409-10, 411-2
Ashraf-i-Zanjání, 184n., 411-2, 465
Asia, 246, 421, 450
Assemblies, *see* Local and National Spiritual Assemblies
'Aṭá'u'lláh, Saráj'u'l-Ḥukamá, Mírzá, 347
Attributes
of God, 17, 46, 99, 137-9, 141-2, 203, 209, 229, 258
Manifestations bear God's, 138, 139
manifested in all kingdoms of God, 209
Australasia, 246
Auxiliary Board Members, 294
Al-Azhar University, 158, 282
Azalís, 86-7, 183, 185, 201, 232, 238-9, 323, 333, 425, 428, 431, 439
machinations of, in Istanbul, 417-40
and Nabíl ibn-i-Nabíl, 420-5
A'ẓam (owner of land in 'Ishqábád), 125, 127
'Aẓím (Mullá 'Alí), 467
'Azím-i-Tafrishí, 270
'Azízu'lláh (son of Varqá), 59, 61, 62
'Azízu'lláh-i-Jadhdháb, 425

Báb, the, 134, 154-5, 218-22
announces station of Bahá'u'lláh, 132, 134
banishment to Máh-Kú, 235
begins Bahá'í Dispensation, 163
bestows station of Imám on believer, 220
birth of, 356
on coming of Bahá'u'lláh, 435
Declaration of, 156, 350, 356n., 459
and destruction of religious books, 174
House of, 17, 127n., 174, 351, 352, 355, 459-61
interment of, 381
in Iṣfahán, 78, 80
and King and Beloved of Martyrs, 78
kinsmen of, *see* Afnán
laws of, 174-5
Martyrdom of, 77
names and titles of, 218, 222
'Point of the Bayán', 217-8, 219

on power of God, 345
prepares the way for Bahá'u'lláh, 85, 154, 435
remains of, 381-3
wife of, *see* Khadíjih Bagum
Writings of, 49, 134, 397, 435
mentioned, 106n., 125, 127, 128, 132, 144, 155, 157, 184, 324n., 430, 433, 466, 467, 468, 469
Bábís, 56, 449-50
allowed to defend themselves, 402-3
attempt on the life of the Sháh, 403
and Bahá'ís, 404
Bahá'u'lláh addresses 'People of the Bayán', 154-5, 184, 217-8, 232, 439
Bahá'u'lláh declares mission to, 350
Bahá'u'lláh focuses message on, 85
Bahá'u'lláh rebukes, 232
and Covenant-breaking, 85-6, 157, 184-5
Ḥájí Mullá 'Alí-Akbar meets, 313
and laws of the Báb, 174-5
march towards Mázindarán, 221
and Mírzá Yaḥyá, 323
persecution of, 6-7
steadfastness of, 147-8
turn to Quddús, 222
and use of force, 402-3
mentioned, 67, 428
Badakhshán, 193
Badasht, conference of, 16, 78
Badí', 40, 77, 318, 324, 412, 465
Badí'u'lláh (son of Bahá'u'lláh), 62, 401, 465
Badí'u'lláh (son of Varqá), 62
Badru'd-Dín Al-Ghazzí, Shaykh, 159
Baghdád, 4-5, 113, 121, 259, 262, 323
pilgrims meet Bahá'u'lláh in, 54, 56, 78, 84, 93, 260, 320, 469
Bahá'í Cycle, 220, 390, 453
Bahá'í Faith
allegiance to, 356
Bahá'u'lláh's vision of, 178
Centre of the Cause, 150
conversion to, 195
development of world administrative centre of, 386-91
Dispensation of, 163
dissimulation forbidden in, 96
enemies of, to be pitied, 97
fostering of, 340
future of, 76, 357
greatness of, 315
growth of, 147-8, 187, 246, 265, 273, 340, 452, 461
independence of, 194
international seat of, 374-97
laws of, 122
love within the, 205
opposition to, 341, 356
prerequisites for teaching, 251
prestige of, 253
principles of, 452
protection of, 295, 305, 308, 341-2
purpose of, is unity, 414
recantation of, 96-97, 184-5
a religion in its pure form, 164
spread of, 74, 181, 187, 246, 265
teaching of, *see* Teaching
those who rise up against, 338, 362
unity of, a model, 200, 389
universal adoption of, 60
Bahá'ís
accusations against, 325, 419-40
acquisition of saintly attributes, 182
in 'Akká, 2
allegiance of, 356
addressed in Tablet of Carmel, 380-81
and Bábís, 404
behaviour of, 337-8
business dealings among, 27-8
character of, 226
companions of the Crimson Ark, 339
concern of, 418
conduct of, 405
counselled to be wise, 342
counsels of Bahá'u'lláh to, 167-8, 202, 359-64

cursing of, 97
deeds of, 226, 337
development of Bahá'í community, 307
dissimulation of, 96, 289n.
enjoined to teach, 291
exhortations of Bahá'u'lláh to, 182, 224-5, 251, 337, 399-402
gatherings of, 336
and Hands of the Cause, 295
Ḥuqúq'u'lláh and, 263-72
identification as, 289n.
imprisoned in Ṭihrán, 404
in India, 187-91
integration of community, 309
intermarriage of, 309
of Jewish background, *illus. 310*; 269, 284, 450
and laws, 304
love among, 205, 337
and love of Bahá'u'lláh, 200, 295-301
in Mandalay, 193
misdeeds of, 238-9, 417
and pioneering, 181
prayer for, 257
prejudices of, 309
prominent, 304
promotion of peace, 364
protection of, 344
and sacrifice, 200
schools built by, 127n.
spiritual character of, 406
standard of Bahá'u'lláh for, 87
standard of detachment, 264-5
station of, 96-7, 302
steadfastness of, 147-8
Tablets to, 344
true, 169, 314
understanding of teachings, 224
understanding of the Testaments, 285
unity of, 200, 202, 204-5
uprisings against, 129
well-being of, 307
Ẓillu's-Sulṭán offers to assist, 106
mentioned, 120, 124n., 196, 444
Bahá'í World Centre, *illus. 387*; 374-91
Bahá'íyyih Khánum, *see* Greatest Holy Leaf
Bahá'u'lláh
'Abdu'l-Bahá shields, from outside world, 1, 4, 5
and Abu'l-Qásim, 30-31
achievements of, 450-3
accused of identifying Himself with God, 131, 433-5
addresses divines of Islám, 102-4
addresses leaders of religion, 224
at Adrianople, 261, 420, 449
and 'Akká, 110, 256-8
Apostles of, 51, 53, 56, 93n., 110, 312, 421, 442, 468
and appointment of Hands of the Cause, 303, 312-34, 335-48, 359n., 452
Áqá Mírzá Áqá meets, 351-8
arrival in 'Akká, 374
Ascension of, 112n., 195, 319, 374, 441-53
in Baghdád, 259-60, 313
at Bahjí, 9n., 89, 108-22, 257, 259, 354, 374, 442, 446, 450
belief in, 205
birth of, 356
Centre of the Cause, 150
children of, 5-6, 296
on Christ, 160
clothes of, 262, 263
on condition of mankind, 75-6
confers title on Quddús, 222
and consultation, 307
counsels of, to followers, 360-4
cursing of, 96-7, 185
as Day-Spring of God's signs, 136
Declaration of, 56, 85, 323, 350
described by Ḥájí Muḥammad-Ṭáhir-i-Málmírí, 9-10
describes station of 'Abdu'l-Bahá, 60
detachment of, 261-2, 270
donkey of, 110, 111, 357
and edict of Sulṭán 'Abdu'l-'Azíz, 254, 255

and E. G. Browne, 263
on equality of men and women, 210-15
exhortation to Bahá'ís, 182
family of, Covenant-breakers, 5-6, 296
and famine in Persia, 318
as the 'Father', 241, 242, 441
feasts held in honour of, 10
on future of the Cause, 76
at Garden of Riḍván, 11-33
and gifts, 261-2
Ḥájí Mírzá Ḥaydar-'Alí's reminiscences of, 4-5
Ḥájí Mírzá Siyyid Muḥammad meets, 350
Ḥájí Yahúdá meets, 12-13
in Haifa, 374
and House of the Báb, 459-61
House of, in Baghdad, 174
humour of, 257, 271
Ibn-i-Aṣdaq meets, 320
imprisonment of, 255-6
infallibility of, 157
and Istanbul, 419-20
Jalíl-i-Khú'í meets, 152
as Joseph, 85
and King and Beloved of Martyrs, 78-9, 84-94
love of, 200, 222, 292, 296-7
magnanimity of, 255-63
at Mazra'ih, 1-10, 77, 110, 191, 196
message to Amínu's-Sulṭán, 195
message to Christians, 240-8
and misdeeds of Bahá'ís, 238-9, 417
at Mount Carmel, 353-8
Mullá 'Alí-Akbar meets, 318
and Mullá Ḥusayn, 221
Nabíl-i-Akbar dear to, 51
Nabíl's poetry about, 112-3
names and titles of, 146, 218, 392-3
orders land to be purchased in 'Ishqábád, 125
the Person of Bahá'u'lláh, 140-2
and pilgrims in the Holy Land, 88-92
praise of, as 'Supreme Mediator', 392
prayer for believers, 257
presentation of His teachings, 398-402
and the process of revelation, 230-1
proclamation to kings and rulers, 449
proofs of, 279
quotes from previously revealed Tablets, 396-8
recognition of, 149, 203, 208, 217-8, 224, 228, 324
recognition of God comes only through, 145-6
on religion, 163-4
response to martyrdoms in Yazd, 365
Revelation of, *see* Revelation of Bahá'u'lláh
and Rúḥu'lláh, 61-8
sends travel teachers, 292-3
sends unaddressed Tablets, 343-5
Shrine of, *see* Shrines
and Siyyid Asadu'lláh, 201
Siyyid Muṣṭafáy-i-Rúmí attracted to, 192
slippers of, 263
speaking as the Manifestation, 339
on spiritual worlds, 216-25
station of, 69, 98, 113, 130-45, 148, 235, 340
stories attributed to, 179
sufferings of, 6, 40, 156, 414-6, 417-8, 429-33
and Sulaymán Khán, 187-95
summons of, to Son of the Wolf, 437-40
as Supreme Manifestation, 141, 143-5, 154, 398, 433-6
Tablets of, *see* Tablets of Bahá'u'lláh
teachings of, *see* Teachings
on unity, 204-8
Universal Manifestation, 141

on use of force, 402-3
Ustád 'Alí-Akbar meets, 125
and Varqá, 60-8
Will and Testament of (*Kitáb-i-'Ahdí*), 414, 448, 449
on wisdom, 340, 340-3
and Writings of the Báb, 50, 397
Writings of, misrepresented, 157-8
Ẓillu's-Sulṭán's letter to, 106
mentioned, 127, 187, 188, 192, 387
Bahjí, Mansion of, *illus. 115*, 116, 117, 118, 451; 32, 108-22, 430, 444
and 'Abdu'l-Bahá, 1, 5, 111, 113
Bahá'u'lláh at, 9n., 89, 108-22, 257, 259, 354, 374, 442, 446, 450
circumambulation of, 112-3
Ḥájí Muḥammad Ṭáhir describes events at, 111-3
Holy Family does not go to, 1, 111
inscription over entrance of, 108-9
Bali, 193
Balkh, 193
Báqir, Mullá, Imám-Jum'ih of Nayríz, 216
Báqir, Mullá, Letter of the Living, 469
Barq, the donkey, 110
Bastinado, 6, 156, 326-7, 415
Bavánát, 347
Bayán, the, 50, 133, 174, 232, 324, 351
People of, 154-5, 184, 217-8, 232, 439
Point of, *see* the Báb
Begging, 171, 268
Beirut, 55, 351
'Abdu'l-Bahá's visit to, 253-4
University of, 32
Believers, *see* Bahá'ís
Beloved of Martyrs (Maḥbúbu'sh-Shuhadá, Mírzá Muḥammad-Ḥusayn), *illus. 82*; 16, 61, 77-94, 95, 104-5, 106, 124, 392, 409, 464
Bey, Nikolaki, 4
Bíbí Ṭúbá (sister of Varqá), 58
Bible, Holy, 49
see also Gospels, Testament, Scriptures
Bihjatu's-Ṣudúr (Ḥájí Mírzá Ḥaydar-'Alí), 64
Bírúní, 3
Bishops, 242-3
Black Standard, 221
Bombay, 112, 188, 191, 351, 411
Book of the Covenant, 73, 414
Books, 397
burning of, 363
destruction of, 174, 175
of God, 224
printing of, 342
Boys, school for, 333
Britain, 106, 279, 280
Browne, Edward Granville, 263, 323
Bruce, Revd Dr Robert, 279-86
Buddhists, 191, 195, 284, 450
Bukhárá, 278
Burma, 191, 192, 194, 199, 322, 450
Burning Bush, 233, 241, 361, 380
Buzurg-i-Afnán, Ḥájí Mírzá, 16, 354, 358-9

Cairo, 24, 129, 158, 446
Calamity, 237, 249
Caliphate, 389
Carmel, Mount, *illus. 387*; 74n., 128, 179-80, 353, 374
Tablet of Carmel, 374-91, 452
Cause, *see* Bahá'í Faith
Caucasus, the, 90, 328
Celebes, 193
Central Organization for a Durable Peace, 323
Certitude, 37
Ceylon, 191, 193
Chicago, 383
Chihríq, 468
Children, 227
education of, 167, 363
suffering of, 97
Christ Jesus, 60, 345
historicity of, 282
reality of, 160, 284
return of, 160, 240-1, 374-5

teachings of, 160
mentioned, 67, 76, 101, 114, 132, 132, 136, 171, 180, 194, 227, 242, 245, 338, 373, 390, 463
Christianity, 160, 163, 172, 240-48, 280-1
administration of, 389
converts to, 280n.
Christians, 280, 282, 373, 374-5, 446
Tablet to (*Lawḥ-i-Aqdas*), 240-8
Churches, 242, 243, 280, 282
Circumambulation, 112, 113, 114
Civilization, 345
Bahá'í, 144, 246, 390, 441, 452
Clergy, 182, 196, 288, 371
and cursing, 363n.
during Muḥarram, 342
Mírzá Abu'l-Faḍl's dialogues with, 279-86
Muslim, 175, 184, 212, 338, 461, 463
S͟hí'ah of Persia, 367
as 'stars' referred to in the Gospels, 242
see also Divines and Priesthood
Commonwealth, Bahá'í, 386
Concourse on High, 301, 316, 336, 371, 376, 389
Confession, 172
Constantinople, *see* Istanbul
Consultation, 124, 250, 307, 309, 338, 342
Counsellors, Boards of, 293, 306
Covenant, 153, 181, 322, 330
'ark', 385
authenticity of, 153
Book of the, *see* Book of the Covenant
Centre of, 149-50, 153, 263, 267, 330, 449
Covenant-breaking, 5-6, 63, 86-7, 90-1, 152-3, 199, 261-2, 323, 394-5, 448-9
establishment of, 452
Ibn-i-Aṣdaq's writings on, 322
steadfastness in, 150, 153, 217, 248, 319
Covenant-breakers, 181, 322
and Hands of the Cause, 319
Jalíl-i-K͟hu'í, 152-4, 156
Jamál-i-Burújirdí, 152, 199, 269, 304n., 341
Mírzá Áqá Ján's downfall, 261
Mírzá Muḥammad-'Álí, 5, 63, 152, 250, 449
Mírzá Yahyá, *see* Yahyá, Mírzá
Siyyid 'Ali and Fúrúg͟híyyih, 430
see also Azalís
Creation, 199, 215, 217, 228, 324
origin of, 40-8, 296
principles of, 38, 295
purpose of, 140, 441
responds to Revelation of Bahá'u'lláh, 376-5
Cursing, 96-7, 166, 363
Cyprus, 425
Czar, 368, 414, 464

Damascus, 446
Daniel, 162, 463
Dáru'l-Funún, 332
'Day of God', 69, 131, 131, 140, 155, 174-6, 220, 226, 230, 243, 252, 264, 273, 275, 321, 332, 398, 433, 441
Day of Resurrection, 218
Dayyán (Mírzá Asadu'lláh), 469
Dead, the, 172-3, 218
Deeds, 251, 265, 278, 306, 337-8, 361, 394, 401, 406
condemnation of wicked, 396
service is greatest of all, 321
unity of, 202
Deputization, 275
Dervish, 53n, 188
Detachment
of Bahá'u'lláh, 261-2
need for, 71-72, 264-5, 269, 306, 337
and successful teaching, 274, 277, 287
Díyár-Bakr, 88-9, 89
Dispensation, 144, 200, 202
of the Báb, 174-5, 324n., 402, 467

developments in the, 344-5
each has a beginning and an end, 163
previous, 361, 463
Dissimulation, 96-7
Disunity, 205, 206, 208
Divines
Bahá'u'lláh's challenge to, 229-30
of Islám, 102-4, 182, 203, 213, 226, 231, 406, 412, 415
see also Priesthood and Clergy
Díyá, Ḥájí Mírzá, 354
Díyá'u'lláh, Mírzá, 62
Dreams, 217
Druze, 446

East, the, 246, 256
Education, 166, 249
of Bahá'í youth, 333
of children, 167, 363
of the human race, 362
Ministry of, in Persia, 333
of women, 212, 331
Egypt, 187, 254, 348, 447
Elections, 308
Elijah, Cave of, 374, 382
Emanation, 42, 46
Encyclopaedia, Arabic, 428
Epistle to the Son of the Wolf (Baha'u'llah), 392-440
study of, 398, 462-9
Equality, 210
of men and women, 210-15
musávát, 206
Esperanto, 467
Essence of Essences, *see* God
Europe, 246, 323

Faith, personal, 37, 150, 166, 225, 229, 292
'Abdu'l-Baha's words on, 229
a relative term, 58, 69
Fá'izih Khánum, 330
Famine, 280, 318
Fárán, 270
Fáris Effendi, 240
Farmán Farmá, 468
Fárs, 346n.
Fast, prayer for, 10
Fatḥ-'Ali Sháh, 234, 322, 463
Fáṭimih, 95n., 463
Fáṭimih 'the Immaculate', 197n.
Fáṭimih Khánum, 316
Feasts, 8-10, 14
'First Mind', 46
Forel, Dr August, 138
Forgiveness, 89-90
Formative Age, 192, 246, 303, 391
Fu'ád (minister of Sultan 'Abdu'l-Azíz), 256
Funds, 263, 268, 271, 275, 280
International, 271
see also Ḥuqúq'u'lláh
Fúrúghíyyih (daughter of Bahá'u'lláh), 430

Gabriel, 95
Galilee, hills of, 1
Gallipoli, 376
Germans, 74, 374, 375
Gifts, 261-2
Girls, school for, 333
God, 177-9, 208, 377
achieving nearness to, 71-4, 149, 222-3
addresses the Son of the Wolf, 395
attributes of, 17, 46, 99, 137-9, 141-2, 165, 209, 215, 258
Bahá'u'lláh accused of identifying Himself with, 131, 433-5
belief in, 28-9, 48
Book of, 224
bounty of, 121, 228, 247, 338
and creation, 40-5
Essence of, 134-9, 436
fear of, 29, 226, 251, 278, 306, 401, 406
greatness of, 277
guidance of, 345
'Humorist', 258
'the Incomparable', 210
knowledge of, 146, 225, 399
laws of, 385
love of, 36, 314

and man, 50, 68, 146, 158, 165, 304
mercy of, 436-9
nature of, 42, 45-8, 134-42, 283
no 'time' in sight of, 178-9
oneness of, 305, 424, 434
power of, 345, 397
Presence of, 436, 466
recognition of, 145-6
reliance on, 343
relationship of, with Manifestations, 134-42
and 'return', 218-20
tests of, 28-9, 262, 304
turning to, 337-8
Will of, 46, 345
Word of, *see* Word of God
worlds of, 216-7
worship of, 37, 175-6
wrath of, 338
Golden Age, 390
Golden Rule, 206
Gospels, the, 45, 74, 132, 160, 242
see also Holy Bible, Scriptures and Testament
Government, 167, 170, 201, 226, 249, 284, 368
Bahá'ís intercede with, 368
British, 279
constitutional, 363
of Persia, 325, 333, 356, 359, 406
presidential system, 170
Graves, 172-3
Greatest Holy Leaf (Bahá'íyyih Khánum), 1, 63, 111, 330, 358, 385-6, 390
Greatest Name, 141, 438n.
Greece, 34, 44, 48
Greek, 48
Guardian, *see* Shoghi Effendi
Guardianship, 390
Gulistán, Treaty of, 463

Ḥabíb-i-Afnán, Ḥájí Mírzá, 106
Ḥabíbu'lláh, Ḥájí Mírzá, 353-7
Hadhramaut, 455
Hádí, Mírzá, 16, 77
Hádíy-i-Dawlat-Ábádí, Mírzá, 50, 184-6, 440, 465, 468
Hádíy-i-Sabzavárí, Ḥájí Mullá, 233
Ḥadiqatu'r-Raḥmán, 348
Ḥadíth (Tradition), 41-2, 221n., 225, 412, 466
Hague, The, 323
Haifa, 74n., 180, 353-4, 358, 369, 374
Ḥájibu'd-Dawlih, 67
Hamidán, 12, 275
Handmaidens, *see* Women
Hands of the Cause, *illus. 297-300,* 309
administrative seat of, 390
appointment of, 192, 332, 359n., 452
development of institution of, 293-4
establish first elected assembly in Ṭihrán, 308, 331
function of, 295-6, 305
and Ḥuqúq'u'lláh, 269
the 'learned', 39
lives of, 312-34
in Persia, 129, 273-4
prayers for, 305, 317, 340, 359
role of, 291-311
service of, 319
Tablets to, 335-48, 359
teachers of the Cause, 273-4
urged to consult, 307
urged to move about and deepen Bahá'ís, 318
Harris, Hooper, 330
Ḥasan, Ḥájí Mírzá Siyyid, *see* Afnán-i-Kabír
Ḥasan, Mírzá (brother of Varqá), 54, 56
Ḥasan-i-Adíb, Ḥájí Mírzá (Adíb), *illus.* 300, 309; 294-5, 330, 331-4
Ḥasan-i-Mázindarání, 468
Ḥaydar-'Alí, Ḥájí Mírzá, 274, 287-90, 343, 346, 462
Kalimát-i-Firdawsíyyih revealed in honour of, 226
met by Ḥájí Muḥammad-i-Yazdí, 26

reminiscences of Bahá'u'lláh, 4-5, 15
reminiscences of Varqá and Rúḥu'lláh, 64
on the Person of Bahá'u'lláh, 142
on teaching, 288-90
teaching work of, 252
Heart, 72, 225, 296, 405
Heaven, 222
Hebrew, 48
Hell, 223
Heroic Age, 124, 128, 192, 246, 390
Hidden Words, The (Bahá'u'lláh), 56, 72, 86, 296-301, 339, 362, 441-2, 463
'Him Whom God shall make manifest', 56, 154, 174, 183, 232, 351, 467
see also Bahá'u'lláh
Hindus, 195, 284
Ḥisamu's-Salṭanih, 468
History, 49, 69, 113
'History of the Faith in the Province of Yazd' (Ḥájí Muḥammad-Ṭáhir-i-Málmírí), 24, 53-4
History of the Martyrs of Yazd, 129, 369
Holy Family, 269, 448
Holy Land
agitation in, 153
pilgrims arriving in, without permission, 88-9, 91-2
prestige of Faith in, 253-5
Templers come to, 74, 374
mentioned, 9, 26, 120, 269-70, 323, 382, 420, 447, 450
see also 'Akká and Haifa
Holy Spirit, 139-42
Houses of Justice, 39, 345, *see also* Universal House of Justice
House of Worship, *see* Mashriqu'l-Adhkár
Húd, 101, 454-8
Humility, 68, 203
Humour, 258-9
Ḥuqúq'u'lláh, 62, 263-72
Ḥusayn, Imám, 212, 342, 372
Ḥusayn, Mírzá (brother of Varqá), 53-6
Ḥusayn, Mírzá (relative of Sulaymán Khán), 191
Ḥusayn, Mullá, 219-20, 467
Ḥusayn-i-Áshchí, 258-9
Ḥusayn Khán, Mírzá, Mushíru'd-Dawlih, 464
Ḥusayn-i-Shírází, 26
Ḥusayn-i-Yazdí, Siyyid, Letter of the Living, 468

Ibn-i-Abhar, *see* Ḥájí Mírzá Muḥammad-Taqí
Ibn-i-Aṣdaq, Hand of the Cause (Mírzá 'Alí-Muḥammad), *illus. 299*, 309; 294-5, 303
life of, 320-3
Tablets to, 269, 292, 294, 314, 335-48
Ibn-i-Fáriḍ, 415, 463
Ibráhím, Mírzá, 78
Ibráhím, Siyyid (Khalíl), 469
Ibráhím-i-Abharí, Mírzá, 323
Idleness, 170-2
Incarnation, 42
India, 187-96, 199, 322, 330, 334, 351, 411, 447, 450
Indians, 188
Infallibility, 150, 152, 156-60
Institutions, 203-4
Integration, 308
Intercession, 368
Iran, *see* Persia
'Iráq, 6, 449
Isaiah, 45, 241, 284-5, 378-9, 382, 385, 435, 441
Iṣfáhán, 61, 105, 124, 183, 184, 279-81, 283, 333, 365
martyrdoms of King and Beloved of Martyrs at, 77-94, 409
prison at, 58
upheavals at, 392
'Ishqábád, 31, 365-6, 367, 413, 450
upheavals in, 365-9
Ustád 'Alí-Akbar in, 124-8, 129
Islám, 45, 93, 95n., 158-9, 194
abrogation of laws of, 194

administration of, 389
converts to Christianity from, 280n.
and cursing, 97
divines of, 102-4, 157, 260
dissimulation allowed in, 96
downfall of, 103
knowledge of Islamic subjects, 399
negation stands above affirmation in, 182
prayer of, 438n.
S͟hí'ah, 185-6, 220, 342, 363
S͟hí'ah orthodoxy undermined, 175
women in, 210-2
Ismá'íl, Mírzá (brother of King and Beloved of Martyrs), 80
Ismá'íl, Siyyid, 412, 465
Ismá'ílís, 193, 194
Israel, 435
Children of, 49, 223, 285
Prophets of, 13, 48, 162, 385
Istanbul (Constantinople), 466
exile of Bahá'u'lláh to, 113, 245-6
machinations of Azalís in, 238, 417-40
Persian Embassy in, 419, 464, 465

Jacob, 415
Jaddih (Jidda), 26, 475
Ja'far, the sifter of wheat, 463
Ja'far, Mírzá, 1n.
Ja'far-i-Kirmání, Mullá, 426
Ja'far-i-Ṣádiq, (Sixth Imám), 466
Ja'far-i-Yazdí, Mírzá, 258-60
Jáhil, *see* Muḥammad-'Alíy-i-Sayyáh
Jalíl-i-K͟hu'í, 152-4, 156
Jamál-i-Burújirdí, 152, 199, 269, 304n., 341
Jamálu'd-Din (Jamál Effendi), *see* Sulaymán K͟hán-i-Tunukábání
Jamálu'd-Din-i-Afg͟hání, Siyyid (founder of Pan-Islamic movement), 363, 428
Java, 193
Javád-i-Karbilá'í, Ḥájí Siyyid, 468
Javáhirí, Mr, *illus. 310*; 308
Jerusalem, 375, 385, 435
Jewish Faith, 163, 269
Jews, 279, 280n., 284, 446
Bahá'ís of Jewish descent, *illus. 310*; 12-13, 269, 284, 450
and martyrs of Yazd, 369-71
at time of Christ, 60, 101, 241, 345
Joseph, 85
Josephus, 282
Junaynih, Garden of, 110, 259, 357
Junyan Gardens, 32
Justice, 35, 102, 163, 182, 184, 206, 228, 234, 238, 242, 285, 372, 394, 400, 408, 415, 438
'Abdu'l-Bahá helps people receive, 3
God's forgiveness outweighs His, 90
of Hands of the Cause, 302
for murderers of a Bahá'í, 366-7
no one can be a human being without, 338
upheld by reward and punishment, 167

Kaaba, 380, 382, 384, 406, 438, 463
Kalimát-i-Firdawsíyyih, 185, 206, 226-39, 398
Kamál Pás͟há, 464, 467
Kámrán Mírzá, the Náyibu's-Salṭanih, 316, 317, 359
Karbilá, 105, 372, 459
Karbilá'í Áqá Ján, 287-88
Kás͟hán, 261-2, 469
Kashmir, 193
Káẓim, Mullá, 410-1
Káẓim, Ustád, 260
Káẓim-i-Samandar, S͟hayk͟h, 93, 188, 201, 421
K͟hádem, Hand of the Cause D͟hikru'lláh, 476
K͟hadíjih Bagum, 350, 352, 432, 430, 459, 460
K͟halíl (Siyyid Ibráhím), 469
K͟halíl-i-Tabrízí, Áqá, 283, 285
K͟hán-i-Maḥallátí, Áqá, 193
K͟hánum Buzurg (S͟háh Sulṭán K͟hánum), 468
K͟hartúm, 24, 26

Khávar, Ḥájí, 357
Khurásán, 105, 221, 221n., 269, 312, 365
Khuy, 469
King of Martyrs, (Sulṭánu'sh-Shuhadá, Mírzá Muḥammad-Ḥasan), *illus. 77*; 16, 61, 77-94, 95, 105, 106, 123, 269, 392, 409, 464
  Bahá'u'lláh's prayer for, 86
Kings, 102-3, 179, 249, 309, 414, 449
Kirmán, 426, 427
Kirmánsháhán, 275
Kitáb-i-'Ahdí (The Book of My Covenant), 448, 464
Kitáb-i-Aqdas (Bahá'u'lláh), 128, 145, 168, 224, 426, 427, 445
  law of Ḥuqúq'u'lláh, 263-72
  laws of, 119, 122, 318, 341-2, 450, 452, 463
  Tablets revealed after, 34, 123, 175, 240-48
  tribute to the 'learned', 39
Kitáb-i-Íqán (Bahá'u'lláh), 99, 143, 146, 160, 162, 218, 225, 314, 342, 350, 411, 449, 456-8, 468
Knowledge, 224, 225, 250, 291-2, 364, 464
  of God, 399
Komaroff, General, 366
Krupatkin, General, 127
Kurdistán, 7

Laddakh, 193
Lahore, 193
Language, 204, 377-8, 398
  universal auxiliary, 167-8, 170, 227, 363
Lawḥ-i-'Abdu'l-Vahháb, 50
Lawḥ-i-Aqdas, 240-8, 375, 376
Lawḥ-i-Ard-i-Bá, 254-5
Lawḥ-i-Bishárát, 166, 167, 169-76, 177
Lawḥ-i-Burhán, 95-107, 454, 465
Lawḥ-i-Dunyá, 305, 350-66, 428, 459
Lawḥ-i-Fu'ád, 467
Lawḥ-i-Ḥikmat, 34-52, 397
  ancient Greek philosophers, 48
  on creation, 40-48
  deplores condition of the world, 35-6
  description of nature, 47
  differs from historical records, 49
  on knowledge of the Manifestations, 51
  philosophical terminology of, 34
  revealed in honour of Nabíl-i-Akbar, 34, 40, 48
  on speech, 202
  teachings to spiritualize the human race, 36-8
Lawḥ-i-Hizár Baytí ('Abdu'l-Bahá), 153
Lawḥ-i-Ishráqát, 23, 152-8, 170, 177, 430
Lawḥ-i-Ittiḥád, 201-6
Lawḥ-i-Karmil, 374-91, 452
Lawḥ-i-Maqṣúd, 249-50
Lawḥ-i-Ra'ís, 467
Lawḥ-i-Siyyid Mihdíy-i-Dahají, 250-2
Lawḥ-i-Sulṭán, 399, 414
Lawḥ-i-Tajallíyát, 123-51, 177
Lawḥ-i-Ṭarázát, 177-86
Laws, 122, 165, 194, 223, 227-8, 273, 304, 450, 452, 463
  application of, 342
  of the Báb, 174-5
  of Ḥuqúq'u'lláh, *see* Ḥuqúq'u'lláh
  laws of God, 385
  obedience to, 149
  physical, 270-1
  publication of, 317-8
'Leaf', *see* Women
Lebanon, 379
Lesser Peace, 167, 170, 208, 390
  Universal House of Justice to promote, 363-4
  see also Most Great Peace and Peace
Letters of the Living, 221-2
Life, purpose and principles of, 203, 295
Local Spiritual Assemblies, 203-4, 292, 293, 308
  of Bahá'í Women, 331
  instituted in Persia, 293
  of Ṭihrán, *illus. 310*; 308-11, 331

Locusts, 31
Lote-Tree, 178, 439, 466
Love, 169, 327, 361, 399
  among believers, 337-8
  of Bahá'u'lláh, 200, 204-5, 248
  of one's country, 362
  prime cause of creation, 209
Luqmán, 466

Madras, 191
Máh-kú, 235, 350, 468
Maḥmúd Mírzá, Prince, the Jalálu'd-Dawlih, 369-71
Maḥmúd-i-Zarqání, Mírzá, 153, 302, 330
Maḥrám, Mírzá, 194
Majdu'd-Din, 448
Majzub, Nuṣratu'lláh, 475
Malaya, 193
Man
  barrier between God and, 304
  capacity to understand God, 158
  each person unique, 209, 210
  a finite being, 228
  greatest achievement of, 86
  human nature, 149-50
  muvását is noblest quality of, 206
  need for detachment, 71-4
  need for humility, 68
  need for justice, 338
  need to live the life, 73-4
  spiritual growth of, 38
  station of, 68
  'Supreme Talisman', 249
  tested by God, 262
  see also Soul and Mankind
Mandalay, 194
Manifestation, 131-2, 139, 144, 466
  attributes of, 260-1
  Bahá'u'lláh is Supreme, 141, 143-5, 154, 285, 398, 433-6
  effect of coming of, 154, 163
  bearers of God's attributes, 138
  can see the end in the beginning, 178-9
  endowed with divine knowledge, 50
  man's capacity to understand, 158
  next, 228
  of the prophetic cycle, 174
  proof of, 114
  recognition of, 148-50
  relationship with God, 134-7
  revealers of God to man, 49, 137-8, 147
  Saviour of man, 203
  'Universal Manifestation', 141
  see also the Báb, Bahá'u'lláh, Moses, Muḥammad and Prophets
Mankind, 143-5, 182, 226-7, 249
  Bahá'u'lláh's counsels to, 167, 359-64
  condition of, 69-76, 158, 164-6
  encompassed by Bahá'í Faith, 273
  fellowship among, 363
  oneness of, 209, 285
  perversity of, 338
  regeneration of, 71, 249
  suffering and tribulation of, 76, 164-6
  unity of, 165, 167, 169, 205, 206-9, 227, 249, 285, 414
  vision of, 178
Man<u>sh</u>ád, 30
Maqálih-Fí-Al-Islám (Treatise on Islám), 158
Maqṣúd, Mírzá, 249-50
Marriage, 171, 212, 309, 330
Martyrdom, 60-61, 147, 184, 246, 281, 342
  of Bahá'ís in Yazd, 129, 198, 354, 368-71
  Bahá'u'lláh on, 408-14
  of Ḥájí Muḥammad-Riḍáy-i-Iṣfahání, 364-9
  of Imám Husayn, 212, 342
  Tablet concerning, 92, 321, 324
Martyrs, 173, 346n., 347-8, 408-14, 450
Maryam Sulṭán Bagum (wife of Áqá Mírzá Áqá), 353, 358
Ma<u>sh</u>had, 221, 312, 314
Ma<u>sh</u>riqu'l-A<u>dh</u>kár, 180, 336n.

definition of, 125n., 336n.
in 'Ishqábád, 125-8, 450
on Mount Carmel, 375, 387
in North America, 383
in Ṭihrán, 336
Master, the, *see* 'Abdu'l-Bahá
Mas'úd Mírzá, the Ẓillu's-Sulṭán, 80, 106-7, 279, 280, 369, 410-1
Mathnaví, 246
Mawlavís, 468
Maxwell, May Bolles, 29
Maydán-i-Khán, 370
Maydán-i-Sháh, 410
Mázindarán, 6, 155, 187, 221, 402, 406, 408, 413, 415
Mazra'ih, Mansion of, 55
Bahá'u'lláh at, 1-10, 11, 53, 77, 108, 110, 191, 259, 450
room of Bahá'u'lláh at, 263
scenery at, 7
Mecca, 389
Memorials of the Faithful ('Abdu'l-Bahá), 430-1
Men, 227
Bahá'í, in great danger, 124
equality between men and women, 124, 215
Mercy, 97, 99, 206, 242
Messengers, *see* Prophets
Midḥát Páshá, 253
Mihdí, Dervish, 53-4
Mihdí, Mullá (martyr of Yazd), 370
Mihdíy-i-'Aṭrí, Ḥájí Mullá, 53-4
Mihdíy-i-Dahají, 250-1, 304n.
Mineral kingdom, 209
Miracles, 114-9, 252, 290, 345
Mír Muḥammad Big, Áqá, 270n.
Mírzáy-i-Afnán, Ḥájí Siyyid, 112
Mishkín-Qalam, 258, 354
Moderation, 71, 202, 227, 250
Monarchy, constitutional, 170
Monks, 171, 242, 375
Moody, Dr Susan, 348
Moses, 49, 114, 132, 136, 233-4, 345, 346
Most Great Branch, *see* 'Abdu'l-Bahá
Most Great Name, 146, 243, 401
Community of the, 181, 251, 253, 273, 385
Most Great Peace, 166, 209, 249, 390
see also Lesser Peace and Peace
Most Great Prison, 5, 7, 109, 110, 256, 356, 428, 439
see also 'Akká
Most Holy Book, *see* Kitáb-i-Aqdas
Mu'ayyad, Dr Ḥabíb, 32, 179
Muballigh (Teacher-proclaimer), 273, 291-4
see also Teachers
Muḥammad, Prophet, 49, 80, 93, 95, 101, 132, 201n., 219, 220, 282, 286, 313, 315, 345, 434
Muḥammad, Ḥájí Mírzá Siyyid, 350
Muḥammad, Mír Siyyid, 78, 79
Muḥammad, 'Abdú, Shaykh, 253
Muḥammad-i-'Aláqih-band, Ḥájí Áqá, 26, 231
Muḥammad-'Alí, Ḥájí Mírzá (maternal cousin of the Báb), 125-7, 420
Muḥammad-'Alí, Ḥájí Shaykh, *see* Nabíl ibn-i-Nabíl
Muḥammad-'Alí, Mírzá (Arch-breaker of the Covenant), 5, 63, 152, 250, 449
Muḥammad-'Alí, Mírzá (father of Munírih Khánum), 77-8
Muḥammad-'Alíy-i-Afnán, Ḥájí, 262
Muḥammad-'Alíy-i-Iṣfahání, 239, 421-3
Muḥammad-'Alí Mírzá (the Crown Prince), 429
Muḥammad-'Alíy-i-Sayyáh, Ḥájí (Jáhil), 106
Muḥammad-'Alíy-i-Tabrízí, 421-2
Muḥammad-Báqir, 261-2
Muḥammad-Báqir (martyr of Yazd), 370
Muḥammad-Báqir, Shaykh (Dhi'b-Wolf), 80, 83, 315, 392, 410
Lawḥ-i-Burhán addressed to, 95-107
Muḥammad-Ḥasan (martyr of Yazd), 370
Muḥammad-Ḥasan, Mírzá, *see* King

of Martyrs
Muḥammad-Ḥasan-i-Najafí, Shaykh, 220, 463
Muḥammad-Ḥasan-i-Sabzivárí, Shaykh, 54
Muḥammad-Ḥusayn, Mír (Imám-Jum'ih of Iṣfahán, Raqshá-she-Serpent), 79-80, 83-4, 95, 101-2, 104-5, 315
Muḥammad-Ḥusayn, Mírzá, *see* Beloved of Martyrs
Muḥammad-Ḥusayn, Shaykh, 216-7
Muḥammad-Ibráhím, Áqá, 31-2
Muḥammad-Ibráhím, Ḥájí (Muballigh), 161n., 430
Muḥammad-i-Iṣfahání (Anti-Christ of Bahá'u'lláh's Revelation), 239, 440, 464, 465
Muḥammad Khán-i-Balúch, 112
Muḥammad-i-Qá'iní, Áqá, *see* Nabíl-i-Akbar
Muḥammad-Qulí, Mírzá, 262
Muḥammad-Qulí, Mírzá (half-brother of Bahá'u'lláh), 257
Muḥammad-Riḍáy-i-Iṣfahání, Ḥájí, *illus. 367*; 364-9, 413, 465
Muḥammad-i-Riḍáy-i-Muḥammad-Ábádí, Mullá, 304n.
Muḥammad-Riḍáy-i-Yazdí, Mullá, 404
Muḥammad Sháh, 234-5
Muḥammad-Ṭáhir-i-Málmírí, Ḥájí, 114
  account of Bahjí, 111-3
  'History of the Faith in the Province of Yazd', 24, 53-4
  memories of Bahá'u'lláh, 9-10, 258-9, 262
  story about Mírzá Ja'far, 259-60
  Tablet revealed for, 344
Muḥammad-Taqí, Hand of the Cause Ḥájí Mírzá (Ibn-i-Abhar), *illus. 298*, 329; 27, 129, 294, 307, 359
  letters of, 326-8
  life of, 323-31
  Tablets to, 335-48
  wife of, 331-2
Muḥammad-Taqí, Ḥájí Mírzá, the Vakílu'd-Dawlih, 125, 127, 128, 420
Muḥammad-Taqí, Mírzá, 24
Muḥammad-Taqí, Shaykh (Son of the Wolf), 83, 184-5, 333
  Epistle of Bahá'u'lláh to, 392-440
  prayer for, 393-5
Muḥammad-i-Yazdí, Ḥájí, 23-6
Muḥammad-i-Yazdí, Shaykh, *illus. 22*; 420, 421, 425
Muḥarram, 342, 355, 356
Muḥsin-i-Afnán, Mírzá, 422
Munírih Khánum (wife of 'Abdu'l-Bahá), 16, 77, 460
Munírih Khánum (daughter of Mullá 'Alí-Akbar), 330-1
Murtiḍá, Mírzá, the Ṣadru'l-'Ulamá, 465
Músá, Mírzá (Áqáy-i-Kalím), 257, 448n., 468
Musávát (Equality), 206
Muslims
  Bahá'ís of Muslim background, 308-9
  clergy, *see* Divines
  and holy war, 169
  in Mandalay become Bahá'ís, 194
  Shí'ah, 195, 367, 446
  Sunní, 194, 446
  mentioned, 158, 181, 279, 281, 285, 356n., 365, 446
Muṣṭafá, Mírzá, 412, 465
Muṣṭafáy-i-Rúmí, Hand of the Cause Siyyid, *illus. 190*; 191-3
Muṣṭasháru'd-Dawlih (Mírzá Yúsuf Khán), 283
Muvását, 206
Mystics, 227, 312

Nabíl-i-Akbar, Hand of the Cause (Áqá Muḥammad-i-Qá'iní), 34, 40, 40, 48, 51, 123, 251, 274, 303, 332
  'Abdu'l-Bahá's tribute to, 34
  travels of, 187
  Nabíl-i-A'ẓam, 89, 111-3, 114, 221, 256, 258-9, 350-1

account of Ascension of
Bahá'u'lláh, 442-6, 447
Nabíl ibn-i-Nabíl (Ḥájí Shaykh Muḥammad-'Alí), *illus. 431*; 421-5, 466
Najaf, 105
Najafábád, 411
Najaf-'Alí, Áqá, 411-2, 465
Najafí, Áqá, *see* Muḥammad-Taqí
Na'mayn, Garden of, *see* Garden of Riḍván
Napoleon III, 99, 264, 414, 464
Naṣír, Ḥájí, 409, 464
Náṣirí (trademark), 188
Náṣiri'd-Dín Sháh, 40, 80, 106-7, 196-7, 316n., 407, 408, 413, 428, 468
attempt on the life of, 129, 403, 404
mistrust of, 404-5
Tablet to, 399-400, 414
Naṣru'lláh, Siyyid, 201
National Spiritual Assemblies, 203-4, 292, 293, 308
of Persia, 333
Nations, 208, 208, 249, 252, 385, 406, 452, 462-3
Nature
animal, 149-50
Bahá'u'lláh's definition of, 47
creates life, 345
human, 149-50
laws of, 270-1
observation of, 209, 270
spiritual, 150
Navváb, 1, 111, 386, 390
Naw-Rúz, 192, 383, 442, 445
Náyibu's-Salṭanih (Kámrán Mírzá), 316, 317, 359, 404-5
Náyib, Jináb-i-, 275
Nayríz, 216, 347, 402, 405, 465
Nazareth, 253
Newspapers, 183, 371-3, 422, 427
Nimrod, 345
Níyáz, Ḥájí, 443
Noah, 454-8
North America, *see* America
Nuclear energy, 237
Núru'd-Dín, *see* Áqá Mírzá Áqá
Núru'd-Dín-i-Zayn, 110

Obedience, 25, 26, 63, 149
Ober, Harlan, 330
Order, World, 119, 146, 227-8, 384, 452
see also Administrative Order
Ottoman Empire, 188, 419-20
court of, 423

Palestine, *see* Holy Land
Pan-Islamic movement, 428
Patchin, William J., *illus. 348*; 347-8, 486
Peace, 414
Central Organization for a Durable Peace, 323
Prince of, 285
promotion of, 363-4
results from unity, 165, 206-9
search for peace of mind, 75
teachings conducive to, 162-3
world, 206-8, 249, 363-4
see also Lesser Peace and Most Great Peace
'People of Bahá', *see* Bahá'ís
Persecution, 92, 281
of Bábís, 6
of Bahá'ís in Persia, 120, 371-3
of Bahá'u'lláh, 180, 417
of Cause of God, 356
of Ḥájí Ákhúnd, 315
of Ḥájí Yahúdá, 13
of Ibn-i-Abhar, 324-8
of Mírzá Hádí, 16
Persia, 96, 106, 120, 265, 363, 367, 372, 382, 392, 405, 428, 447, 450, 461, 463
adoption of surnames in, 311
Bahá'í community in, 325
Bahá'í schools in, 127n.
cradle of the Faith, 247
divines of, 103
effect of the Báb's Revelation on, 174-5

famine in, 318
government of, 234, 325, 333, 356, 359, 406, 428
Ḥájí Mírzá Ḥaydar-'Alí travels around, 287-90
Ibn-i-Abhar's travels around, 325-31
intermarriage of Bahá'ís of, 309
Mírzá Abu'l-Faḍl's travels around, 274-87
National Spiritual Assembly of, 333
Obligatory Prayers sent to, 318
Sulaymán Khán's mission to, 195
teachers in, 187, 269, 273-90, 291-3, 316, 321, 322, 325, 328, 450
well-being of Bahá'ís in, 307
women in, 331
Peter, 463
Pharaoh, 49, 345
Philosophy, 144, 250, 312
ancient Greek philosophers, 34, 44, 48-52
of Ḥájí Mullá Hádíyi-i-Sabzavárí, 233
Islamic philosophy, 44
Pilgrim House, 2, 9, 443
Pilgrimage
conditions for, 89
Ḥájí Mírzá Ḥabíbu'lláh's account of, 353-8
to the House of the Báb, 173, 459, 461
permission for, 87-90
rituals in connection with, 174
Pilgrims, 8-9, 229, 270
'Abdu'l-Bahá makes arrangements for, 2
to 'Akká, *see* 'Akká, pilgrims to
arrive without permission, 88-9
to Holy Land, 34, 87-90, 450
May Maxwell among first group from West, 29
at Mazra'ih, 9-10
at Shrine of the Báb, 179-80
at Shrine of Bahá'u'lláh, 108
visit Bombay, 188
Pioneering, 181, 348
Poems, 9, 68-9, 112-3, 130, 243-4, 332
Politics, 144, 322
Polygamy, 212
Port Said, 353
Possessions, earthly, 206
Prayers, 37, 177, 288, 336n., 438n.
on Essence of God, 136
for the Fast, 10
for Ibn-i-Aṣdaq, 320
influence of, on Mírzá Abu'l-Faḍl, 277
for Ḥájí Muḥammad-Riḍá, 366
for Hands of the Cause, 305, 317, 340, 358-9
for King of Martyrs, 86
Obligatory, 137, 228-9, 278, 318
at resting place of the departed, 172-3
for Son of the Wolf, 393-5
for understanding, 225
Prejudice, 60, 145, 158, 205, 309, 327
Priesthood, 102-4, 171, 204, 242-4, 306
see also Clergy *and* Priesthood
Principles, 207
of the Faith, 119, 153, 304, 340, 399-401, 450
of life, 295
Prisons
Mullá 'Alí-Akbar in, 315-6
of Qazvín, 318, 325, 359, 431, 466
of Tabríz, 196
of Ṭihrán, *illus. 329*; 67, 320, 325-7, 359
of Zanján, 324
see also Most Great Prison
Promise of World Peace. The (Universal House of Justice), 364
Prophecies
of 'Abdu'l-Bahá, 179-80
of Bahá'u'lláh, 164-5, 203, 237
fulfilment of, 161-2, 436, 441, 450
of Siyyid Asadu'lláh, 196
Prophetic cycle, 174

Prophets, 114, 114-9, 131, 132, 246, 384, 424
ancient, 49, 454-8
foretell coming of Bahá'u'lláh, 241, 434, 441
Greeks learned wisdom from, 48
of Israel, 13, 48, 162, 385
revealers of the Word of God, 49
see also Manifestations
Protestant Evangelical Society, 158
Punch, India, 193
Punishment, 165, 167, 223, 250
Punjab, 193
Purest Branch, 386, 390, 450

Qá'im, 184
Qá'im-Maqám (Mírzá Abu'l-Qásim-i-Faráhání), *illus. 236*; 234-5, 236
Qá'im-Maqámí (Mírzá Áqá Khán), *illus. 236*; 235-7
Qará-Guhar, chain of, 6, 415, 465
Qaṣídiy-i-Tá'íyyih, 415
Qaṣídiy-i-Varqá'íyyih, 416
Qayyúmu'l-Asmá, 385, 467
Qazvín, 201, 421
prison at, 195, 318, 325, 359, 431, 466
Qiblih, 386
Quddús, 221
Qum, 197, 288
Qur'án 30, 49, 57, 64, 132, 159, 163, 222-3, 283, 328, 434, 454-7, 463
authenticity of, 286, 290
on certitude, 37
historical accounts in, 49
laws of, 174
prophecies of, 435
on superiority of men, 210

Ra'd, the donkey, 110
Raḍa'r-Rúh, 346
Ráḍíyih, 15-16
Ramadán, 83
Raqshá, *see* Mír Muḥammad-Husayn
Rashh-i-'Amá, 433
Rasht, 118, 201, 408
Rawḍih-khání, 212-3

Recantation, 96-7, 184
Religion, 60, 206, 226, 295
Bahá'u'lláh addresses leaders of, 224
development of, 345
disenchantment with, 75
divisions in, 202, 389
followers of, 362, 389, 452
harmony of science and, 164
and the Holy Land, 389
ignored in its day, 76
loss of power of, 163
past, 170
principles of, 227
purpose of, 167
a 'radiant light', 162-3
reality of, 160
relationship between religions, 163, 169-70
sects in, 144
unity of, 201
unnecessary to turn to other religions, 148-9
'Return', 218-22
Revelation, 48, 94, 139-40, 178, 222, 225, 285, 424, 439
act of, 338, 354, 355
of attributes of God, 17
authenticity of, 64
of the Báb, 174-5, 220, 350
Most Great Revelation, 148
new, 174
of Tablets, 273
of the Word of God, 5
world immersed in ocean of, 73
Revelation of Bahá'u'lláh, 6, 56, 69, 100, 143, 145, 175, 181, 193, 209, 220, 318, 375, 380, 381, 396, 441, 450-2, 467
after martyrdoms in Yazd, 370
Anti-Christ of, 239
Bábís who were heedless of, 85, 155
birth of, 433
canalized through the Administrative Order, 247
climax of, 119

history of, 120-1
distinguishing features of, 362, 389
glory of, 340, 376
greatness of, 69, 114, 131, 133-4, 139, 158, 228, 230, 332, 338, 340, 356
influence of, 376
nature of, 135-6, 158, 414
power of, 251, 414
to priests, bishops and monks, 242-3
process of, 231, 396-7
purpose of, 166, 206, 389, 414
truth in, 148, 159, 360
veils to recognizing, 145
and the West, 245-6
world depends on, 339
Revelation of Bahá'u'lláh (Adib Taherzadeh), 449, 462
'Revelation-writing', 130, 355
Reward, 165, 167, 223, 250
Riḍá, Imám, 197n.
Riḍáy-i-Qannád, Áqá, 448
Riḍá-Qulí, Mírzá, 468
Riḍáy-i-Yazdí, Shaykh, 303
Riḍván, Garden of, *illus. 20-21*; 11-33, 110, 259
Abu'l-Qásim, gardener at, 29-33
May Maxwell's account of, 29-31
passage on trustworthiness revealed in, 16-17
Tablet on, 15-16
Risáliy-i-Síyásíyyih ('Abdu'l-Bahá), 323
Rosenberg, Ethel, 48
Rúḥu'lláh, *illus. 66*; 59, 58-68
Russia, 414, 447, 462-3
Ru'yá, Tablet of, 445

Sacraments, 306
Sacrifice, 147, 200, 206, 450
Sádát-i-Khamsih (The Five Siyyids), 201
Sa'dí, 69
Ṣádiq, Imám (Ja'far-i-Sádiq), 466
Ṣádiq-i-Khurásání, Mullá (Ismulláh'u'l-Aṣdaq), 303, 320
Sadratu'l-Muntahá, 466
Ṣadru'ṣ-Ṣudúr, 333
Ṣafá, Mírzá, 464
Salásil, chain of, 415, 465
Ṣáliḥ, 101, 454-8
Salmán, Shaykh, 346
Salmán, Tablet of, 181
Salsabíl, 370
Samarkand, 278
Sámirí, 48, 223
Saráju'l-Ḥukamá, *illus. 348*; 486
Sardár 'Azíz Khán, 465
Schools, 227, 333
Sciences, 123n., 144, 151, 170, 182, 224, 295, 377, 433, 463
harmony of religion and, 164
Scientists, 377
Scriptures, 49, 50, 51, 131, 143, 230-1, 278, 397
see also Gospels, Holy Bible, Holy Writings, Qur'án and Testament
Sects, 144, 164, 313, 389, 419
Service, 203
to the Cause of God, 37, 296, 309, 316, 321
of Hands of the Cause, 294-5, 318
to human race, 249
station of man is service, 68
and tests, 261
Seven Valleys, The (Bahá'u'lláh), 148, 191
Sháh Khalíl'u'lláh, 290n.
Sháh Sulṭán Khánum (Khánum Buzurg), 468
Shahíd-ibn-i-Shahíd, *see* Ibn-i-Aṣdaq
Shahmírzád, 312
Shahr-Bánú, 468
Shams-i-Ḍuhá, 16
Shaykh-i-Aḥsá'í (Shaykh Aḥmad), 466
Shaykhís, 313, 469
Shíráz, 334, 350, 352, 355, 409, 459-61, 466
Shoghi Effendi
as Centre of the Cause, 150

creation of world administrative order, 386-91
describes end of the Wolf and the She-Serpent, 105
describes events after the Ascension of Bahá'u'lláh, 446
describes importance of Mashriqu'l-Adhkár in 'Ishqábád, 127-8
describes relationship of God to Bahá'u'lláh, 134, 141
discusses Bahjí, 109
encourages pioneering, 181
explains revelation of laws, 122
explains 'rulers' and 'learned', 39
and Hands of the Cause, 62, 244-5, 293, 302
infallibility of, 157
and interpretation of Scripture, 380
interpretation of Tablet of Carmel, 382, 386
and laws of the Báb, 174-5
on love, compassion and sacrifice, 200
permission for pilgrimage sought from, 92
and prestige of Faith, 253-5
recounts martyrdom of Mullá 'Alí-Ján, 413
and Shrine of the Báb, 383-4
and Siyyid Muṣṭafáy-i-Rúmí, 192
statement on Ḥuqúq'u'lláh, 267
stories attributed to, 179
summary of martyrdoms in Yazd, 369-71
and teaching plans, 381
travel teachers during ministry of, 293
ushers in Formative Age, 247
mentioned, 30, 408
Shrines, 459
of the Báb, *illus. 387*, 387; 128, 173, 179-80, 381-91, 448
of Bahá'u'lláh, *illus. 451*; 31n., 108, 173, 179, 386n., 446, 448
of the Immaculate, 197
see also Pilgrimage
Shujá'u'd-Dawlih, 464
Siam, 193
Sidon, 54
Sin, 172
Sinai, 74, 98, 132, 136, 146, 241, 380
Síyáh-Chál, 6, 121, 139, 156, 263, 415, 403, 433
Síyávash, Mr, *illus. 310*; 308
Siyyid of Findirisk, 464
Sleep, 217
Society, 206-9, 214, 363
Socrates, 48
Some Answered Questions ('Abdu'l-Bahá), 42, 47, 160
Soul, 166, 199, 212, 247, 251, 266
equal status of, 214-5
freedom of, 203
holy souls, 336
immortality of, 43
in the next life, 395
one soul in many bodies, 200
prayers for, 172-3
return of qualities of, 219, 220-22
unity of, 316
virtues of, 38
see also Man
Speech, 73, 201-2, 251
Spiritualization, 36-40, 149-50
Station, 202-3, 219-20
Stars, falling of, 242
Steadfastness, 147-8, 337, 339
Ṣubḥ-i-Azal, *see* Mírzá Yahyá
Sudan, the, 187, 290
Suffering, 76, 164-6, 207
Suhráb, 'Ináyatu'lláh, 280
Sulaymán Khán-i-Tunukábání (Jamálu'd-Din, Jamál Effendi), *illus. 189*; 187-99
Sulaymáníyyih, 121
Superstition, 158, 184, 243
Súq-i-Abyaḍ (White Market), 111, 258
Súrih of Tawḥíd, 434
Súriy-i-Haykal, 139, 295
Súriy-i-Vafá, 216-225
Surnames, 311
Syria, 254, 274, 278, 444, 447

Ṭabarsí, 405, 465
Tablets of 'Abdu'l-Bahá
to Áqá Mírzá Áqá, 460-1
on attributes of God, 138
to the Central Organization for a Durable Peace (to The Hague), 323
on consultation, 307
to Covenant-breakers, 153
of the Divine Plan, 381
on equality of men and women, 215
to Dr Forel, 138
to Ḥájí Áqá Muḥammad-i-'Aláqih-band, 26
to Hands of the Cause, 302, 335
on historical records, 48
to Ibn-i-Abhar, 27, 326, 328
on interment of the Báb, 383
to Mírzá Áqá Khán, 235-6, 427
on nature of God, 137-8
on prayer, 173
and resting places of departed, 173
unaddressed, 345-6
of visitation, 173
Tablets of the Báb, 350
Tablets of Bahá'u'lláh, 34, 94
addressed to church aristocracy, 242-3
advice on teaching, 202
to Afnáns, 302
of Aḥmad, 148
to 'Andalíb, 88
for Áqá Siyyid Áqá, 301-2
on auxiliary language, 167-8
for Bahá'í women, 213-4
on Bahjí, 109
on believers as Hands of the Cause, 303
Bishárát, 122, 166, 169-76, 177
on calumnies of Azalís, 426, 429
of Carmel, *see Lawḥ-i-Karmil*
for chief of Templers, 374
on circumambulation, 113-4
compilations of, 275n.
composition of, 23n.
on consultation, 308
on countryside, 8
on creation, 40-42, 44, 47
to Czar Alexander II, 464
delivery of, 343-8
on detachment, 261
to divines, 102-4
to enemies, 99
on equality of men and women, 210-15
explanation of 'stars', 242
on fear of God, 29
on forgiveness, 90
full of significances, 177
on Garden of Riḍván, 11, 15-16
on God the Incomparable, 210
to Hádíy-i-Dawlat-Ábádí, 50, 183
for Ḥájí 'Abu'l-Ḥasan-i-Amín, 121, 301, 307
to Ḥájí Áqá Muḥammad-i-'Aláqih-band, 231
Ḥájí Mírzá Buzurg-i-Afnán, 17
for Ḥájí Muḥammad-Ibráhím, 161n.
to Ḥájí Muḥammad-Riḍá, 364-9
for Ḥájí Muḥammad-Ṭáhir-i-Málmírí, 344
to Ḥájí Mullá 'Alíy-i-Kání, 315
for Ḥájí Mullá Mihdíy-i-'Aṭrí, 54
to Hands of the Cause, 269, 294-5, 301, 305, 335-48
on Hands of the Cause, 305
on the heart, 36-7
on His Revelation, 433
on House of the Báb, 459
on Ḥuqúq'u'lláh, 267-8, 271-2
to Ibn-i-Abhar, 307, 324-6
to Ibn-i-Aṣdaq, 269, 292, 294, 314, 321-3, 335-48
to Indian believers, 191
on infallibility, 157-8
on inner realities of prominent people, 304
of Ishráqát, 17, 122, 152-8, 170
on Islamic prophecies, 161-2
Kalimát-i-Firdawsíyyih, 122, 185, 206, 226-39, 398
to Karbilá'í Áqá Ján, 288
to King of Martyrs, 92

to kings and rulers, 414
Lawḥ-i-'Abdu'l-Vahháb, 43
Lawḥ-i-Aqdas, 122, 240-48, 375, 376
Lawḥ-i-Ard-i-Bá, 254-5
Lawḥ-i-Burhán, 95-107, 454, 465
Lawḥ-i-Dunyá, 122, 305, 350-66, 428, 459
Lawḥ-i-Ḥikmat, 34-52, 202
Lawḥ-i-Ittihád, 201-6
Lawḥ-i-Karmil, 374-91, 452
Lawḥ-i-Maqsúd, 122, 249-50
Lawḥ-i-Siyyid Mihdíy-i-Dahají, 250-2
Lawḥ-i-Sulṭán, 399, 414
on leaving 'Akká, 110
for mankind, 36-7
on martyrdom, 92
to Mírzá Abu'l-Faḍl, 276
on Mírzá Áqá Khán and Shaykh Aḥmad, 426-7
for Mírzá Ḥasan, 56
on misdeeds of believers, 40, 238
on monasticism, 170-1
to Muḥammad 'Alíy-i-Afnán, 262
to Muḥammad-Báqir, 262
to Mullá 'Alí-Akbar, 270, 304, 335-48
for Nabíl and Muḥammad-Ṭáhir, 113
to Napoleon III, 264, 464
of Naṣír, 408
on nature of God and His Manifestations, 140-1
to Núru'd-Dín, 8
on Obligatory Prayers, 318, 318
on plants, 12
on power of unity, 204-5, 207-8
on Presence of God, 435
on punishment of mankind, 165
to Queen Victoria, 464
quote passages from the Báb, 50-51
recounting story of King and Beloved of Martyrs, 77, 84-94
re-revelation of, 396-8
revealed at Bahjí, 119-20
revealed at Garden of Riḍván, 15-16
of Ru'yá, 445
revealed in the home of Áqáy-i-Kalím, 257
of Salmán, 181
on sciences which begin and end in words, 151
to Shaykh Káẓim-i-Samandar, 93
on Shaykh Muḥammad-i-Yazdí, 421
on sin, 91
on steadfastness, 148
on suffering, 110, 165, 429
to Sulaymán Khán, 191
Súriy-i-Haykal, 139
Súriy-i-Mulúk, 28
Súriy-i-Vafá, 216-225
survey of, 240-1
Tajallíyát, 122, 123-51, 177
Ṭarázát, 17, 18, 122
on teaching, 292, 324, 339-40
to *The Times*, 371-3
on a true believer, 169-70
on Trustworthiness, 18-23, 467
twenty-seven, revealed for Ustád 'Alí-Akbar, 130
on unacceptable actions, 169
on unknowable Essence, 136
to Varqá, 18, 54, 68-76, 92-4
for Varqá's children, 62
on 'veils' and 'oppressors', 182
of visitation, 173, 448
in which locations and cities are addressed, 375
on wickedness, 362
on withholding Kitáb-i-Aqdas, 263-4
on worthlessness of world, 264
Tablets of Bahá'u'lláh, 240
Tablets of the Divine Plan, 381
Tabríz, 59, 153, 188, 196, 283, 429, 469
Ṭáhirih, 16
Talkhunchih, 410
Tarbíyat Schools, 333
Táríkh-i-Shuhadáy-i-Yazd, 369

Teachers
Bahá'í travelling, 187, 291-2, 452
Bahá'u'lláh's advice to, 251, 314
notable, 273-90
in Persia, 270, 291-2
teacher training for youth, 333
training institutes for women, 323
with understanding, 273, 292
visiting graves of, 173
see also Muballigh
Teaching, 125, 128, 129, 226, 339-40
Bahá'ís enjoined to teach, 291-4
Bahá'u'lláh counsels Bahá'ís on, 202
detachment important for success in, 274, 278, 337
by Hands of the Cause, 292, 339-40
importance, of, 251, 324, 337
meaning of, 337
methods of, 251, 279
in Persia, 120
pre-requisites for, 51,
Rúḥu'lláh's method of, 61-3
and station of martyrdom, 60
of Sulaymán Khán, 187-99
success in, 274, 278, 337
Tablets of the Divine Plan a charter for, 381
tours of Ibn-i-Aṣdaq, 321-3
travel teaching, 207-8, 251, 273-4, 276-8, 321, 322
wisdom in, 71, 324, 340-3
women encouraged to teach, 213
Teachings
Bahá'u'lláh's presentation of, 398-402
carrying out, 149, 166
on creation, 40-48
designed to spiritualize human race, 36, 39
equality of men and women, 210-15
explained to Náyibu's-Salṭanih, 404
exposition of, in *Epistle to the Son of the Wolf*, 395-6
forbidding contention and strife, 399-407
harmony of science and religion, 164
listed, 167-8, 169-76, 226-7, 363, 399-402
on living the life, 73, 88
on reconstruction of human society, 363
revolve around principle of love and unity, 169
for rulers and ministers of the world, 162
on search for truth, 148-9
understanding of, 224-5
on worship, 37
mentioned, 119-20, 153, 177, 181, 194, 223, 252, 273, 336, 414, 463
Templers, German, 74, 374-5
Ten Year Crusade, 381
Testament
New, 13, 48, 132, 284, 454
Old, 49, 284-5, 454
see also Holy Bible, Gospels and Scriptures
Tests, 262, 304, 327
Thamúd, 101, 454-8
Tibet, 193
Ṭihrán, 104-5, 375
imprisonment of Bahá'ís in, 404-5
Mashriqu'l-Adhkár in, 336
prison of, *illus. 329*; 67, 320, 325-7, 359
see also Síyáh-Chál
release of Bahá'í prisoners in, 14
remains of the Báb in, 318
residence of Ibn-i-Abhar, 325
school for girls in, 333
Siyyid Asadu'lláh in, 196
Spiritual Assembly of, *illus. 310*; 308-11, 331
suffering of Bahá'u'lláh in, 155-6
teacher training institute in, 323, 333
upheaval in, 129, 392, 405
mentioned, 12, 80, 124, 187, 275, 314, 315, 331, 333, 348, 413, 459

Times, The, 370-3
Torah, the, 48
Townshend, George, Hand of the Cause, Canon of St. Patrick's, Dublin, and Archdeacon of Clonfert, 244
Tradition, 70, 145
  see also ḥadí͟th
Transcaspia, 366
Trustworthiness, 16-29 182, 265, 401, 405, 467
Truth, 161, 178, 185-6, 224, 233
  religious, 158, 160
  of Revelation of Bahá'u'lláh, 360
  Spirit of, 240
  truthfulness, 182, 265, 343, 405
  unfettered search after, 148-9, 208, 312
Ṭúbá Khánum, 2-4, 13-14
Turkistán, 127, 276
Turkmenistan, 187
Turkomanchay, Treaty of, 463

'Údí Khammár, 108-9, 113
Understanding, 69, 224, 273, 291, 340
United States, *see* America
Unity, 167, 169, 316, 399, 405, 406
  of the Bahá'í community, 200-6, 337-8, 389
  in diversity, 209
  meaning of, 200-4
  peace unattainable without, 165, 206-10
  not possible in previous Dispensations, 361
  power of, 338
  purpose of Bahá'u'lláh's Revelation, 389, 414
  in society, 206-9, 226, 389
Universal House of Justice, 39, 92, 167, 172, 227, *see also* Houses of Justice
  and the Ark, 384-5
  can enact new laws, 228
  as Centre of Covenant, 150, 271
  duties of, 170
  infallibility of, 157, 345
  and institution of the Hands of the Cause, 293, 306
  and International Funds, 271
  to promote the Lesser Peace, 363-4
  Seat of, *illus.* 387; 386
  and world administrative centre, 386
'Urvatu'l-Vuthqá (newspaper), 428
Uzbikistán, 278

Vafá (Shaykh Muḥammad-Ḥusayn), 216-7
Valíyy'u'lláh, Hand of the Cause, 62, 476
Varqá, 'Alí-Muḥammad, *illus. 65, 66*; 53-76, 283, 285, 286
  Tablet to, 92, 94
  Tablets revealed for, 68-76
Vegetable kingdom, 209, 271
Victoria, Queen, 414, 464
Visitation, Tablet of, 173, 448
Voting, 309
  see also Elections

War, 60, 165, 207, 249, 285, 385, 402-4, 418
  holy war, 169, 175, 462-3
Wealth, 86, 271
  see also Ḥuqúq'u'lláh
West, the, 245-6, 256
Will and Testament of 'Abdu'l-Bahá, 303, 305
Wisdom, 340-3
Women, 227
  education of, 212, 331
  equality between men and, 210-15
  seclusion of, 124, 212
  Spiritual Assembly of Bahá'í, 331
  teacher training institute for, 323
Word, 147, 241, 278
  inner meaning of, 157
  sciences which begin and end in words, 151, 249-50
Word of God, 219, 223, 225, 241, 338, 424, 437, 463

Bahá'u'lláh as Revealer of, 203
glorification of, 395
outpouring of, 355
power of, 251, 461
Prophets revealers of, 48
sources of creation, 44, 295-6
source of heat, 295-301
source of unity of people, 204, 206
at time of its revelation, 231
Work, 171, 276
World
spiritual, 216-7, 270
worthlessness of, 264
Worship, 37, 170-1
see also God
Writings, Holy, 130, 177, 202, 422, 452
of 'Abdu'l-Bahá, 209
anthology of Bahá'u'lláh's, 396
of the Báb, 397, 435-6
of Bahá'u'lláh on Persian authorities, 235
Bahá'u'lláh quotes from His own, 161n., 170
Bahá'u'lláh repeats subjects in, 130
on creation, 44-5
definition of terms used in, 181-3, 230, 456
depicting perversity of humanity, 74
on detachment, 72, 261, 264-5
and equality of men and women, 211
first Bahá'í, printed, 188
high standard of behaviour demanded in, 88
on Ḥuqúq'u'lláh, 268
interpretation of, 154
misrepresented, 157-8
need to recite, 69
not in printed form, 275n.
on power of unity, 204-5, 206-8
printing of, 342
on recognizing God, 145-6
on relationship of God to the Manifestations, 136-7, 138
study of the, 17, 224
teachers well-versed in, 292
on uniqueness of creation, 209
on worship, 37

Yahúdá, Ḥájí, 12-13, 475
Yaḥyá, Mírzá, 56, 85-6, 91, 120, 183, 223, 273, 425, 427, 428, 435n., 439, 450, 468, 469
Bahá'u'lláh addresses, 233
followers of, *see* Azalís
role of, 323
Yarkand, 193
Yazd, 24, 53-4, 123-4, 128, 260n.
Governor of, 123
martyrdoms in, 198, 354, 369-71
massacre of 1903, 199n., 333, 370-1, 392
Tyrant of, (Prince Maḥmúd Mírzá), 368-71
Yazdi, Aziz, 475
Youth, 333
Yúsuf, Shaykh, 253
Yúsuf Khán, Mírzá (Mustasháru'd-Dawlih), 283
Yúsuf Khán-i-Vujdání, Mírzá, 354

Zahrá Bagum, 459-60
Zanján, 64-7, 324, 402, 405, 465
Zaynu'l-Muqarrabín, 110, 258
Ẓillu's-Sulṭán, *see* Mas'úd Mírzá
Zion, 380, 385, 435
Zoroastrians, *illus. 310*; 279, 284, 308, 450

OTHER BOOKS IN THE

REVELATION OF BAHÁ'LLÁH

SERIES

VOLUME 1:
BAGHDÁD 1853–63

The story of the Revelation of Bahá'u'lláh from its birth in the dungeon of the Síyáh-Chál to Bahá'u'lláh's Declaration to His followers on that 'Day of supreme felicity' in the Garden of Riḍván. Some of Bahá'u'lláh's best known Writings, including *The Hidden Words*, *The Seven Valleys*, and the *Kitáb-i-Íqán* were revealed against the background of exile and deprivation, of exhilaration and joy described in this book.

ISBN: 978-0-85398-057-5

384 pages, 19 illustrations
19.8 x 12.9 cm (7.75 x 5 in)

Kindle version available.

VOLUME 2:

ADRIANOPLE 1863–68

From Baghdád to Constantinople, and then to Adrianople the Revelation of Bahá'u'lláh takes on its distinctive character as the advent of the Day of God is progressively proclaimed. Among the Tablets described in this volume are the *Súriy-i-Mulúk* (Tablet of the Kings) and the *Lawḥ-i-Sulṭán.*

ISBN: 978-0-85398-071-1

492 pages, 17 illustrations
19.8 x 12.9 cm (7.75 x 5 in)

Kindle version available.

VOLUME 3:

'AKKA, THE EARLY YEARS 1868–77

This book describes the exile and imprisonment of Bahá'u'lláh and his companions in the fortress city of 'Akká, including the tragic death of his younger son, The Purest Branch. It delineates the major themes of the Kitáb-i-Aqdas, the Most Holy Book revealed behind the walls of that city, and describes many other weighty Tablets, including those sent by Bahá'u'lláh to the kings and rulers of the time.

ISBN: 978-0-85398-144-2

544 pages, 36 illustrations
19.8 x 12.9 cm (7.75 x 5 in)

Kindle version available.

www.ingramcontent.com/pod-product-compliance
Lightning Source LLC
Chambersburg PA
CBHW030102010526
44116CB00005B/63
9780853982708